CW00547787

Cape Town

in the twentieth century

An Illustrated Social History

1919

1945

1948

1976

Cape Town
in the twentieth century

An illustrated social history

Vivian Bickford-Smith
Elizabeth van Heyningen
Nigel Worden

DAVID PHILIP PUBLISHERS
1999

First published 1999 by David Philip Publishers (Pty) Ltd,
208 Werdmuller Centre, Newry Street, Claremont 7708, South Africa.

ISBN 0-86486-384-5

Design and layout by Sarah-Anne Raynham
Front cover art by Lien Botha
Cartography by James Mills-Hicks
Reproduction by Hirt and Carter, Cape Town
Printed and bound by Tien Wah Press, Singapore

Contents

Preface

PAULINE PODBREY, a trade-union organiser and member of the South African Communist Party, lived in Cape Town between 1943 and 1951. In her autobiography (published in 1993) she expressed the belief that each 'city has a personality, a character, a certain aura, and it is always my first impressions of a city that I've learnt to trust ... I'd like to believe that it has nothing to do with architecture, history, shopping. It has, it concerns all these and much more. But mainly, of course, it's about people.' For Podbrey, Cape Town was 'a lovely, enchanting gem of a city', one that would 'smile on the stranger', with Table Mountain cradling the place 'in a warm, protective embrace'.[1]

In contrast Sandile Dikeni, a poet and journalist, claimed he wished to say something flattering about the Mother City in 1996 'but I found nothing, not even the mountain, could bowl me over. Standing in the shade of the night it looked monstrous and scary like an ancient ghost guarding over some evil.' For Dikeni, the city's present evil was rampant racism and streets 'without soul'.[2]

We are very aware that the experience of Cape Town, and a sense of its history, have varied enormously for different people, whether visitors or inhabitants. John Matshikiza, a writer, has recently argued that, as the twentieth century draws to an end, 'the mountain stands like a huge, indifferent moderator between the conflicting worlds of Cape Town. Its face is turned towards the open sea, with paradise – the playground of lush white houses, the business district and the Waterfront – dribbling down its chest. [But] the back of the mountain is like the dark side of the moon.' Here, townships like Manenberg and Guguletu 'huddle sullenly'.[3]

There have been numerous attempts to capture Cape Town's 'character', its spirit of place. Differences of opinion depend as much on the identity of the writer, and consequent individual experiences, as on the particular period in which the visit took place. Most have combined physical descriptions of the city with comments on the nature of its inhabitants. We believe that the answer is to seek the relationship between the two. People make places, but places also make people. In the case of twentieth-century Cape Town, it is perhaps particularly clear that existing geographical features combined with the modern 'science' of town planning and beliefs in 'racial' difference to produce the sometimes very different senses of place that exist among its three million citizens today.

This history is then, first and foremost, about people, about varied human experience. But it attempts to trace the changing and enduring interactions between people and place over time. It is about perceptions as well as reality, the poor as well as the powerful. The titles and themes of chapters begin to reveal how the authors believe that Cape Town's 'spirit of place' has changed through the years. This provides an organising principle for a book which can only be but one version of the city's past.

Cape Town in the Twentieth Century begins where its companion volume, *Cape Town: The Making of a City,* left off: with Capetonians on the eve of the South African War as well as a new century. The two books together form a modern history of the city that has had a lengthy gestation. In 1978 Robin Hallett organised the first of six Cape Town History workshops at the University of Cape Town. From 1990 the Centre for Scientific Development funded research through a Cape Town History Project, located in UCT's History Department. Neither volume would have been possible without the plethora of mostly unpublished academic research on the city's past that both initiatives have generated.

Cape Town in the Twentieth Century also includes considerable original material based both on conventional sources and on oral testimonies and literary accounts of the city. The numerous illustrations form an important part of the text, themselves reflecting multiple visions of the city through the century. Inevitably there are still gaps, and many topics that are included have been treated unevenly. Nonetheless we hope that you will recognise something of 'your' Cape Town in these pages.

IT IS IMPOSSIBLE to write twentieth-century South African history without incurring a debt either to some of the participants of the events described, or to the institutions which have collected the records of a dark time in Cape Town's history.

In the first place, however, our warm thanks must go to our indefatigable editor, Russell Martin, for his constant and warm support, and to all at David Philip Publishers for encouraging this project. Sarah-Anne Raynham, who designed the book, our cartographer James Mills-Hicks, and Jean Brundrit, our photographer, have once again played a major part in the creation of the book, while Lien Botha responded imaginatively to the task of creating the front cover.

Our thanks also go to the Cape Tercentenary Foundation which subsidised the maps. We should also like to thank the Centre for Scientific Development of the Human Sciences Research Council for their support of research into Cape Town history over six years. They are in no way responsible for our opinions.

An invaluable part was played by students who contributed to the research of the Cape Town History Project as well as others in the Department of History and in other departments and universities who have worked on Cape Town history. From the CTHP they include Teun Baartman, Andrew Bank, Naomi Barnett, Harriet Deacon, Marijke du Toit, Kevin Greenbank, Craig Iannini, Mark Irvine, Kirsten McKenzie, Rosemary Ridd, Terri Strauss, Andrew Walker, Kerry Ward and Joanne Winter. In addition, a number of students conducted interviews for us under the aegis of the Tutu Fund Vacation Students, including Paula da Gama, Thavie Mchunu, Victor Modise and N. Radebe.

We could not have written this book without the assistance of Cape Town's libraries and research institutions. Our warmest thanks go to the staffs of Jagger Library, University of Cape Town, the South African Library, the Cape Archives and the Mayibuye Centre, University of the Western Cape. In addition we thank Mary Hartle of the Argus Photo Library and the staff of iAfrika Photos for their efforts in tracing elusive photographs, and *Die Burger* and the Cape Institute of Architects (Delia Colborne and Vivienne Japha) for other illustrations; Cape Town Municipality, particularly the Land Survey and City Engineer's Departments; the Community Arts Project; Diocesan College (Brian de Kock and Anthony Lister); the District Six Museum; the Groote Schuur Transplant Museum (Sue Henderson); MuseumAfrica; the National Library of Scotland; Roberts and Loebenberg (Pat Gonzalez); the South African Cultural History Museum; the South African National Gallery; and Transnet.

Many individuals have also contributed. We thank the following either for the loan of photographs or for their enlightening discussions: Cloete Breytenbach, Dennis Cavernelis, Benny Gool, George Hallett, Mike Hutchings, Roger Meintjes, Chris Schoeman, Mark van Aardt and Obed Zilwa; James Matthews and Stephen Watson for permission to use their poems; Basil 'Manenberg' Coetzee for his music; Andrea Fine for information on The Space; Jill Fletcher; as ever, Vincent Kolbe and Shula Marks for discussions on mid-century Cape Town; Nöel Mostert for inspiration and insight; Bill Nasson for details on what was or was not segregated by the 1960s; Ligia Fernandes and Jonathan Paarman for the loan of family photographs; Nigel Penn for school photographs; Hans Smit for information on Cape Town housing; Julia Teale for the use of her painting; and Amy Thornton both for her photograph and for her insights.

Finally, we should once again like to thank Arthur Davey, Claudia Pienaar and James Patrick for their personal, and practical, support.

THE NEW WOMAN AND A GIRL OF NO CONSEQUENCE

CHAPTER ONE

Challenge to the Imperial Order

Cape Town 1899–1919

Adderley Street in the early twentieth century, with the railway station on the left and the post office further up the street. (UCT BC 1019)

The South African War, 1899–1902

TO Capetonians, the town they lived in at the end of the nineteenth century had become a place of some stature, symbolised by the adoption of the title of alderman by senior municipal councillors. Cape Town, they felt, could claim the right to be regarded as a city. From the outside, though, Cape Town struck a different image. The British journalist G.W. Steevens considered the place agreeable but hardly dynamic or prosperous – 'Denver with a dash of Delhi'. 'All in all,' Steevens went on to say, 'Capetown gives you the idea of being neither very rich nor very poor, neither over-industrious nor over-lazy, decently successful, reasonably happy, whole-heartedly easy-going. The public buildings ... confirm the idea of a placid half-prosperity. The place is not a baby, but it has hardly taken the trouble to grow up. It has a post-office of truly German stability and magnitude. It has a well-organised railway station, [which] has the merit of being in Adderley Street ...'[1]

But by mid-1899 heated debate in parliament and undue activity at the railway station belied this placidity. At the station hundreds of refugees fleeing from the Rand and war clambered down almost daily, stiff and sore, from cattle trucks, clutching their few belongings. Frightened women had to fend for themselves and their children in a strange city. Indians, 'Peruvians' (as East European Jews were sometimes contemptuously called), not to mention Belgian, French and Russian prostitutes – all had to find homes and work. 'Sun-reddened, unshaven, flannelshirted, corduroy-trousered' British working men thronged the offices of the steamship companies and streamed down to

The cattle trucks in which many refugees travelled from the Transvaal to Cape Town emphasised the humiliation of their plight. (CA J536)

Previous pages: James Ford's evocation of twentieth-century Cape Town pictured the town as gateway to South Africa, at once capital city and prosperous holiday resort. The painting was finished in 1899, just as war broke out, changing the face of South Africa, and was displayed to raise war funds. (SA National Gallery)

the docks to board liners to take them back 'home'.[2] All these people were the detritus of war. Over twenty-five thousand poured into Cape Town when the Transvaal Republic went to war against the British Empire and drove the Uitlanders away.

The British government needed victims to justify its war, supposedly fought against Boer ignorance, prejudice and brutality, and the Uitlanders obligingly fitted into this role. At first British Cape Town received them with open arms. Citizens rallied round to set up the Mayor's Relief Fund and the Ladies' Relief Committee. Aid to the suffering was said to know no distinction of race, colour or creed. In practice, though, distinctions were made from the start, between men and women, black and white, deserving and undeserving. Coloured men, for one, received no help at all. Along with African refugees, they disappeared into the ranks of the Cape Town poor, lost to the sight of the relief committees, although coloured women and children were given food and accommodation. Indians fared only slightly better. Already stripped of their possessions by the Boers at the Transvaal border, they were installed in tents in Dock Road on arrival in Cape Town. When disease broke out in 1901, they were shifted to Maitland, from where the Maitland municipality evicted them at the first opportunity, and they drifted into overcrowded District Six.

White male refugees from the Transvaal were housed in the Feather Market, where their lives were strictly regimented. (UCT Macmillan)

White male refugees, on the other hand, were housed in the Produce and Feather Market building on the shore, and later in a wood-and-iron shelter on Dock Road. The 'able-bodied' were expected either to leave the country, find work or join up to fight for the British but a few elderly or disabled men lingered on in the Dock Road shelter until the end of war. Some men were not so accommodating: they were poor, able-bodied and reluctant to fight. Such 'undesirables' – the 'loafers and hangers on of society' – were a constant source of irritation to the authorities. Determined to get them out of town, the government set up relief works on the Cape Flats to build roads.

Uitlander women symbolised innocent British suffering, and their plight came to inform the rhetoric of appeal. By helping them the wives of leading Cape Town citizens seized the opportunity to demonstrate their patriotism and their womanliness. Dr Jane

An Uitlander Refugee in Cape Town

Elsa Smithers was a colonial-born refugee from Koffiefontein in the Free State. After spending her limited savings, she sought help from the Mansion House Fund. 'Relief, charity! it was almost more than I could bear; but if you have five hungry mouths to feed and an ailing mother to provide for, there is no time to be proud.' Although grateful, she was humiliated by the manner of giving. Work was uncongenial. In her second situation 'I was sent to a woman who, it was obvious, intended to beat me down to the last farthing. However, as beggars cannot be choosers, I consented to go, and I worked for her, being paid the niggardly sum of 10s 6d a week. For this I had to scrub floors, whitewash the front steps, help the daughter to peel potatoes and set tables, do the shopping, and clean out the closets.' Subsequently she worked as a waitress in a boarding-house and took in sewing. After several months her husband returned to Cape Town. 'Safely in Denny's arms I felt the happiest person in the world, and I knew at the same time that a woman can have too much independence.'[3]

Familiar open spaces were transformed during the war into canvas towns. Green Point Common became 'a veritable South African Aldershot'. (CA E9356)

Waterston, Cape Town's redoubtable woman doctor, convened a committee to provide shelter, work and food. The women's suffering was real enough. Trapped in Cape Town, separated from their husbands, watching their slender funds dwindling, ill qualified for employment, these white women faced a harsh plight. All the same, unlike some refugees, they could gain access to relief funds, from the Ladies' Committee, the Mansion House Fund (a British relief fund) and, later, the Victoria League.

Distress was one aspect of war; drama was another. During the years of war British troops paraded through the streets, and their commanders were welcomed with ritual and ceremony. Over ten thousand troops were concentrated in the city at times. Familiar open spaces were transformed into canvas towns. Life under canvas was lovingly described by an interested press. Part of the excitement and pride stemmed from the knowledge that Cape Town was host to the empire. 'Cape Town is an imperial city, and ... as such, it has certain obligations and duties to discharge ... as one of the dozen great important centres of Imperial life in the Empire.' This was a 'grand opportunity', for 'in a sense the city stands on its trial before the Empire'.[4]

A welcome to the City of London Imperial Volunteers provided the opportunity for demonstrating Cape Town's hospitality. Businessmen and the general public joined in laying on a grand reception which had 'never been faintly approached in its absolute abandonment of enthusiasm'. En route to the front, the CIV rode from Green Point Common via Somerset Road, Bree Street, Wale Street and Adderley Street to the station, 'flags flew in myriad colours, balconies gaily festooned, and streets were spanned with rows of fluttering bannerets'. The crowds greeted the soldiers joyously, 'such a boom and thunder of cheers was surely never heard before'. (CA E7830)

For many Cape Town men war had a romantic appeal. This was heightened by the desire of colonials to express their uncertain identity through a display of patriotism. In 1899 they hastened to join the volunteer forces. In consequence hardly a business in the city was unaffected. Coloured men were equally anxious to offer their services and were bitter when their aid was rejected. 'Your servants hereby feel greatly at loss that their services are not required to assist in such a trying hour and that they are not called upon to stand by the side of Her Majesty's forces, thus to prevent so many of them to be slaughtered, as we know and feel the work they are doing too will be for the advancement of our own interest, and of civilisation amongst the dark races of Africa.'[5]

In January 1901, when Boer raids across the Orange River penetrated deep into the colony, the governor and high commissioner, Sir Alfred Milner, turned his mind to the defence of Cape Town. Men of good class would enrol for local defence, he assured Joseph Chamberlain. He was right: the call to arms found a ready response amongst

Eventually there were about 5000 men attached to the Town Guard in Cape Town. They drilled, patrolled, practised musketry and were inspected by dignitaries. They also guarded armouries, bridges and key points – and took photographs of themselves. (CA J7126)

The first of the local volunteer forces to be accepted for active service was the Cape Town Highlanders. (CA AG7108)

Capetonians who had not joined the volunteer forces. The first contingent of a new colonial defence force, the Western Province Mounted Rifles, left early in 1901 for Piketberg, to keep the enemy well away from the port.

The Town Guard attracted men who could not leave home. Within a week at the beginning of January 1901, 3000 recruits had rushed to enlist. The first full company was No. 1, that of Garlicks. Cleghorn & Harris provided No. 2, Stuttafords No. 4, and in their wake followed A.B. Reid & Co., J.J. Hills, and Richards & Sons. 'All the shop boys are armed' was the comment of a disapproving John X. Merriman. Soon there were about 40 companies, mainly infantry, but also cyclists, artillerymen, a sailors' company, workshop artisans and detachments of mounted men like the Peninsula Horse.

> There are few portions of this city to which one can go at any time of the day without seeing members of the new force on duty, taking the place of regulars as guards here, there and everywhere; without meeting sections and companies marching to or from their drills, or hurrying to their posts of duty in various parts of the town and suburbs. At night every street echoes to the tramp of the civilian soldiers, and one might not inaptly compare the scenes that are being enacted in the metropolis to those that were to be witnessed in the cities of North and South during the American Civil War.[6]

Playing at war could be wearisome, however. Within a few weeks reports were emerging of sentries being unrelieved and enthusiasm dwindling.

Cape Town coloured men resented their exclusion from the defence of their city. The Coloured Men's Political Protection Association forwarded a resolution to the prime minister asserting their loyalty and willingness to 'repel the treacherous foe'. Milner was not entirely unsympathetic: it was difficult, he felt, to refuse the right of full-fledged British citizens to defend their own property, but the prime minister W.P. Schreiner resisted a demand which he knew would offend the white electorate.

If the war offered Cape Town men the opportunity of playing at soldiers, women were able to test their organisational skills. Philanthropic organisations proliferated: the

Fundraising became a major occupation. Kipling's verses 'The absent-minded beggar', set to music by Sir Arthur Sullivan, were sung on every possible occasion. In January 1900 at the Cape Town wedding of Miss Belle Sytner and Mr Jack Tuchten, Miss Lillie Fisher, accompanied by Master Isidor Fisher, sang it 'in a very feeling and pathetic manner'. £20 was collected from the wedding guests for the war. (Private collection)

Good Hope Society provided comforts for the sick and wounded, and women's working parties made clothing for the men. An early forerunner of women's hospitality movements, common in both world wars, was the 'Tommy's welcome to the Cape' by means of which women supplied refreshments for the troops disembarking and entraining for the front. When plague struck Cape Town, teas were abandoned and soldiers received parcels instead. Later on, the Soldiers' Comforts Fund provided gifts for Christmas.

Cape Town fizzed with political unrest for much of the war. For one thing the presence of the refugees guaranteed a volatile atmosphere. When Conyngham Greene, the British representative in the Transvaal, arrived in Cape Town after hostilities broke out, he was hailed with excitement: 'Mr Greene was recognised at once, and the dense mass of men raised cheer after cheer as he struggled towards the exit. He was shaken by the hand by everybody within reach, patted on the back, even narrowly escaped being car-

News of the war was signalled by the 'peculiar bass note' of the steam siren of the Cape Times Printing Works. When the hooter sounded, thousands made their way 'through the heat and dust of the day or in the cool of the evening to the "Cape Times" office in St George's-street, to get a copy of the special telegram they know is being issued' (*Cape Times*, 20 March 1900). Yet, in a divided city, information was often received in silence. (CA J5304)

The Relief of Kimberley

The news of the relief of Kimberley came through just after 10 in the morning. 'For something like ten minutes on end there was one prolonged roar of cheering, whilst from all parts of the city people left their business and rushed up the upper end of St. George's-Street. Every second the crowd increased in proportions; the National Anthem and "Rule, Britannia" were sung by thousands of voices, and cheer after cheer was given for "The Queen," "Lord Roberts," "General French" and "The Governor."'[8]

(UCT Macmillan)

ried shoulder-high from the train. "God save the Queen" and "Rule, Britannia" were roared forth in splendid volume, and the far greater crowd outside the station took up the loyal chorus, and sang until the whole station vibrated with sound.'[7] Anyone apparently representing the Boer cause received short shrift. The Bond town councillor D.J. Graaff, who arrived at the same time as Greene, was unwise enough to make a remark in the *taal* and had to fight his way through a hostile crowd to seek refuge in the Grand Hotel. The crowd remained outside, yelling and hissing, until they were dispersed by the police.

After initial dismay at the early British defeats, the lifting of the sieges of Kimberley, Ladysmith and Mafeking, and the victory at Paardeberg, all provided occasion for celebration. News of the relief of Mafeking was anticipated keenly. All through April Cape Town waited. Only on the weekend of 19–20 May did the news come through and the government finally announce that Monday would be a public holiday. Rain dampened initial excitement but Monday dawned bright and clear and Cape Town celebrated with zest. Flags became the mark of the occasion, the expression of loyalty and patriotism. 'From end to end of each of the principal thoroughfares one looked down to the sea through a vista of red, white and blue bunting, interspersed here and there with Irish green.' In Greenmarket Square a crowd sang the 'Old hundredth'. Workmen tramped through the muddy streets of Salt River to the sound of a band playing 'The red, white, and blue', while coloured people held a thanksgiving service on the Grand Parade. That night the city was illuminated by Chinese lanterns. At the Town House there were coloured lights and 'long lines of electric glow-lamps, which picturesquely lined the outlines of the building'. Huge bonfires at Kloof Nek burnt copies of pro-Boer papers like the *South African News*. The Cape Garrison Artillery band played patriotic airs while impromptu processions marched through the town. Only in the small hours did the streets begin to empty.[9]

These spontaneous revelries resulted largely from the release of tension in an overwrought city. But Cape Town was to witness during the course of the war a series of

THE RELIEF OF MAFEKING.

Be prepared for this historic event. Have your

FLAG READY.

WE HAVE JUST OFF LOADED:

UNION JACK FLAGS (Cotton),
27 x 20 inches, 6d each
34 x 31 inches, 1/0 each
38 x 32 inches, 1/3 each

UNION JACK BUNTING FLAGS (Roped & Togled),
36 x 18 inches, 3/11 each
2 yards x 1 yard, 12/6 each
3 yards x 1½ yards, 25/0 and 30/0 each.

ROYAL STANDARD BUNTING FLAGS (Roped and Togled),
3 yards x 1½ yards, 52/6 each
6 yards x 3 yards, 7 Guineas each

CAPE COLONY FLAGS (Cotton), 29 x 20 inches, 9d.
PATRIOTIC FLAGS, 27 x 22 inches, 9d.
FOR DECORATIONS: Red, White and Blue Striped Cloth, 33 inches wide, 7½d. per yard
Turkey Red Twills, 6d, 7½d, 9d, 10½d, 1/0 per yard
Plain White Cloths, 4½d to 8½d per yard
Plain Blue Cloths, 6½d per yard
Patriotic Badges, Buttons, Rosettes
Photographs of Baden-Powell, Roberts, Kitchener, Buller, &c.
Red, White and Blue Ribbons, all widths.
Victory Badges, National Flag Belt Buckles.
Union Jack Hat Bands, Khaki Belts, Absent Minded Beggar Ties, Brooches, Charms, Pendants, &c. 1537my

We are Booking Orders, send yours, or Call and See Our Stock.

Cleghorn & Harris,

Adderley and St. George's-streets.

(*Cape Times*, 11 May 1900)

The South African Vigilance Committee planned a great public demonstration in Greenmarket Square on 3 April 1900. The meeting, of over twelve thousand people, was a great success from the point of view of the imperialists. Businesses were closed. The crowd assembled on a blazing day with scarcely a breath of wind. At the sound of a bugle a flag was raised and the assembled multitude lifted their hands to affirm a declaration demanding annexation of the Boer states. (CA E8359)

political campaigns that were much more carefully orchestrated, being designed to protect imperial interests in South Africa. From its base in Cape Town the South African Vigilance Committee (SAVC), founded in March 1900 to counteract pro-Boer propaganda, organised an extensive crusade of petitions, resolutions and public meetings throughout the colony to press for the annexation of the Boer states. Conscious of its imperial status as the 'Metropolis of South Africa', Cape Town took the lead in grandiloquent resolutions: 'the blood of the Sons of the Empire', it declared, 'which had been spilt in upholding the authority of Her Most Gracious Majesty in her South African Colonies and in the defence of the British Flag, demands a voice in the settlement ...'[10]

But by the beginning of 1901 the ebullience which had characterised British Cape Town in 1900 began to wane as the war dragged on. Refugees were growing frustrated and restless. Coloured people, deprived of the right to express their loyalty in concrete form, were becoming politicised. Above all, a new danger to the city was looming: overcrowding and poverty in the town created ideal conditions for an epidemic. Indeed, Cape Town in wartime was living on a powderkeg; nor was the fuse lacking. Sweeping the world at the end of the century was a pandemic of plague – the third since the terrible 'Black Death' of the Middle Ages. Not only was Cape Town, as an entry point of the British Army into South Africa, extremely vulnerable to infection spread by military activity, but Capetonians in fact knew the epidemic was coming, for plague had already spread from China to Sydney, Glasgow and Argentina by 1900.

If Cape Town had plenty of warning to get its house in order, what precisely should be done? Professor W.J. Simpson, once medical officer of Calcutta and now plague adviser to the Cape government, had no doubt where the problem lay. 'Next to Bombay, Cape Town is one of the most suitable towns I know for a plague epidemic,' he wrote. There were, he went on, a large number of old and filthy slums, occupied by a heterogeneous population; the Africans living in the town were unfit for urban life; the poorer coloured people were even dirtier in their habits, while the Malays and Indians pos-

The author of this cartoon, 'Scalpel', was Constance Penstone, South Africa's first female cartoonist. (*The Owl*, 13 March 1903)

sessed the habits of the Asiatic, and the poorer-class Portuguese, Italians, Levantines and Jews were almost as filthy as the others. 'Living in the same insanitary areas, often living in the same houses, the different races and nationalities are inextricably mixed up, so that whatever disease affects the one is sure to affect the other.'[11] In other words, race and culture, as much as poverty, were responsible for disease, or so Simpson believed.

Then on 1 February 1901 E.A. McCallum, a clerk at the South Arm of the docks, took ill. He was taken to Rondebosch Cottage Hospital, where plague was diagnosed. Further investigation revealed a number of disturbing facts. As far back as September 1900 rats had been dying in large numbers at the South Arm, where the British Army offloaded its stores, and several people working there had also died under suspicious circumstances. Plague had come to Cape Town, brought in forage from Argentina by the army.

The plague epidemic tested the bureaucratic efficiency of the colony and its newly constructed health department to the utmost. In some respects it functioned remarkably well. When the disease was identified in the laboratories, the 1897 Public Health Act was invoked, giving health officials great powers. A plague hospital was established at Uitvlugt forest station (modern Pinelands) and a camp was set up nearby for the contacts of victims. Africans living in District Six were rounded up and, under armed guard, taken to a location created at Uitvlugt. Above all, Cape Town's slums underwent the greatest cleansing they had ever known. People were moved in their hundreds from their homes, first to a temporary tent camp on Ebenezer Road near the docks, and later to a more permanent one in Maitland. Houses were hosed down with disinfectant, cleaned and whitewashed. 'No words can, however, paint the indescribable filth in which many of the houses were found to be. On several occasions my men, on entering a room that had been closed for two or three days were overpowered by the foul air within, and in three instances men were dragged out of these dens by their companions in an asphyxiated condition.'[12] Not surprisingly, it was difficult to find anyone to undertake this appalling task and the government resorted to recruiting prisoners from the Breakwater jail in return for a remission of sentence. The convicts responded willingly. The energy with which the clean-up campaign was undertaken prevented the plague from spreading beyond the slums, nor would it ever return – as it did in Sydney, for instance. But there was a price to be paid for efficiency, and the cost to Cape Town was high: the loss of freedom for part of its population.

For years some Capetonians had been urging that African migrants should be segregated. They frequently lived in extremely overcrowded conditions in the town. By 1900 there were about 1500 migrant workers housed in barracks at the docks and another 8000 living elsewhere, mainly in the Horstley Street area of District Six, where a slummer journalist described the 'herring-packing process' in which 'not an inch of space went abegging'.[13] Throughout the city and the suburbs there were scattered 'Kafir haunts'; some even survived in makeshift shelters on the mountain. Another trigger prompting calls for segregation was the occasional episodes of violence involving Africans. For years Capetonians remembered an incident in September 1881 when some 200 Africans 'swarmed up from the locations' in the vicinity of Papendorp and were attacked by a mob of whites and coloureds, who proceeded to destroy African property. African 'savagery', it was believed at the time, had come to Cape Town.[14] But, increasingly towards the end of the century, white concern became focused on the insanitary conditions under which Africans were living and in 1900 the Cape Town medical officer of health urged that they be confined in a location.[15]

Africans were caught in a double bind: the city was both contaminating – 'they were

Plague Cases in the Peninsula in 1901

The epidemic started slowly, the numbers increasing as summer temperatures rose. It reached its peak in the middle of March when 81 cases were admitted to hospital in one week. In all, 766 people fell ill and 371 died, a mortality rate of almost 50 per cent. Coloured people were the worst affected. Africans would have been much more severely infected if they had not been moved out of the town to an area which was free of disease.

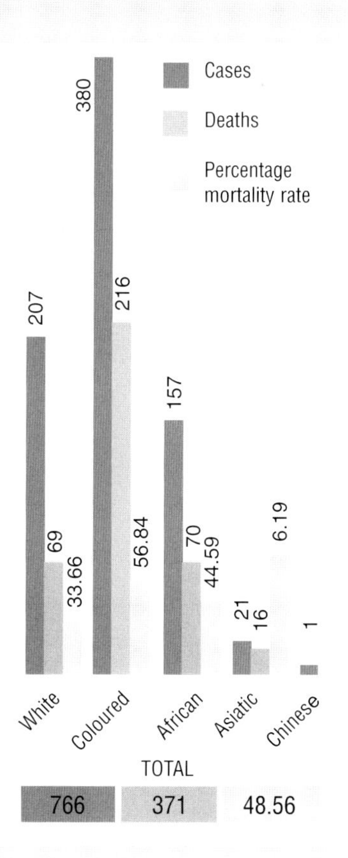

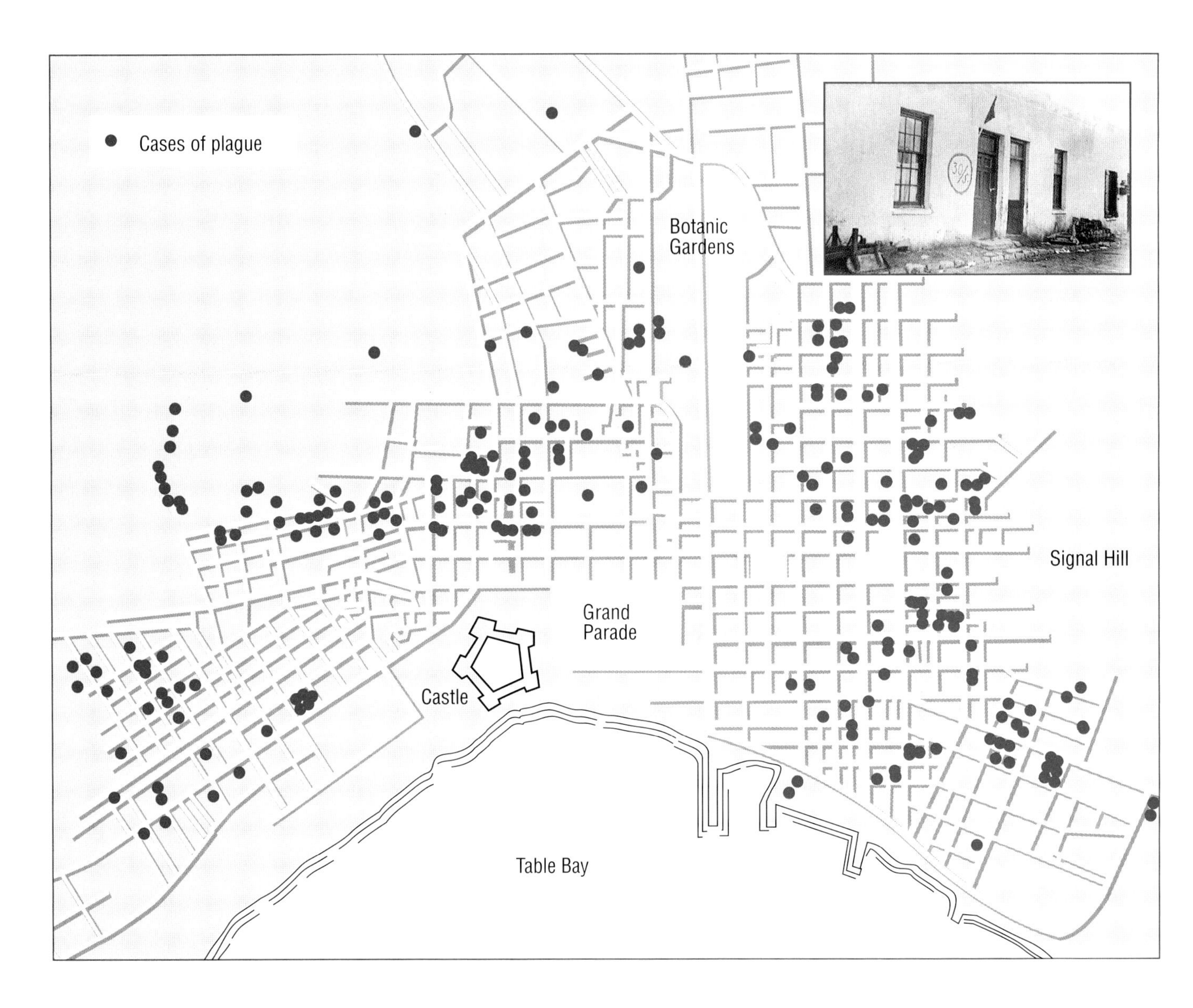

The plague map illustrates poignantly the location of Cape Town's slum districts. A yellow flag denoted an infected house, while the number painted on the house front gave the date of discovery, in this case 30 May 1901. (CA AG4194)

learning all sorts of bad habits through living in touch with European or Coloured surroundings,' said the prime minister W.P. Schreiner – and contaminated – 'uncleanly, half-civilized units' were brought into intimate contact with 'the more cleanly and civilized portion of the community'. Although many employers preferred their employees to live close to work, increasingly the perception of Africans as a threat to the health of the city became dominant, encouraged by the medical bureaucracy.

Yet Africans did not submit passively to their segregation. When plague broke out and black migrant workers found their living quarters invaded by sanitary inspectors, many besieged the shipping offices for tickets to return home to the eastern Cape. Later, when docks employers tried to register them prior to their removal to Uitvlugt, they went on strike. On 13 March 1901 they attempted to hold a protest meeting on the Parade. The call of the agitators, reported the *Cape Times*, had a large response and nearly a thousand of all classes assembled, but before proceedings could get under way, the meeting was broken up by a force of mounted police. In the end African resistance had little effect, for they were rounded up under armed guard and moved by train to the location.

The plague epidemic was the last straw for Uitlander refugees, who had expected their sojourn in Cape Town to be brief. Instead, many were to remain in the city for

Meetings held by Africans on the Parade and on the mountainside to protest against forced removal were broken up by the police, who supervised the removals. Many of the Africans deported lost all their possessions. At Uitvlugt they were kept under guard. (SAL CW J857, J883)

almost three years, resentful of their exile and hating the expensive and plague-ridden town. They believed that they would be able to return once Pretoria had fallen to the British on 5 June 1900, and were encouraged in this expectation by the optimistic tone of the press. 'Hurry up refugees!', a Stuttafords advertisement of early June urged. 'Baskets for the return journey. Tiffin baskets, 3/6d each. We are now in a position to supply all the comforts necessary for the long cold journey. Delay is sometimes disastrous.'[16] But their hopes were dashed when the weeks passed and permission to go home was not granted. Bored, disappointed, demoralised and indigent, the embittered refugees called a series of public meetings in August 1900, established a Refugee Committee, and publicised their cause.

Their agitation was not entirely without effect. Sir Alfred Milner pressed the military to allow some refugees to return and hopes ran high, only to be dashed with the revival of the war. For months this pattern continued, of acrimonious public meetings, official promises and frustrated anticipation. Cape Town was constantly on the boil and Milner became anxious about the political effects of this tension. Gradually a few trickled back while most of the remaining white men were scattered amongst various volunteer corps. From November 1901 Uitlanders began to return to the Transvaal in substantial numbers.

If white refugees suffered, the plight of blacks was far worse. They were excluded from representation on the protest committees and initially even from registration as refugees. Many felt that the equality for which the war was ostensibly being fought had been betrayed. 'They feel this very bitterly. Many a score of them are men who, though coloured, are infinitely above the degraded whites who loafed about ... Naturally they feel much hurt at what seems to them a hard and fast colour line being drawn, especially after all the "equal rights" talk.'[17] Eventually Indian and coloured refugees were allowed to register and return to the Rand, but the plight of Africans was wholly ignored until their cause was taken up by F.Z.S. Peregrino and the Coloured People's Vigilance Committee. Finally the Cape government set up a commission to attend to their claims and they received permission to return home at last.

The recrudescence of the war in 1901 left Cape Town politically uneasy. Edgar Wallace, in his book *Unofficial Dispatches*, expressed some of this tension: 'There are the same old rebellious circles – stronger numerically than they were of yore – babbling the same traitorous sentiments with increasing bitterness. There is the same coterie of traitorous women binding themselves into a thousand and one high-falutin' leagues – little rocks of discontent that serve to indicate the hidden reefs of hate and treason.'[18] An easy target for the expression of these fears was the pro-Boer press – the *South African News*, edited by Albert Cartwright, and *Ons Land*, edited by F.S. Malan. Both newspapers had been attacked by rioters during the celebrations after the fall of Pretoria. Now as the war entered the guerrilla phase they became the object of more sustained hostility. When the *South African News* was unwise enough to stigmatise returning Australian contingents as 'scum', the Australians smashed the windows of the building in Keerom Street, entered the premises and wrecked the place.[19] Finally, both editors were partially silenced when they were found guilty of libel and imprisoned.

Albert Cartwright, editor of the *South African News*. (SAL, *African World*, 17 October 1903)

The vendetta against Cartwright and Malan became part of a larger campaign to have martial law extended to Cape Town. As early as January 1901 when Boer forces penetrated the Cedarberg, it was claimed that rebels were directing operations from 'snuggeries' under the shadow of Table Mountain, and guns and ammunition were being smuggled in part through Cape Town docks. The Cape ministry, however, jibbed at an erosion of their authority through the extension of martial law, and instead introduced the Peace Preservation Act of 1878, a disarmament measure, to little effect.

From April 1901 the governor began to put pressure on the Cape ministry to agree to the extension of martial law to the Peninsula. Few in Cape Town were in favour of such a step; but under pressure from Kitchener martial law was proclaimed in October in the districts of the Cape, Wynberg, Simon's Town, Port Elizabeth and East London.

Although the average pro-British Capetonian probably did not suffer unduly under martial law, foreigners did: for the first time they had to have passports and register with their consulates. Within a short time the authorities suspended the *South African News*. But expectations of identifying spies and smuggled arms all came to nothing. Without any remarkable discoveries martial law continued to be enforced, being eventually suspended in July 1902, well after hostilities had ended.

In Cape Town the new century was inaugurated with a coronation. The Victorian era ended with the death of Queen Victoria and the accession of her son Edward VII on 26 January 1901. This was another occasion for the display of patriotic fervour in a city heightened by the tensions of war. It was followed in August by the visit of the Duke of Cornwall and York, reaffirming the imperial tie. (UCT Macmillan)

The South African War permanently altered the face of South Africa. After hostilities ended, the knowledge that the entire subcontinent was now British gave substance to the belief that El Dorado had been attained at last. South Africa beckoned to those wishing to make their fortune or a new life. Even before the war was over, immigrants began pouring into the country. The Cape government was ambivalent about this influx. White English-speaking immigrants were favoured but many potential residents, from Argentine cattlemen to Indian traders, were considered 'undesirables' – 'foreigners of the usual low type carried by the Union-Castle Co.'s intermediate steamers'.[20] To the xenophobic British, Russian Jews were bad enough, 'but the Italians, South Americans, and Portuguese, and the like are in most respects worse. What civic virtues they have are

A City Hall for the Twentieth Century

(SAL PHA)

In 1905 Cape Town acquired a new city hall. Bordering the Parade, facing the sea, it was designed by the architects Reid & Green in the Italian Renaissance style and built of golden Bath stone. The City Hall marked the apex of the imperial relationship, reflecting the civic pride of Britain's industrial cities, and the final rejection of the Dutch town. Next to it stood the Volunteer Drill Hall, opened in 1885, a mixture of art nouveau, Gothic arches and Tudor castellations, with elaborate cast-iron fanlights and stairways. Here the 'Dukes' and the Cape Town Highlanders, established in 1885, met to reaffirm their imperial military traditions and to uphold order in the colony. Military and municipal authority stood side by side.

The Grand Parade, on the other hand, was no longer the site of military and commercial display. With the Castle in decay and the Commercial Exchange demolished, the Parade had become public space. Here rich and poor mingled at the auctions, still a Cape Town tradition. Here too the unemployed gathered to challenge the established order, which was to be shaken in the next twenty years by war and the re-ordering of political and social structures.

For twenty years until his death in 1902 Rhodes had been a brooding presence on the periphery of Cape Town life. He left his mark on the Groote Schuur estate, and in the alien flora and fauna which he introduced into the Peninsula. Politically Rhodes had divided Cape Town more sharply than it had been for many years. His death marked the passing of the high imperial era and he would be commemorated in a number of statues that depicted him gazing out over his hinterland. (SAL PHA)

of the predatory sort, and their habits are as bad as bad can be. Treacherous, venal, and above all things addicted to the use of the knife, these Dago gentry are people to be kept at arm's length. If making this country "a white man's land" means filling it with such as these, then for goodness sake let us stick to the black worker.'[21]

White women, on the other hand, being in short supply, were to be cherished. The fear that British men might intermarry with Boer or black women helped spur the vigorous promotion of female immigration. The British Women's Emigration Association, which helped 'gentlewomen' to find work as 'lady helps' or 'family friends', was partly motivated by concern for Britain's 'surplus women', but also by the notion that the Englishwoman was racially superior, the model of refined motherhood and a civilising agent.[22] In Cape Town such ideas were fostered by the South African Immigration Committee, set up in 1901 with a hostel in Rosebank to encourage women to remain in Cape Town. Some feminists, however, considered Cape Town, with its Contagious Diseases legislation, a thoroughly unsuitable destination. 'A country where the State Regulation of Vice is in force is no safe place for women,' they argued.[23]

The immigrants, the troops, and all the demands of war quickened the Cape Town economy. For a brief moment, during the course of hostilities, Cape Town seemed to be the hub of empire. The docks in consequence were barely able to cope. All day squads of men were kept busy loading long trains of trucks. Berths were too few, storage was inadequate and so were the facilities for offloading lighters, which had once more been brought into use. Trade – indeed, the whole rhythm of life in the town – suffered when the mail steamers decided that delays were too serious to allow them to stop here.

'The spectacle afforded by Table Bay just now is surely unique in the history of the port ... The flags of all maritime nations, British predominating, fly from the halliards of this great fleet.'

Cape Times,
27 November 1899

> The spectacle afforded by Table Bay just now is surely unique in the history of the port ... The natty barque of seven or eight hundred tons, which has brought corn and flour from the granary of South America, Buenos Aires, lies within a cable's length of the vast Cunarder from Liverpool. Close by is a big 'tramp' from the Antipodes, and further away a swift ocean-goer from New York. The flags of all maritime nations, British predominating, fly from the halliards of this great fleet.[24]

These difficulties could not be blamed entirely on the war. Although the tonnage of

shipping in Cape Town trebled between 1881 and 1899, expansion of facilities had barely kept pace with demand. Now hasty remedies were undertaken. The new coaling jetty, still under construction, was brought into use for the lighters; more stores were built; and the Harbour Board purchased 23 powerful steam cranes to land cargo. As a result of a select committee of inquiry the Harbour Board took over much of the docks contracting, ousting the private companies. Another consideration was labour. The stevedores, profiting from full employment, improved their pay by 1s a day. But in the post-war depression, despite a number of strikes, their wages dropped as strikers were forced out by scab workers from Ndabeni location.

By 1900 most of Cape Town's dock labourers were Africans recruited from the Willowvale district of the Transkei by local headmen, who acted as intermediaries between the workers and the Harbour Board. At the docks they worked under 'native foremen', or 'serangs', a system which continued well into the twentieth century. Although many lived in the city until the plague epidemic, there was a long tradition dating back to 1879 of housing dock-workers in barracks (see detail above). Conditions were bleak, but they were infinitely better than the Kimberley compounds, cheap at 1s a week, and close to work. (CA AG951)

An alternative source of employment for black migrant workers was the construction industry, which prospered in wartime Cape Town. New commercial properties abounded: the Harbour Board and the Chamber of Commerce both erected new offices, the latter 'one of the most striking buildings in Cape Town'.[25] The residential area of Tamboerskloof expanded by leaps and bounds, and City Tramways extended its lines. Their expansion down Hanover Street fostered the development of District Six and Woodstock, making these areas more accessible to the city. In 1900 Woodstock reported 538 new buildings erected including 451 houses, 19 shops, a school, a brewery and a hotel as well as two cold-storage facilities.[26] In these circumstances some Capetonians engaged in their favourite activity of rash speculation, this time in property. Prices soared, only to crash in 1904 when depression struck, and many Capetonians lost their fortunes, including H.M. Arderne of The Hill in Claremont. The centre of that patriarchal family disintegrated.

To a limited extent the South African War also hastened the industrialisation of the city. Some needs of the British Army had to be met locally: B. Lawrence & Co. successfully tendered for the supply of a host of canvas goods like nose-bags, canvas mangers and tarpaulins. Between 1899 and 1904 capital investment in machinery in the western Cape doubled, as did the number of factory workers, reaching nearly 12,000 by 1904. But essentially the pattern remained the same as that of pre-war industry, with the main strength in light manufacture, above all in food and clothing.

Conditions in Cape Town's early industries were unpleasantly similar to the sweat workshops of nineteenth-century London. In 1906 bakers worked at least 84 hours a week. In the clothing industry the putting-out system meant long hours in cramped and

Rhodes commissioned a statue of Van Riebeeck, which was placed at the foot of Adderley Street in 1899. Conceived as a statement about Europe's conquest of savage Africa, it became a site for opposition to imperial power. Here on Sunday mornings socialist speakers, such as J.L. Page, a founder of the SDF (pictured here), harangued the crowd. (W.H. Harrison, *Memoirs of a Socialist in South Africa,* Cape Town, n.d.)

unhygienic homes while the factories, attempting to compete with this cheap labour, demanded equally long hours and offered poor wages. Skilled workers, on the other hand, remained in a favourable position: the average wage for white artisans was between 13s and 16s a day as late as August 1903.[27]

Although high unemployment and casual labour militated against successful combination by unskilled workers, artisans began to challenge existing employment practices. British and Australian immigrants in particular, coming from a more militant labour tradition, established a socialist movement in Cape Town. Several minor socialist organisations had been formed in the town in the late nineteenth century. In 1903 workers founded the Political Labour League, the first genuine labour party in Cape Town. Then in May 1904 there emerged the Social Democratic Federation (SDF), allied to the British SDF, sharing with it an abiding faith in the socialist millennium. By 1906 it was a well-established organisation with its own premises in Barrack Street, and its own newspaper, the *Cape Socialist.* Unlike many local craft unions, the General Workers' Union (GWU), set up in 1906, was both non-racial and open to women.

Perhaps the most significant result of the war was to politicise social groups in Cape Town that had previously been outside the mainstream of political life. In Wynberg coloured people, fiercely patriotic, formed a branch of the imperialist South African League, which, they believed, supported 'equal rights for every civilised man'.[29] In 1901 John Tobin started the Stone meetings at which, regularly on Sundays, coloured people met at the top of Clifton Street in District Six to debate political issues, current affairs and labour matters. A strong black consciousness strain ran through the rhetoric of the Stone speakers and also in the pages of the *South African Spectator*, founded in 1901 with the express intention of encouraging black empowerment and upliftment. The same was true of early political organisations. Through the influence of the Trinidadian advocate Henry Sylvester Williams and the West African journalist F.Z.S. Peregrino, the ideas of American black consciousness leaders and Pan-Africanism were spread in Cape Town.

Women in Cape Town's Cigarette Industry

An indication of the increasing social emancipation of women was the growing number of women who smoked publicly. But in Cape Town women were producers as well as consumers of tobacco. Cigarette manufacturing, often from Turkish tobacco grown in Oudtshoorn, was one of Cape Town's new industries. Conditions were harsh. Policansky's employed children of nine or ten, working 10 hours a day for 5s a week. Premises were overcrowded and insanitary. Backed by the GWU, the women downed tools in 1906 in a widely supported strike which was sustained by a workers' co-operative that made 'Locked-out' cigarettes. Although it could not survive in depression conditions, the episode marked a step in the development of working-class consciousness.[28]

Women working in the Kloof Street factory of the United Tobacco Company in Cape Town. (SAL PHA)

The Stone Meetings

'The Stone is at the top of a circle of smaller stones. These smaller stones are the reserved seats. You must come very early to secure them. The space enclosed by them is vacant, but outside the circle are gathered some hundreds of coloured men – Kafirs, Hottentots, Cape boys, half-castes ... All crowd together and pass newspapers and tobacco bags to each other ... The intellectual standard of the meeting is equal to that of any British labour meeting. You are amazed to see a native with a copy of "Nineteenth Century" in his hand, criticising an article by a London bigwig on the South African labour question. You are equally amazed to hear a native discussing the financial condition of the British colonies, and what is more, to see that audience – as is apparent from the remarks – understand very well what he is talking about.'[30]

Members of a Stone meeting in 1905. Reclining in front was Isaac Purcell, a self-styled 'working-man's candidate' in municipal elections. (SAL PHA)

Born in Accra and educated in England, where he married an Englishwoman, F.Z.S. Peregrino (1851–1919) was strongly influenced by American ideas of black upliftment. He came to Cape Town shortly after the first Pan-African conference in London in 1900 and founded the first black newspaper in the city, the *South African Spectator*. Short-lived, never a financial success, the *Spectator* was nonetheless a voice for the new coloured political elite in Cape Town. (SAL INIL 24184)

Americans and West Africans like Williams and Peregrino thought in 'black' rather than 'coloured' terms. Although in Cape Town their audience may have been mainly coloured, they were concerned with a larger identity. The same was not necessarily true of the coloured elite, ambivalent as they were about their identity, feeling that their language and culture was Asian or European as much as African. While black consciousness and socialism infused the thinking of early coloured politicians, there were other influences at work as well. Organisations like the Independent Order of True Templars and the YMCA provided much of the early leadership, emphasising temperance and moral reform. Furthermore, until the 1930s many coloured politicians still clung to their imperial loyalty perhaps because the empire seemed to offer the promise of non-racial justice and equality, lacking in South Africa.

All these influences were at work in the new party formed in September 1902 in Claremont: the African Political Organisation. The APO was African in name but its predominant appeal was to the coloured elite, above all the teachers who struggled to

The African Methodist Episcopal (AME) Church was another vehicle of black empowerment in Cape Town. It was started in the city in 1897 by the American-born Rev. F.M. Gow and received a boost in 1900 when L.J. Coppin (pictured above) was appointed as the first resident bishop of South Africa. Although the AME Church was primarily a movement among Africans, the founding in 1901 of the Bethel Institute attached to the church in Cape Town, which was inspired by Tuskegee Institution in the United States, made the city an important educational centre for coloureds as well as Africans. (SAL INIL 24173)

maintain their respectability and aspirations on pitiable salaries. The early founders, including small businessmen and a lay preacher of the AME Church, reflected these concerns.

Africans in Cape Town were by no means isolated from these developments but the circumstances of location life produced other reasons for them to challenge the colonial state. Conflict hinged on the right of government to demand rents: 10s a month including a railfare into town. The protest against the enforced use of the train and the call for freehold titles as in the Grahamstown location were soon being led by Alfred Mangena, then teaching at a night school in town and saving to study law in London. Mangena was quick to appreciate the significance of the successful Supreme Court appeal of one Arthur Radas against the payment of rent on the ground that he had been forced to live in the location against his will. On Sunday 29 June 1901, Mangena urged a stand against government demands. The following day a mass boycott of the trains ensued; some commuters were prevented forcibly from buying tickets and glass was broken in train windows. 'The natives', wrote the assistant general manager of railways, 'have taken

Dr Abdullah Abdurahman

In September 1904 Dr Abdullah Abdurahman (*c.*1872–1940) became the first black man to be elected to the Cape Town municipal council, representing District Six. The next year he became president of the APO, holding the position until his death in 1940. In his life and work Abdurahman embodied vividly the dilemma of the coloured people in Cape Town. Highly educated, married to a Scotswoman, Abdurahman was a member of the elite. But although he was personally popular amongst Cape Town's coloured working class, neither he nor the APO was populist and they failed to mobilise the masses of the coloured poor in Cape Town. A skilled and determined politician, Abdurahman maintained his political position in the municipality partly because he was at heart a conservative. Though his moderation alienated him from a later, more radical generation, all the same Abdurahman would dominate coloured politics throughout his life.

Dr Abdurahman sitting on the municipal council on the occasion of the visit of the Prince of Wales in 1925. Behind him is Miriam Walsh, the first woman to sit on the council. (SA Cultural History Museum)

Alfred Mangena in legal garb. He left for England during the unrest of 1901 in Ndabeni to qualify at the Inns of Court. (T.D.M. Skota (ed.), *The African Yearly Register*, Johannesburg, 1930)

Members of the Guild of Loyal Women were drawn largely from Cape Town's British middle-class elite. Underlying the formation of the Guild was the belief that political traditions were maintained in the home. (SAL CW I 544)

charge.'[31] The result of this unrest, which ended with the arrest of resisters, was to put the Cape Town location on a legal footing with the passing of the Native Reserve Location Bill in 1902. By means of the Act, circumstances under which resistance might occur were carefully obviated and the location was renamed Ndabeni after Walter Stanford, head of the Native Affairs Department.

The new political movements gaining ground in Cape Town were male-dominated. At this time black women remained excluded from politics, but white women found a separate path through a host of imperial, suffrage and philanthropic organisations. The Guild of Loyal Women, formed early in 1900, was explicitly imperialist, intended to maintain and foster 'the spirit of loyalty to the Queen and fidelity to the British Empire'.

At the Alexandra Club middle-class women claiming equality with men established their own club, the counterpart of the City and Civil Service clubs. Their aspirations were satirised in the conservative press. (SAL, *The Owl*, 19 December 1902)

Julia Solly

A key figure in the Cape Town suffrage movement was Julia Solly (1862–1953). Educated at Cheltenham Ladies' College and Liverpool University, in Paris and Leipzig, she came to South Africa in 1890 after her marriage to Hubert Solly, a government engineer. Like so many of the women in the suffrage movement, Solly started her public career in the WCTU but her interests were far broader, for she was a founding member of the NCW and the first woman to join the South African Association for the Advancement of Science. Social issues like child welfare and housing occupied much of her attention and, almost uniquely in Cape Town, she was a campaigning pacifist during the First World War. (SAL PHA)

Within these bounds it was also a bridge-building body between British and Dutch. To a limited extent this goal of reconciliation was achieved, for the first committee in Cape Town included a substantial number of Dutch names, most from well-known anglicised families. The core of the membership was provided by the Claremont Nonconformists. The first meetings were invariably held in 'Arderne Dorp' – The Hill, in Claremont – and the Arderne and Fairbridge women were leading members. In many respects the Guild of Loyal Women was a transitionary organisation. Neither explicitly feminist nor philanthropic, it mobilised women for the imperial cause without challenging the existing social order. Emphatically middle class, it held little appeal to women of any other social group. A strong inspiration in the founding of the Guild was Sir Alfred Milner; he played a prominent part in its early public functions. Yet the very fact that men like Milner felt such an organisation had value was an acknowledgement that women had a political role to fulfil.

Many of the Guild women were members of the Women's Christian Temperance Union, the most vigorous feminist body at the Cape before the war. Cape Town feminists also drew on another inspiration: Olive Schreiner, who was a major figure in stimulating the suffrage movement even if her views, broadly socialist and non-racial, were unusually comprehensive. Although Durban led the way in 1902, Cape Town saw the formation of the Women's Enfranchisement League (WEL) in 1907 under the aegis of the WCTU. It remained rather aloof from similar movements elsewhere in the country. Indeed, when a national organisation was formed in 1911, the Cape Town WEL did not join and it continued to operate semi-independently for a long time.

In these years the expansion of women's political rights often occurred without much fanfare. In 1912 a new municipal ordinance granted all women who were property holders the right to a municipal vote on an equal basis with men, although they were still excluded from sitting on council. That privilege came at the end of the First World War, the result of the 'noble work' performed by women during the war, as the administrator of the Cape Province declared.[32] Yet Cape Town's electors were slow to take the oppor-

Those involved in the women's suffrage movement were often drawn from the same elites that provided membership of the Guild of Loyal Women and the WCTU. (SAL PHA)

tunity of enabling a woman to represent them and it was only in 1921 that Mrs Miriam Walsh was elected to the Cape Town municipal council.

A potentially more significant change was the politicisation of Afrikaner women. In this regard some leadership was given by liberal Englishwomen like Georgina Solomon, the British-born widow of the Cape politician Saul Solomon, who founded the Zuid-Afrikaansche Vrouwe Federatie (ZAVF) in 1903. Born out of war, the ZAVF was preoccupied with the politics of reconciliation within the framework of empire, pursuing the ideal of a white South African identity (though there are indications that Georgina Solomon herself held a more all-embracing vision).[33]

A very different trend was revealed in the formation in 1904 of the Zuid-Afrikaansche Christelyke Vrouwe Vereniging (ZACVV), soon to become the ACVV. Typical of the early leadership were Elizabeth Roos, the wife of a Cape Town *dominee*, and Margaretha de Beer, who had been educated in English at the Huguenot College in Wellington, and was the wife of the Woodstock *dominee*. The ACVV had strong rural connections and its interests linked Cape Town Afrikaner women with their sisters in the interior. Notwithstanding its church affiliations it was never a wing of the Dutch Reformed Church and the ACVV women in fact fiercely resisted interference by churchmen in their affairs. Closely associated in the ACVV's activities were the promotion of Afrikaner nationalism and philanthropic work on behalf of women. 'If one asks, what reason does the ACVV have to exist? The answer is: because the *volk* has need of the organisation. It is no chimera but a fact that woman is keen-witted and sure of heart. Her keen eye sees and her tender heart feels. Especially as regards the poor, the sick and the fallen a woman can help more than a man. Our people have need of help ...'[34]

'If one asks, what reason does the ACVV have to exist? The answer is: because the volk has need of the organisation. It is no chimera but a fact that woman is keen-witted and sure of heart. Her keen eye sees and her tender heart feels. Especially as regards the poor, the sick and the fallen a woman can help more than a man. Our people have need of help ...'
De Zuid-Afrikaan,
16 November 1907

These Afrikaner organisations were often deeply divided amongst themselves. The ACVV remained always a Cape-based movement, with a residual loyalty to the Crown. But its incipient nationalism and espousal of the *volksmoeder* concept led it into conflict with Solomon's ZAVF, which did not survive in the post-war political atmosphere. As Olive Schreiner explained in 1905: 'The Africanders are all quarrelling among each other. The two women's organisations hate each other with a hate that passes words, and the Women's Christian Union (not Mrs Solomon's, the other) are fighting among themselves. There has been a bitter newspaper fight raging, no doubt you saw in the S.A. News and the Cape Times, between Mrs Koopmans[-De Wet] and Mrs Roos ...'[35]

Yet another body of note to emerge in these years was the National Council of Women (NCW), formed in 1909 as an umbrella organisation to foster women's interests. Its existence indicated how women's organisations in Cape Town had proliferated. Like the ACVV, the NCW promoted the welfare of women and children, in a move to 'maternalism', which was a feature of international feminism in the 1920s and 1930s. Through the International Council of Women the NCW acquired strong international links, bringing Cape Town women into close contact with women's issues abroad. Despite occasional attempts to co-operate with Afrikaner women, the NCW remained a white, English-speaking, middle-class movement, beneficent in intention but essentially patronising, remote from the mainstream of women's life in Cape Town. Through their marital and social links, however, the women of the NCW had the ear of influential men in the city, making them a force to be reckoned with.

Depression, Poverty and Riot

The emergence of the Social Democratic Federation, the APO, the ACVV and the English-speaking women's organisations all subtly marked off Edwardian Cape Town from the Victorian era. They also posed a challenge to the imperial order. But it was poverty and unemployment that would give rise to even sharper protest in the early 1900s.

Although war had brought full employment to Cape Town, already by the middle of 1903 there were indications that the country was passing into depression. The financial incompetence of the ruling Jameson government did nothing to relieve the situation yet when that stern financial manager, John X. Merriman, took over as premier in 1908, his determination to put the Cape on a sound economic footing before it entered Union made conditions still harsher. He introduced the Cape's first income tax designed, at a flat rate of 10s on all incomes between £50 and £100 as a start, to touch the small man. His 'ten bob' tax was bitterly hated.

The main focus of government concern was the skilled British labourers, threatened by competition from foreign aliens and local coloured artisans. The municipal Citizens' Employment and Relief Committee and the relief work provided by the government labour bureau were both intended to ameliorate their lot. But the unemployed were now more organised and less willing to accept patronising relief. Under J.L. Page of the SDF they founded an Unemployment Committee to look after their interests, an organisation that was soon at loggerheads with the Citizens' Relief Committee, which accused the 'noisy agitators of the so-called unemployed' of being 'loafers'.[36] At the heart of the quarrel lay a number of issues – conditions of relief work, rates of pay and the responsibility of society to the unemployed. 'It was the duty of the community to deal with this problem of the unemployed, and it should not be left almost entirely to the Salvation Army,' Page explained; and at the foot of Van Riebeeck's statue he elucidated their grievances.[37]

Relief works were intended for British artisans, and left the coloured unemployed unprovided for. Now for the first time coloured political organisations took up their cause. Peregrino and the Coloured Citizens' Vigilance Committee initiated soup kitchens in October 1904 to relieve distress in District Six. The soup kitchen, later run by the Salvation Army, was a 'revelation' of the extent of suffering amongst coloured people, the *South African News* considered.[38] Socialists were also sympathetic. Why should coloureds be banned from the relief works? the maverick socialist George Woollends asked. They were ratepayers and citizens of the country and gave generously at collections during meetings beneath Van Riebeeck's statue. Eventually the clear evidence of coloured distress, publicised by Woollends, Peregrino and the newly formed APO, forced the government by the end of 1904 to provide limited relief work for them.

The social crisis in post-war Cape Town led to discussions about the role of philanthropy, a debate which occurred against the background of a British inquiry into the Poor Law. Dependence on the benevolent rich and emergency appeals were no longer adequate, the *Cape Times* argued in March 1905. The city needed a better organisation for raising funds and for investigating cases. While the government labour bureau had become a more professional institution, measuring the state of trade and supply and demand in the labour market, the role of private philanthropy was less clear. State intervention and poor laws, or better-coordinated private charity? These were the issues. In April 1906, before the problem had been resolved, the Relief Committee ran out of money and closed down. Unemployed men were left entirely to the mercies of the government labour bureau.[39]

It was clear that tensions were rising high and hostility was growing – to the Salvation Army; to the relief works where men were 'in a condition of semi-revolt'.[40] Meetings

During the hooligan riots of August 1906 the young James La Guma, stimulated by his discovery of socialism, was in the thick of the action 'hurling armloads of bread out through the smashed windows of bakery shops into the scrambling, clutching hands of the cheering workers' (James La Guma Memorial Committee, *James La Guma*, n.p., n.d., p. 4). (SAL PHA)

increased – in the Socialist Hall in Plein Street, in the Social Democratic Hall in Barrack Street, as well as on the Parade – demanding that work be given to all unemployed workers, that they be paid a fair living wage, and relief fall under government control, not that of religious or charitable institutions.[41]

Finally, on a fine half-holiday on 2 August a crowd of nearly 800 people gathered on the Parade, including 'a large number of low-class people from the slums' and also 'a good sprinkling of respectable looking young white men and a few women'.[42] Carrying placards they marched up to parliament to make an appointment to meet the prime minister. The following Monday, 6 August, people reassembled. This 'wretched-looking crowd' was surrounded by the police. 'Dapper mounted men were stationed at the head and tail of the gathering, their sleek, well-fed horses presenting a striking contrast to the hollow-eyed ragged human beings around them.'[43] In a long meeting the prime minister promised assistance to destitute wives and children and work for a hundred men at a 'farm colony' near Caledon. While the gathering had been mostly orderly, there can be little doubt that there had been some wild words. Urged on by provocateurs, a body of 'hooligans', which 'consisted entirely of coloured persons', dashed up Plein Street, 'shouting and yelling'. They seized boots hanging outside Mr Henry's boot store, and linen and hams from shops in Church Square, and made a 'clean sweep' of the goods outside shops in Caledon Street before moving on to Hanover Street.

For another two days crowds continued to roam the central city, meeting sometimes on the Parade or pouring through District Six, to the fear of the respectable. Socialists anxiously dissociated themselves from the proceedings. As for the Stone leaders, carefully constitutional, they had no desire to be linked with the riot, and urged coloured people to show by their conduct that they were law-abiding and orderly. As with the cemetery riots twenty years before, the Volunteers were called out to help the police and gradually order was restored.

The riots gave a fleeting glimpse of the constituency of Cape Town's poor and of the tensions and changes occurring within this community. Many of those who were arrested were first-generation Capetonians. Women too were active participants and three were arrested although the language of protest had been that of Victorian patriarchy – the defence of starving women and children. Another element was squatters, who swept down from the slopes of Table Mountain on the evening of 7 August. The riots also made it clear that gang formation was well developed in the town. Certainly, coloured leaders were concerned about 'the crowds of coloured youngsters loitering about the streets' who had formed themselves into 'organized bands of thieves with "captains," pass-words and so on!'[44] On the other hand, there were no 'Malays' involved, the *Argus* noted approvingly. This was, the paper believed, an outbreak of coloured rowdies, part of a general manifestation of unrest among the native population in South Africa.

Tuberculosis becomes a Social Issue

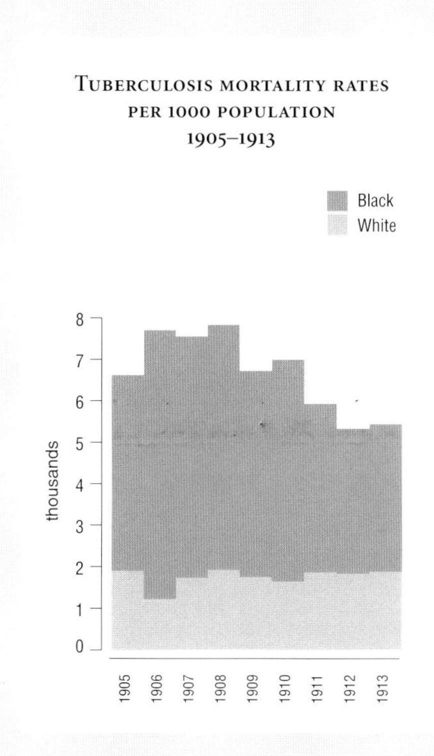

Clear evidence of poverty in Cape Town was the increase in tuberculosis. Although Muslims had long been familiar with *tering ziekte*, there was no doubt that, by the end of the nineteenth century, the disease was spreading, identified by improved diagnostic and statistical techniques. Cape Town took a national lead in the fight against the scourge yet the problem was attributed primarily to the 'ingrained habits of the people' including 'the high rentals of the houses, the thriftlessness of the people, their natural dislike of work, ignorance of the merest rudiments of domestic hygiene, the utter disregard of the necessities of their children ... and an unreasonable extravagance in such luxuries as pleasure and dress. The high rentals may fairly be attributed to the sins of omission and commission of the working classes themselves.'[45] Given the dire financial state of the colony, Cape Town had few resources to fight tuberculosis. Jasper Anderson, Fuller's successor as municipal medical officer of health, led an active educational campaign and struggled to improve medical facilities. Shelters were built at the City (Infectious Diseases) Hospital, which was opened in 1902 next to the New Somerset Hospital.

The Old Somerset Hospital

For many years the Old Somerset Hospital had been the main institution providing for the relief of poverty in Cape Town. By the early twentieth century, however, it was desperately cramped.[47] Its portals were 'forbidding', its surroundings symptomatic of conditions within, 'bounded on one side by a disused, neglected cemetery, and on the others by dirty, narrow streets'. Added to this was 'an extremely undesirable intermingling of white with black, of sane with the insane, and of the healthy with the unhealthy.'[48] Jane Waterston's report in 1902 gave some indication of the suffering within. Many of the patients were congenital syphilitics for whom there was no hope and no future. 'If women knew that they came for cure, and when cured would be sent out there would not be the same hopelessness about their lot ... these unfortunates seem imprisoned for life,' she commented. Her suggestion that the young women be allowed out occasionally was unsympathetically received.[49]

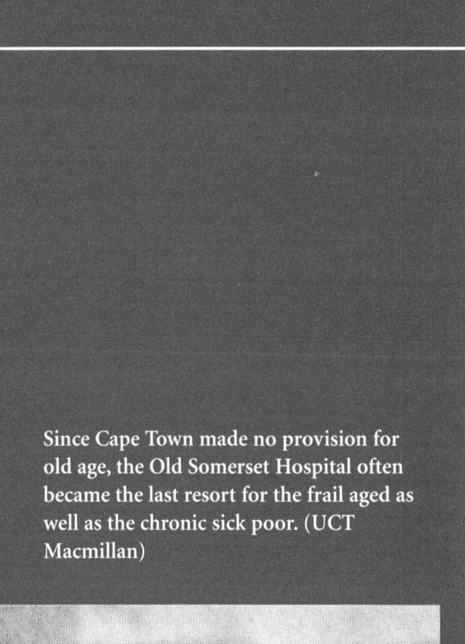

Since Cape Town made no provision for old age, the Old Somerset Hospital often became the last resort for the frail aged as well as the chronic sick poor. (UCT Macmillan)

One result of the 'hooligan riots' was to drive the APO into more active support for the coloured unemployed. Both the municipality and the government agreed to provide relief work for them. Yet in many respects, the hooligan riots took the spirit out of labour protest. Although complaints about conditions on the relief works and demands for state intervention continued, more and more white artisans simply left the country.

The unemployment riots occurred against a background of increasing poverty. The war had pushed up rents, the price of meat and fish had risen, and although inflation was not severe, a sense of deprivation altered perceptions of the cost of living. To be unemployed or even an ordinary labourer almost certainly meant living below a minimum subsistence level.

Overcrowding in Cape Town exacerbated ill health. The average number of people per house had risen from 6.7 in 1891 to 7.6 in 1904. More and more were shacks built of corrugated iron or even wattle and daub. Meanwhile, on the boundaries of the municipality squatting was increasing. Many Africans avoided the location: in 1901 there were 'black spots' on the Rondebosch Flats (West London), at the Elsies River *mok* (squatter settlement) and on the Mowbray Flats. By 1903 Africans evicted from these areas were sleeping in huts on the mountain. But although housing became a matter of public debate after the war, Cape Town's ratepayers were not prepared to fund accommodation for the poor. Virtually nothing was achieved before the First World War.

Debates about poverty broadened in the aftermath of the hooligan riots. The private philanthropy of the Salvation Army and the Ladies' Benevolent Society was no longer acceptable to the articulate unemployed. Whereas the Army lacked 'tact, discretion, privacy and gentleness, all of which are called for', the LBS was worse. 'Anybody who has had experience of charity organisations knows how obnoxious it is to have those well-disposed, idle ladies prying around. They have no knowledge of the poor and very little sympathy with these unfortunate victims of a bad system ... Their kindly superior way of assisting, with their kindly little lectures, always sets the teeth on edge.'[46] Nevertheless, it was in the context of private charity that professional social work developed, against a background of changes in the organisation of British philanthropy. In 1908, inspired by the Charity Organisation Society of London, the Cape Peninsula Charity Organisation (CPCO) was formed to ensure the systematic co-operation of all charities, and to prevent overlapping and a waste of resources. This, it was hoped, would discourage the indiscriminate giving of alms. Whatever its limitations, the CPCO engaged in the first professional welfare work in Cape Town.

Although 'wife desertion' was one problem which came to the fore, it was the plight of children that caused the most concern. Again, international influences were at work at a time when anxiety about national deterioration was leading the middle classes both in England and the colonies to examine more closely the conditions under which children were born and bred. In Cape Town in 1902 the municipality appointed a female sanitary inspector to investigate infant deaths. Other areas of investigation were 'baby farming', especially common for illegitimate babies (who were now sedulously recorded); the rise of gangs; and the practice of employing children in Cape Town's expanding factories. The CPCO was one of the first organisations in the city to raise its voice against this practice.

This new awareness of the plight of Cape Town's children contributed to greater welfare provision for them. In 1907 the Infant Care Protection Act was passed and the following year the Child Life Protection Society was founded. Dr Jane Waterston had established a Ladies' Branch of the Free Dispensary many years before to provide maternity care for women (carefully confined to legitimate births, with the result that 'marriage lines' were common currency amongst poor women of District Six). But the focus continued to be on ignorance and poor sanitation rather than the social conditions that gave rise to these small tragedies.

Of far-reaching significance in determining the prospects of children and reinforcing coloured poverty was the passage of the 1905 Education Act. On the one hand the Act expanded white education for the first time but on the other it restricted coloured children to the underfunded mission schools in the town. As a result segregation and the inequitable distribution of resources were now firmly entrenched in the educational system of the colony.

Although private philanthropy remained a strong feature of Cape Town welfare, the colonial government had long accepted some responsibility for the chronic sick poor. Between 1906 and 1908, moreover, the government spent £60,000 on poor relief. At this time too, interest in state welfare was aroused by the 'poor white' issue, which became publicised in Cape Town by the Transvaal Indigency Commission when it took evidence in the city in March 1907. As the *Cape Argus* explained, poor whites were a danger to the state. 'It lowers the moral tone of both whites and natives, depreciates the value of labour, leads to crime, and breeds a deteriorating generation.'[50] The new prime minister, John X. Merriman, had no doubt that poor whites had to be raised from their condition by the government: 'for the benefit of the natives in the country and for the benefit of our condition in the country we should keep the European races at the top.'

Yet when the Cape entered Union in 1910 there had been few practical changes. The emigration of white artisans had reduced white unemployment and, as the economy began to pick up, conditions improved for those who remained. The same could not be said for the coloured poor, now severely depressed. In a united South Africa conditions were to become even more acute in a society in which 'poor whites' were already being treated more tenderly and the protection of white labour became a high priority. Moreover a Transvaal-dominated Union parliament had little interest in Cape Town's problems or, indeed, in social welfare generally and had few resources before 1919 to tackle such social issues. That would have to wait for after the First World War.

Leisure, Rational and Irrational

In the early years of the century a tense wartime atmosphere, restless refugees and an influx of immigrants of all kinds combined with the erosion of familiar middle-class values to arouse anxiety among the white elite. There was, it was claimed in 1901, a reign

This satirical cartoon made fun of the inability of the police to end the post-war crime wave. (SAL, *The Owl*, 15 August 1902)

of terror in the town, a 'carnival of crime'. Drunkenness, gambling and prostitution seemed to be increasing. In September 1902 the commissioner of police estimated that there were 'about 30 gambling institutions' and 'a few Chinese dens' in the town, as well as about 150 brothels. Of the 600 prostitutes, he thought only about 100 were coloured, a very different profile from the pre-war years.

There was some truth to these perceptions of a crime wave in Cape Town. During the war, criminals from the Rand found their way to the city and European prostitutes were active in petty theft as well as soliciting. Prostitution at 7s 6d 'short time' and £2 to £3 a night proved a lucrative occupation in these affluent years. Stories like that of Frederick Colborne, a retired clerk from Observatory, alarmed respectable Capetonians. At midday one Saturday, walking down Longmarket Street, Colborne was accosted by two women who implored him to come into a nearby house. Inside they solicited him. When Colborne tried to leave, one, Sarah Zimmerman from Russia, caught him by the jacket. After he made his escape he found he had lost his purse containing £17. Capetonians demanded action from the government; church deputations met the attorney-general and public meetings were held. A Purity League was formed to fight vice. There was another aspect to the problem, as the attorney-general explained to parliament:

> From what he heard from clergymen and other who were constantly coming into contact with Kafirs and the natives generally, it appeared that a considerable traffic was being carried on in Cape Town between aboriginal natives and white European women. There were certain houses in Cape Town which any Kafir could frequent, and as long as he could pay the sum demanded, he could have illicit intercourse with these white European women. This was a matter of the gravest importance, for once the barriers were broken down between the European and native races in this country, there was no limit to the terrible dangers to which women could be submitted, particularly in isolated places.[51]

'There were certain houses in Cape Town which any Kafir could frequent, and as long as he could pay the sum demanded, he could have illicit intercourse with these white European women.'

The attorney-general, 1902

It was these fears that led to the passing in 1902 of the Betting Houses, Gaming Houses and Brothels Suppression Act, more simply known as the Morality Act. Forbidding intercourse between black men and white prostitutes, the Act represented another stage in the progress of segregation in Cape Town.

The police force, which was expected to implement the new legislation, remained undermanned and underpaid. More men were recruited during the war but a deputation to the attorney-general in 1903 noted that people had entirely lost confidence in the police. A small number of plainclothes men, the 'morality police', were given the special job of enforcing the new law. They became familiar with the haunts of the organised pimps and brothel keepers, making them vulnerable to corruption.

There was clearly a clash of cultures at work. For Jewish and Chinese immigrants a gathering of fellow countrymen to play cards was not immoral: to members of the Purity League they were engaging in vice. Just how broad definitions of sin were, emerged over the next few years. A Totalisator Bill to extend betting at the races led to howls of dismay: this was seen as the legalisation of vice. Even more abhorrent was the introduction of *fin de siècle* literature into Cape Town. Foreign writers, ranging from Boccaccio to Balzac and Zola, were deplored. The press trod a lofty and confused line. Although works of genius should be preserved, they ought not to be broadcast among the people, the *South African Review* argued. 'Indeed, I have so much faith in the improved taste and moral sense of the people in these days, that I feel convinced nine-

Rosie Zeeman was a young Russian Jewish immigrant who worked for a ladies' tailor in Sea Point. On the evening of 22 March 1904 she was walking up Buitenkant Street on her way home from work when she was accosted by a couple of men, bundled into a cab, assaulted by them and carried off to the Wale Street police station. Here she was booked for soliciting, her address given as 40 Caledon Street, a restaurant owned by a notorious pimp, Max Harris. Barely able to speak English, Rosie Zeeman had difficulty pleading her innocence and it was some time before her family were able to find out what had happened to her. She was rescued only after she had been convicted, but her case aroused great indignation in the Jewish community and led to a widespread investigation into the actions of the morality police.

The Rosie Zeeman case opened a can of worms. It became clear that the morality police were deeply implicated in local crime. Local people were fascinated, for the incident revealed how much Cape Town had become part of a national crime network. At the centre of the investigations was Max Harris, described as a tinsmith and plumber, who also kept a dubious restaurant. Harris was known to run a gambling den and lived largely off the earnings of prostitution. Even more sinister was Joe Silver, one of the most notorious members of South Africa's underworld. In the end both men were sentenced rather lightly, along with David Charteris, a young Scottish policeman who had been closely involved with them. The morality police were disbanded and their work distributed amongst the ordinary police.

The scandal over the Zeeman case by no means ended public concern about crime. Underlying much of the anxiety was hostility to new immigrants. Jews and Chinese were singled out as malefactors. A typical example was that of Benny Silberman, Solomon Son and Woolf Whitkosky, charged with keeping a gaming house at 40 Primrose Street; 21 other men, nearly all Jewish, also appeared in court. They had, they explained, been playing solo whist and 66 but, it was reported ominously, racing and betting cards had also been found.[52]

Chinese 'gambling dens' were raided repeatedly. The 'fan tan case' at 83 Buitengracht Street demonstrated the extent of prevailing xenophobia. Accused of playing 'fan tan' and smoking opium, the assembled Chinese were, so it emerged, members of the Chinese Empire Reform Association, composed of Chinese Christians and potential converts and a number wanting to learn English. The Rev. E. Baker of the Baptist Church confirmed that they had collected money to pay the costs of evangelisation and had contributed to the New Somerset Hospital. Their appeal was unsympathetically received by the attorney-general, who declared that they had been gambling within the definition of the law. Fortunately Baker's solicitations had some effect, for 'Chock's' sentence was reduced from six to three months. In gratitude the Chinese presented Baker with 'a quaint and beautiful Japanese china tea service, and silk handkerchiefs'.[53]

(SAL, *SA Review*, 6 May 1904)

(SAL, *The Owl*, 21 August 1904)

tenths of the men and women who picked up a copy of Balzac's "Droll Stories" would have no inclination to peruse its contents.' At worst, works of genius should be bowdlerised. 'There are many and really good editions of foreign classics which have undergone a judicious process of excision, rendering them suitable for the "popular reader," although they are not sufficiently attractive to the purulent mind which is ever in quest of foul literary garbage.'[54] The unfortunate Ernest Frederick Reichenbach of the Corner House bookshop was fined £10 for selling *Cousin Laura* by Marcel Prévost.

'Rational' pastime was promoted as one means of combating vice. It also had a positive commercial value, especially when it was associated with Cape Town's growing tourist trade. In 1913 Cape Town's reputation as a seaside resort was enhanced by the building of a three-storey pier at the foot of Adderley Street. On the lowest level were bathing boxes, fishing platforms and rowing boats for hire. 'Every lunch hour the pier was filled with men who used to have a daily swim. With some it was a point of honour to dive off it once a day'.[55] The upper levels housed an auditorium, a bandstand with copper-domed roof, restaurant, café and news stand. Entertainment ranged from arcade games to concerts, theatre and cinema. The pier's crowning glory was its observation tower, unhappily also the favourite choice of Cape Town's suicides. Steam yacht trips left from the pierhead and it was here that yacht races started and foreign dignitaries were received.

In a poster competition sponsored by Cape Town's publicity association, the pier featured prominently, emblematic of Cape Town's self-image as a cultured holiday resort. (UCT)

Cape Town gained its first publicity association in 1909 to tap the local and overseas tourist market. In particular Muizenberg was promoted as the 'Brighton of South Africa'. Since the 1880s it had been popular with mining magnates, as the many Baker homes testified. After the railway reached the coast in 1882 boarding-houses and hotels began to attract middle-class up-country visitors. Soon the heart of central Muizenberg was dubbed 'The new Jerusalem' because of its popularity with Jewish holidaymakers. Mixed bathing was now enthusiastically encouraged despite its 'dangers'. 'Nothing could be worse than to get on speaking terms with a stranger in that way. It would be the most indiscreet thing a woman or girl could do' – a comment that was a sure indication of common practice.

Other forms of recreation were encouraged. The town council made land available at Green Point Common for white and coloured sports clubs, built swimming baths and laid out De Waal and Trafalgar parks. For 'working men' the ground floor of the old Town House was converted into a library. In the southern suburbs Cecil Rhodes made the upper reaches of Groote Schuur estate accessible to the public for picnicking in 1890 through the allocation of 200 keys to 'some citizens'; after his death this area was opened to everyone.[56]

For James Ford the Coons had become an integral element of the Cape Town scene. (SA National Gallery)

The New Year Carnival also became a more regulated form of public entertainment from 1907 when a highly organised procession of seven troupes marched from the Parade to Green Point Common on New Year's Day. The names of these troupes were testimony to American minstrel influence, which affected appearance as well as performance – the Jolly Coon Masquerade Troupe, the Jolly Coons, the White Noses, the White Eyes or the Diamond Eyes. Within a few years, probably reflecting the growing reach of the cinema, names and costumes had become more exotic and international. The 1909 carnival featured the Spanish Cavaliers, the King's Messengers and the Prince of Benin's Escorts. On the Common, troupes performed for prizes before a crowd of onlookers. Significantly, the judges were 'mostly white' and included 'several from retail firms'. Although street parading on New Year's Eve returned by 1909, the daylight competitions endured: the tamed Coon Carnival had arrived, assisted by the association of

Rhodes bought large tracts of land on the lower slopes of Table Mountain as a scheme for a national park. After his death the road he laid out through the old Kirstenbosch farm became Constantia Nek Road and the farm itself became the site of the National Botanic Gardens in 1913. This project was one of the first expressions of the new South African national identity, drawing on the rich fynbos vegetation of the western Cape for national symbols. (SAL PHA)

carnival troupes with coloured 'sports and pastimes' clubs. Indeed, it was representatives of seven of these clubs who had met together in November 1906, under the auspices of the Green Point Cricket Club, to plan the 1907 carnival competition.

The hooligan riots made the white middle classes even less tolerant of unlicensed street activities. In 1906 a new council regulation forbade all processions, except those associated with funerals, without the written consent of the mayor, and then only 'by such routes and in the manner specified in such consent'. A hundred coloured men hauled up before the magistrate for 'playing banjos' were told that the town 'had had too much of this sort of procession – quite enough of it. By-and-by the men would not be able to control themselves, and then there would be trouble. They had had riots recently.'[57] Moreover, it had been noted at the time that some of the rioters had 'hair done up in the latest coon fashion'.[58]

Women drivers were relatively uncommon in the early years of motoring at the Cape, but motoring would eventually change their lives as much as it affected the economy and the urban landscape of the city. (Margaret Cairns)

For the coloured elite, also alarmed by the riots, the way to respectability lay thro the internalisation of white middle-class values. To be respectable meant to be morally upright and financially independent; industry, honesty and self-control were the hallmarks.[59] Rejected by whites, the tiny coloured middle class established its own temperance movements and a YMCA. The APO campaigned against drugs, alcohol and immorality in favour of education, sensible recreation and 'race pride'. To promote coloured ethnicity was also to promote respectability. As such, it was entirely appropriate that Mrs Abdurahman and other APO leaders should attend coloured sports meetings and hand out the prizes.[60] Yet this process of asserting respectability widened the cultural gulf between different classes and groups of coloured people. In a letter to a newspaper a Muslim condemned *klopse* and 'the going about the streets singing and the jollification. It is all against our belief and religion, and I feel ashamed that these young people should be knocking about the streets in the way they do.'[61] Respectability was also a matter of choice in which poverty played only a limited role: in the early 1900s an ex-

The Boys' Brigade

The Boys' Brigade, formed in Cape Town in 1894, was a militarist organisation for working-class youths, explicitly intended to regulate male social behaviour. By 1905 there were 16 companies and 500 members. Although membership was mixed, individual companies tended to be segregated. In Cape Town the main focus of the Boys' Brigade was the reclamation of street children, as John Parker, captain of the 1st Cape Town Company, explained – 'we picked them off the streets, of the roughest boys in town, and oh! were they wild!'[62] The name 'The Black Watch' for the 1st Cape Town Company was a reference both to the Scots influence and to the colour of its membership.

'The Black Watch', 1st Cape Town Company of the Boys' Brigade. (*The Boys' Brigade Gazette*, 1 February 1896)

ted a church service in her cottage on the anniversary of emancipation, ı of some fishermen was to get drunk in the Queen's Hotel.

ıg men of the emergent gangs chose to actively challenge dominant val- re not new to Cape Town. Already in 1826, 13 slaves and free blacks, eries of burglaries, had been described as a gang. But the term only came into regular use, associated with a criminal 'class', in the late nineteenth century. In the 1880s the Rodgers gang specialised in theft, and all its members had criminal records; in the 1900s there was at least one gang among squatters on Table Mountain whose members 'make their livelihood from crime'.[63] Although a very different breed from modern urban gangs, as early as 1876 'the Hanover Street gang' in District Six was 'becoming quite a terror to the neighbourhood'.[64] In the 1890s another Hanover Street gang received considerable publicity for street fighting and preying upon Christian congregations on Sunday night. According to a police inspector, members of the gang lounged on street corners and 'no respectable person could pass without being interfered with'.[65] In the same decade another gang terrorised the Harrington Street neighbourhood on Saturday nights; a 'Malay mob' was 'at work' in Buitenkant Street hijacking vans; and a gang in Somerset Road fought with police when the latter tried to disperse them. By the 1900s Cape Town had gained a reputation among southern African cities for the extent of its organised gangsterism, one it has not lost. Until the 1960s most of the gangsters were coloured and much of their activity centred on District Six, although there was at least one African gang in West London on the Cape Flats in 1905. Gangs came to dominate illegal gambling, liquor and drug dealing as well as theft.

Young men like this group in Bo-Kaap formed the core of early twentieth-century gangs. (UCT Macmillan)

Disrespect for authority was reflected in a subculture characterised by particular forms of organisation, appearance and language, including satirical names. One gang in Woodstock in the 1900s called itself the Rough gang. Another in District Six was the Hanover Street Burglars' Club and there was also the Steal Club that met outside a hotel where members worked as musicians. Gangsters also spoke a disreputable *tsotsi taal*, or 'thug language'.[66] The journalist George Manuel remembered that gangsters in Cape Town between the two world wars wore caps back to front, trousers at half-mast and jackets, shirts or belts that displayed emblems. In this way they proudly identified themselves as *tsotsis* or 'skollies' – literally 'scavengers', people who did not have to work for a living.[67]

Across the town, and segregated from the mainstream of town life, was Uitvlugt location, where a new community slowly emerged, stunted by the nature of its creation. The location grew rapidly after it was established in February 1901, and by the end of March it was home to 6000 people. With the depression numbers dwindled to an average population of just over 1000 until the First World War. The residents were mainly male migrants although about a tenth were women, many described as 'of Hottentot, Malay and mixed races' rather than African. Churches, emblems of respectability, sprang up rapidly; within a year there were six. A government primary school was opened in 1902 but the Anglicans had already founded St Cyprian's Day School the year before. Seven night schools catered for adults. Employers were often unenthusiastic about this passion for education, complaining that it attracted their domestic servants to the location in the evening; and, because children were at school, 'it is naturally very difficult to recruit servants from the ranks of the juveniles'.[68]

In the location, which had in fact been established by the colonial health department, accommodation was bleak, overcrowded, insanitary and regimented. Control was the keynote of the administration, symbolised by the grid of streets patrolled by African

Ndabeni Location

Ndabeni was Cape Town's first planned township but its residents were outcasts from the town, still tainted with the stigma of the plague camp. The main structures were five large dormitories, each accommodating 500 men. In addition 615 unlined lean-to corrugated iron huts housed 8 people each. There was no privacy and cooking and washing facilities were inadequate. There were no floors and until the huts were raised on banks, they were subject to flooding in winter. There was 'plenty of ventilation' through which the south-easter might 'gaily' enter (*The Cowley Evangelist*, July 1901). (CA NA 540; L. Rousby, *Under Table Mountain;* SAL)

constables, the fences surrounding the location, and the constant surveillance of the location inspector and his staff. Yet, before Uitvlugt's establishment some of Cape Town's African residents had believed that a 'model location' might offer them opportunities less easily available in the competitive town. After its establishment a petition asked for government, rather than municipal, control; that 'Native Police' be employed; that all business in the location should be conducted by Africans; and that residents be allowed to buy and build their own houses.[69] But the government was unsympathetic. 'As no Native is capable of carrying on business as a Shopkeeper on a large scale, I am not in favour of these people being allowed to trade here – except on the same conditions as Europeans,' the magistrate at Uitvlugt advised the Native Affairs Department.[70] Instead, Jewish traders became part of the fabric of Ndabeni life. Africans were, however, allowed to run bakeries and eating houses but under such restricted conditions that they struggled to survive in the bleak depression years.

It is probable that the existence of the location inhibited the development of a permanent African population in Cape Town. Whereas an unemployed man might previously have lived in the town, possibly marrying into the local community, and struggling along, unemployed location residents were soon forced to leave and return to the Transkei. The municipality preferred that the supply of labour be regulated by the state by means of the number of passes issued in the Transkei. As for employers, the existence of the location relieved them of the need to provide accommodation for their workers, and they could thus pay lower wages. Despite all this, by 1926, when the location was closed, Ndabeni residents had established a permanent community which was attached to its restricted home.

Union and Unification

The early 1900s were years when the old colonial certainties disappeared. Unification was in the air. On 31 May 1910 the Cape Colony became the Cape Province of the Union of South Africa. Cape Town became the legislative capital of the new state, continuing to host parliament, to be a site of representations to the governing authorities, to see ceremonial processions wending their way up Adderley Street. But Union meant fundamental change as well. Economic dominance had already been lost to the Rand while the value of shipping in Durban's harbour, so much more accessible to the Transvaal, already far outstripped that of Cape Town. Now in 1910 executive authority was also lost to the north. The liberal Cape franchise, attenuated though it might have been, was confined to the province and a few municipalities, the exception rather than the rule in the new South Africa.

But unification was not confined to the nation. In 1913 Cape Town joined with most of the suburban municipalities, from Kalk Bay to Sea Point and also Maitland, to form a single municipality. Only Wynberg stood out until 1927. The *raison d'être* could be summed up in a single word: water. As far back as the 1880s lack of water had dominated Cape Town's political life. For Cape Town itself the dams on the top of Table Mountain had temporarily solved the problem but the South African War and the plague demonstrated how narrow the margin of safety was. The suburban municipalities were not viable at all and constantly had to buy water from Cape Town. Although a parliamentary commission of inquiry in 1902 had made it clear that unification was the only way to go, the suburban municipalities clung fiercely to their independence, convinced that their interests would be neglected in a larger body. By 1902 it was clear that Cape Town would have to look beyond the Peninsula for future water supplies but only

The Dawn of Union

In 1910 *The Dawn of Union* was a popular Cape Town play that promoted the new South African nationalism – one that embraced Boer and British alike, as long as they were white. In contrast the socialist Stephen Black's equally popular *Love and the Hyphen* (1908) lampooned the prejudices among English, Afrikaner and coloured Capetonians alike. One of the few sympathetically delineated characters was the unpretentious coloured gardener, Frikkie January, who closed the play by addressing his social superiors – but moral inferiors – with the words 'You can all go to hell'.[71]

Harry Stodel as John Bull in *The Dawn of Union.* (Jack Stodel collection)

To young Barbara Mackenzie, the Union Pageant was the great celebration of her childhood. 'Everyone seemed involved in the 1910 Pageant, the distinguished and the humble, the Afrikaans speaker and the English speaker, the coloured and the black' (B. Mackenzie, *Salt River Doctor*). Barbara Mackenzie formed part of the court of King John II of Portugal receiving Dias after his successful voyage round the Cape in 1487. Lady Juta was the queen and Mackenzie's mother was a court lady. (UCT BC 1019 G4)

Cape Town could actually afford to bring its water so far. This realisation was gradually and reluctantly forced upon the suburbs.

Nor was Cape Town entirely in favour of such an expensive undertaking. In a division similar to the Clean and Dirty Party conflicts of the 1880s, councillors representing smaller local interests, including Dr Abdurahman and the merchant Hyman Liberman, opposed the larger merchants and businessmen, led by the architect John Parker, the retailer William Duncan Baxter and the past mayors Thomas Ball and Sir William Thorne. It took all Parker's negotiating skills combined with the multiple vote of the

The Union Pageant presented an heroic view of South Africa's settler history. Here indigenous inhabitants, immigrants and Voortrekkers are all captured in a single scene. (SAL PHA)

Born in Greenock, Scotland, John Parker (1866–1921) emigrated to Cape Town in 1883. After working for the architect Charles Freeman for a number of years, in 1890 he opened his own practice. He was one of Cape Town's most influential architects, his distinctive style embellishing a host of Peninsula buildings. (UCT Macmillan)

John Parker represented the progressive forces while the former mayor Hyman Liberman championed those opposed to expensive water schemes. (SAL, *The Owl*, 6 September 1907)

merchants to carry the day. In the face of critical water shortages in the dry months of 1913, Cape Town was finally united with the suburbs.

As the city entered upon a new role, symbolic tribute was paid to Cape Town's imperial era with the opening of the Rhodes Memorial on the slopes of Table Mountain in 1912. Designed by Herbert Baker in a monumental style echoing the classical architecture of Greece and Rome, it was built of granite to last eternally. 'The South-Easter will pour its white cascades dissolving half-way down the mountain; the North-Wester will come with rain-wet wings buffeting with genial ferocity the flanks of Table Mountain, but the Temple shall endure as will the undying work of Rhodes while the years fade and flit.'[72] G.F. Watts's bronze statue of 'Physical energy' represented Rhodes's 'boundless energy, drive, vision and determination' while the eight lions were modelled after Egyptian monumental lions 'to give the highest expression of calm strength and reserve power'. The whole was a statement about imperial conquest of Africa, located on the spot where Rhodes had liked to brood on his vision for Africa.[73]

In another respect too, Cape Town came of age in these years when it acquired the first fully fledged university in South Africa. In 1873 the University of the Cape of Good Hope had been established in Cape Town but this had been purely an examining body. Post-matriculation teaching took place in such boys' schools as the South African College. By 1900 there were over 200 students, including a number of women, attending courses at the SAC and the foundations of a university college had been well laid. A bequest from the mining magnates Otto Beit and Sir Julius Wernher made expansion possible and in 1916 an Act was passed creating the University of Cape Town. The new university was formally established in 1918. Although the original campus was in town, another bequest, from Rhodes, made part of the Groote Schuur estate available for further expansion. In 1929 the vision of a new university on the slopes of the mountain was given concrete form by J.M. Solomon, one of Herbert Baker's associates.[74]

Solomon's vision of UCT's Groote Schuur campus, considerably modified, was eventually completed in 1930. (UCT Macmillan)

Opposite: From Rhodes Memorial, the statue of 'Physical energy', flanked by lions, gazes out over the Cape Flats. (UCT Photographic Society collection)

Cape Town and South Africa had barely entered Union when they were confronted by the crisis of another war. If one may judge from the columns of the local press, in July 1914 few Capetonians had any idea of what lay ahead. Reports of events in the far-off Balkans evoked limited interest. Only on 27 July, as the great powers began to mobilise, was the possibility of war seriously discussed. Even so, most people hoped that South Africa would not be involved. If they should be, the *Cape Times* declared bellicosely, 'none of the nations of the Empire will gird on the sword with greater alacrity, or with greater certainty of the righteousness of the cause, than the South African nation'.[75]

'None of the nations of the Empire will gird on the sword with greater alacrity, or with greater certainty of the righteousness of the cause, than the South African nation.'

Cape Times,
5 August 1914

Within a few days of the outbreak of hostilities a routine had been established: the arrival of news was heralded by the shrill call of the siren. Cable messages would be displayed on screens to the sound of lusty cheering and the nation anthem sung 'with great earnestness'.[76] Censorship of the English-language papers was hardly necessary: the newspapers willingly promoted patriotic propaganda, excluding any serious discussion of the issues of the war. Instead they virulently attacked traitors, made the most of victories, and played down disasters.

Although Cape Town was so far from the centres of war, military considerations soon dominated the life of the town. By the end of July 1914 defence measures were in force and ordinary Capetonians found their movements restricted. Lovers' moonlight strolls on Signal Hill were among the first to go. Soon most of Table Mountain and large parts of the beach at Milnerton were off limits. The Public Welfare and Moratorium Act gave the government wider powers to intervene in civil life: prices of food could be regulated, the sale of liquor controlled, and censorship of 'any form of matter calculated to spread false intelligence, to create alarm or to excite public feeling' introduced.[77] Gradually the provisions of the Act pervaded Cape Town life.

South Africa had no right of neutrality; its only choice was the extent of participation. Given the bitter divisions among whites, the South African government confined itself at first to responsibility for the defence of the Union. Local forces were hastily mobilised for the defence of the 'all-important' Cape Peninsula against the enemy to the north in German South West Africa, and against attack from the sea. Enemy aliens were also rounded up, a difficult task since Cape Town's many German residents were an integral part of the community. Although many had become naturalised, others had retained their German nationality. Now such prominent townsmen as the retailers R. Müller and John Burmeister were deported to camps in the north, along with the men of the Philippi settlement. Their families were left to struggle on as best they could, receiving little sympathy from the public.

Possible African responses were anticipated nervously by white Capetonians. A meeting was hastily convened at St Columba's Home in District Six at which Senator Walter Stanford addressed the assembled gathering in Xhosa, describing the Triple Alliance and arguing that Germany was jealous of Britain's large colonial possessions. White alarm in this respect was unnecessary, for black leaders in Cape Town remained loyal.

Where the conflict affected most people was in their purses. Rumours abounded that shipping would be interrupted. Most of Cape Town's foodstuffs were still imported including, astonishingly, fruit, vegetables, butter and cheese, eggs, fish and biscuits. Shopkeepers and housewives began to hoard food and prices shot up alarmingly. Cries of profiteering arose, forcing the municipality to intervene. A committee of representative citizens, including Mrs E.B. Fuller, Miss Woods (a journalist) and some merchants,

The Midday Pause

The observance of the midday pause started late in the war on 14 May 1918. Three minutes were soon reduced to two. The last pause was honoured in December 1918. 'The sound of the bugle dies away on the last sad, heroic note. Then, complete silence for a hundred seconds or so. They seem like a thousand ... The motionless detachment of the crowds is emphasised by a succession of sounds that emerge out of the background of silence ... But I think that what to me most emphasised the solemn stillness of the occasion was that while I stood in the roadway, midway in the "pause," there came from some shop or office behind, the ringing of a telephone bell ... It rang and rang and rang with a faint distant tinkle, but there was no one to answer it ...'[78]

'Cape boys' who had been working in German South West Africa were forced to return home, only to find that their money was worthless. Early in September 1914 over 100 men gathered outside the offices of the German East Africa Line in Adderley Street in the hope of being able to cash their pay. Eventually they were dispersed by the police with the assistance of Dr Abdurahman. Although they never recovered their losses, by October they had been absorbed into the local economy. (SAL PHA)

Recruits for the Western Front came largely from the English-speaking middle classes. War was often a family enterprise, with brothers from Rondebosch High, 'Bishops' or SACS at the front and their sisters from St Cyprian's or Rustenburg engaged in war work. Of this group of the 'Bishops' cadet corps pictured in 1914, 19 ran away from school to join the army. (UCT Macmillan)

were appointed to hold a watching brief. Prices were published in the press to prevent a 'certain class' from undue price fixing. 'Business as usual' became the order of the day as employers were urged not to dismiss staff and consumers not to withhold spending.

When Cape Town became the base for the Union Expeditionary Force to German South West Africa in September 1914, the face of war changed abruptly. Initially, mobilisation was confined to the Active Citizen Force but on 9 October the prime minister, General Botha, called for volunteers. A few days later, on 12 October, martial law was proclaimed. But German South West Africa was not a popular cause and the Afrikaner rebellion as well as South Africa's invasion, which preceded it, opened up old wounds. Much more glamorous was the prospect of serving in Europe. A few young men, including some coloureds, had enlisted independently in Britain. By the middle of 1915 more and more local men were demanding the right to assist their beleaguered compatriots on the Western Front. Eventually in July 1915 a South African Overseas Expeditionary Force was announced. Recruitment became more vigorous, and central Cape Town was covered in recruiting banners. The department store Cleghorns had two running the entire front of its building: 'Botha's boys, the Empire needs you, join the Overseas Contingent to-day' and 'Clinch your glorious victory here by fighting for liberty overseas', they read.[79]

Recruiting often took place in the streets. (SAL PHA)

The first portion of a contingent to Europe sailed on the *Dunvegan Castle* on 13 November 1915. Recruiting drives became common for the next three years, energetically promoted by the local press, which published lists of successful applicants daily. But many Capetonians had no desire to go to war. As the months passed recruiting slowed, and women were called upon to assist. At recruiting rallies emotions often ran dangerously high and the practice was introduced of alternating speeches with patriotic songs and rousing choruses, to provide the audiences 'with a safety-valve for their superfluous energies and emotions'.[80]

As the war dragged on, recruiting lost its exuberance. Indeed by September 1917 the local recruiting committee was seriously considering resignation. They struggled on: war had become a grim business. Even so, whites were extremely reluctant to put guns into black hands. In terms of the 1912 Union Defence Act blacks were explicitly excluded from carrying arms. Yet for blacks, beguiled partly by propaganda that this was a war against oppression, the First World War offered the hope that through participation their full rights as citizens would be realised. Dr Abdurahman emphasised that under the British flag blacks had at least some small measure of liberty; if the empire fell they would lose even this.[81]

When recruitment for the South African Native Labour Contingent began in September 1916, Peregrino threw himself into the task with enthusiasm. To Peregrino army service was educative, instilling pride and cleanliness in black men. (F.Z.S. Peregrino, *His Majesty's Black Labourers*, Cape Town, [1918], p. 10)

The APO led the way in coloured support for the war yet the government was reluctant to use their services. Finally in September 1915 the imperial government, desperate for manpower, agreed to take the responsibility of raising an infantry battalion for service overseas. It was very much a Cape Town affair, with Dr Abdurahman, the Anglican clergyman Sidney Lavis and the coloured politician James Currey on the recruiting committee. Pay and terms were poor, pegged to the rates of the British West Indian contingents. Above all, the army wanted single men. At first there was no separation allowance, as paid to white soldiers for the support of their wives. Not surprisingly, despite initial enthusiasm, the response was poor in Cape Town. Unable to improve service conditions, the recruiting committee resorted to bands, street parades and stirring posters. Notwithstanding the effort to recruit men without dependants, when the coloured soldiers departed on the *Armadale Castle* on 9 February 1916 it became clear that many women had been left unprovided for. Reluctantly separation allowances had to be organised.

Cape Town Women's Recruiting Drive

After Cape Town failed to produce its quota of recruits for German East Africa in April 1916, women were called upon to rally men to the cause. Boy Scouts led the great women's recruiting drive of 13 April 1916. Some women invaded the tearooms to recruit unwary men drinking tea, accompanied by others who recited or sang patriotic poems and songs. Responses were mixed. Capetonians, who 'dearly [love] ... anything in the nature of a procession', watched, but the faces of the men were 'apathetic' and some 'obviously looked the other way'. A meeting followed at the City Hall in which leading women appealed to patriotic duty and the honour of the city. Young girls were urged not to 'walk out' with men fit to fight.[82] 'There are many of us girls of the Empire who feel as intense a desire to help in the great war as any man who has willingly given his life. It has been hard to feel, as we all have, that after all there are very few ways in which a girl can help ... Let us follow the example of the patriotic business firms, and be prepared to write over the doors of our homes and hearts: "No man eligible for service need apply here."'[83] But the girls were requested to be 'gentle and ladylike in their methods'. The main message was that the honour of manhood resided in women.

(SAL PHA)

For the patriotic who remained at home there was ample room for work. Fundraising became part of the fabric of life for many Capetonians, filling every day with a host of activities. For numbers of middle-class women, working outside the home on this scale was a new experience. Moreover, almost for the first time their contribution was publicly acknowledged when they served on the same committees as men. Nevertheless, it was felt that some forms of support were peculiarly appropriate for women. It was 'women's work to care for the sick and wounded', Lady Innes explained when launching a campaign for the Women's Hospital Ship and Convalescent Homes Equipment Fund. Through their efforts a hospital ship, the *Ebani*, was fitted out.

Relief funds played a crucial role in softening the edge of economic deprivation for soldiers and their families and in relieving the state of the burden of providing for dependants and wounded; at the same time public involvement maintained morale on the home front. Almost any occasion was suitable for fundraising. 'Belgian Day' assisted Belgian refugees and 'Botha Day' collected for the Governor-General's Fund, the most prominent of all the funds. Money was disbursed cautiously but it soon became clear that the need was greatest amongst coloured people. By the end of 1914 they were receiving about half the funds collected. By October 1916 Capetonians had already contributed almost £250,000 to the war effort.

Throughout the war Cape Town hosted thousands of men passing through, often tired, cold and hungry. Australians and New Zealanders were a particularly lively presence. A variety of recreation centres was established by different organisations including a refreshment room in the Feather Market 'Liberty Hall', staffed by women volunteers, and an Australian Rest House with a posse of Australian Military Police. The entertainment of troops also provided much of the recreation of the city during the war years. Visiting Australasians were particularly fêted, especially the wounded veterans of Gallipoli, for whom the city turned out in large numbers. Such cars as Cape Town possessed drove the visitors round the Peninsula, seen off by a 'big and fraternal' crowd. In the streets the New Zealanders received 'distinguished consideration' from passers-by and 'many friendships were struck, which cannot fail ... to tighten the bonds of Empire' (*Cape Times*, 21 February 1916). (SAL PHA)

The return of General Botha at the end of the South West Africa campaign in July 1915 was the first of many victory processions. In the drenching winter rain thousands thronged into the city to welcome the general. Adderley Street buildings were decorated, Garlicks 'gracefully hung with multi-coloured flags, the pillars being draped with palm fronds'. Disregarding the downpour, Botha, the mayor and their wives drove in an open car to the City Hall. The spirit was one of 'magnificent resignation' until the procession appeared, when the crowds 'with waving handkerchiefs and deafening cheers, welcomed the conqueror home' (*Cape Times*, 23 July 1915). (SAL PHA)

Lapel stickers for street collections during the First World War. (SAL AF 1980-80)

Together with fundraising went celebration and commemoration. These rituals sustained morale and the pace of recruitment. As casualties mounted, observances were introduced to commemorate the dead, comfort the grieving and inspire citizens to the cause. Within a remarkably short time after the battle, Delville Wood became one such moment to be remembered. It was South Africa's answer to Gallipoli, enabling the white nation to lift its head with pride after the shame of the 1914 Rebellion; it was an experience uniting white South Africans of both Dutch and English descent.

The war also sent a tremor of fear through the ruling establishment about the stability of the society. In sermons and speeches it was observed repeatedly that this was a 'time of unusual excitement', that a 'wave of ... emotion' was sweeping over the whole community, with a resultant want of self-control; the very air was 'quivering with excitement'.[84] For one thing, considerable changes had taken place in women's lives in the decade since the turn of the century, at every level of society. Perhaps for women rather than men, these changes offered opportunities. 'The life of the girl to-day is far more complicated than was the sheltered life of the girl of former days, and she has many difficulties to contend with', Lady Buxton, the governor-general's wife, told one group of young women.[85]

Middle-class women attempted to guide their juniors in this brave but dangerous new world. A League of Honour was established in 1915, aimed predominantly at white women, schoolgirls and young women in commerce. Founded by the National Council of Women, the League drew on the methods of the temperance movement to pledge members to 'prayer, purity and temperance'. Extravagantly high-minded, appealing both to religious feelings through its intercessionary meetings, and to the desire of girls for companionship and patriotism through work parties, the League proved surprisingly successful.

Young white women were not the only ones whose 'equilibrium' was 'upset' by the war and the presence of soldiers in their midst. The 'Adderley street girl' aroused the concern of the South African branch of the International Federation for the Abolition of State Regulation of Vice.[86] Its members, such as Julia Solly, shared an evangelical high-mindedness which drove them to improve women's lot at all levels of society. Women of their class and time, they did not seek to overturn the structures of their society, but to improve it from within. Concern about prostitution, combined with opposition to the Contagious Diseases Act, led the NCW to propose the introduction of volunteer women's patrols – respectable women who would patrol the streets, using 'moral force' to reclaim young people. The object was to approach girls who were 'indiscreet' and 'carried away by the excitement of the moment' and direct their enthusiasm into 'wholesome' channels.[87] This unlikely proposal, based on a similar movement in Britain, gained ready support from Major Gray, the deputy commissioner of police in Cape Town. The organisation soon fielded over 65 patrols and it had two permanent consequences: one was the appointment of a woman to the police force to deal with women's issues; the second was the formation of the Marion Institute.

Patrolling the Cape Town streets rapidly brought white middle-class women to recognise the plight of young coloured girls, now widely employed in business and industry. After long hours in offices and factories, they were driven by overcrowding in their homes onto the streets for recreation. Poorly educated, lacking resources, there was little for them to do. A club seemed the answer. The fortuitous arrival of Deaconess Julia, an Anglican sister, and the gift of £100 got the Marion Institute off the ground. At 23 Chapel Street in District Six, a night school provided basic education; here too, musical

The Marion Institute. (UCT Macmillan)

drill, singing and Morris dancing gave exercise after sedentary days in the factories.[88]

In the overheated atmosphere of wartime Cape Town, dissidence had no place. Germans suffered most. Prominent German residents with South African nationality, like the Spilhaus family, proclaimed their loyalty loudly and contributed generously to war funds. Poorer families like the women of the Philippi settlement had a more difficult time. Initially the Mayor's War Relief Fund helped South African women married to Germans, but there came a growing resentment against this use of funds, however, and German-born women were left to the mercies of compatriots until the Union government took over this responsibility.

Although the war led to bitter divisions in Afrikanerdom, Cape Town Afrikaners were less affected than their compatriots further north. The city was not completely untouched, however. In 1915 Afrikaner women in Cape Town established the Nasionale Vrouwe-Weldadigheidsgenootskap to raise funds for the families involved in the Rebellion. A few months later the Helpmekaar Vereniging van die Kaapprovinsie was founded to coordi-

Peter Coetzee, last survivor of Delville Wood, died in Cape Town in 1996 aged 98. Born in Chiappini Street, Coetzee typified Afrikaner Capetonians who retained a lifelong allegiance to Smuts, the South African Party and the empire. (*Argus*, 17 July 1996)

A German Childhood in Wartime Cape Town

Mrs Herud's father, C.L.A. Haupt, was interned at the start of the war. His wife had died and the children were alone, apart from the grandparents who had come from South West Africa to look after them. Mrs Herud, then aged 9, and her 11-year-old brother attended Mowbray Public School. Although they had shared in wartime activities like making bandages and knee-guards for the troops, they were teased by the other children, who surrounded them saying, 'You Huns, you Huns, we'll hang the Kaiser on the apple tree.' Eventually the tension forced the family to move to Woodstock where they were closer to the German community, and the children went to the German School, then in Queen Victoria Street. The family kept to itself. The children played in the garden and were forbidden to speak German on the streets. School attendance was circumspect. Even here they played at the back of the school, where they were out of sight, and spoke English. When a troopship put into town, the children were sent home early and not allowed to attend school at all.[89]

The *Lusitania* Riots

Anti-German hostility in Cape Town reached its apogee during the *Lusitania* riots of 1915 after the sinking of the passenger ship, the *Lusitania*, off the British coast on 7 May. As a seaport Cape Town was particularly sensitive to the tragedy and there had been growing criticism of the government's tender treatment of enemy aliens. Early closing had just been instituted and pubs were closed at 8 p.m. on the evening of 13 May 1915, Ascension Day and a public holiday. As a result workers, notably the Salt River boilermakers, 'a boisterous set of people ... if they get full up with liquor', were in town. The troops in Rosebank camp and sailors in port provided incendiary elements. Feelings had been running high all day. When the bars shut large numbers of people 'pretty full of liquor' began to incite one another to attack German shops. Müller's and Spilhaus were burnt to the ground; Koch & Dixie's was badly damaged. In the end 41 buildings were attacked, and a total of £46,726 damage done, mainly to British property. Few rioters were identified or punished. After the riots the government tightened up with new measures against the enemy, interning more Germans and restricting German business.

(SAL PHA)

nate local efforts. This movement proved remarkably successful. The Cape Helpmekaar was the most vigorous of all such societies and the fundraising it became involved in was to form a basis and model for later Afrikaner business enterprise.

The issue that in fact engaged Afrikaners most closely during the war years was the struggle over the birth of Afrikaans. Conservative Dutch Reformed ministers, in other ways the leaders of their communities, still clung to the Dutch of the Bible and the church. Leadership in the language movement in Cape Town lay, consequently, in the hands of younger middle-class Afrikaners, often resident in Tamboerskloof and centred on the Oranje Klub. With the founding of the National Party the desire arose for a representative newspaper and on 26 July 1915 the first issue of *De Burger* was published from Keerom Street with Dr D.F. Malan as editor. Although it was mainly in Dutch, from the beginning it also contained Afrikaans material.

De Burger took over the offices of the *South African News*, now defunct. The Keerom Street building once occupied by the *South African News* became synonymous with the Afrikaner nationalist voice. (*Burger* library)

The only organised groups to protest against the war were socialists and pacifists. The war in fact badly divided the left in South Africa. In 1913 the South African Labour Party, then affiliated to the Socialist International, had endorsed its anti-war stand, but when hostilities started the party came out in support of the war. In Cape Town, however, the Social Democratic Federation emphatically condemned the conflict. During the war an International Socialist League was formed in Johannesburg to promote the values of international socialism. Non-racial from the start, it was to become the forerunner of the Communist Party of South Africa. In Cape Town, slightly aloof from these developments, the old SDF continued to hold sway, although there was also an 'ultra-left' revolutionary group in the town, the Industrial Socialist League.

Cape Town's leading pacifists were the Rev. R. Balmforth of the Unitarian Church and Mrs Julia Solly. Their gentle, reasoned voices gained little hearing in the press. Together they established the South African Peace and Arbitration Society, which shared international opposition to militarism and to secret treaties and alliances, and promoted international organisations of arbitration and peacekeeping. Unable to hold public meetings, the Peace and Arbitration Society confined itself mainly to issuing pamphlets.

Armistice Day celebrations outside Stuttafords in Adderley Street. (SAL PHA)

Balmforth's *The War and the Coming Peace* offered one of the few considered discussions of the causes of war and the need for peacemaking in the new world, but it fell largely on deaf ears. When Mrs Solly stood as a candidate for the municipality in Salt River in August 1918, the *Cape Times* described her as a member of a 'hole-in-corner' organisation: her work was 'pernicious' and it would be a public disgrace if she were returned as a member of the council. It was hardly surprising, in view of the overwhelming public support for the war, that she was not.[90]

By the time hostilities ended in November 1919, the course of war had forged a tentative South African identity, still closely tied to the empire. But it also left Cape Town more divided than it had been since the early nineteenth century. Despite the boost which the war gave to local industry, poverty became even more deeply entrenched and the national government had few tools in place to combat distress. The outbreak of the influenza epidemic in October 1918 was to demonstrate these failings tragically.

Memorials to War

(The Diocesan College, Rondebosch)

The rolls of honour in schools and businesses in Cape Town commemorated Capetonian loyalty to the empire. Such memorials often attempted to enshrine a new South African identity. In the war memorial chapel at Bishops, the older Gothic style was abandoned for a plainer Byzantine influence. 'There is nothing distinctly African about the design, but equally there is nothing distinctly English. Is it fanciful to believe that the architect desired that his chapel should emphasise the truth that the religion of Christ is neither English nor Dutch, but universal and all embracing? Boys who have prayed and sung together under these great arches ... may, some of them, learn too that it is no part of Christianity to foster either racial pride or racial intolerance.'[90] Some 800 Bishops boys had served in the war, of whom 110 had died. Rondebosch Boys' High shared the same commitment to empire: at least 250 pupils enlisted.

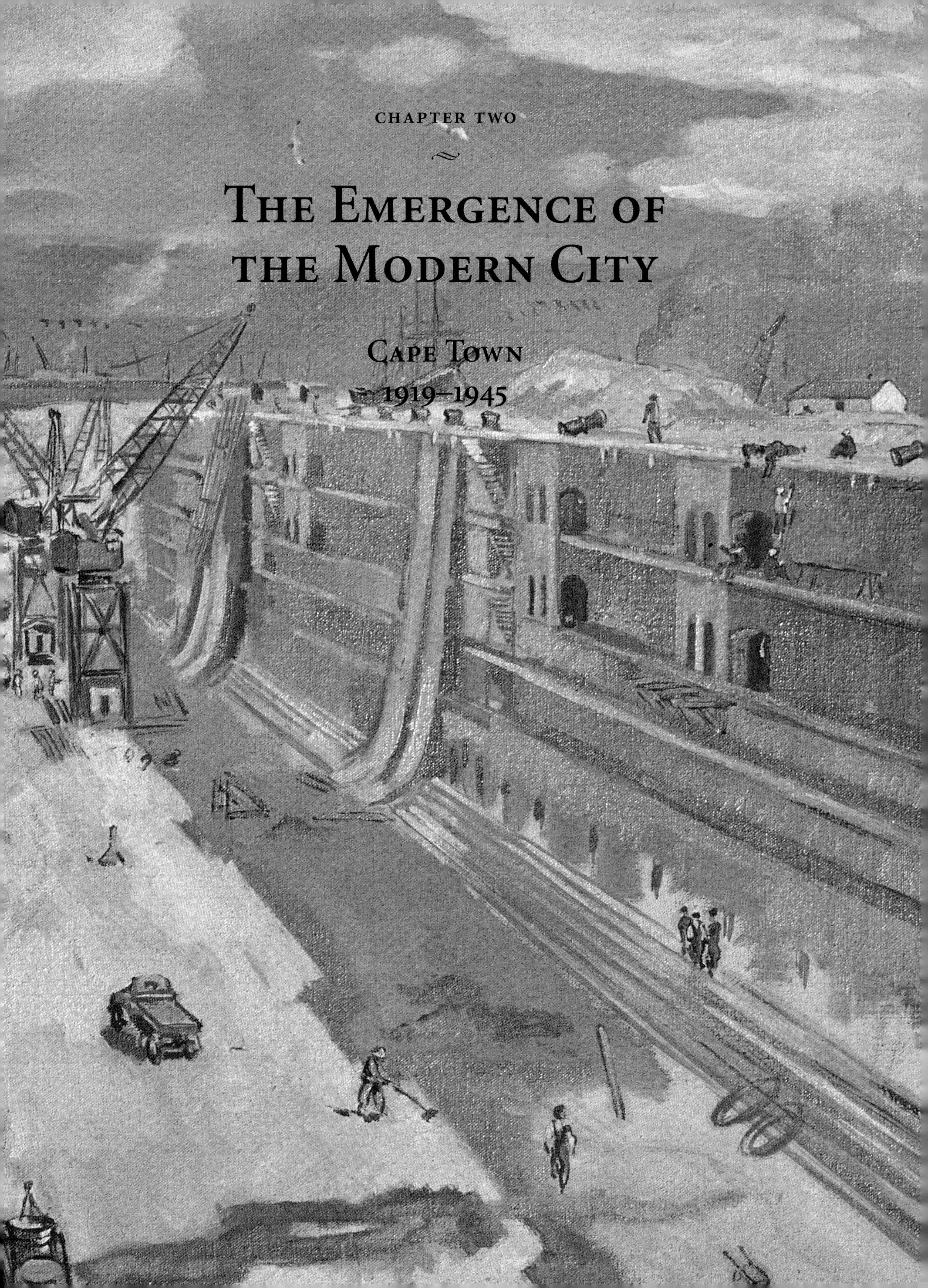

CHAPTER TWO

The Emergence of the Modern City

Cape Town

1919–1945

THE First World War hastened the modernisation of Cape Town. While its basic structures had already been set in place before the Great War, between 1919 and 1945 the town was transformed into an industrial city particularly with the development of the docks and the growth of new manufacturing areas. These years also saw the introduction of many of the facilities and conveniences of modern life such as electricity, motor cars and the cinema. At the same time Cape Town grew into a fresh role as cultural, provincial and legislative capital. A monolithic Provincial Administration building replaced the Wale Street police court, which moved to Caledon Street, to the site of the old barracks. In the Public Gardens the newly built National Gallery, fronted by a fish pond and a boulevard of war memorials, provided testimony to Cape Town's status as cultural capital of South Africa. This transformation was symbolised by the decision of the Place Names Committee in 1930 that the city should officially be styled Cape Town, thus rescuing it from the 'indignity' of 'Capetown'.[1] Nor was Cape Town immune in these years to the great events and forces of the twentieth-century world and of the country as a whole. Depression, Afrikaner nationalism, segregation, ethnic conflict, and protest politics all left their mark on the town. Moreover, national legislation began to divide the city more sharply on racial lines, poverty deepened, and the gap between rich and poor and between black and white widened.

Previous pages: The Sturrock Dry Dock, funded by the Royal Navy during the Second World War to accommodate bigger ships, represented the modernisation of Cape Town's waterfront – ironically at the point when air travel began to reduce the importance of the harbour. Painting by François Krige, who worked as a war artist. (Transnet Museum)

Although the pier stood only for a quarter of a century, it became associated in the minds of older Capetonians, black and white, with a pre-apartheid Cape Town in which remembered social relations were more friendly and intimate, the pace of life was slower, and the town still in touch with the sea. The pier was demolished in 1940 to make way for a major reclamation scheme which isolated the city from its waterfront but provided it with a modern harbour. (SAL PHA)

The Table Mountain Cable Car

The remote majesty of Table Mountain was breached. Until 1929 the mountain had been out of reach to all but the most energetic. In that year a cable car was completed and 'Table Mountain top, hitherto the close preserve of the youthful in body and spirit who have been prepared to face an arduous climb, is to-day accessible without any climb at all'. The journey by air was a delightful experience: 'Thus the comparative impregnability of the old mountain is at an end. Its top will become familiar ground to thousands who would not have had the strength, or the time, or perhaps the inclination to climb there ... Nor were the elders, to whom the top of Table Mountain has been a wistful and inaccessible place of vision, far behind the children in their eagerness to take the journey.'[2]

Between the wars Cape Town grew from a small commercial port to a modern industrial city. The merchants who had dominated the nineteenth-century economy gave way to a new breed of businessmen and industrialists, protected by Union economic policies. Yet despite the increase in industrial establishments in the western Cape, the local economy remained relatively undiversified and modest in scale. Manufacture was still concentrated in the production of food, drink and tobacco, clothing, and paper and printing, as it had been in the early years of the century. Compared with the Rand, Cape Town was not wealthy. In 1939 there were 9000 income-tax payers, compared with over 19,000 in Johannesburg alone. Although incomes over £300 were taxable, the tax rate was low with the burden falling mainly on single men. After 1939 the tax base broadened when changes in legislation led to an increase in the number of taxpayers. By the end of the war there were over 22,000 in Cape Town paying over £11 million in income tax, compared with about £225,000 at the start.

As a result of the combination of 'civilised labour' policies, the search for cheap

THE SECOND TRANSPORT REVOLUTION

In the 1930s Cape Town streets still saw the occasional hansom cab, and trains departed from the railway station (originally built in 1878), but the last tram ran – from Adderley Street to Sea Point – in January 1939. Now, those with £258 to spare could purchase a Hillman Minx. A small car cost about six times the annual wage of an unskilled worker. Motor traffic added a new hazard to Cape Town streets; it also created a host of new jobs in the city, from salesrooms to repair workshops.

Although air travel eventually proved a nail in the coffin of Cape Town's proud claim to be the gateway to Africa, in the early post-war years Cape Town was still the natural destination for pioneer flights. Communications with other parts of the country improved when Union Air Mail was inaugurated on 26 August 1929. On that day Major A.M. Miller left Maitland (the future Wingfield aerodrome) at 7.24 a.m., with 168 lb of mail, planning to reach Johannesburg via Port Elizabeth and Bloemfontein. Although he was unable to complete his mission on that occasion, it was not long before regular air communication was established with the other major cities.

Above: Despite the introduction of motor transport, hansom cabs lingered in the city until the 1930s. (UCT BC 718 A32)

Right: Lt. Gearing arriving at Green Point Common with the first air mail, after a flight from Wynberg. (SAL PHA)

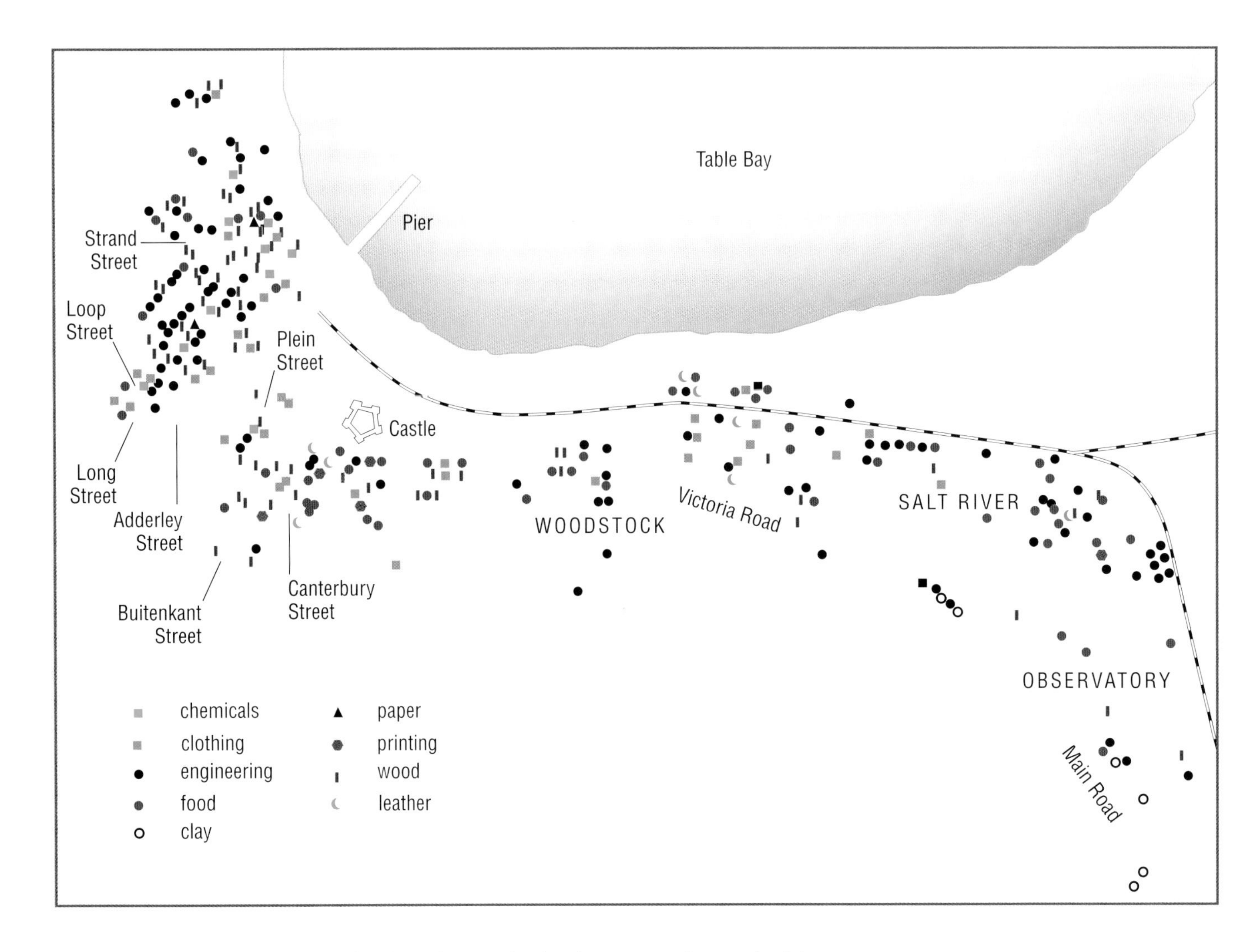

The geography of Cape Town's economy in 1920. The development of industry in the inter-war years reshaped the structure of the city. Economic activity began to move from the dockside and inner city to new industrial sites, in Woodstock and Salt River, and out to Paarden Island, which was reclaimed from the marshes. Ndabeni, once an African location, also became an industrial area. (After Whittingdale, 'Location of industries in Cape Town')

labour and the predominance of light industry, the local economy favoured whites, Africans and women as employees above coloured men. Coloured youths were often excluded from apprenticeship because of their poor schooling; on the other hand, coloured women were far more widely employed than anywhere else in the country. With the Depression years came a substantial shift in the character of Cape Town's workforce: black numbers in general declined in relation to white, with coloured men suffering most. In addition, by 1936 over half the white working population of Cape Town was Afrikaner. Skilled occupations were mostly filled by white men but there was an ethnic overlap in semi-skilled occupations, in which coloured men still held their own. Given this distribution of ethnicity and skill, poverty and colour continued to be closely correlated in Cape Town in the late 1930s.

During the inter-war years the clothing industry became a dominant feature of the Cape Town economy. The first modern clothing factory, A. Fraser & Co., began operation in Salt River in 1907. During the war new enterprises benefited from the demand for military clothing. The conditions of war also enabled factory owners to exploit workers, particularly young coloured women: this would eventually lead to strike action.

Notwithstanding the boost which the First World War gave to the Cape Town clothing industry – at this time local factories produced a quarter of South Africa's clothing requirements – business did not flourish in the early 1920s. Influential retailers like J.W. Jagger & Co., Cleghorn & Harris, Garlicks, and Hepworths still imported most of the clothing they sold. However, the local industry benefited from a campaign to promote tariff protection waged by the South African Manufacturers' Association (later the Cape Chamber of Industries), which had been founded in Cape Town in 1904. All the same it was only after 1924, when the Pact government enacted legislation to protect workers and removed customs duties on raw materials, that the clothing industry really grew. By 1939 about half of all new clothing was manufactured locally, with nearly 6000 people employed in all branches of the industry.

Until the 1930s working women's wages were extremely low. When the more advanced factories began to use specialised machinery and introduced sophisticated production techniques, wages improved, bringing white women into the clothing industry in greater numbers. By 1934 they made up about 40 per cent of the female workforce in the Cape and some firms gave them preference. Work was a means by which migrants were assimilated into city life. New horizons were opened up for them by the workplace. For Mrs Rousseau, an Afrikaans-speaking shop assistant, work at Stuttafords brought her into contact with the English-speaking middle classes for the first time:

> O, dit was heerlik werk. Want kyk, daardie dae was jy nie, jy was nie 'n toonbank, jy't nie agter 'n toonbank gestaan nie, dit was daardie dae toe's dit 'n bietjie select,

A Wartime Clothing Workers' Strike

Wartime conditions led to a clothing workers' strike in favour of improved wages which started on 22 October 1917. The protest was led by a short-lived union, the Tailors' and Tailoresses' Union. Members were based mainly in two firms, A.E. Mendelsohn in Burg Street, and Hogsett, Stephens & Bishop in Loop Street. At a mass meeting in the Metropolitan Hall, attended by the dean of Cape Town, Sidney Lavis, and supported by Dr Abdurahman of the APO, participants protested against conditions which allowed the employment of girls and boys as young as 12, earning as little as 3s 6d a week. By the end of October virtually all clothing workers in Cape Town had come out.

Just after midday on 30 October the strikers marched through Cape Town streets, singing 'Britons never shall be slaves' and carrying banners reading 'Down with sweating'. Two days later an agreement was reached, 'satisfactory to the employees'.[3]

Workers at A. Fraser & Co. about 1930. By this time Fraser's had adopted the policy of employing only white women. (SAL PHA)

Robert Stuart

Robert Stuart (1870–1950) was the 'father' of trade unionism in Cape Town. From 1913 to his death in 1950 he played a dominant role, resisting all attempts to unite the South African labour movement in a single national body. While his criticism of racism in the Transvaal unions gave him worker support locally, opponents accused him of being a bosses' man who sold out the workers.

Stuart had little formal schooling, starting work at the age of 14 as an apprentice to a monumental mason. He worked in Canada and the United States before immigrating to Cape Town in 1901. Although he was a founder member of the SDF, he was little interested in revolutionary Marxism, preferring to solve 'the economic problems of the workers through organization into trade unions'. The Cape Federation of Labour Unions, which he was instrumental in forming, was 'conservative, reformist and Cape chauvinist'.[4] E.S. (Solly) Sachs described him thus: 'unscrupulous and uncouth, cunning, crafty and crooked, without culture or education, he bossed over the majority of workers of the Cape for twenty-five years'.[5] His dominance of Cape trade unions was broken only in the late 1930s when Transvaal-based unions successfully established themselves in Cape Town.

(*SA Baker and Confectioner*, October 1933)

... as jy in ... 'n afdeling werk, in 'n showroom. Want daardie dae het hulle 'n showroom wat net 'n hele vloer op homself [was]. En, man, dit was ook maar, hoe sal ek sê ... it was very snobbish. Die mense wat in 'n showroom gewerk het, het nooit met die ander gemeng nie. Want dit was nou, maar sê 'n spogwerk daardie, daardie dae. Want kyk, daardie dae het jy min goed gekry wat hier gemaak is, omtrent niks ... Want al ons goed was, vernaamlik Stuttafords, al die goed het van oorsee af gekom.[6]

The Second World War reinforced Cape Town's dependence on light industry, particularly the food and clothing sectors. Still trailing behind them was shipbuilding, even though now more important than it had been. Apart from the needs of the South African Defence Force, the convoys passing the Cape created a heavy demand for food, both fresh and tinned. By 1944 the output of the Cape canning industry grew from 96 million lb in 1940 to 198 million lb. The number of workers in the clothing industry increased. By October 1940 Cape Town was also manufacturing aerial bombs and munitions, often in makeshift converted factories and engineering workshops. Eventually about 75 firms and factories were involved in such activities.

Successful industrialisation was the key to victory in the Second World War, as the government was well aware. Once South Africa was thrown onto its own resources after the Nazi invasion of Scandinavia and the Netherlands in 1940, the war was marketed as a showcase for South African industry. Post-war prosperity, it was urged, would rest on present efforts and recruiting drives emphasised the country's industrial potential.

The Steel Commando, a three-mile-long 'commando on wheels' which toured South Africa in November 1940, proved 'a revelation and an inspiration' to South Africans.[7] 'And this army is more truly South African than any in the past: its lorries, its armoured cars, its field guns, the ammunition it would use if it were facing the enemy, are all of South African manufacture. It wears South African uniforms; marches – when it has to march – on South African boots; sleeps under South African blankets.'[8] The Steel Commando was greeted in Cape Town with wild enthusiasm, its stay lingering long in the memories of small boys.

The Steel Commando comes to Cape Town. (SAL Poster collection)

The change to motor transport opened up new opportunities for employment. Motoring came to Cape Town when Garlicks Cycle Supply imported a Royal Enfield Quad in October 1898. It was bought by Alfred Hennessy for £110. (UCT Macmillan)

During the war the docks, now closed to the public, were greatly enlarged. After a massive reclamation scheme which swept away Roggebaai harbour and the pier, the new Duncan Dock was opened in April 1943. At Wingfield aerodrome the Royal Navy equipped the best repair base in the southern hemisphere against Japanese attack, attracting during its construction large numbers of black and white immigrant labourers to Cape Town. This boom in employment absorbed impoverished Afrikaners, African migrants, and women above all.

Leisure in an Industrialised Society

During the inter-war years Cape Town saw a new world emerging as the fruits of modern technology became more widely available. Before the war there had only been a handful of motor cars in the city. After 1918 their numbers increased steadily, transforming the culture of the middle class and opening up new employment opportunities. The motoring pages in the press provided some indication of this transformation. Unfortunately, along with the increase in motoring went car accidents. In September 1929, when there were 17,000 licensed motor vehicles in Cape Town, on average seven accidents occurred a day.

Even more pervasive by 1924 was the wireless. The *Cape Times* began to feature technical notes in its columns and at the end of the year a local radio station was in place. Programmes were painstakingly highbrow. A typical schedule on 25 September 1924 featured a talk on the League of Nations, children's hour, the news and market prices, a Beethoven and Wagner concert in the City Hall, and a talk during the interval by W.J. Makin on 'Adventures in journalism'.[9] When war came in September 1939 the wireless proved a more immediate and potent source of news than the press, and the BBC six o'clock news became a regular feature of Cape Town's wartime life. Cape Town's fish-horns, whose raucous sound the white middle class had railed against for so long, were incorporated into the 'respectable' folk culture of the nation through Cecil Wightman's radio programme 'Snoektown calling'.

For women the electrification of the home constituted the most dramatic change in the 1920s and 1930s. The 'Electricity pages' of the *Cape Times* were introduced to edu-

Globe Engineering

Founded in 1907 by W.I. Perrot in Wright Street, Woodstock, Globe Engineering became engaged during the Second World War mainly in ship conversions and repairs. With Gearings, Globe converted the P&O liner *Cormorin* from a passenger ship to an armed merchant cruiser. During the war Globe was acquired by Anglo-Transvaal Consolidated Investment Co., one of South Africa's foremost mining and financial houses; this strengthened the investment of Transvaal mining capital in the Cape Town economy.

Music making in Cape Town

Music making was a still feature of many lives, from Mrs G. of Parow, whose family sang along to their home organ, to the aficionados of the British Bioscope in District Six, where the audiences sang 'Just a song of twilight' to words on the screen. The band at Delmonico's restaurant appealed to the more select. A District Six resident remembered, 'My father and my mother and my granny were fond of music, they would go to listen to the bands at Delmonico's, which was in Riebeek Street. They were very fond of the Tivoli, I can remember that. And the Opera just on the opposite side.'[10] For Italian immigrants music was also part of their identity: 'Culturally, our family, somehow or other, retained quite a lot of the Italian culture, musically. While I wouldn't say that any of us were great musicians, I do have two brothers who were very musically inclined. They both played brass instruments in a band, not an Italian band.'[11]

In Langa music making was equally popular. There were a number of bands, the oldest of which was the Merry Macs, a jazz and ballroom dance band which played 'dignified music' favoured by the more educated. Younger people preferred the Cordettes and the Disciples. *Mbaqanga* (*marabi* music), strong in Johannesburg, had only a limited appeal in Cape Town.[12]

Cape Town's Municipal Orchestra was formed in 1914 with Theo Wendt as conductor. It was criticised for its highbrow programmes but, the orchestra claimed, it played light and popular music on Tuesday nights and did not disdain to perform 'even dance music' on occasions. Part of high culture the orchestra may have been but its appeal reached the working classes of District Six. (*The Cape*, 17 September 1915)

Wolfram's was the most successful of the early cinemas in Cape Town, charging 6d for continuous shows. The term 'bioscope' lingered on in South Africa into the 1960s. (UCT BC 206-504)

Cinemas were often in the forefront of modern design. The Plaza had a stylish art deco interior. (SAL PHA)

(UCT BC 709)

(SAL INIL 14969)

The Jewish immigrant family pictured above could muster sufficient players for an entire small string orchestra. In District Six guitars were among the favoured instruments.

cate the housewife, as a journalist recalled a decade later: 'I certainly did not then visualise the army of more than 27,000 women who would be doing their cooking electrically in 1939! Nor could I have imagined that in ten years the number of hot water installations would be approaching the 15,000 mark.'[13]

Cape Town was in the forefront of this development, setting the pace for other South African cities. The capacity of Cape Town's first power station at the Molteno Reservoir was later extended by a further station in Dorp Street. The original Dock Road power station was opened in 1904 and its successor, built in 1908, became a prominent feature of the waterfront. By the end of the First World War the sale and supply of power was an important supplement to Cape Town's revenues. Eventually Table Bay power station was built in 1936. The stylish art deco Electricity House in Strand Street became the public face of this profitable municipal enterprise.

The New Year Carnival, on the other hand, had changed very little although by the late 1930s it had become more formally organised. It persisted throughout the bleak years of the war as a 'Visitor from England' observed with relief in 1940: 'Thank goodness for the Coons. They are a real high-spot in the flatness of Cape Town life.' By then a Western Province Jubilee Carnival Board had been instituted to work for 'the betterment of the coons, to improve its organisation, and to keep it under Coloured control'. Despite dissent from some troupes, remarkably large sums of money were donated to war funds in these years, giving the carnival a new respectability in the eyes of the authorities. Their garb took on Allied colours, with the Union Jack, the Union of South Africa flag, and the Stars and Stripes worked into the satin outfits which they wore as they sang patriotic songs.[15]

Women had little place in the carnival, except in support roles, but the cinema gave them new leisure opportunities. By the end of the First World War the cinema was firmly entrenched in Cape Town life, the Globe as much a part of District Six life as the luxurious Alhambra with its Moorish décor was for the wealthier. 'That strange invention', the talkies, were first shown in the Alhambra. In District Six the 'bioscope' was such an integral part of local culture that one couple recorded in 1957 that they had visited the cinema at least three times a week for 48 years. At the height of its popularity, crowds queuing for performances outside the Avalon cinema were so large that buses had to be re-routed. The City Cinema (the 'Brood-en-Wors bioscope'), the National Theatre, the British Bioscope and the Star Bioscope all played to local audiences. In District Six the Avalon was the most superior – it had softer seats and ushers, and patrons were not allowed to take their fish and chips inside. But the popularity of the cinema destroyed older forms of live entertainment: both the Tivoli, home of music hall performance, and the Opera House closed in the inter-war years.

An Immigrant City

Immigration changed the demographic composition of the city. By 1945 the British influence had become noticeably diluted, even if English remained the lingua franca. For the first time since the early nineteenth century the number of blacks overtook that of whites. Most were coloured people but rural impoverishment also drove large numbers of Africans to the western Cape. The influx too of 'poor white' Afrikaners gave a new profile to the working-class districts of Woodstock, Salt River and Observatory, and they flowed as well into the dormitory suburbs of Goodwood and Parow. Whereas Parow had less than 500 white residents in 1911, by 1945 there were over 10,000 and four municipalities burgeoned to the east of the city – Parow, Goodwood, Bellville and

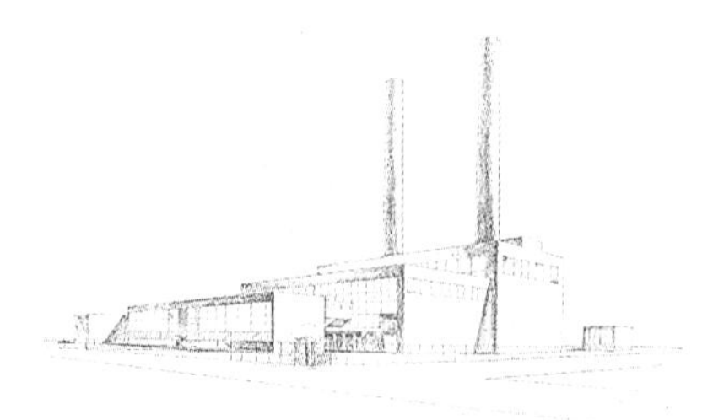

The style of the 1936 Table Bay power station epitomised modern industrial design. (UCT BC 206–504)

G.H. Swingler

The person largely responsible for the expansion of Cape Town's electricity between the wars was G.H. Swingler. A self-educated British immigrant, he shared the post-war belief that the 1920s had ushered in an era of social progress and economic prosperity through technology. One of a new breed of professional managers planning and developing large organisations which used the most modern technology, Swingler forged an effective electrical supply for Cape Town by linking the existing scattered systems. He pioneered marketing methods, running his department like a business, and building up a strong corporate spirit; at the same time he fiercely resisted the absorption of Cape Town's electricity department by the national Electricity Supply Commission, which was then being established. He also launched a publicity campaign to popularise the use of electricity in the home, including a hire-purchase scheme which enabled consumers to acquire domestic appliances. Within four months, at the height of the Depression in 1931, 763 appliances, mainly stoves, were sold, and household consumption of electricity increased by 21 per cent.[14]

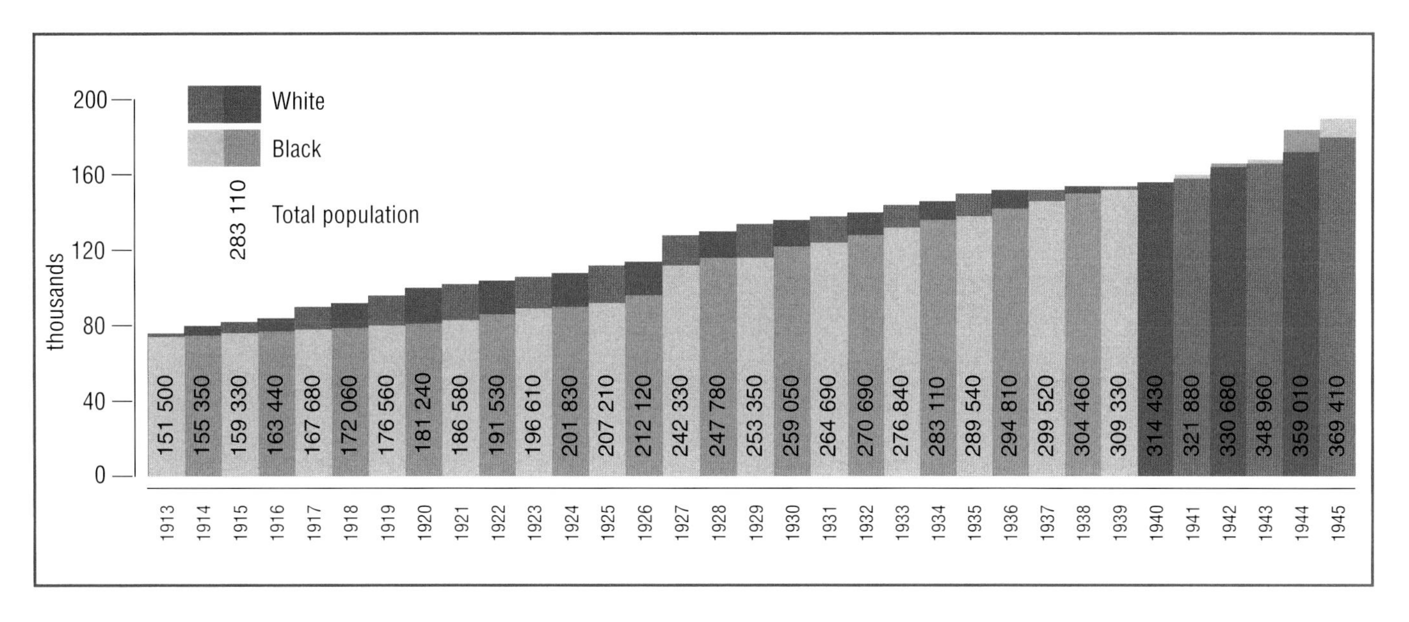

The population of Cape Town, 1913–1945. In 1940 the size of the black population overtook that of the white for the first time since the early nineteenth century.

Durbanville. Gardens, the residential area in the city, became another Afrikaner stronghold between the wars.

For black and white the experience of immigration was often similar. Their various customs and traditions severally and jointly helped dilute Cape Town's Englishness. In District Six, for instance, coloured and white Afrikaner rural migrants rubbed shoulders with Jewish and Indian shopkeepers; West Indians introduced the language and ideas of African America; and St Helenans lived cheek by jowl with Cape Muslims and the descendants of Filipino fishermen. As fishermen and cooks in boarding-houses and hotels, Italians introduced hidebound white Cape Town to the rich variety of fish off the Cape shores. 'People then didn't know about crayfish ... They ate only stockfish ... they didn't know about sole ... The Italians, they ate it, but the others didn't know anything. And calamari ... oh ... people saw them, but no one would eat them. Other fish, no. No, only snoek ... this we sold. [The Italians] understood about crayfish, and bit by bit they brought it in ... The hotels had Italian chefs and Italian *maitres d'hôtel.* So, through

Birthplace of whites in Cape Town in 1936

If white Cape Town became less British, it remained a parochial and provincial town. In 1936 most Capetonians, black or white, were Cape-born. Whites coming from abroad were still predominantly British but a white person in the street was as likely to hail from Lithuania as from the Orange Free State, and more likely to be Russian than Natalian.

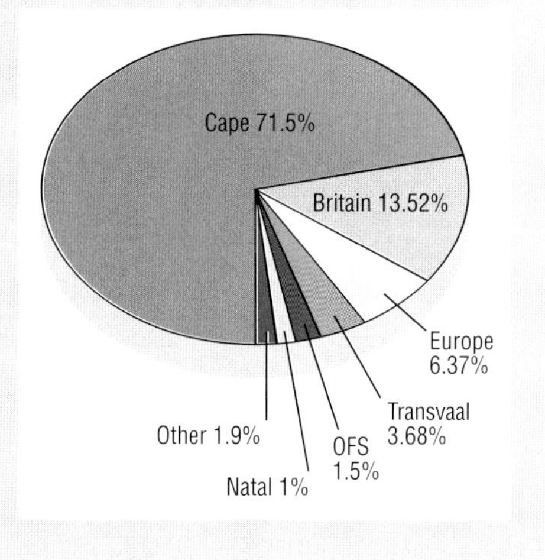

The Madeiran Immigrants

Let the experience of the Madeirans, a small group of Portuguese fishermen, speak for Cape Town's immigrants. The Madeirans left their island home because of economic distress, summed up in one bitter word – *miseria*. The pioneers in the 1930s and 1940s were fishermen who settled in Woodstock because it was conveniently close to the harbour. The stories they told lured others. 'Most of our village, Ribeira Brava, believed that the streets of Cape Town were paved in gold because of letters we received, like other people who also had family overseas, from husband or brothers that were making more money than we could ever make in Madeira.'

Brothers brought out brothers, and nephews followed uncles; wives and children came later. In Woodstock the Madeirans created an ethnic community centring on St Agnes's Catholic Church in Dublin Street. Proximity brought comfort and aid. 'If ever you needed something like the name of a reliable doctor if somebody was sick or a lift to Cape Town with a Portuguese who had a car, it was easy to go and ask a Portuguese neighbour about these things. If they couldn't help you there was always somebody else further down the road or somewhere else in Woodstock who could help you.'

(Private collection)

In Madeira women had been able to contribute to the family incomes through their embroidery but there was no sale for such work in Cape Town. Here they remained at home. For them the church became central to their lives. 'I would very often walk down Roodebloem Road to go to daily mass at St Agnes. It was a custom, call it that, that I was used to from having gone to mass everyday in Madeira.' It was in the home that women consciously nurtured their ethnic traditions. 'A mother is responsible for raising her children in the way that she was brought up, which means that I raised my children as Portuguese. I taught them how to speak Portuguese and how to value what I was taught to value. A tradition is passed down from the mother to her children.'

Fishing was important in their local economy. When Lusitania Sea Products was established in the 1960s, the Portuguese owner made a point of employing his compatriots. 'I looked specifically for Portuguese fishermen and skippers because I wanted my company to get a name as a Portuguese company ... As a "Portuguese," I felt the company could be run better with Portuguese labour because we could communicate in our language and relate to each other better.' Such patronage eased the way for immigrants when quota restrictions in the 1920s and 1930s imposed limits on the numbers of Southern Europeans.

Many Portuguese soon moved out of the fishing industry, preferring the independence of small businesses, especially cafés. Here wives could contribute their labour, in the process breaking down traditional household structures and integrating families more closely into Cape Town neighbourhoods. Even so, many Madeirans were reluctant to leave the familiarity of Woodstock, although they might move up the hill to University Estate. 'My father came out in 1935. I came with my mother and brother later in 1944, by which time he was renting a house in Ebenezer Road. I grew up in Woodstock and to move out meant breaking ties with friends that I went to school with at St Agnes and Queen's Park High as well as family who moved to Woodstock after us.'[17]

them, they brought it into the hotels.'[16]

Apart from the West Europeans favoured by official immigration policy, Jews were the largest group to enter the country in the twentieth century. The poorest established themselves in District Six or Woodstock and Salt River, moving later to Oranjezicht, Gardens and Tamboerskloof, or Sea Point. Many found it easier to assimilate in heterogeneous District Six than in white English-speaking Cape Town.[18] Those who had already learnt the ropes passed the local lore and know-how on to newcomers. While the older people cherished the traditions of their homeland, younger people felt the tug of the modern world. In Ann Kreitzer's gregarious home in Oranjezicht, *landsleit* (kinsfolk) from Kupschik and Dvinsk were constant visitors. Mrs Kreitzer, still believing in the evil eye (*anhores*), practised fortune-telling and dispensed traditional wisdom and advice. The songs and stories she told her children confirmed their East European Jewish culture. But the younger generation preferred cricket, a game old Mr Kreitzer found ridiculous.[19]

The strength of literate Jewish culture in Cape Town was evident in the Yiddish theatre in William Street, District Six; a Yiddish press including David Goldblatt's *Yiddisher Advocat* and N.D. Hoffman's *Der Afrikaner*; an English-language paper, *The South African Jewish Chronicle*; and three Hebrew bookshops, including Beinkinstadt's, which still survives on the fringes of District Six. (CIA Wissema collection)

Older Jewish immigrants often retained East European dress but younger people soon assimilated into the local society. (UCT BC 709)

The Portuguese and Italians, as Catholics, shared a religion with other Capetonians, which eased their assimilation into local society and encouraged marriage with the local population, coloured as well as white. But church and language isolated the immigrant Greeks. As 'sojourners', intending to return home, they were slow to establish their own cultural institutions. As a result their children grew up knowing little Greek. Many left the Greek Orthodox Church for other denominations, the Jehovah's Witnesses being popular. Unwilling to invest heavily in their temporary home, they found the independence of small business, especially café ownership, particularly attractive. Hours were long, hard and lonely. When they decided to remain, Greek families had no desire that their children should follow in their footsteps. Lacking the ties of church, neighbourhood and family, second-generation Greeks were highly mobile socially, moving rapidly into the professions.

Jews also prized education fiercely. 'Oh, they were tremendously in favour of it because they had missed out. My mother had missed out on her education. All they wanted ... [was that] we should be educated one way or another.'[20] In the inter-war years, the Normal College on the corner of Buitenkant and Roeland streets and secondary school at SACS were particularly favoured for boys. Medicine and law were the preferred professions; to a lesser extent this also applied to girls.

Yet the Cape Town Jewish community was not uniform or undifferentiated in composition. The original English Jews often despised the East European newcomers; the Lithuanians on the other hand valued their Yiddish culture and were scornful of the English-speaking Jews' ignorance of Hebrew and talmudic knowledge. As for the German Jews they were 'more German than they were Jewish'. Class reinforced these cultural differences: the Gardens *schul* was 'a posh place' while in the Roeland Street *schul*, attended by East Europeans, 'they really prayed – they spoke to God'.[21] Cape Town Jews found in Zionism a focus beyond their immigrant home and Zionist organisations flourished. The blue collecting box of the Jewish National Fund to buy land in Palestine was a familiar sight in many homes. Notwithstanding these allegiances Jews played a vigorous part in Cape Town's political life, especially on the left. Men like Sam Kahn and A.Z. Berman contributed a radical flavour to the council when they were elected to the municipality in the 1930s.

In general white immigrants, however poor and uneducated, enjoyed opportunities which were not available to any coloured or African. But discrimination was not confined to blacks in Cape Town and immigration did not mean equality. The Immigration Quota Act of 1930 had Eastern and Southern Europeans as its target, while the Aliens Act of 1937 excluded German Jews. Once in the country these immigrants, moreover, found themselves the objects, at the least, of subtle social discrimination. Jewish immigrants arriving in Cape Town in the 1930s were horrified to find the streets lined with posters declaring, 'Kaffirs and Jews indecently assault white girls'.[22]

The *Stuttgart* Incident

At the end of October 1936 the *Stuttgart* was due to arrive in Cape Town with Jewish refugees on board. At the Dagbreek university residence in Stellenbosch a number of academics, including the future prime minister H.F. Verwoerd, planned a protest march, and on 26 October the Greyshirts, Cape Town's largest fascist organisation, held a well-attended meeting of protest at the Koffiehuis next to the Groote Kerk. Later that evening, when rumour had it that the *Stuttgart* had arrived, a thousand people poured down to the docks. Their efforts were wasted, for the ship eventually docked the following day, when rain dampened fascist enthusiasm. Only immigration officials and porters were there to meet the *Stuttgart*.

The stormy politics of their European homelands often preoccupied immigrants. Fascism had fairly widespread appeal for Cape Town Italians, although its attraction was an expression of national identity rather than a political credo. When Italy entered the war in June 1940 the Italian consulate became a target for anti-fascist feeling. A crowd of young men collected outside the Italian consulate on Grey's Pass at the top of Queen Victoria Street. They tore the Italian coat of arms off the building, amid catcalls and hooting and, when the police arrived, made off with it. (*Cape Times*, 11 June 1940)

Ethnic Identities

Between 1919 and 1945 war, economic depression and ideology were to influence the ways in which Capetonians conceived their various identities in a united South Africa.

Long after it ended the Great War left a lasting mark on whites, coloureds and Africans and came to be commemorated in different ways, which were bound up with their several identities. For much of white Cape Town, the war was the true expression of South African nationalism, representing a fight for South Africa's freedom and the cause of civilisation. These sentiments would be embodied in Delville Wood Day. A more concrete commemoration of the war was to be found in the memorials erected after 1919.

Symbolically, perhaps, blacks had no expensive stone memorial. The Cape Corps held an annual service in the City Hall, commemorating the capture of Square Hill in Palestine on 19 September 1918. In December 1920 a plaque was unveiled in the vestibule of the City Hall by General Lukin in memory of the coloured men of the South

The Adderley Street War Memorial

In 1920 a conspicuous site at the bottom of Adderley Street was chosen for Cape Town's main war memorial, for here 'our gallant South Africans took their last glance back at the old city and mountain and heard the cheers of friends as they marched down to the Docks or passed on to the train from "Potch" to embark on their great adventure'. The memorial took the form of two bronze figures on either side of a central needle; this supported the symbolic figure of Victory, modelled on the torso of the Winged Victory of Samothrace, which was chosen as 'one of the noblest examples of Greek art, wrought before that art had spent its creative force and had begun to direct a subtle and technical mastery to serve private luxury and pomp'.[23] The Winged Victory had long fascinated Olive Schreiner, who had 'a lovely big picture of the Winged Victory hanging over my mantel piece'. 'No picture has ever been to me what this [is] ... Broken, defaced, without head or arm – and yet so strong, moving on to victory!'[24]

The memorial figure, now complete with head and arms, fell short of Greek standards, Sir Percy FitzPatrick thought. 'The face is, if I may so express it, pretty rather than majestically or divinely beautiful.'[25] Two bronze fighting men were, however, 'perhaps the very best I have ever seen'. At the base was a roll of honour, covered by a bronze door which had a bas-relief design of Delville Wood. The memorial was unveiled in August 1924.

For the Earl of Athlone, the governor-general, the shrine surmounted local loyalties. 'I cannot but believe that the existence of these visible memorials, which are to be found throughout the world – silent witnesses to the desolation of the war – will through the years to come, be potent advocates of peace and will eventually serve to draw all peoples together in mutual understanding.'[26]

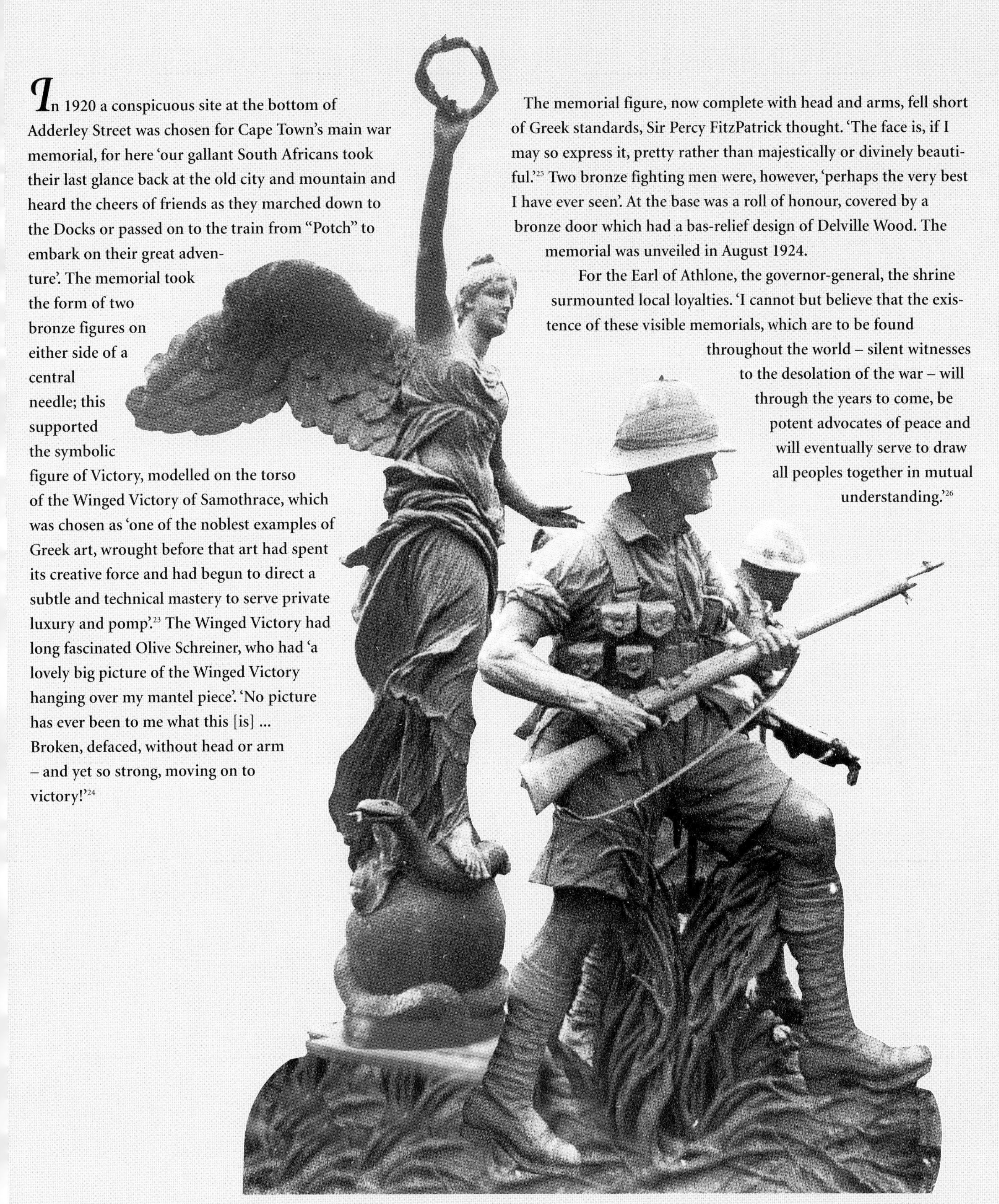

(SAL PHA)

African Field Artillery who had died in German East Africa and Palestine. Yet as late as 1973 the Coloured Ex-Servicemen's Legion was still trying to raise funds for a war memorial for the Cape Corps.

Cape Town's African residents mourned their losses in the Mendi Day commemorations on 21 February each year. In Cape Town the Mendi Memorial Club was started in 1920 by S.M. Bennett Ncwana, one of the founders of the Industrial and Commercial Union, and I.B. Nyombolo, editor of the *African Voice*. Ncwana secured such notables as the eastern Cape journalist Tengo Jabavu and the Cape Town merchant J.W. Jagger as patrons. Mendi Day had a national rather than a tribal basis, unlike many other township celebrations. From the start it also had strong connotations of 'black upliftment', for the experience of war had given veterans like Ncwana 'a heightened sense of black nationalism'.[27]

For many white Capetonians, English and Afrikaans, their South African identity was interwoven with a pride in their Cape heritage. This rediscovery of Cape Town's neglected past was a peculiarly modern project, and had first been initiated by Cecil Rhodes, who had commissioned the young English architect Herbert Baker to reinterpret Cape Dutch vernacular architecture in his house at Groote Schuur in Rondebosch. In 1905 the South African National Society was founded to protect historical artefacts. Among the results of its activities were the preservation of the derelict Castle and the Old Supreme Court, the establishment of the National Botanic Gardens at Kirstenbosch, the restoration of Groot Constantia, and the purchase of the Koopmans-De Wet House in Strand Street. For many years the Society's successor, the Historical Monuments Council, continued to define South Africa's heritage mainly in terms of its white, Cape origins.

The preservation of a Cape Town heritage took many forms, from the restoration of buildings to the publication of historical documents and the erection of memorials. Whereas Herbert Baker wanted Government Avenue to be re-created as a boulevard with monumental vistas, the National Society preferred that it be retained in an unspoilt

DOROTHEA FAIRBRIDGE

(SAL PHA)

Dorothea Fairbridge (1862–1931), a founder of the National Society, was one of a group of architects, artists and historians dedicated to the idea of a united South Africa within the British empire. Influenced by Edwardian 'modernism', Fairbridge's view of the western Cape was Mediterranean in inspiration rather than African. Cape Dutch architecture represented in her eyes the product of European settlement; in the revival of Herbert Baker it was reworked in the Arts and Crafts tradition of William Morris. This mixed heritage was to bridge the divisions between English and Afrikaner, creating 'a new, ameliorative South African identity'.[28]

Baker's scheme for Government Avenue was more grandiose than the simpler memorial eventually erected and which was a copy of the Delville Wood memorial in France. (UCT BC 206-380)

form. The preservation of the Old Supreme Court was another source of conflict: improvers wanted to widen the upper part of Adderley Street by demolishing the 'ramshackle old barn',[29] but for leaders of the conservation movement, like the archivist C. Graham Botha, the site had venerable associations. Eventually, as a compromise, the building was moved back several feet.

The Van Riebeeck Society was another Cape Town-based institution which reflected attempts to create a South African identity out of its Cape heritage. Conceived by A.C.G. Lloyd of the South African Library and John X. Merriman, its formation stemmed from the discovery of the diary of Adam Tas, the eighteenth-century western Cape farmer and rebel, in the holdings of the Library in 1911. The Society was formally constituted in 1918 to publish historically significant South African manuscripts. Most of its early publications were associated with the western Cape Dutch heritage – the reports of De Chavonnes and Van Imhoff, Mentzel's *Life at the Cape*, and De Mist's *Memorandum*, to name the earliest.

A South African identity could not be entirely divorced from the African environment. In 1929 the South African Association for the Advancement of Science, founded in Cape Town in 1902, convened a joint congress with the British Association in Cape Town and Johannesburg. This was a landmark event in defining South Africans as progressively Western and also in confirming humankind's African origins. An important feature of the discussions was the recent discoveries of early hominids at Taung. Although Cape Town could not produce such spectacular fossil remains, Peers Cave at Fish Hoek, an archaeological site excavated between 1927 and 1929, gave Capetonians some share in this African uniqueness.

In the 1920s writers and students would meet on Saturday mornings at the Koffiehuis, next to the Groote Kerk, to drink coffee, eat pancakes and talk. Here, at the Oranje Klub, they explored Afrikaans as a literary language. The Oranje Klub, from which sprang the literary group the Dertigers, was partly based at the University of Cape Town. The Dertigers also included Herman Charles Bosman, the maverick Transvaler, and the English writer Pauline Smith. (SAL PHA)

The inter-war years also saw the growth of a more exclusive Afrikaner identity, which was partly associated with the Afrikaans language movement. In Cape Town English was usually the medium for writing and business for Afrikaners while Dutch was the language of the church. Afrikaans was confined to intimate domestic use, for it still had connotations of a *kombuistaal* (kitchen language), the language of the poor. If Afrikaans was to become 'respectable' it had to be re-created, to acquire a more formal grammar and vocabulary, to achieve cultural status, and divest itself of its slave origins. In this process journalists and writers employed in the local universities or in the emergent Afrikaans press based in Keerom Street played a significant role. The poet and doctor C. Louis Leipoldt returned to the city in 1925, to practise as a paediatrician. In 1929 the poet Jan Celliers moved to Cape Town. As a member of the Provincial Council and, later, parliamentarian, C.J. Langenhoven, one of the strongest proponents of Afrikaans as an official language, spent long weeks in the mother city. The home of the writer I.D. du Plessis at 22 Montreux in Tuynstraat (Grey's Pass) became the centre of a lively cultural circle.

It was a Cape Town lawyer, W.A. (Willie) Hofmeyr, secretary of the Afrikaanse Taalvereniging, who emerged as the 'kingmaker' of Cape Afrikaner nationalism when he persuaded the wealthy wine farmers of the western Cape to invest in a series of business ventures. In 1914, with funding provided by Cape farmers, De Nasionale Pers was established; its major publication, *De Burger*, first appeared in 1915. It was the success of the Cape Helpmekaar movement, which had raised almost a quarter of a million pounds from ordinary Afrikaners to pay the fines of Afrikaner rebels during the First World War, that suggested to Hofmeyr a means of broadening the base of Afrikaner investment in business. In November 1917 he formed the Suid-Afrikaanse Nasionale Trust en Assuransie Maatskappij (Santam) with capital provided by the same Cape farmers who had funded *De Burger*. The life assurance company, the Suid-Afrikaanse Nasionale Lewens

I.D. du Plessis

I.D. du Plessis (1900–81) was a prolific writer in many fields. Much of his work was flavoured by the romantic appeal of the Orient, influenced by Cape Muslim culture. He has been described as 'enchanted by the flamboyantly colourful, glowing, exotic words, the echoing refrain and the external splendour of the traditional ballad verse'.[30] As 'friend of the Malays' he popularised 'Malay' culture mainly to whites through such books as *The Cape Malays* (1944).

(UCT Macmillan)

Assuransie Maatskappij (Sanlam), followed in 1918. To secure its growth, nationalist sentiment was mobilised to release Afrikaner funds. 'Sanlam is an authentic institution of the Afrikaner *volk* in the widest sense of the word. As an Afrikaner, you will naturally give preference to an Afrikaner institution. I would just remind policy holders that we are busy furnishing employment to young Afrikaners, and training them in an assurance field. We hereby intend to provide a great service to South Africa. If we want to become economically self-reliant then we must support our own institutions.'[31]

This organic growth of Cape nationalism diluted any allegiance western Cape Afrikaners might have to republicanism. With the Keerom Street 'mafia' firmly in place and a rich Afrikaner cultural and commercial life abounding in Cape Town, the Transvaal secret society, the Broederbond, and its allied institutions were slow to penetrate the Peninsula. Only in 1931 was a Broederbond branch formed in the Cape. Nor was much interest evoked in Cape Town in the 1920s by *Geloftesdag* celebrations, commemorating the Trekker victory over the Zulu at Blood River on 16 December.

By the start of the Second World War these differences between north and south had diminished. For one thing the experience of the Depression had sharpened extremism in Cape Town. Although the 'shirt' movements were not confined to Afrikaners, their ideology helped shape the more radical elements of Afrikaner nationalism. It was at the Koffiehuis, the cherished meeting place of Afrikaner nationalists, that Louis Weichardt – a former hairdresser and later a National Party parliamentarian – set up in October 1933 South Africa's largest fascist organisation, the South African Gentile National-

The stark lines of the Santam building in Wale Street expressed the modern forces of Afrikaner nationalism. (SAL INIL 14953)

Socialist Movement (the Greyshirts). As it happened, South Africa's Nazi Party was founded, in 1932, in the heart of English liberalism, by the professor of electrotechnics at the University of Cape Town, Dr Hermann Bohle; this appealed mainly to some Germans.

One may ask why it was that moderate, 'liberal' Cape Town produced these reactionary organisations. Undoubtedly the hardships of the Depression created fertile soil

The 1938 Voortrekker Celebrations

The 1938 centenary re-enactment of the Great Trek led to an upsurge of nationalist fervour amongst Peninsula Afrikaners. It was at this time that D'Urban Road, the main road through Goodwood and Parow, was renamed Voortrekker Road. The trek started from Cape Town on 8 August 1938. In an attempt to play down the potential separatism of the movement, English-speaking Capetonians joined in offering homage to the pioneers. The British Empire Service League presented a Bible which would be carried on the ox wagon 'just as Piet Retief had carried with him a Bible given by the English settlers of Albany'.[32]

At the first outspan at Goodwood a crowd of over 10,000 attended a *braaivleisaand*. Although some white speakers again stressed the importance of a spirit of tolerance and the need for the formation of a nation free of race or language differences, coloured people, excluded from the event, were unconvinced: 17 coloured youths appeared in court for throwing stones at a lorry-load of women and children in Voortrekker dress. Later an Afrikaner youth was stabbed in a fracas involving a number of white and coloured men. He explained that he had seen 'coloured men making trouble' and attempted to put a stop to it.[33]

(SAL Ossewatrek (CT) album)

for discontent. Perhaps, too, Cape Town's ethnic mix was unusually troubling to those who felt they had their backs to the wall. Certainly the 'shirt' organisations were not lacking in local support. Greyshirt demonstrations in 1933 were reported to attract 'thousands' while at a meeting of Greyshirts in 1934 the Koffiehuis was 'crowded mostly with tram-drivers, railway workers, unskilled labourers, shopwalkers, etc.'.[34] There is little doubt that some South African Germans were also deeply disaffected. Between the wars they were subjected to an 'avalanche' of propaganda through schools, churches, 'reading circles' and the German newspaper *Deutsch-Afrikaner*, which had fallen into Nazi hands. German communities like the Philippi farmers, largely isolated from the mainstream of Cape Town life, were vulnerable to the blandishments offered by the new world order. Yet, when war broke out, few were interned despite the fact that Philippi was regarded as a hotbed of disaffection by local soldiers.

During the Second World War the Reddingsdaadbond (RDB), a Broederbond cultural and economic movement, emerged to weld the major western Cape farmers firmly to Afrikaner capitalism. Through the RDB 'a cultural mesh was woven around the local Afrikaner community in which all cultural activities were controlled by the RDB, and all were encouraged to take an active part in such activities'.[35] The effect of this was to create Afrikaner 'ghettoes' in all aspects of life and isolate Afrikaners from any real contact with English speakers. It also placed boundaries on art, which became defined in Afrikaner nationalist terms, although writers like Elisabeth Eybers opposed this turn of events. Nevertheless, compared with the Transvaal, Afrikaner national identity in Cape Town was moderate. Certainly Afrikaners valued their language, yet many were fluent in English as well. As important as language in defining identity was the church. What is more, many Afrikaners remained faithful to Smuts and the United Party: even the northern suburbs were drained of men during the Second World War. Although *Die Burger* gave implicit support to Germany throughout the war, the case of Ds. J.D. Vorster of the Nieuwe Kerk in Bree Street was unusual in Cape Town: a member of the Ossewa-Brandwag, he was found guilty of contravening the Official Secrets Act in 1940.

If Afrikaner identity was complex, the notion of 'coloured' identity was still more fluid and ambiguous. Rejected by whites, coloured people were forced to redefine themselves. What were they: 'African' or 'European', 'Christian' or 'Muslim', 'English' or 'Afrikaans', 'Coloured' or 'Malay', working class or middle class, conservative or radical? Political affiliations reflected these dilemmas. But categories were by no means watertight. Cutting across ethnic boundaries or class lines was also a notion of inter-racial political unity which contributed to the intricacy of relationships in the city.

By 1919 the APO was already on the wane although, as long as its leading figure, Abdullah Abdurahman, was active, the party retained the loyalty of many Capetonians. Ralph Bunche, an African-American notable who visited Cape Town in 1937, remarked on Abdurahman's continuing popularity. But Bunche was contemptuous of the pusillanimity of the APO leaders in general: 'A very mild group. No aggressiveness indicated; merely polite speeches. A rather pitiful sight, if these are, as I was assured, representative of leading public-minded colored citizens.'[36] The Commission of Inquiry into the Cape Coloured Population of 1936 (the Wilcocks Commission) also commented on this lack of direction and clear focus. For the commission (which included Abdurahman), unable to define 'coloured' except in negative terms, being coloured constituted a 'problem'. They had some justification, for the commission's findings indicated only too clearly that years of collaboration had done little for Cape Town's working population, trapped as they were between competition from African labourers and Hertzog's 'civilised

Miss E.M. Woods, a journalist on the staff of the *Cape Argus*, refused to pay her income tax as a protest against her disfranchisement. While blacks in Cape Town were increasingly excluded from political representation, white women obtained the vote at last in 1930. But it was a tainted victory, for it weakened still further the political influence of African and coloured voters. (SAL PHA)

Coloured people also claimed identities for themselves in the inter-war years. The centenary of the emancipation of the slaves in 1934 was commemorated in a pageant which traced the diverse roots of Cape Town's coloured people. Despite Dr Abdurahman's patronage, it was a Christian celebration which ignored the heritage of Islam among coloureds.

labour' policy, a concept which was insulting to many coloured people. Abdurahman could in fact protect the interests of only a few hundred city council employees.

Yet Abdurahman cannot be categorised simply as a lackey of white capitalists, as his detractors considered him. Although he might participate in white political structures, he did consistently oppose segregation. Moreover, unlike the political left he did not reject working-class popular culture. Between 1921 and 1940 he was one of the organisers of the Green Point carnival competition and his satirical 'Kaatjekekkelbek' columns in the *A.P.O.* newspaper illustrated his sensitivity towards the voice of the poor. Describing himself sometimes as a socialist, Abdurahman actually tried to form an APO trade union after the First World War, but it was too middle class and tepid to be successful. All the same this attempt explains his willingness in the early 1920s to co-operate with the newly formed black trade union, the Industrial and Commercial Union (ICU). Although the ICU is usually thought of as an African movement, in Cape Town it was the one organisation that gained substantial support amongst coloured workers. Only after 1926, when its headquarters moved to Johannesburg, did this coloured constituency diminish. The passing of the ICU left a gap in city politics which no other party succeeded in filling before the Second World War.

Yet many coloured people were deeply conservative, still clinging to imperial values. A journalist remarked in 1936 that in Bo-Kaap 'every second house has a picture of Nelson's last order, "England expects that every man will do his duty" hung reverently on a cracked wall'.[37] Conservative leaders like N.R. Veldsman, wary of Abdurahman's 'radicalism', sought another option: in return for their electoral support, the Pact government under Hertzog offered them a 'New Deal', which would protect their separate ethnic interests. Such collaboration had some effect, for Veldsman, appointed inspector of coloured labour at the docks, was able to ensure that coloured men were employed there

THE ICU AND THE 1919 DOCK-WORKERS' STRIKE

The ICU was formed in January 1919 by a white labour leader, Alfred Batty, and a young Malawian, Clements Kadalie. Batty recognised in Kadalie the talent to attract the dock labourers, Cape Town's largest body of unskilled and semi-skilled workers.

Within a few months opportunity arose for a strike. Angered by the export of South African foods when the cost of living was so high after the war, dock-workers refused to load any more. They were supported by the Cape Federation of Labour Unions and the National Union of Railwaymen. 'On the appointed day [17 December 1919] ... I went straight to the docks at the East Pier where mail steamers were then berthed. Immediately on my arrival at the docks I boarded the *Norman Castle* and got into touch with Joe Paulsen, a Coloured man who was the first chairman of the ICU and who was one of the foremen of the Union Castle Company. I ordered him to "down tools" as a signal to others. He, however, hesitated, as he was not sure whether the native workers employed by the Railways and Harbours Administration would respond to strike action. Eventually, Paulsen ceased work and was followed by his "gang." The *Norman Castle* was immediately deserted by its non-European employees. I managed to borrow a bicycle and cycled throughout the docks calling on workers to down tools and to follow me outside the dock gates.'[38]

Clements Kadalie. (MuseumAfrica)

The strike lasted for three weeks though the white unions withdrew their support after the initial goal of stopping food exports to Europe was achieved. The ICU stood out for improved wages until it was forced to come to terms. Nevertheless, the considerable publicity achieved by the strike gave the ICU new status.

I.D. du Plessis's associate, C.A. Lückhoff, took a number of fine photographs of 'Malay' life. In this scene in Longmarket Street in Bo-Kaap, a Muslim couple represent the respectability and family values of the 'Malays'. (UCT Macmillan)

in preference to Africans. But he could not halt the impact of Hertzog's 'civilised labour' policy, which blatantly set out to protect white interests.

Coloured Muslims in Cape Town were also encouraged by the government to see themselves as ethnically distinct. The Cape Malay Association (CMA), drawn largely from the skilled artisans and a few property owners, supported Hertzog. Their reward came in 1924 when Dr Malan told the CMA at its first conference that, unlike Indians, 'Malays' were true South Africans with 'a distinct status'. The CMA was particularly susceptible to I.D. du Plessis's 'reinvention' of the 'Malays'. In his influential writings Du Plessis constructed an archetypal 'Malay', derived partly from nineteenth-century writings and partly from current theories about race types. The 'pure Malay', he claimed, was 'introspective, kind towards women, children and animals; inclined to speak slowly, to be passive and indolent. When aroused he may lose all self-control and run amok.'[39] Du Plessis's conception of the 'Malay' was given content by folksong and other cultural forms. His encouragement of choral singing gave rise to the Cape Malay Choir Board in 1939. Along with this creation of tradition went moves to preserve the Bo-Kaap, supposedly the 'old Malay quarter'.

Such political options as pursued by the CMA lost their viability after white women were granted the vote in 1930 and the Nationalists no longer needed to bargain for the coloured vote. Yet when war broke out in 1939, ethnic pride could still be mobilised for the imperial cause. Recruiting was aided by detachments of the Cape Corps and the Indian and Malay Corps, which 'created great enthusiasm' in the Peninsula in September 1942. Emotional commemorations could also encourage recruits: at the Square Hill commemorative service in September 1942, taken by Canon Lavis, 'hundreds' of coloured people were turned away from a packed City Hall.[40]

In the 1930s the shadow of segregation began to lengthen across the country. Opposing it was a new generation of young coloured leaders, who emerged from the inner-city schools. Although overcrowded and ill equipped, these played an important part in creating the cosmopolitan cultural vitality of District Six. At the Lutheran General School in Searle Street, for example, German *lieder* were sung at Monday assemblies to the accompaniment of a violin, and teachers were often remembered with affection despite the strict discipline, which enforced punctuality and neatness. The high schools established in town in the early years of the century attracted remarkably articulate teachers and pupils. Trafalgar Second Class Public School, founded in 1910 as the only school in the city to offer secondary education to coloured students at that time, had the brilliant young Harold Cressy as its principal. Hewat College, begun in 1941 in Roeland Street as the first coloured tertiary institution, provided another focus of intellectual resistance to white segregation.

Another oppositional force to make its mark in Cape Town was socialism, which had existed in the city before the First World War. In 1921 the Cape Town Social Democratic Federation combined with other socialist organisations to form the Communist Party of South Africa (CPSA). Although the CPSA was linked to Soviet Russia's Comintern the Cape Town left were often reluctant to bow to Soviet dictates. Cape Town, more than any other part of the country, was the 'home territory' of 'independent South African Marxism'.[41] Strong disagreement and divergence of opinion over leading issues of the day led to the repeated fragmentation and re-formation of political groupings. Should radical organisations be dominated by blacks or whites, coloureds or Africans? What was the meaning of 'unity' in the South African and Cape Town context? Driven by issues like these, Capetonians formed the Lenin Club in 1933 and, when it splintered in 1935, launched the Spartacus Club. Disenchanted with Stalinism, these groups were always minuscule and poorly resourced. Although largely ineffectual in themselves, they contributed to the 'purist' attitudes of later organisations like the National Liberation League and the Non-European Unity Movement.

As segregation became more entrenched in the social and political life of the country, the younger generation of coloured people increasingly rejected the moderate strategies of the APO. The National Liberation League of South Africa (NLL), founded in Cape Town in December 1935, expressed this more militant spirit. Its members were a closely knit intelligentsia, linked through family and marriage, educated in the same schools, many of them teachers with a university training. Leading lights included both Dr Abdurahman's daughters; his first wife, Nellie; his son-in-law Dr A.H. Gool; Gool's wife Hawa Ahmed; Gool's brother, Dr Goolam Gool; and the sisters Minnie and Jane Gool, the latter married to I.B. Tabata. The NLL was a 'unity' movement which called for a political alliance of all the oppressed against the common enemy, the 'white capitalist imperialist', though it was not explicitly socialist. Its slogan and emblems appealed directly to Cape Town's slave past. Launched on Emancipation Day (1 December), it adopted as its emblem a black slave with severed chains, holding aloft a flaming torch, with the slogan 'For equality, land and freedom'.

Unity was further advanced among the groups on the left when in March 1938 delegates to an NLL conference formed a Non-European United Front (NEUF) of Africans, coloureds and Indians to oppose all colour bars. Their weapons were to be 'the strike, the boycott and peaceful demonstrations'. However, the NEUF had little success in attracting membership away from the ANC and remained a predominantly coloured organisation. In 1939 the NLL itself split, expelling the hard-left members of James La

The Hyman Liberman Institute

Self-education was as important as formal schooling in the coloured communities. The Hyman Liberman Institute became the centre of 'high' culture in District Six. It had started in 1934 as a reading room and community centre for the poor on the strength of a bequest by the Cape Town mayor Hyman Liberman. Established on the model of Toynbee Hall in London, it developed links with the University of Cape Town: by 1938 a stint of field work there had become an integral part of the training of social science students from UCT. Professor Batson, the honorary warden, was one of the regular lecturers, along with UCT's eminent economist, W.H. Hutt.

The librarian, Christian Ziervogel (1903–57), was a self-taught man, who had originally begun a library for coloured people with his own collection of 3000 volumes. He complained to Ralph Bunche that the board of the Institute would not let him keep his collection on the shelves of the Institute library because he had too many 'dangerous' books – Ziervogel was a member of the radical discussion circle, the Fifteen Group.[42]

(SAL INIL 14722)

The Liberman Institute was also the first home to the Eoan Group, which sprang from elocution classes started in 1933 and expanded into a drama group, the Liberman Players. The name 'Eoan' was given by its founder, Mrs Helen Southern-Holt, who hoped that it would presage a new cultural dawn for coloured people.

In 1957 a funding crisis ended the Institute's UCT connection, and control was formally handed over to the city. The Institute was absorbed into existing municipal departments such as the municipal library service. By the end of the 1960s the Institute had ceased to exist.

Two Radical Leaders in Cape Town

James La Guma (1894–1961) was born the son of Madagascan parents who died when he was a baby. In Cape Town, where he arrived as a young boy, he had his first taste of unemployment protests and read such working-class literature as R. Tressell's *Ragged Trousered Philanthropist*. As a 'Cape boy' he later worked in German South West Africa and only returned to Cape Town when Kadalie invited him to become assistant general secretary of the ICU in 1921. In 1924 he joined the Communist Party. La Guma was wary of the moderating influence of whites in the organisations with which he was involved. Despite his close ties with the CPSA – he visited Russia twice, met Bukharin, and was responsible for the 'Native Republic' slogan which divided the CPSA – he was expelled during the 'purification' of the Party in 1930. In 1934, along with John Gomas and Cissie Gool, he started the NLL and composed their anthem, 'Dark folks, arise!' After war broke out, La Guma enlisted with the Indian and Malay Corps, arguing that this was a fascist rather than an imperialist war, and served up north.

Johnny Gomas (1901–1979) was born at the Anglican mission of Abbotsdale near Malmesbury, a child of the 'respectable' coloured working class. His formative years were spent in Kimberley, where he was introduced to socialism, and he joined the ANC, the ICU and the ISL. In 1921, after a brush with the law, he moved to Cape Town. Gomas shared La Guma's views on the need for black leadership in South African working-class organisations, a perspective which took him into the Communist Party and also led to his expulsion from the ICU. Like La Guma, he was expelled from the 'purified' CPSA. In the late 1930s he moved closer to the Trotskyites, denouncing the war as an imperialist conflict. In 1943, in one of the most bitterly fought of municipal elections, he contested the seat for Ward 7 (part of District Six) but eventually withdrew to prevent a split vote.

(SAL, *The Liberator*, September 1937; *Cape Standard*, 10 August 1943)

Guma, Dr Goolam Gool and Hawa Ahmed. At the same time local communism was strengthened when in 1938 the headquarters of the CPSA, hard pressed by the authorities on the Rand, transferred to Cape Town. Communist leaders like W.H. Andrews and Moses Kotane became part of the local political scene. Removed from the centre of industrial conflict, the CPSA reorganised its administration more effectively and a paper sympathetic to the communist line, the *Guardian*, was started in Cape Town in February 1937, edited by Betty Radford.

By the time that Dr Abdurahman died in 1940 the political identities of coloured people had changed substantially. Desperate poverty excluded the majority of the population from participation in the political life of the country, while the small coloured elite had become more beleaguered. The war was to divide them further. Communists, bound by the Nazi–Soviet Pact, initially denounced the conflict. The NEUF also at first opposed the war and Cissie Gool, reflecting this attitude, refused to support a motion of

Dr Abdurahman died on 20 February 1940 at the age of 69. His funeral was one of Cape Town's great occasions. Hundreds of Muslim men, bearing Abdurahman's body, walked from his home in Kloof Street to the Mowbray cemetery in the searing February heat. For three hours Cape Town came to a standstill, even the trams being unable to run because of the crowds. (SAL PHA)

loyalty in the city council to the king and Smuts. The fight for democracy and freedom must be carried out at home as well, she declared. By 1942 such opponents of the war had changed their tune. Concentrating on better conditions for black soldiers and the right to bear arms, they now argued that the war was a 'threat to the whole population', a war which could not be fought by whites alone.

The year 1943 was a turning point for those opposed to segregation. Although South Africans were being asked to fight for freedom, wartime slogans appeared not to apply at home. As one young student remembered: '[The war] was in all the papers ... The British, in order to get people behind the war effort, had to make anti-Nazi propaganda. So we were made aware of the fact that our conditions were the same as the horrors of Germany. We were so conditioned to our status and lack of rights, we had never fully realized this. But the war was being fought for freedom and democracy, an anti-Nazi, anti-Fascist war and it was this realisation that made people aware of their position.'[43] By 1943 it became clear that the prime minister, Smuts, did not intend to abandon segregationist measures. For in January 1943 it was announced that a Cape Coloured Permanent Commission would be established to advise the government on matters related to coloured people. This announcement bitterly divided Cape Town's coloured community. Threatened with the prospect of a separatist Coloured Affairs Department, militants from the NEUF and other radical organisations formed an Anti-CAD movement in February 1943. Its main tactic was a boycott of the supporters of the proposed Coloured Affairs Department, like Dr F.H. Gow, now president of the APO. The vituperative language which the Anti-CAD deployed would also be characteristic of its successor, the Non-European Unity Movement (NEUM). Gow and his fellow commissioners were castigated as 'traitors', 'imposters' and 'quislings' engaged in a 'shoddy deal', a 'swindle'. But the Anti-CAD, which consisted of a wide range of organisations from the Trotskyite Fourth International Organisation to the Boy Scouts, proved politically unstable. However much it might attempt to build bridges with other protest organisations, it was essentially sectional in its interests. Moreover, its base was narrow, resting mainly on coloured intellectuals who had little contact with coloured workers and were unable to attract their participation, and it had few objectives beyond negative opposition.

I am riding high-horse all over the land;
I call on my C.A.C.-men to feed from my hand.
They go where I want them,
They do as I please,
They even say 'Yes, Sir' whenever I sneeze.
(SAL, *Cape Standard*, 11 May 1943)

Zainunnissa (Cissie) Gool

(SAL PHA)

One of the major campaigns of the left in Cape Town in 1938 was the election of Cissie Gool (1897–1963) to the city council. The daughter of Dr Abdurahman, she married Dr Abdul Gool in 1919 before completing her university education. She continued to study for the rest of her life, being finally admitted to the Bar shortly before her death. Her first public meeting in 1930 was to protest against the extension of the franchise to white women only. By the mid-1930s she was heavily involved in political activity but, although she became a communist, her concerns were more practical than theoretical. In 1936 she formed a liaison with the Jewish lawyer Sam Kahn that was to influence her non-racialism and widen the growing rift with her father. This personal association, radicals suggested, contributed to her 'political unreliability' and her tendency, for all her passionate eloquence, to compromise with dominant white politics.

In 1938 Gool stood for Ward 7 (Woodstock) as a municipal candidate, winning 1109 votes against her opponent's 739 votes. On council she fought bitterly against growing segregation. Although she refused to support the war effort, she gradually shifted her position to protest against inequities in pay and to demand food rationing and a ministry of food.

Another attempt to link coloured politics with wider South African interests was the NEUM, founded in December 1943, yet it also remained local and sectional. For all its ten point programme urging such basic rights as land reform, it was most significant for representing an intransigent 'purist' element in coloured political life, and for its vigorous influence on many young coloured people. In the long term the NEUM's most distinctive contribution to the character of Cape Town's left would be its emphasis on non-collaboration and its passionate commitment to non-racialism.

By the first half of the twentieth century a substantial African population had made its home in 'Ikapa'. It was a distorted growth, for Africans, still regarded by the authorities as alien to the city, were hedged about by controls at every turn. Painfully they built their urban community, making the most of the fragments of independence allowed to them. By 1945 resistance, often passive, had become a way of life. With the wartime resurgence of the ANC a fresh militancy was added to their protest.

During the inter-war years the regulations of the 1902 Location Act were expanded to create a more formal structure for African urban administration. And in 1923 the Urban Areas Act was passed to enforce the compulsory residence of Africans in locations. Segregation, like other elements of twentieth-century planning, was in this sense an aspect of the modernising society. Although Cape Town's municipality was never as keen as that of Durban to milk beer-hall revenues to pay for location administration, it did prove eager to invoke those clauses of the 1923 Act which controlled African immigration into the city and enabled it to expel 'the idle, the dissolute and the disorderly'.

By 1920 Ndabeni, overflowing from an influx of people during the First World War, was indescribably filthy and derelict, 'a place without a soul ... a confession of the failure of civilisation'.[44] Most Africans, however, no longer lived there. Contemporaries noted that practically no street in District Six was without its African residents; others spilled out onto the Cape Flats. Those that remained in Ndabeni were viewed unenthusiastically by their white middle-class neighbours in adjacent Pinelands, while developers eyed the site for industry. Consequently a new location, Langa, was built to replace Ndabeni. It was officially opened in 1927, in 'healthy ... idyllic surroundings' next to Cape Town's sewage works – though, or so concerned citizens were assured, a band of trees would disperse the smell.

'Langa' (meaning 'sun') was also a shortened form of 'Langalibalele', the name of the Hlubi rebel who had been imprisoned in Cape Town in 1875 after rising against the Natal government. The irony of its name extended to the design of the location. Langa was to be a planned township, very different from 'the ghastly desolation which is called Ndabeni'.[45] In reality, control became the watchword. The barracks for migrant labourers were to be separated from one another by a high, unclimbable fence with only one point of access. The layout proposed that 'a man on point duty at the centre of what you might call the Central Square will be able to see not only from end to end of the Central Avenue, but will be able to look into each of the large Compounds and directly up to the Station Square, and a Police Patrol on the roads running north and south would get an immediate view East and West down all the other roads and across the open spaces.'[46] There was little privacy and the main barracks were condemned later as an assault on the individual's privacy.

In the location, regulations prohibited trading, forced all visitors to report to the superintendent, and forbade gatherings without the superintendent's permission including dances, public meetings, tea meetings or special gatherings on Sundays. Perhaps the most bitterly resented of all the controls were the restrictions on the brewing of sorghum beer *(utshwala)*, integral to local African culture. Langa residents resisted the introduction of municipal beer halls, which were like 'drinking in a cage'; in addition, residents argued, they destroyed control over young men, who were forbidden by traditional custom to drink beer. The scale of illicit brewing, the endless police raids and the resentment of residents forced the municipality to abandon total prohibition by 1930 – one of the few victories gained by Langa residents before 1945. Only in the 1940s were municipal beer halls built.

Like other Capetonians, Africans did not have a single identity. In the years before the Second World War 'tribal' affiliations were at least as strong as national and political identifications. For many, 'tribal' affirmation offered one means of coming to terms with urbanisation. The Fingo celebrations, observed on 14 May, commemorating Mfengu loyalty to the British Crown, and their position as early Christians and recipients of Western education and culture, enforced Mfengu separateness from the Xhosa. In Langa the Mfengu Memorial Association explicitly celebrated the 'liberation' of the Mfengu from the Xhosa. Such rhetoric naturally aroused hostility amongst the Xhosa majority in the township.

For some, tribal affiliations were radically reshaped by their urban experience. By the early 1920s a small African petty bourgeoisie was emerging in Cape Town, consisting largely of teachers, court interpreters, clerks, a few nurses, traders and ministers of religion. This elite was by no means confined to Ndabeni. Mrs Ndollo had an 'African restaurant' in Wale Street and took in weekly and monthly boarders. Advertisements in the black paper the *African World* were suggestive of an African presence in the city: they included W. Solomon, 'The Bantu Butcher'; J. Dude, baker; Kumalo, a general dealer; and Sipondo, a shoemaker. The Venture Bus Service, which ran out to the township, offered special rates to ANC members.

Langa Location

Langa was built in phases, the 'Old Location' being the first. It was shabby, with unpaved roads and without electricity. The 'New Location' – Bhongweni (People's Pride) – for married couples, with slightly better houses, was completed about 1927. Thembani (Trust) followed in 1935 and Bubani in 1941. Bulawayo (To Kill), less spacious than the 'Old Location', was so called because, as one Mr Sigwana explained, 'what we were all concerned about is that they are sort of trying to kill the blacks in a polite manner, giving them small houses where they had no comfort'.[47]

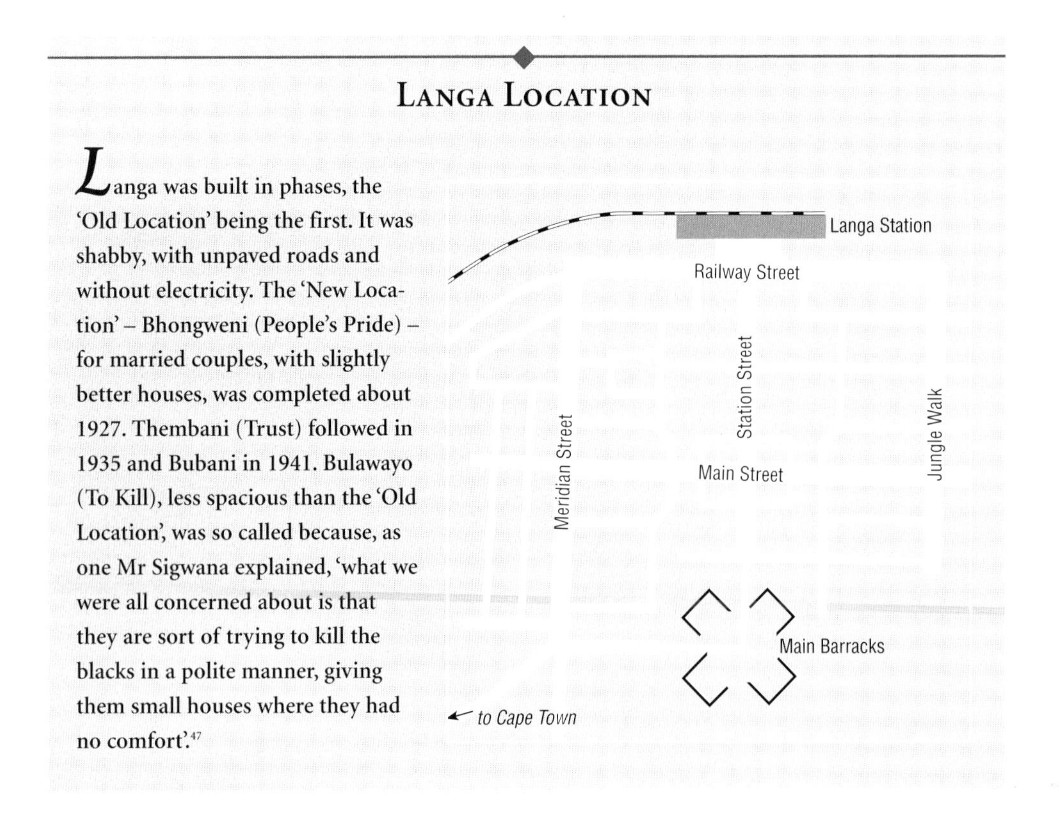

The Ntsikana celebrations, most closely associated with Xhosa identity, were started about 1933. Observed annually on 14 March, they commemorated an early pre-Christian Xhosa prophet. From the start participants emphasised the national features of the commemoration: St Ntsikana represented 'all Bantudom'. In Langa the movement also had a strong self-help element, for money was often collected to sponsor deserving students. (R. Botto, 'Some aspects of the leisure occupations of the African population of Cape Town', M.Soc.Sci. thesis, UCT, 1954, p. 138a)

But it was in Langa that Africans could create their own institutions and organisations most effectively. The enforced intimacy of the location played a role in this: 'Neighbours shop together, eat in each other's homes and accompany one another to meetings of different kinds; they afford each other help by lending various articles and performing favours for each other. Neighbours assist each other on all occasions of note, such as births, marriages and deaths, and at various parties, like those held at baptism and initiation.'[48] One basis for the creation of community institutions was 'home-boyism', the bond of common geographical origin. This was reflected in the rugby and soccer clubs, some of whose names were obvious, like the Basutoland Happy Lads, the Bechuanaland Swallows and the Transkeian Lions; others were less so – the Busy Bees came from King William's Town. In the location inter-ethnic marriage was common, both men and women from Langa rejecting country partners. The terms they used witnessed to the fact of urbanisation: country girls were considered 'backward, uncivilised, coarse' while the women thought the male counterparts 'too coarse and raw'. Townsmen preferred women who were 'brighter and more polished' while women considered that city men were more 'smartly-dressed'.[49]

Churches were probably the most important of all social institutions in Langa, especially for women. The Women's Christian Association (*Umanyano wabafazi*) of the Bantu Presbyterian Church had 90 members and was, in the words of the Rev. S.P. Lediga, 'the spark of life in the church'. Most of these *manyanos* also ministered to the sick and needy – a crucial element of self-help in this impoverished community. In general, churches were a significant agent in imposing discipline and Western moral values on the society. So the Women's Association of the Ethiopian Church of South Africa prayed 'to help those who walk disorderly' and members of the Young Men's Association of the same church were expected to refrain from leading a 'loose existence'.[50] Yet the churches also provided a focus for a reworked African culture, as Ralph Bunche observed with interest. Religion and politics coexisted in a complex amalgam, he noted:

> Saw a native group of about 25 in baptism ceremonies in sea at Woodstock beach. Church of Christ group. Cold, raw, windy day. Singing hymns (strange) and Bible printed in Xhosa. Weird harmony. Only three women; one with a baby on her back. One English speaking native in the group – a little cringing, bearded fellow, dressed like a dandy, told me they are from Langa and have about one hundred members in their flock. Pastor was a tall, brownskinned, serious-eyed, bearded native. In short testimonial sermons after the baptisms (in English), one native, while quoting the scripture like Ford [a black American communist] quotes the party line, stated that the scriptures and religion made no provision for the color-bar.[51]

'Saw a native group of about 25 in baptism ceremonies in sea at Woodstock beach. Church of Christ group. Cold, raw, windy day. Singing hymns (strange) and Bible printed in Xhosa. Weird harmony. Only three women; one with a baby on her back.'

Ralph Bunche, 1938

Education was greatly prized in Langa. Primary schools were established early on but the authorities steadfastly resisted demands for a high school. Eventually in 1937 an interdenominational group of clergy, backed by some parents, succeeded in winning permission to start secondary classes. The education that Langa High School offered was lively but firmly Eurocentric, and an important role was played by sport. Above all, the rugby team was the school's pride and joy. Of 51 early pupils at Langa High School, most had modest middle-class ambitions – to become nurses, teachers or church ministers. Dr Mbombo, the product of one of these first classes, later commented on how many of them realised their aspirations.[52]

Location conditions, the experience of the First World War, and the influence of local and overseas political movements all contributed to the politicisation of Cape Town's African residents in the early twentieth century. Although the authorities attempted to isolate them, African political life in Cape Town was never entirely aloof from broader movements in the city. Before the First World War there was little overt protest but by 1919, when the ICU was gaining adherents in Ndabeni, the South African Native National Congress (SANNC), forerunner of the ANC, was also active in the town. In March 1918 a mass meeting rejected the principle of urban segregation. Bitterness was expressed more vigorously in 1923 when the Urban Areas Bill came before parliament. As Selope Thema of the SANNC told Smuts in Cape Town, 'We have a share and a claim to this country. Not only is it the land of our ancestors, but we have contributed to the progress and advancement of this country ... we have built this city.'[53]

A potent influence on Africans in Cape Town was wielded by the Jamaican political figure, Marcus Garvey. By the end of 1921 there were four branches of Garvey's Universal Negro Improvement Association (UNIA) in the Peninsula, and eventually divisions existed in Goodwood, Parow, Claremont, Woodstock, West London (Rondebosch) and Cape Town. 'Black unity, black consciousness, black liberation' were the slogans of the movement. Its populist style and emphasis on self-help appealed to men like Clements Kadalie of the ICU, although Kadalie rejected its ethnic exclusivity. Garvey's message offered an apocalyptic vision of black liberation emanating from America, as the *Cape Argus* observed in 1923: 'They (the natives) are looking day after day when the 400,000,000 Negro Americans will arrive here.'[54] But there was also an element of modernism in Garveyism – a rejection of British liberal values in favour of American influences, which reached Cape Town mainly through contemporary music and cinema.

By 1930 Garvey's appeal in Cape Town was waning. One reason for the decline of Garveyism was that, ironically, its adherents believed Hertzog's segregation offered opportu-

I.D. Mkize

ID Mkize put his stamp on Langa High School during the difficult years of the Second World War. Politically conservative (though he was a member of the ANC), Mkize appealed shrewdly to white prejudice when struggling to fund his school, reminding his sponsors that secondary school made pupils 'better servants, or gain the opportunity to become clerks, nurses and teachers'. Mkize built up a scholarship fund backed by such institutions as Toc H, the Fingo Memorial Committee, the Golden Arrow Bus Service and Simon's Town municipality.

A Garveyite Leader in Cape Town

In the city two figures were instrumental in spreading Garveyism. One was Ncwana, the founder of the Mendi Memorial Club and a member of the ICU, who started the paper *The Black Man* in 1920. The second was 'Professor' James Thaele, a remarkable and eccentric figure, dressed all in white, with his 'spasms of twisted eloquence and weird posturings'.[55] His idiosyncrasies were misleading, for Thaele, a former Lovedale student, was a graduate of Lincoln University, a black American college, and of the University of Pennsylvania. The South African Police described him as 'intensely anti-white in sentiment' and noted that he 'has refused point blank to co-operate with European Communists, stating quite openly that he does not trust or wish to associate with any white man'.[56] Like Ncwana, Thaele at first tried to combine the interests of the ICU and Garvey's UNIA but eventually found them incompatible and abandoned the ICU. As president of the Cape branch of the ANC he infused the organisation with the symbols and rituals of Garveyism. The official organ of the Cape ANC was thus named the *African World* in tribute to Garvey's *Negro World*, while the ANC headquarters in Cape Town were named 'Liberty Hall' after the UNIA centre in New York.[57]

James Thaele addressing a crowd on the Parade, Cape Town's 'speakers' corner'. (SAL PHA)

nities for black self-determination. Moreover, for all Garvey's populism, men like James Thaele were more concerned to preserve the interests of the educated African elite than to protect the working mass. This was not, in the last resort, a working-class movement.

A crucial factor in politicising Cape Town's African population was the Native Advisory Board, set up in terms of the 1923 Urban Areas Act. Under this system Langa

In 1925 Edward, Prince of Wales, visited South Africa. This was yet another opportunity for the display of patriotic fervour but such occasions had become much more sectional in their celebration than they had been in the nineteenth century. The Cape branch of the ANC boycotted the visit. A satirical letter in *The Cape*, addressed to 'His Warship the Mare of Capetown', explained the resentment which blacks felt at being excluded from some of the official celebrations. 'It is also an insult to Him not to see us in our coloured skin which we are not ashamed of yet proud to be seen in.' (SAL Prince of Wales (1925) album)

The Second World War

THE Second World War marked a watershed in the modernising of Cape Town identities. At first old loyalties were confirmed but war soon became the forcing house of new attitudes and affiliations. For many Capetonians war reinforced imperial ties. The report that South Africa was to participate in the war, after a division in parliament brought in Smuts as prime minister, came as a relief to many. The good name of the Union of South Africa had been saved, the *Cape Times* declared. For an older generation the war also offered the opportunity to reassert conservative values which they felt had been eroded in recent decades: 'After the last war, while Europe became over-militarised, we became over-democratised. We dare not hand ourselves over again to an era of jazz-band music and crooning. The heritage of freedom, for which our young men are now sacrificing themselves, will have to be guarded day and night by a stern generation of young men and women. We shall require stronger personal and national discipline.'[58]

Few young people in Cape Town saw the conflict in such heroic terms. Those who joined up did so because their fathers had

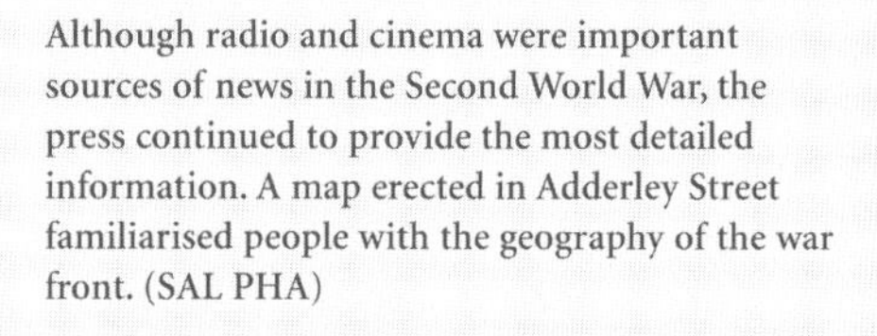

Although radio and cinema were important sources of news in the Second World War, the press continued to provide the most detailed information. A map erected in Adderley Street familiarised people with the geography of the war front. (SAL PHA)

Above: Civilian defence, intended to protect Cape Town from bombing or – a more likely event – attacks from enemy raiders at sea, was primarily concerned with air-raid precautions and first aid. The Civilian Protection Service mobilised patriotic feeling and enabled coloured people to participate more fully in the community life of the town. (*Cape Standard*, 13 May 1941)

fought in the Great War, through peer pressure, or out of a sense of adventure. But, whatever their reasons, middle-class Capetonians were often eager to do their bit. As early as April 1939, three thousand white women had met at the Alhambra to form a local branch of the South African Women's National Service Legion. While moderates urged these women to train at once and not sit back with folded arms, Margaret Ballinger, 'native representative' in the Senate, saw the war as an opportunity to reflect seriously on social reform. She trusted that the Legion would lead people to consider the root causes of war and to build up a state worth fighting for, which in peace would be worth preserving. Although English speakers predominated at the meeting, a number of Afrikaner women signed up as well.

Civilian men organised themselves a few weeks later. When a register of volunteers for the Citizens' Reserve Force was opened in Cape Town there was a steady stream of applicants, many of them ex-servicemen. After October 1940 'key men' (who were of military age, engaged in vital services at home) formed a 'home guard', the National Reserve Battalion. For their elders, mainly war veterans, black and white, there was the Essential Services Protection Corps. This was a full-time, paid unit of the defence forces, which guarded essential works, relieving the police and defence force of routine chores. But the main civil defence organisation for men and women of all races was the Civilian Protection Service (CPS). Cape Town was divided into zones, led by area commandants – 'men of ability, who are able to devote a great deal of their time to this work, in an honorary capacity'.

For those like the Rev. F.H. Gow of District Six, the position added to their local status.

Moments of commemoration and celebration confirmed social, ethnic and political bonds. The Delville Wood Day and Mendi Day ceremonies reminded participants that this war, like the last, was being fought to preserve freedom and democracy within the British empire. Prayer was another means of asserting traditional values and offering hope for a better future. By 1942 the world was well informed about the Jewish genocide in Europe. In Cape Town a National Day of Mourning was held on 29 December 1942. 'Two million souls, each one created in the image of God, have been destroyed from this earth,' the chief rabbi reminded his audience. Bitter at the treatment of their co-religionists, Cape Town Jews took up the Zionist cause with fresh fervour, renewing their mourning annually in a Jewish National Day of Prayer and Dedication.

After June 1941 Soviet sympathisers, so long on the fringes of Cape Town society, were also drawn into the wartime community. May Day, observed for the first time in 1920, was celebrated with new vigour. In 1942 at a workers' rally and concert in the City Hall, two thousand people expressed their solidarity with 'the workers of all lands' and with 'the oppressed peoples of the world'.[59]

The primary duty of the Union government during the Second World War was to defend the Cape sea route but its resources were limited. South Africa had no navy and the few shore batteries were antiquated. Nor were Capetonians security-minded. When modern guns were fired at full charge from the Lion Battery, local residents complained that their property was being damaged. Although the artillery was eventually improved, Cape Town's defence rested mainly on its citizens.

Right: After the German invasion of Russia in 1941 supporters of Soviet Russia acquired a respectability in Cape Town life which they had never had before. (SAL Poster collection)

Opposition to the Noonday Pause

(SAL PHA)

In Cape Town tension between loyalists and those opposed to the war was never as great as it was in the Transvaal although an excess of loyalty occasionally generated anti-Afrikaner feeling. After a recruiting meeting at the end of July 1940 several hundred men collected outside the hall, sang patriotic songs and, when someone shouted 'Keerom Street', they marched on the offices of *Die Burger.* But there was no serious attack.

Cape Town was also one of the few cities in South Africa to revert to the practice of the noonday pause. For a brief period in 1940 the pause became a battleground between pro- and anti-war protesters. Afrikaners claimed that squads were beating up people who did not observe the pause and the mayor's appeal for restraint fell on deaf ears. When a Stellenbosch student walked provocatively up and down Adderley Street during the silence, a soldier knocked him down after reveille, to cheers from onlookers. Free fights followed. Such confrontations occurred several times, giving rise to Nationalist protests in parliament. Finally the churches appealed for peace, reminding Capetonians that the purpose of the pause was prayer.

Volunteers

Above right: Since South Africa never introduced conscription during the Second World War recruitment campaigns were vital to maintain the forces. In this scene in 1940 an uneasy group of volunteers were being signed up for the Cape Town Highlanders. (SAL PHA)

Recruiting was often reluctant even though the government offered more attractive terms than it had in the last war. December 1941 brought the call to 'fill the gap' in Libya, but it was mid-January before Cape Town had met its quota of 1000 men. In June 1942 came the 'Avenge Tobruk' campaign, when Smuts called for 1200 gunners from Cape Town. A month later Cape Town men were labelled the 'shame of civilian manhood', for, with the exception of the Transvaal countryside, the western Cape recorded the lowest response to the appeal. Facilities at the Castle were hastily remedied. A week later there was a new regime of 'cheerfulness and hospitality' with popular and patriotic music playing and tea supplied to recruits. Numbers jumped and in mid-August the quota was finally reached. Younger people were the main target for recruiters. The University of Cape Town acquired an unsavoury reputation as a haven for 'slackers'. Since medical and other students were excused from enlisting, the university was believed to be used as a 'shelter', an imputation that had some truth since the proportion of Afrikaner students at UCT was high during the war years.[60]

Left: Air-raid practice provided some light relief for District Six children. In March 1941, when an alarm was sounded, children from Trafalgar High School were marched to the plantations near the Roeland Street fire station. They dispersed rapidly into the bushes and were recovered by their teachers with some difficulty. (SAL PHA)

Below left: In a port city with a substantial German and Italian population and a number of Afrikaners hostile to the war, security was a constant consideration. 'Don't talk about ships and shipping' became the familiar warning. (SAL PHA)

Air-raid and Black-out

Although bombing seemed a remote possibility, air-raid precautions were introduced, if haphazardly. Early practices were lighthearted. Cape Town's first air-raid rehearsal was conducted one Saturday afternoon at the end of September 1940. 'We knew World War II had come to Cape Town when the authorities erected an air-raid siren in the vacant plot beside our house in Clifton. The first time it went off the cat ran straight up the wall and my small brother wet his pants ... No one quite knew what to do when the siren went off. We hadn't been told to dig trenches or bunkers, or anything like that. Nor was it ever made clear how we were to tell if the alarm was a practice or the real thing. Never mind, we were at war, and we had an air-raid siren, and Camps Bay did not.'[61]

The rapid Japanese advances and the bombing of Pearl Harbor lent new urgency to civil defence in 1941. For months the municipality discussed ineffectually better protection for the poor who lived close to the docks and power station. Should they use city basements? But this was little help at night. At one stage it was decided to provide 'slit trenches', whose utility had been proven in the North Africa campaign. Sample trenches were dug in Government Avenue, the Public Gardens and Trafalgar Park. By the end of July 1942 the municipality had decided that it could not afford communal shelters. The poor must be protected, free, in their own homes. Finally shelter tables – 10,000 at a cost of £2 each – were acquired.

Black-out was even more contentious and the wrangle went on for years. The ardent wanted permanent, total black-out; the anti-war lobby wanted none. Occasional scares strengthened the hand of the hardliners but, in reality, the danger was greater for shipping off the Peninsula coast than for the city. Regulations lacked uniformity, for every port city in South Africa made independent decisions. The quarrel did Cape Town little credit, so the general officer commanding coastal area considered: 'Wartime prosperity has not improved the fibre of Cape Town's character.' At long last, the city settled for a 'dim-out', intended to eliminate the 'loom' above the city, which silhouetted the mountain, providing sea raiders with vital directions. Cape Town's suffering did not last long. By September 1943 strict car black-out was suspended and dim-out only began at 11 p.m. A year later the black-out was ended completely.

Women at War

Below: A SAWAS work party in Claremont. War work provided companionship in a time of stress and loneliness for many women. (SAL PHA)

Bottom: Visiting Maoris provided an occasion for young coloured women to share the gaiety of wartime entertainment. (*Cape Standard*, 18 February 1941)

Opposite right: In the early years of the century a surprising number of women could fly. By the end of May 1940, 300 were training as aviators. (SAL PHA)

Women again took the lead in a variety of philanthropic causes which gave practical expression to their imperial patriotism. This time their activities were more professionally organised than they had been in the Great War. In August 1939 women's voluntary organisations were united within a single body, to become the South African Women's Auxiliary Services (SAWAS) with over ten thousand members in the Peninsula. They would have preferred air-force blue uniforms but a surplus stock of tobacco brown converted them into 'Grown-up Brownies'. SAWAS was to be the linchpin of all women's volunteer services. It co-ordinated the entertainment of convoys and organised comforts sent to soldiers. It was also an umbrella body, linking a host of white women's organisations which reflected the ethnic and religious diversity of the city. Under the SAWAS umbrella fell the British Empire Service League, Catholic Women's League, Fairhaven Work Party, the Great Synagogue Ladies' Guild, Glendore Holiday Home, Magic Needle Guild, Navy League Wartime Workers, New Hebrew Congregation Ladies' Society, Sons of England Women's Association, Union of Jewish Women, the Victoria League, the Women's Hospital Auxiliary and the Women's Christian Temperance Union, amongst others. Middle-class black women,

excluded from these predominantly white organisations, established their own counterparts to provide for African and coloured soldiers, including those from visiting transports.

Contrary to what had happened in the previous war, women replaced men during the Second World War in shops, offices and factories – up to 70 per cent of munitions workers were women. Conditions were not necessarily satisfactory, however. Wage Board inquiries in the Cape Peninsula revealed that some women were still severely underpaid. A typical example was Mrs D. Williams, a widow with three children, who received £1 15s a week. Every Thursday she had to borrow bread to tide her over until pay-day, so she testified. She did her own cooking and washing and had to pay a woman to look after her children. In spite of struggling hard, she could not keep out of debt. Under such circumstances employers preferred single women on the assumption that they lived with their families and did not need a living wage.

The war also altered attitudes to the employment of white women in the armed forces. When war broke out, there seemed to be no place for them. At first they were expected to 'keep the home fires burning' but soon white women were actively recruited into the forces in preference to blacks. Military rhetoric changed when twenty thousand women were urgently needed in November 1941: 'Why had the women not come forward? ... It should burn through a woman's coat if she was not making her greatest effort to help.'[62] The language of honour had altered too. 'For girls, as for men, the only place of honour, unless valid reasons hold them at home, is the army,' the *Cape Times* urged at the end of 1942.[63]

But if this was a step towards equality, it was far from complete. The government refused to pay dependants' allowances to women on the ground that it was contrary to government policy that women should join up. Only when the need for women became pressing did this policy change. Even then, as the National Council of Women protested in September 1942, allowances were much lower than those paid to the dependants of men.

By 1945 the pattern of women's employment in Cape Town had altered, and opportunities widened for white women. Yet on almost every front the advances were limited. The conditions of women's employment continued on the whole to be inferior to those of men, and few women in wartime employment retained their positions, for many returned to domesticity after the end of hostilities.

Fundraising

Fundraising was vitally important to the war effort and competition between the cities stimulated local efforts. The most ambitious of all the wartime schemes in Cape Town was the Liberty Cavalcade. Modelled on previous cavalcades in Johannesburg and Port Elizabeth, it took months of planning. The Soviet Pavilion was 'a dignified building in the simple modern style. Towering high above it and floodlit at night will be seen the five-pointed Red Star and hammer and sickle, emblems of the gallant Russian people. Murals for the interior, painted by well-known South African artists, depict phases of life in the U.S.S.R. A poster and photographic exhibition will feature photographs of Red Army generals who have risen to fame on the Russian front.'[64] The real importance of the cavalcade, the *Cape Times* reflected, was not the fundraising but the community effort in which all sectors of the population shared. Opening on 25 March, stretching over 103 acres, the Liberty Cavalcade was attended by record crowds. The centrepiece, which gave Cape Town its only direct taste of war, was a mock invasion of the town, with 'the greatest concentration of fire-power ever to go into action in Table Bay'. The fierce engagement, lasting nearly an hour, involved almost two thousand people and was witnessed by huge crowds.[65]

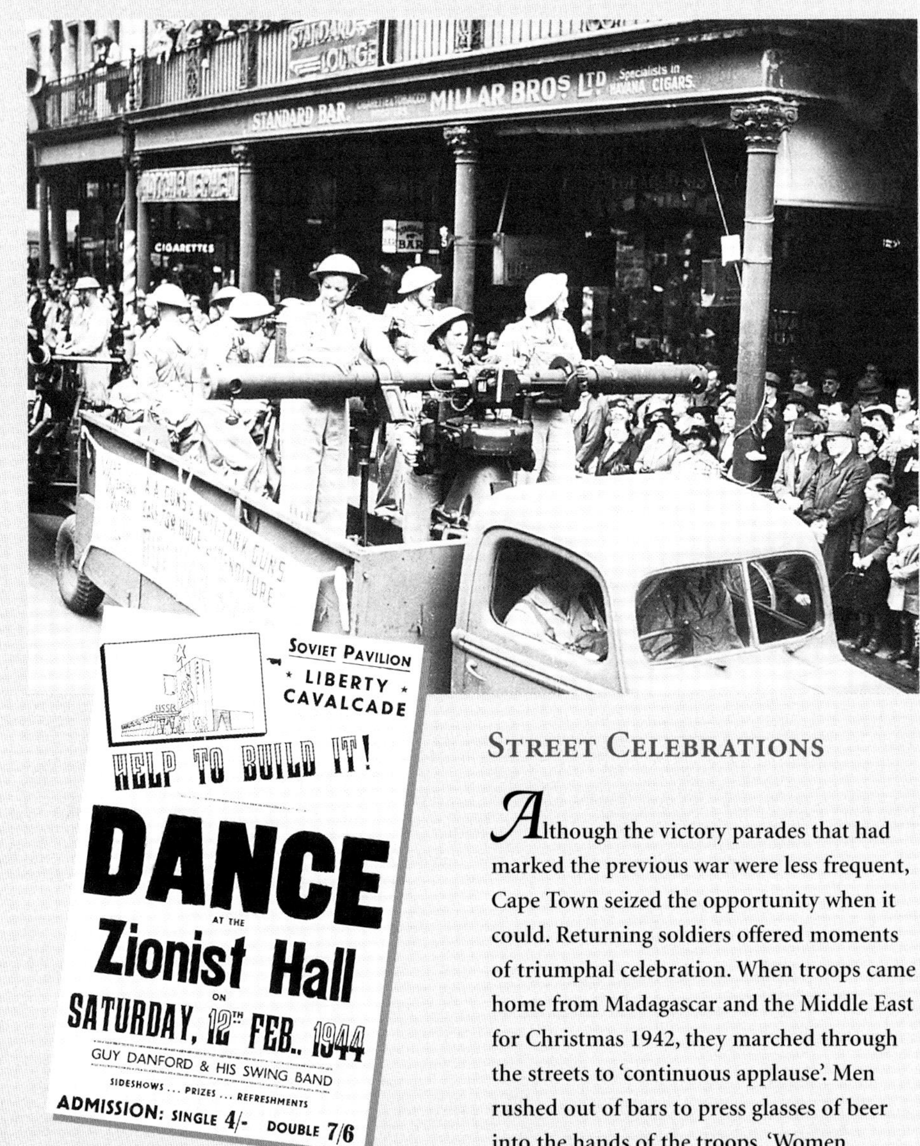

Top: War Weapons Week in October 1942 encouraged the small investor with £5 to spare to contribute to the 3 per cent local registered stock issued by government to raise loans for the purchase of war materials. The cost of weapons was carefully spelt out, from a tank at £17,000, through machine guns (£100) to Bren guns (£70), rifles (£10) and stretchers (£2 10s). It was hoped that Cape Town would be able to raise at least £3 million but subscriptions often failed to meet their target. (SAL PHA)

Above: The Soviet Pavilion at the Liberty Cavalcade was one of the most stylish, representing communism as a force for modernism. This poster also indicates the close links between the Jewish left and socialism in the 1940s. (SAL Poster collection)

Street Celebrations

Although the victory parades that had marked the previous war were less frequent, Cape Town seized the opportunity when it could. Returning soldiers offered moments of triumphal celebration. When troops came home from Madagascar and the Middle East for Christmas 1942, they marched through the streets to 'continuous applause'. Men rushed out of bars to press glasses of beer into the hands of the troops. 'Women Christmas shoppers in their bright, summery frocks stood in the streets cheek by jowl with their bedecked washerwomen and maids – all joining without thought of colour or creed in cheering Cape Town's fighting manhood.'[66] But soldiers were often embarrassed by the adulation and the military authorities were hostile; consequently the practice of public welcome was gradually abandoned.

The End of the War

For Capetonians VE day marked the end of the war, for it brought home most of the troops and prisoners of war. There were no victory parades for returning soldiers in 1945. Instead families greeted them privately at the station or the docks. (SAL PHA)

Capetonians received news of the German surrender with mixed feelings. On 8 May 1945 – VE day – at 3 in the afternoon, ten thousand people packed the middle of Adderley Street to hear the broadcast of the declaration of peace announced simultaneously by the three Allied war leaders. The press reported that it was, on the whole, 'a sombre, pensive gathering'.[67] But celebrations were less bland than the white papers suggested. While the crowd was waiting on the Parade, Cissie Gool addressed them: 'The victory of the United Nations is no victory for us. Our war has begun, war on the unjust, war on the segregationists, war on the promoters of racialism, and injustice through colour bars and racial barriers.'[68]

The dropping of the atomic bomb and the final end of the war could not produce unadulterated relief, although Capetonians did not immediately grasp the implications of this new weapon. In other respects times had also changed. Public expenditure on elaborate war memorials no longer seemed justified. Instead calls were made for a more appropriate and useful commemoration that embodied wartime demands for a new and caring society. This demand emerged as early as 1940 when a speaker at the Delville Wood Day service urged: 'After the war we shall have to raise greater memorials to our dead than the memorial of Delville Wood. We shall have to raise better houses for the homeless, better food for those who suffer from malnutrition, better hospitals for the suffering and better education for the ignorant. If we, together with all our countrymen, were to put the same energy and determination into this task of social reform as we are now spending on national defence, we should find our victories of peace even more glorious than our victories of war.'[69]

acquired a board consisting of six members – three elected by the African residents and three nominated by the local authority, with the location superintendent as chairman – which would be consulted by the municipality on proposed regulations dealing with African affairs. The boards were never a success: they lacked real authority, and consultation between the boards and the municipalities was often perfunctory. Langa response to the system was ambivalent. On the one hand council nominees for the board (usually ministers of religion, safely conservative) were regarded, particularly by the young men of the bachelor quarters, as collaborators, 'spies' for the council. Yet board members, like the Rev. C.N. Citashe, had real status in the community, leading such independent oppositional institutions as the Langa Vigilance Association.

From the late 1930s young radicals began to explore the path of collaboration, operating within the constitutional structures provided by the government. In 1940, for instance, the NLL successfully fielded candidates for the advisory board elections. Soon thereafter, the Langa board, supported by Cissie Gool, claimed a minor victory in persuading city council officials to tour the township. For the first time white council members were confronted by the sooty, smoke-filled barracks and their cold concrete floors. At this time too, the tactics of participating in the existing system of local government were used by both the ANC and the Communist Party. Moses Kotane, who began active work in the townships when the CPSA headquarters were transferred to Cape Town in 1938, explained that political consciousness was not yet sufficiently advanced to make use of the boycott. The CPSA, for example, co-operated in the advisory board elections of December 1944, defeating the anti-communist Rev. C.N. Citashe handsomely.[70]

Deepening Poverty

The First World War left a bitter legacy. In the last week of September 1918 the 'Spanish flu', then sweeping the world, broke out in the city. Although its stay was brief, it proved one of the most traumatic events in Cape Town's history. As early as 6 October burials in Maitland cemetery had increased from an average of 10 a day to 60; between 9 and 15 October the number rose to over 250 burials daily. Many people had to be buried in blankets because there were not enough coffins, and a minister was on permanent standby to conduct funerals. In the city business came to a standstill; the streets were still and empty. Shops, offices and factories were closed entirely or open for only a few hours. Cape Town became 'a veritable city of the dead'.

The city struggled to cope with the calamity: 'We are letting things slide. Dead bodies, from which life has been extinct for 4 or 5 hours, have been left lying on the pavement uncovered. This is to be seen from all parts of the City from Sea Point on.'[71] Hastily, relief operations were put in place. In each ward a district committee was formed to open depots for free medicine and nourishing food. Those who were well rallied to help. Indeed, white Cape Town began to pride itself on the way in which all sectors of the population came together in the face of this disaster.

The truth was that the medical profession had little idea of how to cope with the onslaught – 'We had a rough idea that care was necessary, that fresh air was an essential, but as to medical treatment our minds were fogged,' one medical practitioner later admitted.[72] Viruses were still unknown and there was no effective remedy for the disease. Chemists flourished, selling anything which might remotely help. Commando brandy was advertised as specially 'For victims of Huns or flu'; others placed their hope in garlic, camphor bags, or herbs.

By the beginning of November the epidemic had abated, leaving a distraught and

'The Pestilence in Cape Town'.
Clockwise from top left:
1. Victim being placed in an ambulance.
2. Poor people awaiting the distribution of medicine and soup.
3. Motor cars waiting to take the sick to hospital.
4. People besieging the City Hall for medical comforts.
Inset: A patient being removed to a temporary hospital. (Initially all cases reported to the City Hall.)
(*Stage, Cinema and SA Pictorial*, 1918–19)

shocked city, for over 4600 people had died – a staggering mortality rate of nearly 35 per 1000 people. A few individuals like chemists had profited while insurance companies reported a great increase in business.

The influenza epidemic of 1918 highlighted how impoverished many Capetonians were – poorer even than they had been in 1901, for despite full employment, the rate of urbanisation had increased in the Great War, the cost of living had risen, and no houses had been built at that time. In the inter-war years unemployment remained a feature of the Cape Town economy. White applications for work at the government labour bureau in Cape Town stood at over 10,000 for much of the time, reaching nearly 30,000 in 1933 during the Great Depression. Even after full recovery in 1936 Cape Town was less prosperous than the Rand. Ironically, at least one factor in Cape Town's weaker economic performance was the relatively high wages paid locally, compared with other South African cities. This did not mean that there was less poverty, for Cape Town had a settled urban proletariat faced with high rents and families to feed, unlike other centres with their predominantly migrant workforces. 'The problem was not that unskilled wages in Cape Town were abnormally high, but rather that wages elsewhere were artificially low.'[73] Moreover, food prices were kept above international levels through the protection of white agriculture. Such a battery of control boards was introduced into South Africa in the inter-war years that the poet Roy Campbell remarked of Afrikaner beards at the 1938 Voortrekker celebrations that they were 'the only crop grown in my country without a government subsidy'.[74]

Public discourse about poverty during the inter-war years was distinguished by an emphasis on poor whites. Yet the extent of their poverty should not be exaggerated: by the mid-1930s whites in Cape Town were significantly better off than coloured people.

Professor Edward Batson was appointed to the University of Cape Town chair of social science at the age of 29. He introduced two pioneering techniques in the measurement of poverty: the use of sampling theory and the poverty datum line. His methods made Batson and the department known throughout South Africa. Soon he was asked to conduct similar work elsewhere, was consulted on the formulation of social policy by the Smuts government during the Second World War, and was elected a Fellow of the Royal Society of South Africa. (SAL PHA)

Opposite: In the 1930s the social worker, usually white, became a familiar figure in District Six. (UCT Macmillan)

For the latter, opportunities for casual labour or self-employment in such occupations as fishing and tailoring were increasingly restricted by mechanisation and competition from organised industry. Generally, the poor, both black and white, enjoyed fewer opportunities than previously, and poverty was harsher and more widespread. With the South African economy more firmly than ever integrated into the world economic system, there was no escaping the devastating effects of the Great Depression.

In response to the crisis of the flu epidemic, the Depression and concern for poor whites, poor relief became professionalised in the inter-war years. In May 1919, in the wake of the flu epidemic, the Cape Town and Wynberg General Board of Aid was established. Drawing its support from charitable organisations, the Provincial Administration and the municipalities of Cape Town and Wynberg, the Board of Aid inaugurated a co-operative system of poor relief. In the late 1920s, in another development, the American sponsors of the Carnegie Commission began to encourage the appointment of professionally trained sociologists in South Africa. In 1932 Dr H.F. Verwoerd was nominated to a new chair of sociology and social work at Stellenbosch University. Strongly influenced by American methods, Verwoerd laid emphasis on the need not so much for fundamental economic change as for individual upliftment.[75] Supported by the ACVV, he promoted the importance of 'scientifically' trained welfare work, and campaigned for a national Department of Social Welfare. This was established in 1937 under a Broederbonder, G.A.C. Kuschke.[76]

In its turn the University of Cape Town established a chair of social science in 1935. The person appointed to the new chair, Edward Batson, was above all a statistician. Batson was responsible for the first scientific measurement of poverty in Cape Town. This revealed the full extent of coloured rather than white poverty. His social surveys showed as well that the distribution of poverty in Cape Town was widespread although – perhaps unexpectedly – the southern suburbs were worse off than the inner city. By 1939 commentators were also remarking on uncontrolled peri-urban squatting on the Cape Flats, in Windermere and in Retreat. Like poor people elsewhere, Cape Town's poor experienced 'life-cycle' poverty: young, single workers and those whose children were off their hands might find life supportable, but families with young children and the old suffered severely. Most people struggled with a constant burden of debt exacerbated by the introduction of hire purchase.

While the position of whites in Cape Town was certainly better than that of black people, many poorer white families managed only through the contributions of their children. As a young woman Mrs Swart's contribution to the family income, when she worked at Jaggers, assisted in maintaining respectability in the 1920s. 'Ons kinders het maar gewerk, en ons het die geld ingebring, en hulle het gekyk vir 'n ordentlike huis ... ons het gewerk en hulle het die geld van ons gevat, daai dae moes die kinders gewerk het vir die ouers ... Party dae 'n ou kleinigheidjie het sy [her mother] sommer agtergelaat, maar hulle het vir ons als gekoop wat ons nodig gehad het. Ons het nie in weelde groot geword nie, ons het, sal ek maar sê, spaarsamig. Armoedig en spaarsamig en netjies en skoon.'[77] Mrs Driver, who lived at Ysterplaat beyond the Paarden Island industrial area, and who had left school at 14 to work as a domestic servant, made ends meet in the 1930s through her sewing, working three hours every morning. Smocked children's clothes were most lucrative, bringing in 10s for a little dress, the fabric being provided by the customer. This was an enormous assistance when her rent was £2 a month.

In conditions of deprivation crime assumed new forms. Commentators remarked constantly on the lack of educational opportunities and employment which drove

Parkwood Estate

(Rabkin, 'A socio-economic study of Parkwood Estate, Cape Flats')

Parkwood Estate on Prince George Drive was an area of 43 acres with 185 houses sheltering over 1000 coloured people. A study of the community in 1941 described it as 'the Middletown of the Cape Flats' – 70 per cent were living below the poverty datum line (more than in District Six), with an average income of 30s a week. Despite such destitution, most were buying land on hire purchase at 10s a month. This was a fairly stable community, with an equal ratio of men and women, although young women were thin on the ground, living away from home as domestic servants. Indeed, more women were in regular employment than men, who worked mainly as general labourers. A few eked out a living selling fruit or flowers while an even smaller number were the proud owners of a horse and cart. Boys could earn a few pennies caddying on the nearby golf course.

Living as they did in draughty shacks with earth floors, people in Parkwood Estate endured illness and death as their common lot. Mortality rates were substantially higher than those of Cape Town – at 32.6 per 1000 in 1940, compared with Cape Town's 19.9 – and over half the deaths were those of children (180 per 1000). Bronchitis and pneumonia, rather than tuberculosis, were the main causes of death.

Despite the levels of deprivation, crime and 'hooliganism' were not problems. These were home-owners, most had some form of employment, and the local primary school, the only solid building in the area, was believed to contribute to the 'social morality' of the area.[78]

coloured youths into crime. In 1923 there were nearly 4000 convictions for juvenile crime in Cape Town – worse than Chicago with its 2700 convictions, the deputy commissioner of police declared.[79] Small-scale crime enabled even very young children to become economically independent of their families. In 1918 a 7-year-old from District Six could earn 6s a week selling newspapers in the city centre; combined with petty theft, this provided an adequate income, as gangs of children on the Grand Parade discovered in the 1930s and 1940s. From street child to gang member could be a short step.

In their black studded caps, worn back to front and padded for protection, their *hop-*

Conditions of life in Cape Town's slums encouraged the formation of gangs. (UCT Macmillan)

pels (wide-hipped trousers), and their leather belts bristling with brass studs, Cape Town gangsters acquired a fearsome reputation. Prior to the Second World War these were mainly 'loosely knit groups of hooligans' but the war saw the formation of more dangerous gangs, armed with guns rather than knives and using dogs in their battles with the police. Most notorious of all was the Globe gang, which emerged during the war years, allegedly from a 'group of decent blokes' who had organised themselves in reaction to the threat of the Jester gang. By 1948 it could deploy a fighting force of 300 and had acquired a reputation which few, including the police, were ready to challenge. Like many such groups, these young men had their own codes, language, modes of dress, territory and women, which they protected fiercely. They were also increasingly aware of their status. 'The skolly is a rubbish in the gangster's mind. I remember once a judge told a gangster: "You're a rubbish, you're a low class, you're a skolly!" And the gangster said: "Ekskies, oubaas, ek is nie 'n skolly nie! Moenie my insult nie."'[80]

'The skolly is a rubbish in the gangster's mind. I remember once a judge told a gangster: "You're a rubbish, you're a low class, you're a skolly!" And the gangster said: "Ekskies, oubaas, ek is nie 'n skolly nie! Moenie my insult nie."'

George Manuel, 1979

Intemperance among the poor was a continuing preoccupation of respectable Cape Town. In the years before the Great War, District Six had 30–40 bars and bottle stores, ranging from the four hotels owned by Ohlsson's Breweries to smaller licensed canteens. Here a glass of Castle beer could still be purchased for 3d and Commando brandy for 3d a tot, while the 'penny stores' sold Madeira, Blossom and Hawk wines equally cheaply. The terminology had changed – the word 'shebeen' had come into use, referring to unlicensed premises anywhere from District Six to the Cape Flats. Drugs, in the form of dagga, were also becoming a matter of concern. In July 1929 there were 544 cases before the local courts. The weed usually came by luggage from Basutoland or Swaziland, and was an increasingly important factor in criminality, or so the police believed.

The Second World War brought different levels of deprivation. 'It was hell,' the journalist Peter Younghusband wrote of his experiences as an 11-year-old boy. 'We suffered severe hardships. Chocolate logs and peppermint crisps went up from threepence to

Sister Nannie

Notwithstanding the professionalisation of welfare, private philanthropy continued to provide for some of Cape Town's poor. Anna Tempo (1867–1946) – depicted here as a young woman with members of the Schreiner family – was described by Ralph Bunche as 'the mountainous black sister who got the King's medal recently ... for her work in running a hostel for "unfortunate girls."' Born in Worcester, the daughter of slaves from Mozambique, she became the matron of the Stakesby-Lewis temperance hostel for coloured women in Harrington Street. Increasingly she became interested in work amongst prostitutes and unmarried mothers, and in 1922 she opened her own home, Sister Nannie's House, funded by the Dutch Reformed Church. She received the King George Coronation Medal in 1937 for her work, which is today remembered through Die Nannie Huis, for unmarried mothers, in Athlone.[81]

(SAL PHA)

fourpence.'[82] In general the loyal middle classes, relatively well off, accepted the sacrifices that war implied. Even for the most affluent, however, the start of war meant the disappearance of white bread, to be replaced by the 6d national loaf, which was described by some as 'tasting like damp sawdust'; housewives spent the rest of the war illegally sifting their flour. The poor suffered more since rice, a major staple in their diet, was often in short supply.

While these shortages were irksome, for car-owners they were less troublesome than the petrol restrictions. Petrol rationing, introduced in February 1942, had been made inevitable by Japan's entry into the war. As petrol supplies diminished, Capetonians had to resort to lift clubs and public transport. The shortage of rubber for tyres and the lack of spares also made it increasingly difficult to keep ageing buses on the road. When services were curtailed, tensions rose in District Six and tram-drivers were assaulted on several occasions.

Much more frustrating than the rationing of petrol and tyres were the food shortages, which seemed to arise from sheer mismanagement. Despite the plethora of control boards, prices crept up and food disappeared from the shelves. First it was only imports but by 1942 the cost of local goods was increasing, the problem compounded by drought and poor distribution. By July 1943 meat was in short supply. 'Meatless days' were introduced on Wednesdays and meatlessness became a measure of patriotism. 'Few good South Africans will grumble seriously about having to eat meatlessly one day a week,' the *Cape Times* argued. But the poor suffered: the scarcity and high price of fish made the winter of 1943 a harsh one, and the winter of 1944 proved still worse. The week of 12 August 1944 was reported to be Cape Town's worst food week yet: meat was scarce, there was no butter and cheese, the price of potatoes had increased, and fish was in poor supply.

'European women must not be too proud to join non-European women in the general demand for rationing ... Unity of this kind between the races is terribly important.'
Pauline Podbrey, 1945

By August 1943 trade unionists and women's organisations were calling for better management of food supplies. At a special city council meeting in 1944 Cissie Gool urged the establishment of a ministry of food and the introduction of food rationing, but the government prevaricated. Smuts wished to avoid rationing, 'which in our country, with its different classes of population, was a much more difficult problem than in most other countries'. By February 1945 many Capetonians had had enough. After a lunch-hour meeting on the Parade housewives decided to march on parliament to demand food rationing and a ministry of food. As a result price controls were instituted at Salt River market and mobile markets were introduced in the poorer districts.

Protests against food shortages did not end with the war. Standing for long hours in queues for once enabled housewives to organise protest. By the end of 1945 a Women's Queue Committee, later the Women's Food Committee (WFC), had been formed. In the *Guardian* the communist Pauline Podbrey urged that 'European women must not be too proud to join non-European women in the general demand for rationing ... Unity of this kind between the races is terribly important.'[83] The WFC played a significant role in politicising coloured women. Katy White, a domestic worker from Harfield Road, Claremont, had never been involved in politics before. Elected to represent her food queue on the general committee, she went on to become a leader in Cape Town of the Federation of South African Women in the mid 1950s. The motto of the WFC echoed the earlier suffragists: 'Today we fight for food, tomorrow for the vote and then for freedom for all.' Once relative abundance returned, the WFC could not maintain its momentum. By the early 1950s it was virtually defunct and in 1953 it was transformed into a Christmas Club, offering Christmas food hampers at wholesale prices – a minor,

The food shortages provided the CPSA with a useful platform to campaign for better living conditions. (SAL Poster collection)

Part marshland, part sand dune, sandswept in summer, boggy in winter, the Flats were ill suited to human settlement, but by 1939 thousands of people were making their homes here on the city boundaries. (UCT Macmillan)

but not insignificant, element of the culture of the Cape Town poor.

In addition to the temporary restrictions and shortages, which added to the burdens of the poor in particular, the Second World War created a new dimension to poverty in Cape Town. So many Africans migrated to the Peninsula during these years that even wartime industry could not absorb them and the African unemployed added to the already swollen ranks of the poor. Although in September 1939 Cape Town had been declared a 'closed city' by the Native Affairs Department, which was tired of municipal procrastination on the matter, and Africans without permits were consequently excluded from the western Cape, the regulations fell into abeyance once the war brought new demands for labour. Estimates varied wildly but in 1941 it was thought that 12,000 Africans were working in Cape Town; yet only 3000 lived in the location. Windermere had become a small town while Epping Forest and Blouvlei had settlements of over 20,000 people each. Living conditions here were so scandalous that they were debated in parliament.

In a move to control the migration, the municipality planned a 'reception depot' in Langa. The proposed facilities spoke worlds about the management of African labour, for they included 'a native labour bureau, barracks, fumigating chamber and plant, deverminising facilities, clinic and isolation ward'. Betty Sacks, Cissie Gool and Sam Kahn were the only municipal councillors to oppose the scheme. 'The natives wished to be dealt with on a basis of equality, and not of separate treatment from the rest of the population,' argued Sacks. But despite their protests the depot was opened in 1945. Although it paid lip-service to opposition to passes, the council also decided to repatriate all unregistered Africans; the reason, it emphasised, was the extreme housing crisis.

By 1945 white Capetonian responses to influx control were in fact more uncertain than they had been before the war. The English-speaking press, reflecting confused liberal opinion, recognised that Africans were no longer 'aliens in the city', to be treated inequitably, and were falling outside the ambit of the wartime 'new deal'. What was to be done, short of recasting South Africa's social and economic structure? According to the *Cape Times*, 'Segregation in respect of this class of natives [permanent urban dwellers] is at best a frantically hopeless counsel of perfection; they are members of the urban community as much as the Europeans or coloured whose acknowledged partners in commerce and industry they hope to become.'[84] More vociferous protests came from socialists, trade unions and liberal organisations like the South African Institute of Race Relations. In the immediate post-war years 'enormous' meetings were held throughout the Peninsula to call for the scrapping of influx control and many organisations appeared before the city council's Native Affairs Committee to remonstrate.

Influx control was only one official response to the scandalous conditions on the Cape Flats; attempts were also made to regularise the conditions under which people had settled. In those areas controlled by the Divisional Council, land tenure was haphazard and facilities, apart from a few roads, were almost non-existent. Although a few residents like the Philippi farmers had lived on the Flats for many generations, more recently speculators had sold or leased plots in an unregulated, and often illegal, fashion. Some settlers, looking for stability, bought plots of Flats sand, to be repaid in low monthly instalments. They would combine payment for the ground with payment for building materials and improvise a dwelling but they could not afford transfer fees to acquire fixed tenure. Out of concern that property owners should have some right to legal protection, in 1945 parliament passed a bill to give greater security to some Cape Flats squatters.

With so many people resident on the Flats, regular winter flooding became a serious matter. Severe conditions in the winter of 1941 provoked action. The Divisional Council set up soup kitchens and a Flood Relief Board was established. Private philanthropy also stepped in. Shortly afterwards the Cape Flats Distress Association (CAFDA) was formed under the chairmanship of Mary Attlee, sister of the future British prime minister, with a 'native representative' in the Senate, Donald Molteno, as president. Basic health and welfare facilities were also provided by students at the University of Cape Town in an endeavour which would burgeon into the Students' Health and Welfare Committee (SHAWCO).

Nevertheless, control of the flooding was a difficult and expensive engineering problem, beyond the capacity of the Divisional Council. It was in these circumstances that the municipality began to consider the ambitious project of absorbing the 'festering sore' of Windermere. On 1 May 1943 Windermere and Factreton Estate were officially transferred to the municipality. As a result better facilities and relief services were immediately available to the people of the settlements, and the medical officer of health began a detailed survey of the area. In April 1945, however, the central government decided to take full responsibility for the provision of housing in South Africa, motivated mainly by the desire to enforce segregation. In the words of a spokesman, 'Apart from the overcrowding, the mixing of coloured people and natives in such conditions is regarded as one of the most serious aspects of the problem.' It was consequently decided that Windermere become a model coloured township. But the Divisional Council problems remained, for there were still 15,000 people living in condemned *pondokkies* in the area under its jurisdiction in the winter of 1945.

The moves to improve conditions on the Cape Flats were precipitated not only by local wartime crisis. Throughout the Allied world, the war had been marketed as a fight for freedom and democracy – ideals that were embodied in the Atlantic Charter. In October 1941 Smuts pleaded that there should be a new deal for South Africa, based on the adoption of the social policies of the Atlantic Charter. It was Cape Town that paved

'Segregation in respect of this class of natives [permanent urban dwellers] is at best a frantically hopeless counsel of perfection; they are members of the urban community as much as the Europeans or coloured whose acknowledged partners in commerce and industry they hope to become.'

Cape Times,
2 May 1944

the way. Professor Batson published his social survey of Cape Town in 1941, and this was followed by an influential conference in February 1942, the avowed purpose of which was to bring the thinking and research of educational institutions to bear on government in the formulation of a national policy to reduce poverty. Britain's landmark welfare report, the Beveridge Report, reached Cape Town in February 1943 and was also influential in promoting welfare reform in South Africa. Batson, however, had reservations about the applicability of the Beveridge Report to South Africa – poverty was too widespread and the population too heterogeneous for South Africa to be able to apply similar remedies, he considered. 'To provide for one section of her people and neglect the other will not give South Africa social security.'[85]

While liberal Cape Town thought of social reform in terms of the alleviation of poverty, government planning was more ambiguous. Although Smuts appeared to support the campaign for better social conditions, he also argued that social reform was to be imposed on coloured people through a policy of 'trusteeship'. At the end of January 1943 he outlined his plans for social security but when the final report of the parliamentary select committee was published in May 1944, economic realities disappointingly prevailed. Social security, it was announced, was to start in a limited fashion as it was too expensive to introduce at once.

Meanwhile the medical profession called urgently for 'a new medical order', preferably a state health system based on the British model. Through the Gluckman Commission, the Department of Health pressed for a system with a surprisingly modern ring – to establish preventive health services rather than the expensive hospital-based curative system, which was draining the local authorities. Although Smuts once again abandoned the Gluckman Commission's main recommendations of a free national health service, in Cape Town at the end of August 1945 a small health centre was opened at Grassy Park. 'Here, for the first time in the Cape Peninsula, a medical team will make all-round health, instead of illness, its business ... for the first time in the Peninsula, health workers will go out to study the families of the area, and to see how their way of life, as well as their attendances at clinics may be ordered in the interests of their physical well-being.'[86]

Pondok dwellers of the Cape Flats

In the eyes of the middle classes, most *pondok* dwellers acquired a disreputable name. A contemporary interview reflects the widespread stereotype: on the bush-covered dunes of the False Bay coast was 'a dissolute and lawless conglomeration of coloured and native persons' living in primitive housing; they had been classified in economic terms as 'desperately poor' but it would be more correct, said the *Cape Times*, to regard them as being in the lowest 'cultural' category.[87] Although they had no stable employment, very few were dependent on poor-relief agencies; shebeening was their most lucrative occupation; strike at shebeening and the problem of unauthorised squatting would largely disappear. As the Parkwood Estate study had indicated, many shanty dwellers were in fact families struggling to survive respectably under miserable conditions. But the municipality saw the mixing of Africans and coloured people as degrading to both groups: 'There are more mixed abodes here than anywhere in the country', it noted.[88]

(UCT Macmillan)

Opposite: Windermere *pondoks* taken from the air in 1946. (UCT Macmillan)

But for the most part health reform in Cape Town emphasised the hospital services. Despite the introduction of mass radiography and BCG immunisation during the war, tuberculosis was a growing hazard. In response the municipality pressed for more beds and for more nurses. The greatest need, however, was for a children's hospital. The want was particularly great amongst black children, for whom in the Peninsula there was only one bed for every ten deaths amongst them, and few nursing facilities at home. In 1944, when there was an outbreak of poliomyelitis (infantile paralysis), a minor panic arose in Cape Town and demands grew for a children's hospital. Eventually the Red Cross War Memorial Children's Hospital was built in response to the need.

The war put additional strains on relief services, which became the object of reform during the war years. In August 1939 the Cape Co-ordinating Council of Welfare Organisations was formed as a 'clearing-house' for social work in the city when central government took over poor relief from the provinces. The result was a more bureaucratic management of relief. Encouraged by the new Department of Social Welfare, the municipality established its own social work department under the medical officer of health. Wartime fundraising also contributed to a closer regulation of welfare, strengthening central government control over fundraising and forcing all welfare bodies to be registered. Cape Town was not happy about the new legislation and in particular Batson was concerned by the powers claimed by government, including the right to close down organisations of which it disapproved.

By 1945, then, Cape Town had become a modern industrialised city, but it was far from solving the social problems which beset it. Bitter poverty was the reality for many in an environment which was to become much more harsh in the post-war years. Yet this is not how many Capetonians would remember their city. In contrast with the apartheid era, post-war Cape Town seemed a warm and harmonious community.

CHAPTER THREE

'Those were Wonderful Days'

Cape Town
1945–1948

ROXANE, the well-bred heroine of Joy Packer's romantic novel *Valley of the Vines*, slipped on deck at dawn as her mailship arrived in Table Bay after the war: 'Here is where I belong ... where I have grown up with so much beauty.'[1] Such identity with place, and admiration of setting, were not confined to the social elite of Constantia or those born in the city. Pauline Podbrey, member of the Communist Party arriving in 1943 from Durban, thought Cape Town a 'lovely, enchanting gem of a city'. In addition 'the air was freer, the atmosphere more relaxed ... the comrades were warm and welcoming.'[2] Phyllis Ntantala, a teacher from the eastern Cape, judged the place she discovered in 1945 'a beautiful city ... its majesty dazzles the mind. My soul found a resting place here and I knew I would make Cape Town my home.'[3]

Previous pages: Brommersvlei Road, Constantia. 'In all the world there could be nowhere more beautiful than the Valley of the Vines. Nobody ever disputed that' (Packer, *Valley of the Vines*, p. 9). (SAL BRN 114876)

In the recorded memories of working-class Capetonians there is similar enthusiasm.[4] There is also the belief that, 'back then', life was safe and pleasurable, that race relations were good – despite, as we shall see, the objective existence of widespread discrimination and poverty. The exact chronological limits of this golden age vary with individual experience and, often, the different timing of apartheid removals. But the years between the ending of the war and National Party victory in 1948 provide a convenient moment in which to explore city life during those paradoxical 'wonderful days'.

A Tourist View

In the late 1940s the city bowl area of Cape Town was still relatively unscathed by either apartheid removals or the visions of town planners. The reclaimed foreshore remained devoid of skyscrapers, car parks, broad boulevards and flyovers, which came to form such an effective barrier between city and sea over the next three decades. Woodstock and Paarden Island beaches retained their role as recreational lungs for the inhabitants of working-class areas like District Six, most of whom continued to live close to their places of work as well as all the amenities of the city centre.[5]

By 1946, some 15,000 overseas tourists were visiting Cape Town annually.[6] What were their impressions of the city? Two of them published lengthy descriptions. H.V. Morton,

Born in the Transkei, in relatively prosperous circumstances, Phyllis Ntantala was educated at Fort Hare University and wrote about Cape Town in her autobiography, *A Life's Mosaic*. Active in the Cape African Teachers' Association and Cape Town politics, she also raised four children, who included Pallo Jordan, a future ANC cabinet minister. (P. Ntantala, *A Life's Mosaic*)

Pauline Podbrey

Born in Lithuania, Pauline Podbrey lived in Cape Town between 1943 and 1951. She helped unionise sweet-workers and became a Grand Parade soap-box orator on behalf of the CPSA. Her difficulties in getting married provided just one of her brushes with racial discrimination in the city. She and fellow communist H.A. Naidoo eventually turned to a Baptist minister in District Six. All marriage officers at the magistrates' courts had refused them because they were 'pure white' and 'pure Indian'. If one of them had been of 'mixed blood' it apparently would have been easier. They had similar difficulty in finding suitable accommodation, eventually building their own home on a plot in Noreen Avenue, Newlands. Yet in her autobiography, *White Girl in Search of a Party*, she describes the Cape Town years as the best of her life: 'On my heart you shall find "Cape Town."'[7]

(Podbrey, *White Girl in Search of a Party*, p. 122)

Cape Town, still 'almost on the water's edge'. (SAL Cape Times collection)

The art deco Old Mutual building, of 300 feet, was the highest in Cape Town and 'probably the finest modern building in South Africa' (Morton, *In Search of South Africa*, p. 44). It was designed by Louw & Louw in association with F.M. Glennie, with friezes by Ivan Mitford-Barberton. (SAL Cape Times collection)

Many visitors to Cape Town experienced the Gardens, Table Mountain, and the now famous Marine Drive to Cape Point. (SAL Cape Times collection)

a professional travel writer, was reminded of Athens. The most remarkable thing about Cape Town was 'the fine clarity of air, that bathes this city as it does Greece'. Morton found it difficult to believe that 'this was Africa'.[8] So did Douglas Reed, a journalist, for whom the Cape Peninsula was 'distinctively an outcrop of Old Europe'.[9]

Of course such visitors came with their own particular outlooks on the world, but they were also influenced by the writings of previous visitors, local newspapers and tourist publications. These, as today, typically established the tourist circuit as one of old buildings and scenery, and included pictures of the Malay Quarter, 'Coons', fish-horns and flower-sellers.

These photographs portrayed coloured Cape Town as 'exotic', unthreatening but different. They were extremely important in influencing a visitor's view of the humans they saw. Thus the likes of Morton or Reed saw only two kinds, 'white people and people of every colour'.[10] Those 'of every colour' were made stranger by the anthropological lenses through which they were seen, and the occasions on which much of this closer viewing took place: the 'Malay' wedding, the Coon Carnival or District Six.

Both Reed and Morton hazarded District Six, now another exotic experience for European visitors and local middle-class whites alike. Morton did so accompanied by an armed police sergeant. Reed confirmed the impression created: this was where 'the police go in pairs and only if they must', 'where the skollies live, the roughs or hoodlums'.[11]

The notoriety of District Six had been recently enhanced by its off-limits status to passing soldiers and sailors during the war. In 1949 it was given more weight by a series

Depictions of Coloured Capetonians in the 1940s

Opposite: According to the *Cape Times* in November 1946, the 100 licensed flower-sellers were 'as much part of the city as the flat-topped mountain under whose shadow they were born and raised'. The occupation was handed down within families, many of whom lived in Constantia. They made an average of about 5s most days, but about 10s on Saturdays. (UCT Macmillan)

Left: Both the travel writers Morton and Reed attended a Malay wedding, a common attraction for visitors from the days of Lady Duff Gordon onwards. Even before I.D. du Plessis – and Reed recommended Du Plessis's *The Cape Malays* to his readers – several generations of travel writers had helped to establish the 'Malays' as part of Cape Town's exotic essence, something besides the mountain for such visitors to explore. Reed commented that the 'old songs' sung at the wedding were filled with the 'melancholy of captivity, or exile'. 'The name of the "Baas" ran through them – like Poor Old Joe's lament' (Reed, *Somewhere South of Suez*, pp. 165–6). (SAL Cape Times collection)

Carnival in 1947. In the 1940s there was less variety between troupes. The so-called 'privates' of inter-war years – like the Zulu Warriors or Beau Brummels (who 'whiten their faces ... put on beauty spots and often wear wigs') – had disappeared. After the Second World War, carnivals were dominated by Coon troupes – the exceptions being the *atjas*, or Red Indians, and the Bits and Pieces, who could not afford fancy costumes. Post-war troupes, 150 to 300 strong, included the Loyal Ex-Volunteer Darkies (wearing Union Jack waistcoats) and the Zonk Swingtown Minstrels. They consisted of men and boys; 1950 saw the admission of a 5-year-old as the first drum majorette. Prizes for *ghommaliedjies* had been reintroduced in 1949, but Reed recognised a mixture of hymn tunes, 'the dirges of Tin Pan Alley' and a Vera Lynn song. It was the rhythm with which all were performed that evoked 'inarticulate memories, and hopes seeking expression. They were the gypsy violinist's song of homelessness and the Styrian peasant's song of home, the childish melancholy of the negro spiritual and the tom-tom's call.' For Reed (*Somewhere South of Suez*, pp. 153–5), street parading was about claiming a 'right of way' in the city centre. (UCT Macmillan)

This photograph of a young girl collecting *waterblommetjies*, a local delicacy used in stews, was in keeping with an alternative image of the Cape Flats still prevalent in 1946. *Cape Country*, written by an angler, focused on its scenic beauty and rich fauna. Nonetheless its author, E. Middlemiss, noted that 'few motorists ever stop in the Flats. It is like a quarantine belt that must of necessity be passed through and negotiated as soon as possible' (Middlemiss, *Cape Country*, Cape Town, 1946, p. 19). (UCT Macmillan)

of articles in the *Cape Argus* called 'How they live', which revealed the contrast between a respectable 'us' and an unrespectable 'them'. This time the investigator was taken round by a welfare officer rather than a policeman, but the evocation of District Six remained menacing: 'Off Hanover-street there is a cobbled, sinister little alley that crawls like a filthy reptile towards the mountain. Flanking it, the drab buildings seem to lean towards each other in an effort to shut out the sun.'[12]

The emphasis of the articles was on appalling living conditions and what, if anything, could be done about them. 'Dirty hovels' were always 'an insult to humanity',[13] but the tragedy was worsened by 'the non-European population': 'Circumstance has herded these unfortunates into a forgotten corner of civilization, and over them have grown the cobwebs of our own inability to help them.'[14] Pieces like this sustained the idea among many local whites of a Cape Town divided between an active 'us' – who controlled the destiny of society – and a helpless, coloured 'them'. The writings of Morton and Reed both reflected and perpetuated this dichotomy. White Capetonians were like them and 'no different to those seen in any European city before the last war' – even if they spoke English with a 'twang' and were obsessed with going to the 'bioscope'.[15] Blacks were menials, almost a different species. These views were not random prejudices. They also reflected the near correlation between class and pigmentation that continued to characterise Capetonians.

A back street in District Six. (Cloete Breytenbach)

A Statistical Portrait

By 1946 the population of greater Cape Town was about half a million. The area within the municipal boundaries contained almost 400,000 people. Places outside, which were now counted as suburbs for census purposes, ranged from Fish Hoek (3000) in the south to Milnerton (500) in the north. Also included were the 'northern suburbs' of

Bioscope offerings in 1946 included a 'spine-chiller' called *The Spider*, *The Story of Bernadette* – dubbed a tale of 'religious ecstasy' – and Errol Flynn as a Mountie in *Northern Pursuit*: 'it is virile stuff, abounding in German guile and brutality and Canadian toughness and devotion to duty' (*Cape Times*, 16 August 1946). Musical interludes were provided between double features.

The Alhambra (pictured on the right) was one of the city's most popular cinemas. But since custom-built theatres had disappeared under the onslaught of the silver screen, it also served as a venue for many forms of stage entertainment. In 1946 the famous British ukelele player, George Formby – having been greeted by huge crowds as he drove through the city – entertained his Alhambra audience by singing 'Sarie Marais' 'in a strong Lancashire accent' (*Cape Times*, 12 November 1946). (SAL Cape Times collection)

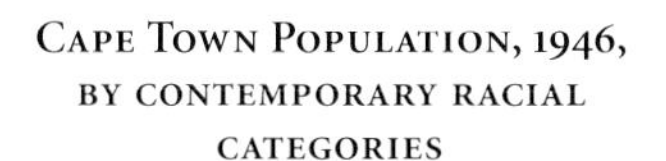

CAPE TOWN POPULATION, 1946, BY CONTEMPORARY RACIAL CATEGORIES

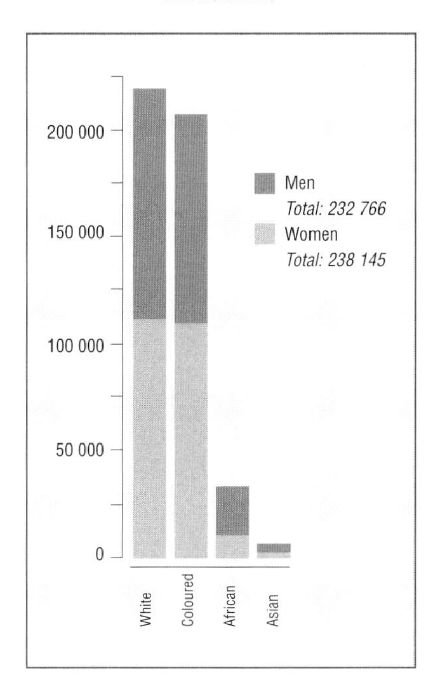

Goodwood, Bellville and Parow – all municipalities in their own right by 1940 – with a combined population of 62,000. The municipality of Durbanville (1600) was still considered a separate village.[16]

Census figures certainly undercounted the number of Africans and coloureds in greater Cape Town, probably because 'illegal' Africans would have wished to avoid enumeration. So would many of those who were 'legally' in the city – as well as thousands of coloureds not subject to influx control – if they were living in the unlicensed squatter settlements. These housed between 50,000 and 150,000 people by 1945.[17] Equally the census was naturally going to undercount, if count at all, those employed in unlawful occupations like beer-brewing or prostitution.

Nevertheless, the official preponderance of Indian and African men suggests the influence of male migrancy, though African female urbanisation increased in the 1940s. About 77 per cent of Africans came to Cape Town having first lived or worked in other urban areas.[18] That women outnumbered men among whites may have been more in keeping with greater female longevity, as well as being a consequence of the war. But the extent of coloured female preponderance may have been enlarged by female migrancy, as young women continued to be sent from rural areas into 'respectable' employment in Cape Town.[19] The small number of Indians in the city was due both to the government's strict immigration policies and the fact that Indians from Natal needed a permit to enter the Cape.[20]

White males still dominated in government, commerce, industry, the professions and many skilled trades, as they had done in the nineteenth century.[21] Yet in at least some professional occupations their monopoly had been challenged by white women, and a few coloured and Indian men. In a pattern similar to Portuguese immigrants, an astonishing 15 per cent of Indians were employed in largely independent, family concerns as shop-owners or assistants. Becoming a teacher or clergyman – for Africans, often the

New Municipalities

Fish Hoek, like Pinelands, had its own town council and a whites-only franchise. In Fish Hoek, 'non-Europeans' could own land, but not live there. Brickfield and domestic labourers squatted beyond the municipal boundary. Already a popular retirement place for English-speaking whites, with safe bathing from a beautiful beach, Fish Hoek was characterised by a booming property market. Liquor licences were not permitted.[22]

Goodwood was also booming, with growth unparalleled even by the gold-mining centres, according to its town clerk. As with other northern suburbs, the Second World War had been a particular stimulus. Founded in 1905 as a horse-racing town – though the first and last races took place that year – Goodwood was called after its namesake in England. It was the first of the 'northern suburbs' to be granted municipal status – with a non-racial franchise – in 1938. By the 1950s, six councillors and 40 per cent of the municipal electorate were coloured.[23]

Goodwood was a working-class and lower-middle-class community, dominated by its churches and schools. (SAL Cape Times collection)

result of establishing an independent church – remained one of the few available roads into at least the lower middle class for black men.

Teaching and nursing predictably offered the best chance for women. But the vast majority of women in paid employment were still in traditional jobs such as laundry work or domestic service, although factories continued to provide a growing alternative for whites and coloureds.

The decline of traditional occupations – which included the virtual disappearance of jobs involved with horse-powered transportation – was largely the result of technological change that had gathered pace in the twentieth century. Only four horse-drawn cabs remained in the city by 1950, none in the 1970s.[24] But by 1946 Wingfield airport offered a regular service to Britain and a daily, 'non-stop' one to Johannesburg. In 1954 a new airport, D.F. Malan, was opened near Bellville, just one year after Jan Smuts on the Rand.[25] New categories of job, particularly in the field of communications, naturally accompanied these developments. Each had its own pattern of employment along lines of 'race' and gender.

Selected occupations in Cape Town, 1946

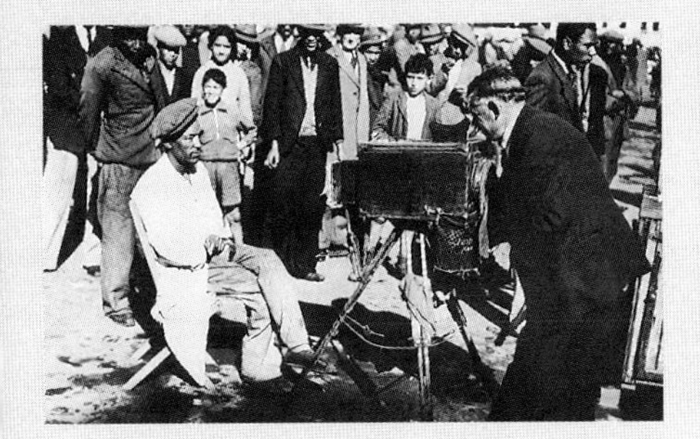

Newspapers reported that street performers were on the decline. The few who remained included the 'kerbside harpist', some 'Coloured string bands' and beggars with gramophones. They competed for space on the pavements with ice-cream vendors, shoe-shine boys, and fruit and vegetable hawkers. (SAL Cape Times collection)

Most wash-houses were originally placed on the fringes of built-up areas, where washerwomen had used natural water supplies to perform their work since the days of slavery. This one, built in 1905 on the site of a spring, was in Hanover Street, District Six. It was closed in 1971. (UCT Macmillan)

White women now also filled almost a third of the clerical jobs in the city, and provided more than 99 per cent of typists and stenographers. (SAL Cape Times collection)

	White		Coloured		Asian		African	
	men	women	men	women	men	women	men	women
Company director	597	2	1	1	–	–	–	–
Banker	371	–	–	–	3	–	–	–
Accountant	242	2	3	–	–	–	–	–
Doctor	532	68	8	1	2	–	–	–
Lawyer	441	8	–	–	–	–	–	–
Journalist/writer	230	35	4	–	–	–	–	–
Clergy	320	33	56	–	8	–	23	–
Lecturer	152	64	–	–	–	–	–	–
School teacher	713	1493	659	516	12	4	34	28
Nurse	17	1795	6	145	–	2	3	32
Shop-owner	3370	403	245	52	708	21	27	1
Clerk	9119	4146	194	26	19	1	22	–
Typist	22	4368	3	23	–	–	–	–
Electrician	1083	–	95	–	–	–	–	–
Fisherman	220	–	688	–	–	7	–	–
Domestic service	22	393	1558	15221	11	82	3705	3507
Laundry work	7	36	96	484	3	–	79	7
Factory hand	105	563	713	1856	7	24	895	8
Railway/dock-work	1798	–	2494	–	97	–	1570	–
Labourer	776	28	16017	777	163	8	8279	49

(1946 census)

One traditional occupation that survived was crayfishing. Indeed it enjoyed a boom once crayfish ceased to be considered fit only for the poor and became 'red gold'. Yet crayfishing was hard and hazardous work: '[fishing] grounds are nearly always situated in places which become perfect death-traps should the wind blow on shore with any force'. As stocks near Cape Town diminished, boats had to travel further afield. Quotas and regulations governing legal length were imposed. Cape Town became one of the centres of an illegal trade supplying restaurants (Bickford-Smith and Van Heyningen, *The Waterfront*, Cape Town, 1994, p. 63). (UCT Macmillan)

TECHNOLOGICAL CHANGE AND NEW OCCUPATIONS, CAPE TOWN, 1946

	WHITE		COLOURED		ASIAN		AFRICAN	
	men	women	men	women	men	women	men	women
Aviator	21	–	–	–	–	–	–	–
Cinema operator	130	–	14	2	2	–	2	–
Telephone operator	57	218	1	2	–	–	–	–
Motor-vehicle driver	15282	2007	3	25	1	–	214	–

(1946 census)

Men had kept the 'skilled' crafts as their preserve. But whites still managed to exclude almost all 'non-whites' from those that needed most training and attracted the highest wages. In contrast there were proportionally far fewer whites in unskilled occupations than 70 years before. For instance, the number of white women in domestic service had shrunk from 30 per cent of the total to less than 2 per cent. Equally, whites had formed 18 per cent of general labourers in 1875; they formed only 3 per cent in 1946. So with the help of government policies since the 1890s, a very small percentage of whites indeed were now in menial jobs. And most of those that still were had their position enhanced by 'civilised' wage legislation or preferential social-welfare benefits.

Crucial in explaining white advantage in Cape Town was government provision of superior, compulsory and free education up to junior secondary level. Such provision was only extended to coloureds, but not Africans, in 1945. By the end of the 1940s – in the whole of the Cape Province – there were 60 high schools for whites, 37 for Africans (mostly provided by churches), but only 7 for coloureds. Indians usually had to find places in coloured schools.

Even with a secondary education, employment opportunities for blacks were highly restricted. Central and provincial governments had effective job reservation policies that privileged whites. Black Capetonians were employed as teachers or nurses to minister to the needs of members of their communities, but were paid less than whites. In terms of other positions the outlook was bleak. Only after the Second World War did the Smuts government allow Capetonian coloureds to become postal assistants (in 'predominantly coloured' areas) and expanded their recruitment to the police. Otherwise blacks were usually employed as messengers or manual labourers.

In contrast every position in the Cape Town municipal government was in theory still open to all. This was largely thanks to the continued existence of the non-racial municipal franchise and coloured councillors. But in practice the highest post held by a black Capetonian (a coloured) was senior clerk. Few were employed above the lower grades 'as this might put them in a position of authority over European employees'.[26]

Reinforcing state policies were the ongoing prejudices and protectionism of many white male employers and trade unionists. Also crucial in determining careers and access to business ownership were inherited patterns of family socialisation and wealth. All these factors helped determine that it was mostly white men that were sent to the University of Cape Town and the Cape Town Technical College.

NUMBER OF APPRENTICES (ALL MALE) AT THE CAPE TOWN TECHNICAL COLLEGE, 1946

	White	Coloured
Engineering	2596	25
Printing	204	1
Building	575	86
Total	3375	112

(S. Patterson, *Colour and Culture in South Africa*, Appendix O, p. 371)

Racial segregation remained crucial to the maintenance of white social supremacy. For instance, *de facto* segregated workplace facilities had been given legal sanction in 1941.[27] Equally, the provision of racially exclusive municipal housing had helped to increase *de facto* residential segregation.

Both local and central authorities continued this trend after the war. Flats were built for coloured fishermen in Kalk Bay; semidetached cottages in Hout Bay. Meanwhile 56 flats and cottages exclusively for white ex-servicemen were provided in Gabriel Road, Plumstead, and a further 60 at Maitland. Whites generally benefited financially from the government's racially preferential demobilisation packages. This helped many establish themselves in suburbs being developed exclusively for their use, like Meadowridge and Bergvliet.[28] Here segregation was achieved by means of restrictive title-deeds, a device which had been used in several parts of the city since the turn of the century and which

LANGA AND NYANGA

Following the wartime increase in African urbanisation, two three-storey hostels for single men had been built at Langa. A further six were under construction by the end of 1945. So was the first phase of an additional location at Nyanga, completed in 1948.[29] Divisional Council officials had called the site Smit's Quarry. It was residents of the nearby shantytown of Sakkiesdorp that came up with the name Nyanga, or 'Moon'. The first 210 houses, later called the Old Location, each had four rooms, a small garden, water and electricity. But there were no wooden floors, only one interleading door and unfinished walls. The weekly rental was 7s 6d compared with about 6d for a squatter shack. So shanties remained – many licensed after an agreement between the government and local authorities in May 1948 – and a large number of Nyanga's first residents came from crowded houses in the inner city.

The second phase of Nyanga was completed in 1953 and consisted of 350 dual occupancy units for 700 families. Residents of the Old Location dubbed this place 'Mau-Mau'. Some said that this was because the new occupants – now forced there after shack demolitions – looked as scruffy as Kenyan 'terrorists' and 'were violent, they liked to fight and we were not used to that'. But perhaps the new residents accepted the name because they were happy to identify with people who could cause panic among whites.[30]

A reception depot was functioning in Langa by 1946. It contained a barracks (for those seeking employment), labour bureau, clinic, isolation ward and fumigating chamber – for 'routine delousing and deverminization'. Location staff herded passengers straight there from the Wednesday afternoon *mbombela* train. (SAL Cape Times collection)

Like Langa, Nyanga was a rigidly planned township providing for easy access and maximum surveillance. (SAL Cape Times collection)

now included all or parts of Camps Bay, Oranjezicht, Vredehoek, upper Woodstock, Pinelands, Rondebosch, Milnerton and Fish Hoek.[31] When the African-American Ralph Bunche visited Cape Town in 1937 he stayed with Cissie Gool in Exner Avenue, Vredehoek. He noted that 'the block in which Mrs Gool's house is located is full of white families, but the property is not covenanted and colored[s] cannot be kept out. Beginning at the corner, however, the property is covenanted vs. colored. These [covenants] have been upheld in the courts.'[32]

'The block in which Mrs Gool's house is located is full of white families, but the property is not covenanted and colored[s] cannot be kept out. Beginning at the corner, however, the property is covenanted vs. colored. These [covenants] have been upheld in the courts.'

Ralph Bunche, 1937

Other factors increased *de facto* residential segregation. The greater upward social mobility of working-class whites, thanks largely to government policies, enabled them more easily to move away from racially mixed inner-city areas. This helped to make places like District Six or Salt River predominantly coloured. There was also the 'voluntary' expansion of black residential areas – affected both by whites-only title-deed restrictions and the matter of affordability – particularly on the Cape Flats. The better-off moved into brick houses in places like Athlone or Crawford; the poor into *pondokkies* in places like Windermere or the large number of squatter camps between Bellville and Retreat.[33]

In addition, influx control over Africans coming to Cape Town, temporarily relaxed during the war, was now reimposed. Africans from the Transkei required 'passes' even to enter the Cape Province. Whether 'foreign' or 'local', most African men had to apply for temporary visitors' or 'seek-work' permits (valid for a maximum of fourteen days) to enter the city. If they found employment, their contracts had to be registered to prove their legal status. So although 'Cape' Africans did not yet need 'passes' to move about their province, they still had to have copies of such permits or contracts and produce them on demand or risk arrest. The 4098 men granted exemption from these regulations in 1945 were parliamentary voters, owners of property or those with Standard 8 education and above. Women were still free from restrictions: although those from the Transkei were supposed to apply for a permit to join their husbands, this was not enforced.

All of this was in keeping with the provisions of the Natives (Urban Areas) Act of 1923, which allowed local authorities to decide whether or when to proclaim their areas subject to its provisions. Cape Town council had done so in 1926, yet Africans outside the municipal boundaries avoided its strictures – only Transkeian Africans required passes and the Cape Divisional Council had a mere six mounted policemen to patrol the area. But following the decision to accept the Divisional Council as an urban local authority in 1944, the whole of the Peninsula and the Cape Flats was made a proclaimed area two years later. From 1937 Africans were forbidden to buy land outside the reserves except from other Africans. The only apparent concession was made to A.C. Jordan, a lecturer at the University of Cape Town, who was able to purchase a plot in Athlone. This was probably because the chief native commissioner had known and admired his uncle. Bureaucratic control was beefed up and police raids launched to check for 'illegals'. At the same time railway authorities in the eastern Cape were allowed to refuse Africans the right to travel to Cape Town. And in 1947 Cape Town employers were offered a disincentive for employing Africans – they bore the cost of repatriating such employees once their contracts had expired.[34]

So there were many areas of Cape Town by the late 1940s that were effectively segregated before the coming of apartheid. The older suburbs did contain an almost equal number of coloureds and whites. But most coloureds (together with a few Indians and Africans) lived in 'pockets' like Newlands Village or Belletjiebos and the Vlak in

Claremont, surrounded by wealthier whites. In some cases a 'pocket' consisted only of one or two streets, like Tramway and Ilford roads in Sea Point.[35] In at least two areas, a wall divided white and coloured residents – along Lady Anne Avenue, in Newlands, and Suffolk Street, in Harfield Village. One coloured resident of Newlands recalled it as 'our Berlin wall'.[36]

But residential mixing involving whites and 'other races' had not been entirely destroyed. If Cissie Gool herself lived in Vredehoek, she also shared a beach cottage with her parents, the Abdurahmans, at Camps Bay – albeit that they were at first 'vigorously resented' by their white neighbours.[37] Considerable 'mixing' of this kind also still existed in the old inner-city area of Salt River and some of the newer housing developments on the Cape Flats.

If mixing between whites and blacks had nonetheless been reduced, this was probably less true among different categories of blacks. Perhaps four-fifths of Africans still defied the law and lived outside townships. Many were in predominantly African shantytowns. But other shanty areas, like Windermere, contained both coloureds and Africans. Equally there were Africans and Indians in most of the 'formal', predominantly coloured residential areas like District Six. The importance of shopkeeping among Indians meant that they were perhaps most scattered among 'other races', albeit that the vast majority of their shops were in older, 'low-grade' housing areas.[38]

'It was bad enough not to be able to take [our child] to the swings ... but to be humiliated in front of the child was intolerable.'

H.A. Naidoo, 1940s

Public gardens, zoos, libraries, museums and galleries were generally open to all, though some parks were not. This H.A. Naidoo and his daughter discovered when confronted by a park keeper and 'whites only' sign at one in the Gardens: 'it was bad enough not to be able to take her to the swings ... but to be humiliated in front of the child was intolerable.'[39] Until 1948 there was also no official discrimination or segregation on buses, trams or suburban trains. But whites, coloureds and Africans largely travelled in first-, second- and third-class railway carriages respectively. And if the city council had not established separate public lavatories, there were different municipal swimming baths for 'whites' and 'non-whites'. The mountain, perforce, remained unsegregated, which is probably why it was loved by all Capetonians.

Segregation was certainly a feature of most government-run institutions like hospitals, schools and jails, as it had been since the late nineteenth century. Podbrey and Naidoo had enormous difficulty in finding even a private maternity hospital for the birth of their daughter Sandra, let alone a mixed day-nursery. At the law courts, there were separate waiting-rooms for white and black witnesses. And there were separate lavatories at Cape Town railway station, if not at Mowbray.[40]

The novelist Richard Rive was still able to enjoy a swim with friends at the Boulders in Simon's Town. (UCT BC 1032 A3 Rive collection)

As the African-American visitor Ralph Bunche put it even before the war: 'it gets powerfully painful ducking all these signs – for "non-Europeans" and for "Europeans Only."'[41] Yet segregation along these lines was increasing with the growth of new facilities, even if still seldom reinforced by legislation. Many cinemas were whites-only while others, in effect, were the virtually exclusive preserve of coloureds. Some put whites upstairs and coloureds in the stalls. One, in Rondebosch, reserved two rows upstairs for 'respectable' coloureds every Tuesday night.[42] Most white-owned cafés, hotels, restaurants and hairdressers did not serve coloureds or Africans at all – and the first hotel for blacks was only opened in 1949. Up to then they had to rely on the Stakesby-Lewis hostel.[43] At many snack bars, blacks were served at separate counters and had to eat their food in the street.

The 'main' beaches were segregated, others were not. In the case of Kalk Bay, a part of the beach had recently been 'reserved for the fisher families and their friends' and was

Parallel organisations, units or companies existed among the Boy Scouts, Girl Guides and South African Legion, as they had done in the YMCA since the 1890s. Blacks were only admitted to the Girl Guides at all in 1936, and 'non-white' Brownies were called 'Sunbeams' in case the former 'might have been thought offensive' (Patterson, *Colour and Culture*, p. 296). And at least one coloured member left the St John's Ambulance Brigade when given a different uniform from that of whites. (SAL Girl Guides collection)

consequently 'looking better', according to the *Cape Times*.[44] At Muizenberg beach, segregation included a further informal separation between Jews and Christians. Such anti-semitism continued to characterise the city's English-speaking establishment, and thus the Kelvin Grove social club in Newlands.[45] It was also part of the ideology of many Afrikaner nationalists, as Podbrey discovered when canvassing a Cape Flats farmer on behalf of the Communist Party: '"you Communists and we Afrikaners should join forces. Together we could drive the kaffirs and the coolies and the Jews into the sea." I didn't stay to ask if he would vote for us. I fled.'[46]

Even most religious bodies had some form of segregation, be it separate training of ministers, congregations, seating arrangements or confirmation classes – even when these were not part of official policy. Anglican Bishop Peacey, of Christ Church, Constantia, used the Dutch Reformed Church argument that it was unchristian for coloureds to sit at the back of churches – they should have separate buildings.[47] The racialised nature of African Independent Churches was partly a response to such exclusivity. Residential patterns that went largely along racial lines greatly reduced the extent of mixed congregations and mixed church activities, even when these were not formally precluded. But there were exceptions. In the Roman Catholic church at Heathfield, there was 'the unwritten reservation of the front pews for children of all races ... At the ... fête last Saturday, no sign of the colour-bar existed. Lunches and teas were served on the Monastery stoep to all races. Children of every shade queued together for pony rides.'[48]

'[In the Roman Catholic church at Heathfield, there was] the unwritten reservation of the front pews for children of all races ... At the ... fête last Saturday, no sign of the colour-bar existed. Lunches and teas were served on the Monastery stoep to all races. Children of every shade queued together for pony rides.'

Cape Times,
5 November 1949

Even in those mixed residential areas that survived in the 1940s, there may have been less inter-racial fraternisation than a generation before. Although quite possibly influenced by nostalgia for their youth, several coloured informants told a white academic in the early 1950s that they had once played with the children of their white neighbours. They also recalled that in those days their families had been invited into white homes, while there was now little of such neighbourliness in mixed streets.[49]

Government policies aimed at raising 'poor whites'– particularly separate and unequal education – made child and parental friendships less easy. Equally, white school syllabuses promoted racialisation and prejudice: topics for primary students included 'the non-European population and the missionaries' and 'difficulties with the Natives'.[50] That the proportion of Afrikaans-speaking whites from rural areas increased compared with that of British immigrants may also have been significant. Such Afrikaners were used to the simpler and more rigid racial divisions of labour in farming. Their racial prejudice was actively encouraged by the Dutch Reformed Church, Afrikaner nationalist politicians and journalists. As an 'Afrikaner mother' wrote to a local Afrikaans newspaper in 1949: 'Here I live amongst these Coloureds in the same flats ... What is going to become of my children? ... May God rescue our people.'[51]

Educational segregation also aimed at separating coloured from African children in a three-tier system. If disqualified children wished to attend a superior school, they usually had to be able to 'pass for' (pretend to be) members of the 'right' race.[52] But in some of the newer private housing developments below the southern suburbs railway line, cross-racial fraternising of Africans, coloureds and whites still occurred, as Phyllis Ntantala recalled of Lincoln Estate in Athlone: 'our children played together in the sand – there were no roads yet – and in the bushes around. Through our children we, the parents, soon got to know each other and some of us became close friends ... my house soon became the place where the neighbours' children came to read and be read to.'[53] Contacts like these were certainly more possible before the advent of apartheid. Friends of different races could still travel together on public transport to those public amenities that would admit them. These included restaurants in District Six or plays and concerts at UCT's Little Theatre, Maynardville and the City Hall – even if blacks at the City Hall were 'usually seated in special blocks'.[54]

'Our children played together in the sand – there were no roads yet – and in the bushes around. Through our children we, the parents, soon got to know each other and some of us became close friends ... my house soon became the place where the neighbours' children came to read and be read to.'

Phyllis Ntantala,
reminiscing about the 1940s

The university itself was open to all races and provided a potential meeting place across the colour line. But this potential was considerably reduced by the fact that whites provided the vast majority of staff and students. *De facto* segregation also characterised hostels, refectories, and sport and social functions: a coloured student attempting to join the Dramatic Society in the late 1930s had been told, 'We're not doing *Othello* this year.'[55] In the same decade the university Council had even considered establishing a separate campus for blacks.

Yet some white staff members and students undoubtedly rejected racial discrimination. They included liberal academics who began the process of re-writing South African history to suggest that racism and segregation were wrong, or at least outdated. Such liberal ideology gained currency among some white South Africans in Cape Town who had fought against Nazism, and who accepted the tenets of the United Nations Charter. Indeed it was the war that probably partly revived and reinvented Victorian Cape liberalism – on the very eve of apartheid.

Naturally there were variations of thought within such liberalism. Some white correspondents to English-language newspapers wanted blacks to acquire and enjoy equal opportunities 'now'.[56] Yet editorials were more cautious: they closely resembled the United Party's Fagan Commission findings of 1946. Total segregation was like 'divorce solving marriage'; 'continual adjustment' was the correct racial policy.[57] Locations would remain, but become 'model villages'.[58]

Another minority influence against racism was Marxism. One strand was more obviously Trotskyite, honed in the New Era Fellowship, which gave birth to the Non-European Unity Movement. Its mouthpiece was the *Torch* newspaper. Hosea Jaffe, a student at UCT in the 1940s, popularised some of the movement's ideas in his book *Three Hundred Years.*

The other strand was Leninist, and disseminated by members of the Communist Party and *Guardian* columnists. Apart from Podbrey and Naidoo, comrades included the trade unionist Ray Alexander and her husband Jack Simons, a UCT lecturer. The Simonses were friends of the Jordans, and the latter held parties that included African township residents, white UCT students and 'street-corner boys'.[59] Pauline Podbrey recalls similar occasions and the entertainment provided when 'the volatile, beautiful, irrepressible maverick' Cissie Gool accompanied herself at the piano in a 'high, clear soprano'.[60] Three novels that evoke Cape Town at the advent of apartheid – by Richard Rive, Reshard Gool and André Brink – all encompass not only the range and fervour of left–liberal politics but also this sometimes frenetic inter-racial socialising.[61] Life was not just about work or fighting discrimination but, as Podbrey put it, also about 'play, friendship and love'. Yet always 'just outside our circle, there loomed the chill winds of hate and prejudice'.[62]

Ben Kies

Ben Kies was one of the NEUM's leading intellectuals. He propagated the argument that South Africa was controlled by a white 'herrenvolk' on behalf of British imperialists. Their successful strategy from the start had been divide and rule – with some black groups being treated better than others – and the promotion of racial mythology. This had provoked only ineffectual, sectarian and reformist opposition. (Private collection)

Living Conditions and Experience

The fact was that most Capetonians lived, loved, played and made friends within highly segregated communities. Yet relationships with other 'races' or ethnic groups were more commonly paternalistic, distant or deferential than openly hostile. Whites and blacks were largely exposed to one another through unequal workplace experiences, and race interacted with class identity. Most whites expected to be addressed as 'Baas', 'Master' or 'Madam', and called blacks of whatever age 'boy' or 'girl'. Many stereotyped coloureds as witty and musical – but also promiscuous, and susceptible to dagga and alcohol. As a coloured man remembered: 'I think that was the attitude of many of the whites that, you know, they were sympathetic as long as you knew your place.'[63] In turn many coloureds saw Africans as beneath them, and disparaged them as 'uncivilised'. Africans often responded by stereotyping coloureds as drunkards and 'nobodies', without their own culture.[64]

Tony Heard, a future editor of the *Cape Times*, recalled 'sitting at the sandalled feet' of Jack Simons and finding his 'Native Law' class 'highly politicised' (Heard, *Cape of Storms*, pp. 74–5). Together with his wife, Ray Alexander, Simons wrote *Class and Colour in South Africa* (Harmondsworth, 1969). (UCT BUZV)

Living conditions and experiences could obviously vary enormously within and between members of different racial categories. Sometimes people of similar class had more in common. The life of the Jordans was not far removed from that of very many middle-class whites or coloureds – which partly explains their eclectic parties. Pallo Jordan and his siblings read, recited and played the piano, or were taken to shows at Maynardville. Their 'African' childhood was obviously very different from that of a squatter camp resident like Sindiwe Magona.

Of course there were numerous divisions of wealth and status among Capetonians of all races. They were still marked by differing material and recreational cultures as they had been in the nineteenth century. Possession of a car, and the revolutionary power of movement it conferred, had become a modern status symbol. So too, increasingly, had possession of a particular make – especially when the end of war meant that new cars came into the country. Dr Jean Walker revelled in her 'gorgeous new black Studebaker coupé which we called "Ginny" because she looked like a shiny gin palace'.[65]

In 1946 Miss Talbot was available to teach a new dance craze sweeping Cape Town, the jive – 'descended from the livelier Jitterbug' (*Cape Times*, 30 July 1946). Both were succeeded in the 1950s by rock 'n' roll. (SAL Cape Times collection)

Where one lived was important. There was a spatial dimension to the social distance and tension between many Afrikaans-speaking, DRC-attending Capetonians and their English-speaking fellow citizens. Increasingly, this was along the lines of residence in the northern and southern suburbs respectively. In particular the north was virtually *terra incognita* to many in the south. And Afrikaner political and ethnic mobilisation was reaping greater rewards in Cape Town in the course of the 1940s. Returning English-speaking veterans found that white politics was significantly more polarised: violence frequently characterised both United Party and National Party meetings.[66]

Many Capetonians across racial divides still shared a sense of Britishness. In retrospect, the Royal Visit of 1947 was the last and greatest piece of pageantry that promoted this identity. The first visit of a reigning monarch helped generate a sense of anticipation in the local media throughout 1946. One titbit fed to eager Capetonians was that Princess Elizabeth darned her own austerity stockings and liked Bing Crosby. To greet the royal family's arrival in Table Bay, children from Sea Point schools formed a living 'Welcome' sign on Signal Hill. On shore, the royal motorcade travelled through the crowded main streets and across the Parade – 'the picturesque centre of the non-European welcome' (*Cape Times*, 18 February 1947) – before ending at Government House. In the evening the biggest fireworks display ever seen in the city lit up Green Point Common. The Cape Town visit was filled with state banquets, civic balls, reviews and garden parties. A ball for 4000 coloured Capetonians in the City Hall featured a 'Malay' pageant – including a mock wedding – introduced by I.D. du Plessis. (SAL Cape Times collection)

Sindiwe Magona

Sindiwe Magona came to Cape Town in 1947 at the age of 5 and recorded her experiences in *To My Children's Children*. Initially she lived with her family in a single-roomed tin shack at Blouvlei, near Retreat, with its 'stagnant, garbage-filled, vermin-infested ditches'. Her childhood was one of domestic chores, including the arduous task of fetching water. But it was also 'stable and happy' with a 'reasonable mix of tragedies, both minor and major'. She fondly remembered playing games in Blouvlei, walking to the 'azure waters of Muizenberg' or collecting 'boxfuls of hanepoot, the sweetest grape in the world' from Constantia. Later she read comics given to a neighbour by her white employer – learning of Mickey Mouse, Donald Duck and Billy Bunter – before graduating to *Treasure Island* and *Great Expectations*. Magona first experienced real whites as doctors, women from charity organisations – handing out toys, and who seemed to be 'from another world' – or as policemen raiding for illicit home-brewed liquor.

(Corrie Hansen)

Whites in Camps Bay lived, physically and socially, a world apart from their counterparts in the municipal housing estate at Epping. Geographically at least, coloured residents of District Six and the adjacent Walmer Estate were much closer. But status and lifestyles generally rose with the ground towards Walmer Estate. It was known as the coloured Bishopscourt (the most elite white suburb). In Richard Rive's description it housed 'Upper-class Coloureds with electric stoves, refrigerators and venetian blinds on their windows. As soon as a family established itself, it moved to Walmer Estate and made a definite point of forgetting the past.'[67]

Between most predominantly coloured areas there were similar wealth and status differences. People in Harfield Village, Claremont, looked down on District Six. In the opinion of Mrs M.S., there 'wasn't quite nice people living there ... it had a reputation ... my father always thought all the gangs lived there.'[68] But another resident of Harfield

Cricket was still played and watched in widely different ways. The New Year cricket game between Western Province and Transvaal at Newlands had become an annual social occasion for many whites. Those who sat 'under the oaks' still enjoyed a magnificent view of Table Mountain when the cricket was dull. Coloured spectators sat in their 'traditional' segregated area, the Planes, next to the railway stand. (SAL Cape Times collection)

Between the wars tennis had become the outdoor recreation that epitomised middle-class status for all communities. For many white housewives, bridge was its indoor equivalent. Here four women described as 'socialites' enjoy a game at the Glendower Hotel, Rosebank. Newspapers were full of descriptions of 'society' parties and fashions: at one held on HMS *Nigeria*, a British warship, Miss Jean Robertson 'twisted a single turquoise ostrich plume hat-wise in her hair as a contrast to her black frock' (*Cape Times*, 24 August 1946). (SAL Cape Times collection)

remembered that in turn 'the people in upper Claremont, they always look down upon us, because we in the Vlak [Cape Flats], they mos up there, "Ja, julle kom van die Vlak, julle is rou" [Yes, you come from the Flats, you are rough people] ... the people [up] there were always reserved ... almost like they were more refined.'[69] Rive satirised the snobbishness that could result, in his fictional character Mrs Millicent Carollissen of Grassy Park: 'over-dressed, over-bearing, over-powdered, she was a pillar of the local Dutch Reformed Mission Church ... In the passage hung two reproductions, one of Christ holding his bleeding heart and another of Queen Elizabeth II.'[70]

The fact was that perceptions were often based on material distinctions. 'Up there' in Claremont, the 'relatively better-off' area of Belletjiebos was adjacent to Protea Road. Here people earned 'reasonably good wages' and there was 'a considerable amount of home ownership'. One house even had built-in cupboards, an American kitchen, inside bathroom and toilet. But there was also the 'quite painful poverty' in patches around the Main Road and the area between the railway line and what became Oaklands High School.[71] There were generally less dramatic differences in wealth in Harfield Village, but in some cases 'sons and daughters sometimes built iron shacks in the backyards of their parents' homes', and around Durham Street there were the notorious tenement houses of the 'Langry'. The greatest poverty was in the unlit streets, shacks, shebeens and dagga dens of 'Ghost Town', lower down and towards Kenilworth.[72]

In Newlands Village, residences ranged from some detached, owner-occupied, 'large properties' in Palmboom Road – like that of the politically active Dudley family with its garden big enough for 'a sort of market gardening operation' – to much smaller, semi-detached cottages off Kildare Road, about half of which were rented rather than owned.[73] In Mowbray, the equivalent of the Langry were the 'Buildings' in Bruce Street; in Black River, Rondebosch, it was the 'Coetzee cottages'.[74]

But status was not just a matter of wealth, occupation or where one lived. Also important were religion, education, the use of language – including a particular dialect or accent – and lightness of pigmentation. If anti-semitism characterised many white Christians, amid general mutual tolerance there was also discrimination between coloured Christians and Muslims. This was expressed in separate sporting leagues or social distance in clothing factories.[75] Mrs M.G., a Muslim, knew many Christian neighbours but 'I would not go eat by a Christian friend because I don't know what they eat.'[76]

Ralph Bunche had noted how important education was to a coloured elite with little financial muscle: 'the teachers tend to affect the psychology of the bourgeois class, but have no economic foundation'.[77] Educational achievement continued to breed disdain for aspects of popular culture. The New Year Carnival came in for particular criticism from left-wing activists – which begins to explain their limited popular support – who saw it as degrading and helping to confirm white stereotypes of coloureds. The *Torch* refused even to publish descriptions of the carnival in 1949 and 1950.[78]

A sign of superior education was usually expertise in English. Many coloured Capetonians could speak both English and Afrikaans, and switch freely between the two. But having English as a home language, or even the ability to use it at all, was undoubtedly a status symbol. So was the way one spoke it. As Richard Rive wrote about a visitor to District Six: 'She was pretty and fair-skinned and spoke English with a Walmer accent.'[79] Similarly, there were and are identifiably different dialects of Afrikaans, from the respectable to *tsotsi taal* (gangster language).[80] English was usually seen and valued as a sign of superior education, of being a 'city slicker' rather than a 'country bumpkin'. It was also valued as a means to upward social mobility, including the possibility of 'passing' for white.[81] For their part, some Afrikaans-speaking coloured residents of District Six mocked those who spoke English, as a Ms B. remembered: 'We came from

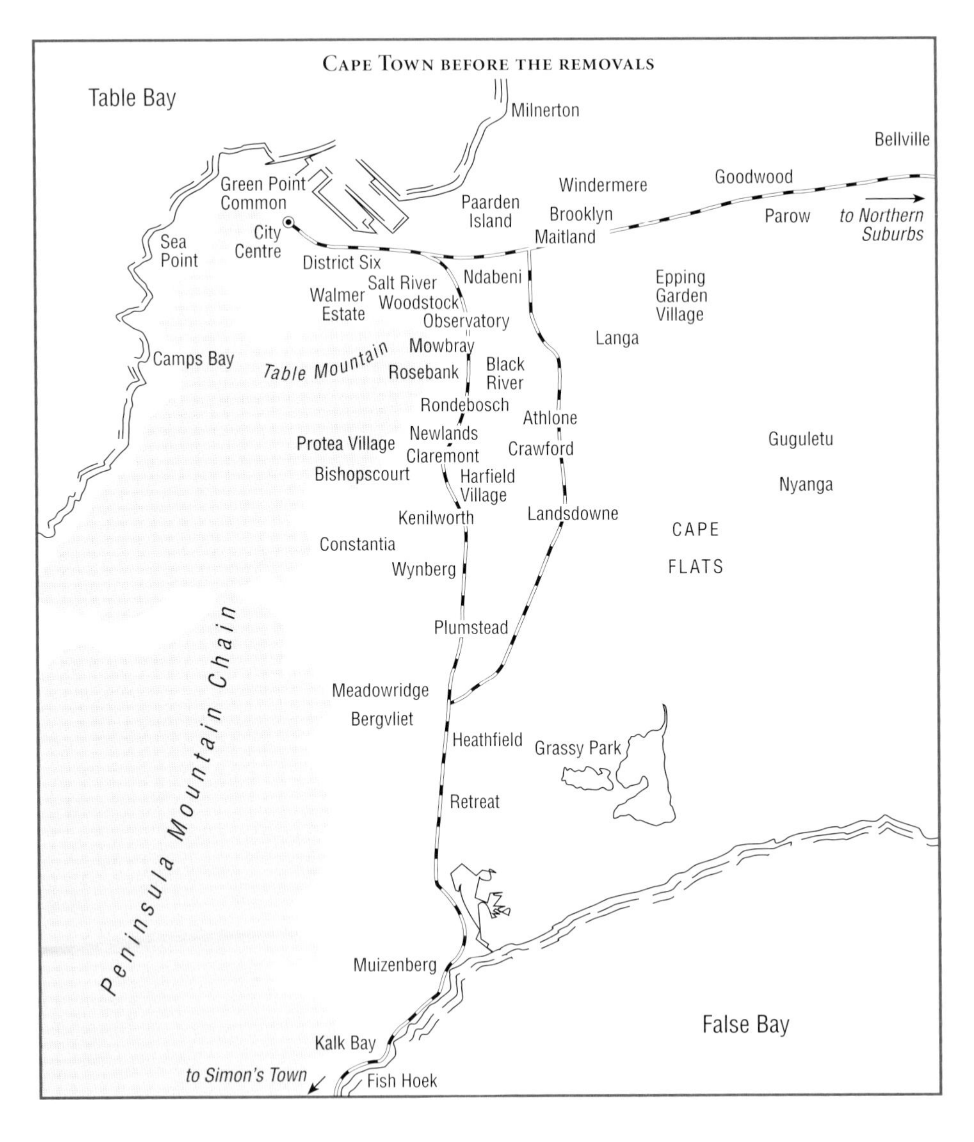

District Six

District Six was a mainly working-class area. Retail services in such places catered for the needs of a predominantly poor community, be it selling cheap stale bread or other commodities in small amounts. If you offered to help at the nearby vegetable and fish markets, you were rewarded with fresh food, if not money; and scavenging was a possibility after they closed. People also made soup and stews from very cheap but nutritious ingredients like crayfish shells and marrow bones.

Toilets were usually outside in the backyard, and people took turns to bath in tubs in the kitchen. Most members of a family were expected to provide some kind of income from an early age. Children could earn money as 'messengers, carry washing, wash cars, do charring, cooking and sewing', as well as having to help their parents with similar domestic chores. Living conditions often varied enormously. Some of the terraced or semidetached houses contained only one small family; others had several, with up to 16 people in a single room.[82]
(CIA Wissema collection)

an English-speaking home. When we first came here the children used to laugh and say in Afrikaans, "Huh! Wat dink hulle, hulle's wit? Waar kom hulle vandaan?" [What do they think they are? White? Where do they come from?]'[83]

Such hostility, or envy, apparently stemmed from the association of the use of English with power and privilege. Rive's *Emergency* argues that similar attitudes often surrounded the possession of lighter or darker skin colour.[84] Certainly a light skin and 'European' features were essential for any attempt to pass for white. In the process of trying, darker-skinned relatives or friends had to be visited discreetly or relegated to the past. In turn, those passing for white were nicknamed 'play whites' or '*venster kies*', because of their alleged sudden interest in shop displays while trying to avoid meeting coloured acquaintances in the street.[85]

Passing was not confined to 'play whites'. Africans passed for coloured for the better educational and economic opportunities as well as the freedom from greater residential restrictions that this provided. The anthropologists Wilson and Mafeje provide some detailed cases of African men who came to Cape Town in the late 1940s and passed for coloured, largely because they were lighter-skinned and fluent in Afrikaans.[86] Phyllis Ntantala recalls about St Mark's English School in Athlone: 'There were many other black children in this school, as was the case in most of the mixed neighbourhoods. The difference was that all these had registered as Coloured and ours were coming as African.'[87] This concession to the Jordan children was made because the principal had told the inspector that they were too young to take the bus to Langa.

Gender remained a pervasive social division whatever one's class or one's race. A

'We came from an English-speaking home. When we first came here the children used to laugh and say in Afrikaans, "Huh! Wat dink hulle, hulle's wit? Waar kom hulle vandaan?" [What do they think they are? White? Where do they come from?]'

Ms B., reminiscing about the District Six of the 1950s

Langa society

UCT anthropologists Monica Wilson and Archie Mafeje provided the first detailed study of social group identity in Langa, based on fieldwork in the late 1950s and early 1960s. They found that there were divisions between migrants (*amagoduka*: 'those who go home'), the semi-urbanised (*iibari*: 'uncouth countrymen'), and also the townspeople. The last were also apparently divided according to age, jobs, education and gender into the disreputable, uneducated, manual labourers (*ikhaba*), the artisans and petty bourgeois (*amatopi*), and the professionals and highly educated (*ooscuse-me*).[88] According to contemporary estimates, about 30 per cent of Langa's population were townspeople.[89] Yet recent work based on oral evidence has cast doubt on the rigid categorisation of residents into 'townspeople' or 'migrants', arguing that a degree of migrancy was almost universal.[90]

A trader and dance manager of the *ooscuse-me* class. (Wilson and Mafeje, *Langa*, pl. 7)

To-day's Hat Parade in Cape Town

Hats were hot items in post-war Cape Town. Controversially, bird of paradise feathers were also much in demand. (*Cape Times*, 13 September 1946)

newspaper article of 1946 talked of the 'two worlds' of Kalk Bay, the 'sedate suburbia of baby carriages, shopping baskets, nursemaids' and the 'masculine world over the railway line – of fishing, oilskins, motor boats'.[91] Fashion, and fashion pages, helped to maintain visible distinctions. Controversy was raging over whether women should wear trousers in public.[92] At the same time photographs of women in increasingly revealing bathing costumes were already being used to sell newspapers. Magazines and newspapers were full of new styles for both men and women. In August 1946 the *Cape Times* announced that corduroy was 'storming' the city, apparently popularised by ex-servicemen who had worn it in the Western Desert.[93] Fashion items defined both gender and social status.

Cape Town's Golden Age?

With all the social divisions, disparities of wealth and widespread discrimination we have recorded, it is hard to believe that eve-of-apartheid Cape Town could be remembered as a golden age. From contemporary newspapers we know that many middle-class people worried about much the same issues that caused concern in post-apartheid Cape Town: planned municipal rate increases, the state of SABC radio and the high rate of divorce (blamed on the war).[94] The residents of Joy Packer's Valley of the Vines feared that property development would destroy its beauty and tranquillity, as their successors did in the 1990s. At both times, crime was of paramount concern, murders given gruesome coverage.

Lower-class Capetonians also worried about crime, as well as poverty and illness. Black Capetonians had the added concern of racial discrimination and their lack of full citizenship. Yet even poorer Capetonians, of all races, recollect the city at this time in glowing terms. Hundreds of their testimonies have been collected by the Western Cape Oral History Project at UCT. True, several acknowledge the existence of social divisions – usually the testimonies of more politically aware teachers or social workers. But for the most part they are overwhelmingly positive.

Despite the fact that 70 per cent of 'serious crime' took place in District Six, Kensington and Windermere, crime and violence are generally downplayed or denied. A policeman who worked in District Six remembers the number of gangs and crime escalating there after the Second World War.[95] But most ex-residents recall things differently. For them, even women and children were 'very safe' on the streets at night, while people left the doors of their houses open, and gangs 'were gentleman's gangs ... they wore suits' and warned residents to clear the streets if a fight was about to happen.[96] Gang members 'never used to rob people, only exceptions when whiteys get there and sailors'.[97] Similarly, for most ex-residents Harfield Village had 'no murders'. 'You had your friends there, it was safe.'[98] Yet one admitted witnessing a man being stabbed to death with a mattress needle one Christmas morning, and another spoke of the frequent fighting in Second Avenue.[99]

District Six was remembered fondly in many ways. Ex-residents seem to agree that though people were poor, they coped, and formed part of a cohesive, tolerant and mutually supportive community whatever their individual identity: 'I suppose we belonged to the middle group or somewhere like that. We were taught to treat all people nicely – you got to treat them all the same.'[100] Memories are full of tales of the vibrant street culture of games, gossip, buskers, characters and choirs; of home entertainment round old pianos or gramophones; of turning somersaults on Woodstock beach; of rugby on Green Point Common or swimming at the Trafalgar baths; of courting at the beach or the bioscope; of gambling and drinking; of classical concerts at the City Hall; and,

Perceived increases in violent assault – particularly on the elderly – and theft were of particular concern in the 1940s. Whites were asked for their responses in one of the country's first opinion polls. They mostly wanted more police, greater control of 'natives' coming to towns and stricter sentences. But the Cape did have a higher rate of approval for more liberal measures such as the provision of better houses and education. Trials like this one of Salie Lineveldt attracted considerable public attention. (SAL Cape Times collection)

inevitably, of a less commercial, less violent and more enjoyable carnival at New Year:

> Oh, oh, those were wonderful days. That days I never forget, because that was when we had a lot of pleasure, man ... it's Old Year's Eve, then my Auntie would make all ready, food and everything, then she would say we must go down and keep our places ... The Malay choirs were the first to come down ... The Coons come marching through, some on stilts, and some were Redskins, they were dancing and prancing; and they also rode horses, just like the old days ... and the people would dance on the street.[101]

'Oh, oh, those were wonderful days. That days I never forget, because that was when we had a lot of pleasure, man ... it's Old Year's Eve.'
Mrs G.J.,
reminiscing about District Six

Even the gangsters of District Six were remembered as harmless: 'I was sitting in the Star bioscope and the Globe gang heard that one of their enemies was ... [there] ... then they rushed in ... We sat and we saw the swords and the commotion. But they [the gangsters] were after their enemy. They would never hurt other people.'[102] Contemporary newspaper reports give a rather different view. Thus in November 1946 there was a 'vicious' combined attack on a cinema by the 'United Gang' and a new group, the Jesters, in revenge for a previous assault on their members by the Globe. 'Innocent men, women and children' were injured by gangsters 'befuddled on dagga and drink' wielding knives, bicycle chains and pitchforks. A prominent social worker said that there was lawlessness in the District 'as never before'. The core of the 'skolly' gangs was drawn from street children, many of whom scraped a living from selling newspapers.[103]

But it is to a magical District Six that the oral testimony of ex-residents continually transports them and their listeners. Here is a place where the community was cohesive, supportive and tolerant, which was poor but fun, and which was safe. In many ways it is very similar to the Black River (Rondebosch), Valley (Mowbray), Newlands Village or Claremont revealed in the oral narratives of their coloured ex-residents. It is also similar to how Nyanga's Old Location or Windermere has been remembered by former African inhabitants.[104] As Mrs M.G. said of Claremont people: 'look, they were not really poor. People never used to complain like they do today. You didn't, because everybody was happy. They might have been poor in material things, but they were rich in spiritual things and in character and so forth ... If I can help you and you help me and so it went ... [Claremont was] a very safe place.'[105]

Street games were played by children and adults and children alike. Kerem was a game not unlike billiards, but played with discs not balls. (Mayibuye Centre)

Part of the explanation for such glowing descriptions must lie in the way that people usually tend to romanticise the past, and think of their childhood or youth as having happened in an unrealistically 'golden age'. In the Cape Town context there was an added ideological and political edge to such memories, sharpened for ex-residents by the experience of enforced removal. In the course of the apartheid years, District Six became the pre-eminent symbol of a more racially harmonious and communal city of the past.

Thus the first major post-war defence of District Six – in a newspaper aimed at a predominantly white, English-speaking audience – came after the National Party had been elected to power. A series of articles in the *Cape Times* of January 1950 – on the eve of the Group Areas Act – was overtly aimed at demythologising the District's 'notoriety' as a place of dirt, gangsters, shebeens and brothels. In the process, the series may have helped to establish myths of its own. Certainly, many of the ways in which District Six was represented in the paper resemble oral, written and theatrical accounts of the District produced in the 1980s and 1990s.

The toddler, Bobby April, pictured here with gangster relatives in the late 1930s, became the leader of the Mongrels gang in the 1960s. (UCT Macmillan)

According to the *Cape Times*, District Six had become the home of coloured people. Thereby it held a unique position in Cape Town and South African history: whereas the likes of Adderley Street could be found in 'any of the world's big cities', 'District Six could only be where it is'. The majority of its inhabitants were simple, hard-working folk. They struggled valiantly to live respectable lives, endlessly scrubbing floors to keep them clean and helping those in distress. 'Almost every Coloured person' wanted to live decently, 'to enjoy the simple necessities of life and a few of its luxuries, and to have some leisure to dance and sing'.[106]

In a view echoed by Dr Jean Walker in her autobiography *Skin Deep*, no one of virtue

A famous graffito in District Six read: 'You are now in Fairyland'. (Cloete Breytenbach)

or who was helping the District was ever beaten up there: only those who deserved to be, like exploitative landlords or sailors visiting prostitutes. The occurrence of gang fights or overcrowding was in fact only 'the natural outcome of conditions over which the people of District Six have no control'. The series concluded that District Six deserved to be saved for its 'decent citizens'.[109] Later articles in English-language newspapers supported this view by emphasising the uniqueness of the place. They depicted it as boisterous, vibrant and ultimately harmless by means of picturesque cameos of street life and individual characters.[110]

In the 1950s and 1960s, this narrative provided an ideological counter to the perception of the area as a crime- and vice-ridden slum that first threatened, then justified, its destruction. By the late 1970s, the positive narrative became an epitaph. It served as a powerful indictment of what Richard Rive called 'Cape Town's Hiroshima', and thereby

Memories of District Six

Popular reminiscences about District Six are very similar to the depictions that resurface in various media from the 1970s: in Abdullah Ibrahim's poem 'Blues for District Six', in Brink's novel *Looking on Darkness* or Rive's *Buckingham Palace, District Six*, in the musicals of David Kramer and Taliep Petersen, as well as the oral and written testimonies of ex-residents.[107] It would seem as though each has helped to inform the other and to produce a popular orthodoxy. The bleak, violent and desperate place of Alex La Guma's *Walk in the Night* or David Muller's *Whitey* is all but forgotten.[108] Instead there is the narrative of a unique, essentially 'good' District Six.

In most pre-apartheid Cape Town communities crime rates were undoubtedly lower.

Murder Rates in Cape Town in the Twentieth Century

Year	Murders	Population	Rate as per 100, 000
1904	5	170, 000	3
1946	25	470, 000	5
1978	447	850, 000	52
1995	1962	2,800, 000	70

of apartheid in general. Subsequently, similar epitaphs and indictments were attached to other destroyed communities, throughout the southern suburbs, as their histories were told to the political enemies of the National Party, like English-speaking academics or journalists. In the process, pre-apartheid Cape Town in general was remembered with nostalgia. Few recollections made any mention of racism, segregation or any other unpleasantness. Instead, in these imaginings or memories – themselves partly shaped by the uncertain world of the 1980s and 1990s – Cape Town on the eve of apartheid was a crime-free, happy, tolerant place. This was the world that was lost.

Yet to dismiss all recollections as entirely imagined would be foolish. New Year Carnivals must have been more wonderful when winding through the streets of District

Cape Town also enjoyed substantial political tolerance. The Parade remained a place for large-scale protest meetings or more intimate soap-box oratory. Although police attended Communist Party meetings and raided the offices of the *Guardian*, the party remained legal and the newspaper had documents returned after a court case. Unsuccessful objections to the Friends of the Soviet Union screening a Russian film at the Odeon, in Sea Point, stemmed as much from worries about Sunday observance as from fears of communist propaganda. (SAL Cape Times collection)

Six, if not necessarily less commercial or violent – in 1948 the mayoress had to present prizes from behind a steel-mesh screen.[111] Lengthy residence, neighbourliness or complex kinship and occupational ties frequently did produce a sense of community and local identity with place among poorer Capetonians. So did relatively old and familiar institutions and organisations, whether they were sports clubs, churches or schools. Households were generally within cheap and easy distance of essential services and work. In the case of coloured and Indian people living in Mowbray pockets and Black River in Rondebosch, oral testimony to this effect has been supported by detailed academic research.[112]

What probably increased a sense of community for many was the belief that they were part of 'black' islands surrounded by a foreign, but not yet overtly hostile, white sea. This may help to explain the tolerance people reportedly displayed towards 'different' social behaviour by insiders. Prostitutes and *moffies* (homosexuals or transvestites) were an accepted and visible part of District Six, and not just at carnival time. The flam-

'"Not Goodbye but Tot Siens": He speaks for all South Africa'. As the next decades were to show, he did not. (*Cape Times*, 24 April 1947)

boyant conduct of *moffies* – like the famous hairdresser 'Kewpie', the subject of a 1990s documentary – probably served to deter potential detractors.

At the same time many Capetonians, particularly among blacks and English-speaking whites, still had a sense of Britishness – undoubtedly reinvigorated by the visit of the royal family in 1947. Part of Britishness was the feeling of belonging to an international community which, rightly or wrongly, was perceived to foster civilised values. For all these Capetonians, and in a different and more promising way for many Afrikaners, the general election of 1948 marked the end of an era.

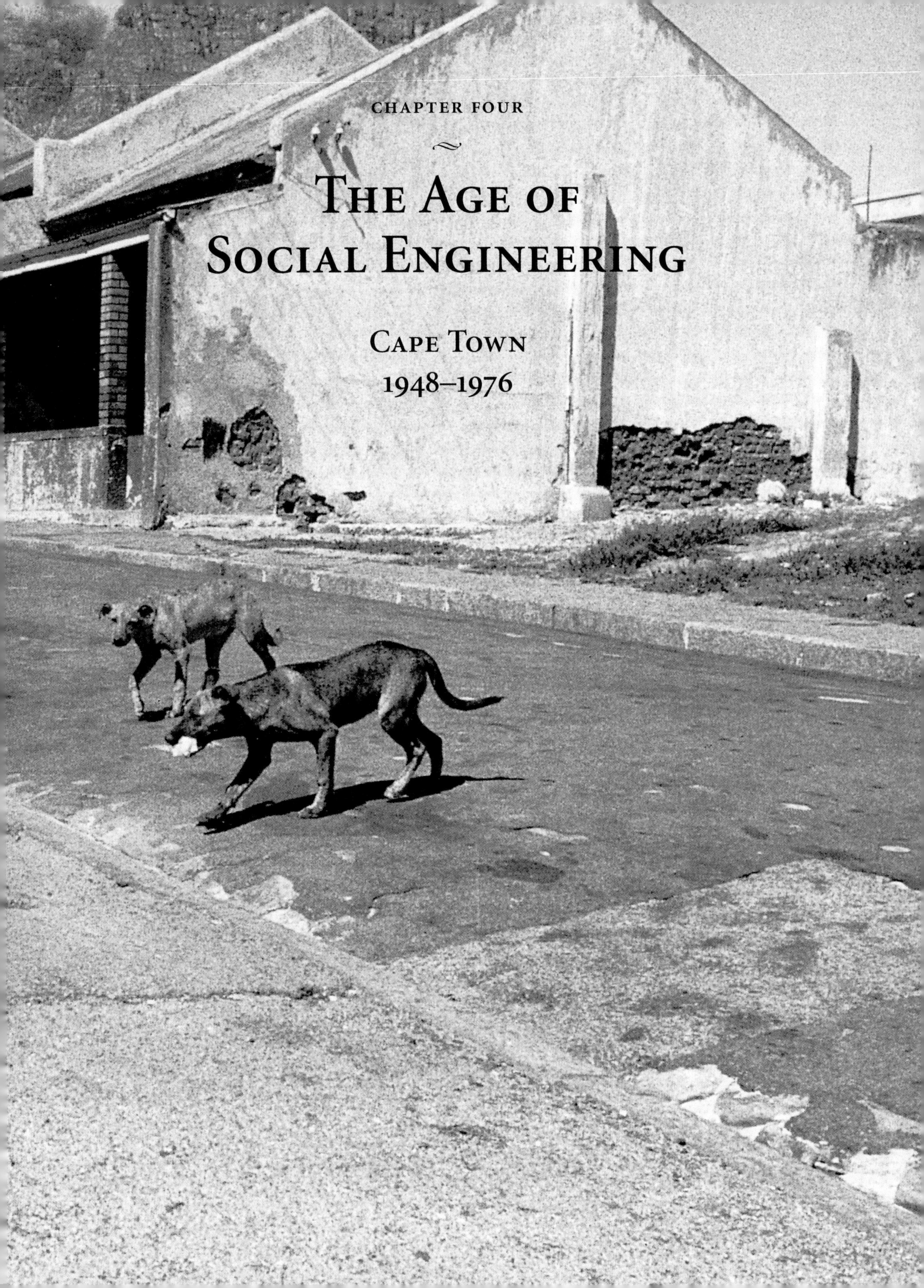

CHAPTER FOUR

The Age of Social Engineering

Cape Town 1948–1976

IN 1956 the Cape Provincial Institute of Architects put together a photographic exhibition on Cape Town. Sir William Holford, a guest speaker from Britain, gave the keynote address. His talk was on 'Diseases of the modern city', which he believed had infected Cape Town. Chief among these was 'monumentality', an abstract and vast rather than human scale in architecture and town planning. Holford was particularly critical of the recent 'folly' of disconnecting the city from the sea. In addition he disliked the 'wirescape' caused by the spider's web of trolleybus cables, the proliferation of advertising boards and the way in which the proportions of old buildings were overwhelmed by the new.[1]

Monumentality was both the aesthetic and political product of twentieth-century 'modernism'. Central and local governments the world over, armed with increased technological and bureaucratic powers, were attempting to plan the lives of citizens more completely than ever before. Modernist town planning also fitted in well with segregationist thinking. Both were concerned with zoning, with placing people in appropriate space, moving them from inappropriate localities.[2] In Cape Town they combined to reach a mutual zenith between 1948 and 1976. After all, the National Party's apartheid project – with its aim of complete 'separate development' – was an attempt to produce a racist, but coherent, masterpiece of urban planning. Towards this end, central government ideally wanted the co-operation of local authorities. But if necessary, the autonomy and powers of bodies like the Cape Town City Council would be severely eroded. The feelings of most citizens would be ignored and protests dealt with in an increasingly autocratic and brutal fashion.[3]

Previous pages: Dogs roaming a street in District Six after the residents had been removed. (Mayibuye Centre)

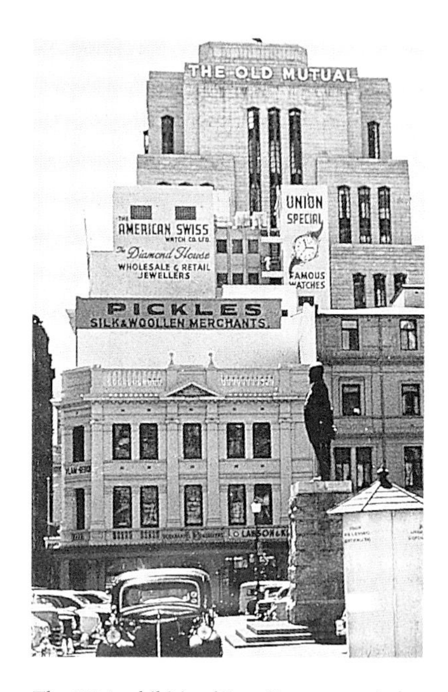

The 1956 exhibition 'Cape Town your city' intentionally illustrated the problems of 'modernism'. Some remedies Sir William Holford suggested were vertical car-parking (to save space), well-designed 'street furniture' (like benches) and the use of 'floor' texture (such as cobblestones). He was also in favour of tree planting, the guarding of existing green spaces and pedestrian precincts. (*Cape Town Your City*)

Planning Twentieth-century Cape Town

Forms of town planning, like forms of racial segregation, had existed in Cape Town long before 1948. While the early Dutch city had been laid out on a grid pattern, British colonial Cape Town was allowed to grow haphazardly, shaped by the whims of developers. By the twentieth century, such organic growth was denounced as inefficient and backward by modern planners.

Two international styles, often in combination, dominated attempts to find solutions. The first was Britain's 'garden city' movement, influenced by Ebenezer Howard and the rural dream. Its moving spirit in Cape Town was the businessman and politician Richard Stuttaford, who instigated the non-profit-making Garden City Trust in 1919, which helped establish Pinelands. In pressing for a successor to Ndabeni, the *Cape Times* had hoped that even this would be a 'Garden village'[4] – when completed, Langa would, of course, disappoint. For its part, Maitland Garden Village, designed for coloured people, had its admirers.

Yet because of the pressing need for low-cost housing, the 'city practical' style of the United States gained greater importance. This emphasised the logical arrangement of urban space through 'zoning' – into separate residential, commercial or industrial areas – for more efficient economic production. The favoured architectural design was stark and spacious, with the use of industrial materials (like concrete) in their rawest form.

Early twentieth-century planners in Cape Town were motivated by concern for public health and the maintenance of social order – and residential segregation was usually seen as part of the solution. In 1927, when the city council put forward plans for a new coloured housing scheme near Maitland Garden Village, the administrator of the Cape Province objected because it was too close to Pinelands: 'Scattering the Non-Europeans from one end of the city to the other was not in the best interests of Cape Town ... The city should be completely zoned ... so that certain sections should be set apart as European areas, others as Non-European areas and areas where noxious trades might be established.'[5]

At this time the main difficulty faced by planners stemmed from the embryonic state of South African legislation. Authority was divided between different local and central institutions. This raised the thorny question of who would have to bear financial responsibility. Such motives and problems were present during the creation of both Ndabeni and Langa. In addition, the absence of regulations encouraged private speculation and urban sprawl, and prompted the Cape Institute of Architects to send a deputation in 1915 to the recently enlarged Cape Town municipality. Their demand was for a comprehensive redevelopment scheme for the whole Cape Peninsula, including the Cape Flats. It was here, by the early 1920s, that 'Township after township springs up and grows haphazard. Speculators are interested only in the division of land into the maximum number of saleable plots; they care nothing for preserving the beauty in which the embryonic cities are set.'[6]

The first town-planning ordinance was passed in 1927. But it was only in 1934 that further legislation established a municipal town-planning branch, attached to the City Engineer's Department. This led to comprehensive urban zoning being adopted for the

Garden Cities of Cape Town

Pinelands was Cape Town's first garden city and also the first place where 'zoning' was introduced. Competition rules for its design specified areas for housing, roads and open spaces. Provision also had to be made for markets, churches, shops, a museum, town hall, post office and schools. Land for commercial use was not sold to private individuals but leased by the Garden City Trust. No. 3 Medway, costing £1050, was the first house to be occupied, in February 1922. The foundation stone of Central Square was laid by General Smuts on 5 May 1923. Like all housing schemes in the city up to the 1990s, whites-only Pinelands was racially segregated.[7]

Maitland Garden Village, the earliest housing estate to be built by the municipality for its own coloured employees, formed a strong contrast. The African-American visitor Ralph Bunche thought it 'not so attractive as Bokmakierie [a later housing estate] since the streets are unpaved, but it is a vast improvement over the crowded living conditions in the colored sections in town. There is plenty of fresh air out there, tho the dust is picked up plenty when the southeasters sweep over.'[8]

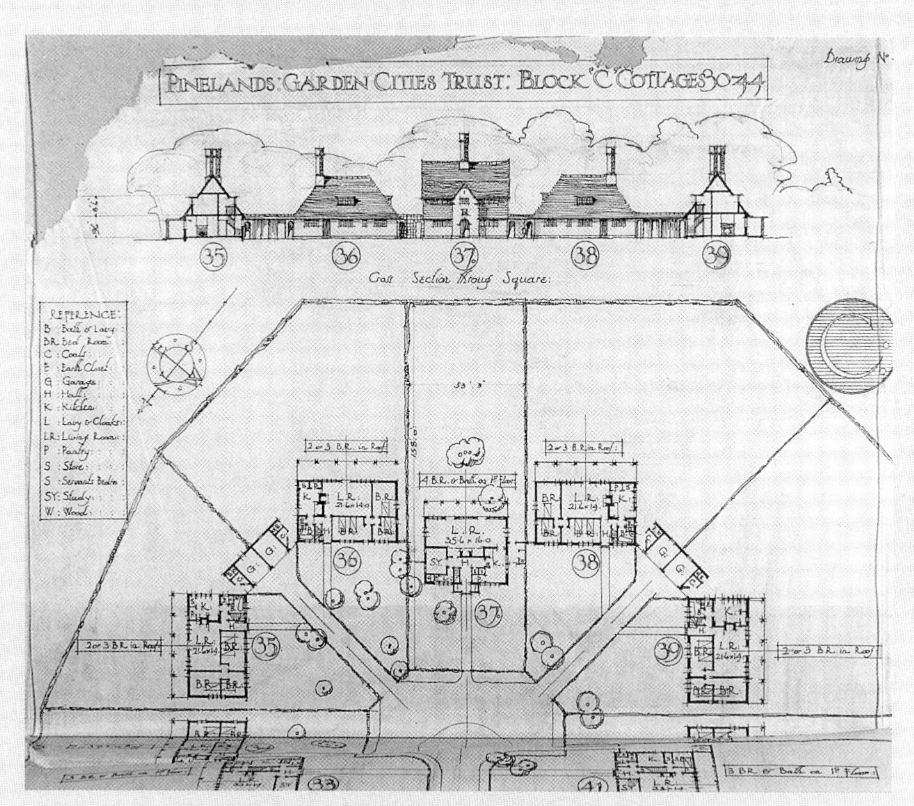

Pinelands was elaborately planned to foster the rural dream. (UCT BC 206-211 A&B)

whole municipality in 1941. Foreshadowing the observations of Sir William Holford, critics disliked the fact that the plan allowed buildings of up to seven storeys in 'general residential' zones, and over-generous 'bulk allowances' in 'commercial' areas.[9]

Before 1948, much of town planning was about slum clearance. Two factors made housing a particularly contentious issue in Cape Town. One was the influence of individuals who publicised the plight of the poor; the second was the evidence suggesting that Cape Town's inner-city slums were the worst in South Africa.

Wartime urbanisation, the 1918 influenza epidemic, and the drift of poor Afrikaners into the city all helped make inner-city housing a political issue. Social reformers of the Afrikaanse Christelike Vroue Vereniging (ACVV), like Zerilda Steyn, were horrified at District Six's cosmopolitan mix. In the Anglican Church the Rev. (later Bishop) Sidney Lavis, mildly socialist, was an outspoken voice for the poor. The municipal council acquired a more militant tone in this regard in 1938, when Cissie Gool ('left-wing and talks a mile a minute') was elected. The powerful figure of the municipal medical officer of health, Dr Shadick Higgins, also fought fiercely for improved housing.

The Rev. Sidney Lavis, depicted here in 1953 after he had been enthroned as a bishop. The working-class suburb of Bishop Lavis on the Cape Flats was named after him. (SAL Cape Times collection)

Repeated surveys had given concrete evidence of Cape Town's overcrowding. Professor Edward Batson of UCT estimated that of 25,000 coloured households in Cape Town, three-quarters were living in three rooms or fewer. In most cases one-room households included at least three people. Virtually none had any bathroom. Rent Board cases also publicised the housing problem. As Sidney Lavis complained, 25s, 35s, even 45s a month was being paid for a single room, by people who rarely earned more than 5s a day as casual labourers, and were uncertain of regular employment. 'The slums are crowded with little children whose chief fare is plain bread and coffee day in, day out – and this because so large a part of the meagre wages of their parents is extorted in rentals for slum tenements.'[10]

Zerilda Steyn and Lavis helped form the Citizens' Housing Council as early as 1919, and later the Citizens' Housing League and the Utility Company of 1929. Most of these initiatives favoured whites. Although Utility Company housing was plain, some were grateful for the homes it provided. Mrs D., who had been a domestic servant before her marriage, remembered her home in Ysterplaat with affection: 'Engels en Afrikaans het gebly daarso. Engels en Afrikaans. Maar ... [the Company was] ... a real godsend to our poor people you know, die minderbevoorregtes. Hulle was, waarlikwaar.'[11]

Yet none of these schemes really solved the problem of the very poor. The munici-

In 1929 the businessman E.R. Syfret donated land in Crawford where one of the few Housing League schemes for coloured people was built. Here Lady Clarendon, wife of the governor-general, opens the scheme in March 1931. (SAL PHA)

pality continued to complain that it lacked adequate legislative powers. Widespread complaints of this kind lay behind the passing of a Slums Act in 1934. This gave both municipalities and government the powers to acquire slum properties for demolition and rebuilding.

One of the effects of the Slums Act was to encourage landlords to spruce up their buildings. But the Act also made it possible to demarcate areas for development, a course favoured by the City Engineer's Department. From its perspective, District Six presented special problems. The street system was so badly laid out that 'order, amenity and healthy conditions can only be derived by a complete replanning of the whole area ... the area must be carefully zoned in the light of the proposed foreshore extensions with allowance for commercial interests. At this stage it would appear that a high degree of decentralisation will be necessary.'[12]

Following W.S. Lunn's appointment as city engineer in 1936, the council began to draw up comprehensive plans for the remodelling of the city slums. Most inhabitants would have to leave the inner city. Lands along the Klipfontein Road, originally acquired by the municipality for sewage disposal, were cheap and 'healthy'. Here could be created a 'garden city ... where all facilities of a town are available to its inhabitants – shops, busi-

'Slum' clearance in Cape Town in the 1930s

Wells Square epitomised all that was worst about District Six slums from the perspective of 'respectable' observers. Impenetrable to outsiders, 'The whole of Wells Square can be likened unto a fort, having a number of narrow inlets, which easily lend themselves to barricading.'[13] Despite its later romanticised reputation, neighbours also feared it. In 1916 a petition from 250 citizens complained of 'brothels and other unmentionable activities in the area'.

In 1932 the first bricks were laid for a new housing scheme, to form part of the Canterbury Square–Bloemhof housing scheme. In the heart of District Six there was to be an 'elegant area, with a layout such as might be the envy of any suburb'.[14] Few of the existing residents could afford the new rents, however.

Above: Wells Square. (SAL PHA)
Right: Bloemhof Flats, built on the site of Wells Square, was an example of enlightened municipal housing. (SAL Cape Times collection)

Solidly built but stark, Kew Town was one of the best of Cape Town's early housing schemes. (SAL Cape Times collection)

ness premises, schools, churches, public buildings, places of recreation'.[15] Lunn envisaged a dramatic reconstruction that would 'completely transform the whole of District Six, replacing narrow streets and congested buildings with wide thoroughfares, open spaces and gardens'.[16] By February 1939, shortly before war broke out, a total of 1127 homes had been built, including 324 flats in Bloemhof–Canterbury Square, 260 in Alicedale and 500 in Schotsche Kloof. Another 10,879 remained to be built.

Q-Town (later Kew Town) was the prize project of the war years, a symbol of well-planned segregation and the social upliftment of the coloured people. 'Wide boulevards and open spaces are characteristic of this new city on the Cape Flats, where slum life will be forgotten,' it was announced proudly in 1941. Q-Town was to be a 'self-contained planned city', a carefully thought-out scheme for 'rehabilitating that [slum] population and for developing among its present numbers and their successors the degree of "social consciousness" essential to good citizenship'. Appropriate planning was seen as the key ingredient of success. Costs and rentals would be carefully controlled, as would the residents, for the scheme was to be operated on the 'Octavia Hill system', with a staff of women, specially trained in housing management, who would exercise close supervision over the tenants. The housing inspector, a latter-day lady of the manor, was the key to

'Wide boulevards and open spaces are characteristic of this new city on the Cape Flats, where slum life will be forgotten.'

Cape Times, 4 July 1941

Opposition to Segregated Housing

It was the United Party government that introduced a 'Class Areas Bill' in 1939. This would have enforced urban residential segregation throughout the country. The NLL and NEUF organised a massive protest meeting for 27 March 1939 on the Grand Parade. Thousands streamed into the city from the suburbs and surrounding areas after work. At ten in the evening the protest culminated in a torchlight march on parliament, led by the Moravian brass band, singing the anthem of the NLL, 'Dark folks, arise!', waving flags and banners. The *Cape Standard* estimated 20,000 people were on the Parade; about 5000 marched. On the steps of parliament MPs were booed and several cars were damaged. The police and military came out in force and the demonstration ended in a 'riot', in which District Six residents were attacked late into the night. About 50 were injured.[17] Such protest and the coming of war delayed legislated residential segregation.

this planned 'new order' for the poor.

By 1939 a real start had been made in tackling Cape Town's housing problem. Although the war was clearly going to delay progress, housing remained a central tenet of the government's 'new order', which it soon began propounding in line with the Atlantic Charter. 'The "new order" to which we must look forward rests not so much on a revolutionary upheaval as on the acceleration and extension of social improvements which the much-maligned democracies have already set in motion. The less war interferes with these improvements, the further advanced we shall be when the time comes to plan the peace.'[18] It would, the *Cape Times* urged, be 'a tragedy and a scandal' if the work were slowed down after decades of neglect. This was a 'crusade' against 'one of the great social evils of our time'.[19]

In the inter-war years, distance from white areas became firmly established as the desirable criterion for all sub-economic housing schemes. When Mowbray and Rondebosch residents rejected a site for coloured housing at the top of Klipfontein Road, coloureds were driven further out onto the Cape Flats. Bokmakirie Township had to be placed 'beyond the Cape Flats railway line adjoining the Hazendal Estate'. Others followed in the same direction – Bridgetown, Silvertown, Gleemoor and Alicedale (the last to be an elite suburb). Yet the council successfully helped to oppose a provincial ordinance of 1938 that would have enforced segregation in the city, labelling it an 'attempt to further encroach upon the liberties of the Non-Europeans in the Province'. The left was most vociferous, but opponents also included local members of the ruling United Party.[20]

The development of Cape Flats housing schemes thus went hand in hand with residential segregation. English-speaking whites were ambivalent about such a policy. On the one hand they were opposed to the 'thorough-going' plans of the Nationalists for segregation, 'whose effect would be to deprive them [coloured people] still more of opportunities for advancement and so clamp more firmly on their already aching shoulders the burdens described by the [Wilcocks] coloured commission'.[21] On the other hand, as the MP Harry Lawrence explained to his constituents in Woodstock, the present position could be pegged. The spread of mixed areas would be prevented.

> The method by which this will be done will be the natural and just method of encouraging the coloured people to live in areas where they will be assured, firstly, of all the amenities of decent and healthy life, and secondly, of a much fuller opportunity for employment and economic development than they have at present ... it will be the policy of the Government, in these areas, to give that encouragement and opportunity to coloured ambition and competence which the Coloured Commission recommended in its report.[22]

'The method by which this [the prevention of mixed areas] will be done will be the natural and just method of encouraging the coloured people to live in areas where they will be assured, firstly, of all the amenities of decent and healthy life, and secondly, of a much fuller opportunity for employment and economic development than they have at present.'

Harry Lawrence, 1939

It was the National Party's Group Areas Act that ended this age of ambivalence. Nationalist victory in 1948 was crucial in facilitating the highly planned city that emerged in the post-war era.

But so was the effect of changes in forms of transport – particularly the greater size of ships and the rapid increase in motor cars. The demands of modern shipping, and the need to enlarge the docks, led to the decision to reclaim the foreshore in 1937. The venture was a joint effort by the South African Railways and Harbours (SAR&H) administration and the city council. Those involved in the scheme saw it as an exciting opportunity:

E.E. Beaudoin and the Foreshore Reclamation

EE Beaudoin was given special leave from the French Army to take up his new appointment as Cape Town's planning adviser since his government considered this 'an honour and a compliment to France'. He was an 'Architecte en Chef du Gouvernement' and 'Ancien Pensionnaire de l'Académie de France à Rome'. Previous experience ranged from The Hague, Brussels and Cuba to Persia, Moscow, Montreal and Ottawa.[23] As a Parisian he incorporated sweeping vistas into his plans. For Beaudouin, Cape Town lay 'on one of the pivotal points of the world's [sea] routes' which gave it 'a very special value among the sentinel towns of the globe'. Its status as 'mother city' of South Africa should be symbolised by 'a monumental approach'. Wide boulevards would replace much of District Six and the Malay Quarter, and create a 'circle of beauty'.[24]

The Civic Centre, finally built in the late 1970s, was described by a critic as 'straddling the main arterial approach to the city like a giant cricket screen' (De Villiers, *A Tale of Three Cities*, p. 67). Conceived within the idea of the harbour remaining the Gateway to Africa, the design aimed at preserving the view of Table Mountain from the harbour. Unfortunately most Capetonians merely experienced its intimidating bulk from Hertzog Boulevard. The modernist architectural style was echoed in many other imposing edifices erected in Cape Town in the 1960s and 1970s. Several – like the 1976 Reserve Bank building in Burg Street – were built in a style that 'turns its back on the street', according to the architect and critic Jack Barnett. From the pedestrian's perspective they appeared to be windowless and inward-looking.

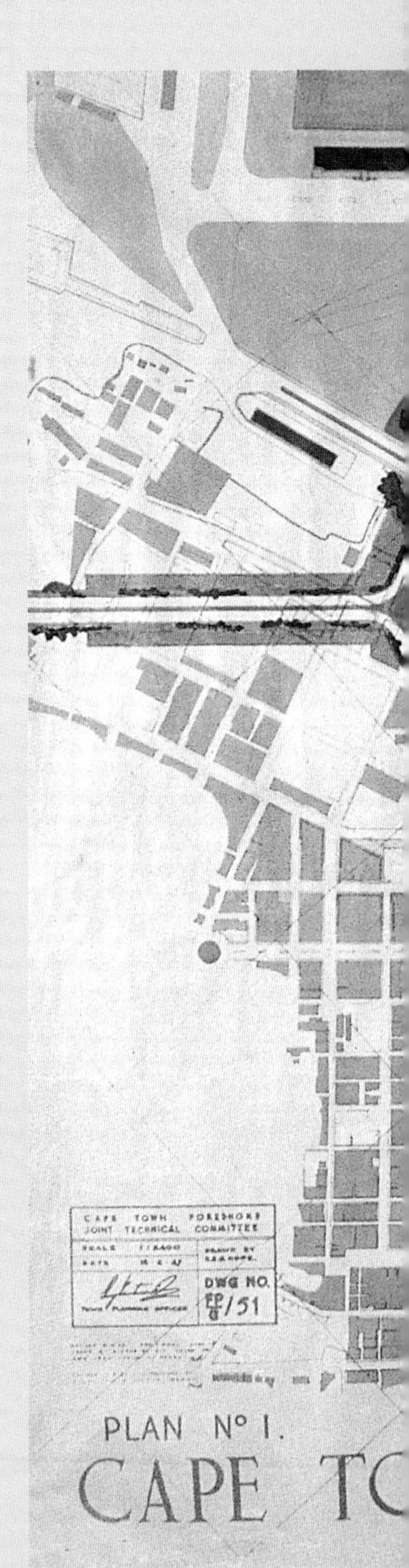

The foreshore plan, 1947. (CTCC)

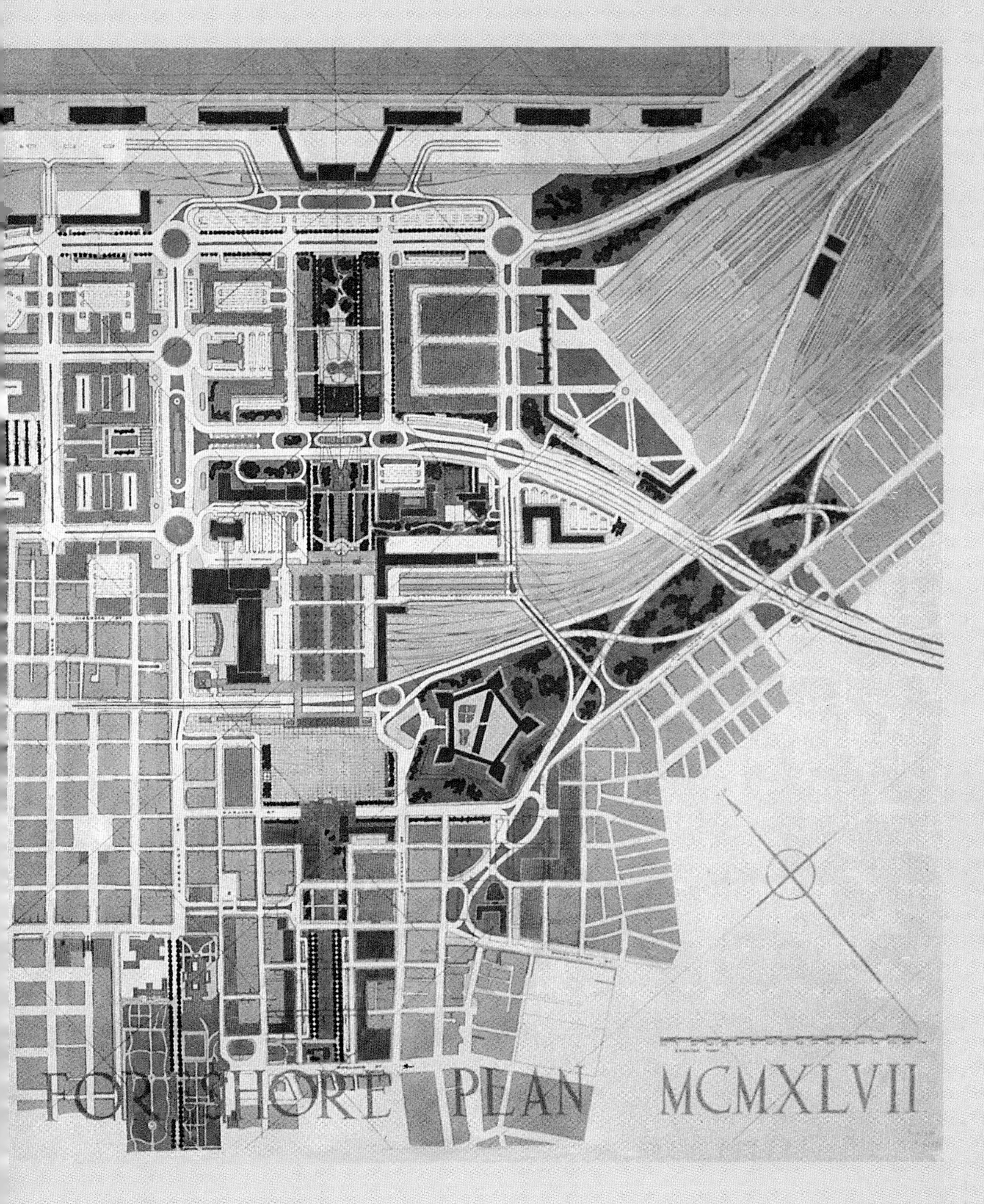
FORESHORE PLAN MCMXLVII

> Here, a vast area of virgin land has suddenly become available immediately contiguous to the seat of the city's greatest difficulties, and this land is held in single ownership by a progressively-minded Government Administration. Here is clearly the chance to recapture the lost ground (both physical and metaphorical) of the last century, and to re-create Cape Town for the needs of modern life whilst at the same time preserving and respecting its tradition of an earlier day.[25]

'Here is clearly the chance to recapture the lost ground (both physical and metaphorical) of the last century, and to re-create Cape Town for the needs of modern life whilst at the same time preserving and respecting its tradition of an earlier day.'

Foreshore Joint Technical Committee report, 1940

The SAR&H appointed a notable British planner, F. Longstreth Thompson, and Professor L.W. Thornton White of the University of Cape Town as advisers, while the municipality drew on the services of a French planner, E.E. Beaudouin.

In 1937 a Dutch company was given the contract for dredging and reclaiming two square kilometres of land. Work progressed steadily, but by 1943 it was clear that a serious difference of opinion existed between the railways and the municipality, centring on the location of the new station.[26] Eventually a government committee of inquiry decided that the station should remain where it was, decked over, 'thus meeting the City Council's requirements for unity of design, town-planning efficiency and adequate provision for traffic facilities and control'.[27]

After the war, implementing the foreshore plan fell to Solly Morris, the city engineer. Beaudouin's monumental approach – which had attempted to link a new 'civic centre' with the national, sacred sites of parliament and the Public Gardens – was abandoned, because the vista from the harbour was obstructed by the station roof. Morris approved the revised siting of the proposed civic centre between the station and the yet-to-be-constructed Grand Boulevard because its 'central position ... enables it to tower forth as a dominating feature, visible from every corner of the central city area. In this commanding position it would serve as a focus of attention and a constant reminder to citizens of their commercial aspirations.'[28]

A crucial consideration for Morris was the problem of traffic circulation. He wanted a ring road which would enable traffic to circulate round the central city. The implementation of the plan dragged on into the 1960s as report after report was submitted and rejected. The final result was an unhappy compromise. Broad boulevards cut the foreshore up into wind-blown stretches of asphalt and concrete, filled with car parks and roaring traffic, inaccessible to pedestrians. Wind tunnels created by skyscrapers were fierce enough to blow over buses. Little remained of the original version of the 'Gateway to Africa'.

From 1959, and with the opening of De Waal Drive and Table Bay Boulevard, dual carriageways and flyovers made their contribution to dehumanising the built landscape. In 1968 the Eastern Boulevard cut a swathe through the newly condemned District Six and ten years later the Western Bypass, complete with missing section, became a further visual and physical barrier between city and sea. As the town planner Peter de Tolly said of Cape Town's foreshore by the early 1980s: 'It offers monumentality and spaciousness, orderliness and predictability, mugging and wind; it can be characterised as ... a suburban office park trying to muscle in on a busy downtown.'[29]

Town planning continued to display a neat dovetailing between racial and spatial ideology. The foreshore scheme spawned the idea of more comprehensive urban replanning, including the destruction of District Six. As a council report of 1941 had stated: 'all the buildings, except those that are of sufficient value to preserve, will be demolished as part of the slum clearance scheme and the land acquired under the Slums Act, so that [a] ... desirable street system [can be] devised as though a new area were being dealt

'Gateway to Africa'

The growth of air travel determined that the 'Gateway to Africa' would soon lie inland. This was not in the minds of the 10,000 Capetonians who witnessed the last public celebration of harbour building in September 1945. Ferried from Van Riebeeck's statue in Adderley Street, they watched the opening of the largest dry dock in the southern hemisphere. A military band played both 'God save the King' and its Afrikaner nationalist successor, 'Die stem'. The ceremony symbolised 'the faith' of a 'young' white South African nation in 'its future', according to Minister De Wet, and was broadcast on the radio. Aircraft flew by overhead and the HMSAS *Good Hope* sailed into the dock to 'loud cheers raised ashore, accompanied by the wailing of sirens from all ships afloat'.[30]

But in the next few decades a mixture of changing technology and politics led to the dehumanisation of the harbour. Vast supertankers meant 'monumentality' in dock construction. They required the building of a huge tanker basin in 1963. Many more ships visited Cape Town when the Suez Canal was closed between 1967 and 1975, with ship building enjoying a minor boom. This led to yet more harbour expansion involving the reclamation of another 173 acres of land.

The new Ben Schoeman Basin was opened in 1977. But by this time government obsession with security ensured that the ceremony took place in front of only a handful of guests. In the same year the *Windsor Castle* left Table Bay for the last time as mailships became redundant. This ended a tradition of arrival and departure, and entertainment, that stretched back 120 years. As Laurens van der Post, a passenger on that final voyage, remembered: 'I have not yet made my peace with the event and doubt if I ever shall ... [Table Bay] ... is still full of shipping but not the kind which made it, for me, one of the most exciting harbours both in the world and history.'[31]

Because of apartheid, another diversion was also eroded – far fewer foreign warships visited Table Bay or Simon's Town. The harbour's commercial fortunes declined in the 1970s because of economic recession, the reopening of the Suez Canal and containerisation.[32]

The arrival and departure of mailships was a tradition that had lasted more than a century. (UCT Macmillan)

Black sailors from the aircraft carrier USS *Franklin D. Roosevelt* being interviewed in February 1967 after the United States Navy had refused them permission to go ashore because of South Africa's apartheid policies. (SAL Cape Times collection)

with.'[33] The plan was to be implemented by the Post-War Reconstruction Committee established in 1944. As Morris argued, it was most economical to put roads through 'low-value dwellings' which were not too costly to demolish.[34] In the tradition of Ndabeni, the same argument applied to the siting of factories or industrial zones – thus the Rex Trueform building replaced a demolished 'slum' in Salt River.

Residents of District Six became aware of the threat as soon as the municipality published its first redevelopment plan in 1940. At a crowded meeting in the Liberman Institute, Cissie Gool claimed that the council's scheme was the introduction of racial segregation by another means.[35] 'Alas, poor District Six,' wrote a columnist of the *Sun*; 'They are planning your downfall. They wish to make an end of the live, throbbing, pulsating ward that always adds to the joys and terrors of candidates for municipal and political honours and that, incidentally, sends (as a rule) such troublesome representatives up. They are making Darling Street a dagger pointed straight at your heart.'[36]

In the event it was the National Party that steered the blade home. After many years of inactivity, the declaration of the District as a 'White Group Area' in 1966 allowed all but religious buildings to be demolished – as 'slum clearance', not just in the name of apartheid. The National Party MP Joyce Waring was unrepentant:

> It is all very well for a well-fed well-housed Coloured leader or business man, who owns his own property, to hold forth on this 'tragedy of the Coloured people', but what of the mothers who see their sons become skollies, their daughters prostitutes, their baby children thieves and hooligans, filthy and lousy because the street is the only playground, the water doesn't run, the privy is overflowing and derelict and children see and hear their parents drinking and fornicating, doing the only things left in a slum for the poor to enjoy. Are they not entitled to a new start, another chance? Or is sentiment going to keep them in a slum?[37]

Under Group Areas legislation about 150,000 people – mostly coloureds and Africans – were forced to move from older, often unplanned residential areas to the Cape Flats.[38] There, many found themselves in new municipal townships designed on 'scientific lines', close to industrial zones.[39] This was no accident. In a symbiotic relationship, new industrial estates – like Retreat West Industrial Area – were usually placed next to locations or new townships, and vice versa, along the main rail and road routes to the north, east and south.

Epping Industria, all of 342 hectares, was the first major industrial estate of the post-war era. Its initial phase was planned in 1947, at the same time as Nyanga, which, like Langa, lay just to the south. The first coloured 'industrial township', Tiervlei (later Elsies River Estate and Industrial Area), was also placed conveniently close off Epping Avenue. For a while, Epping remained undeveloped and the outer ring road – Gunners Circle – was used as an unofficial motor-racing track. Factories were established after 1954, at more or less the pace at which the African and coloured populations were growing nearby – a rate hastened by apartheid legislation.

In the 1960s Caltex Oil and the Fedmis fertiliser factory were confined to the outskirts of the city at Milnerton – a municipality since 1955, with its own industrial zones – because their products were considered 'noxious'. The land was flat and relatively cheap, which aided the growth of Montague Gardens Industrial Area after 1966. Meanwhile the northern municipalities established the likes of Beaconvale and Parow Industria. Most economic sectors had been important since the inception of Cape

Great concrete flyovers isolated the city centre and drove through the heart of the inner-city residential areas. The age of social engineering produced a soulless city centre, virtually lifeless after office hours save for some restaurants and clubs catering for visiting sailors. Virtually the only people seen on the streets after dark were prostitutes. (UCT Macmillan)

Town's industrialisation in the nineteenth century, but the city's chemical industries only rose to prominence during the Second World War.[40]

Dividing new townships from each other, and from older areas – by industrial estates, green belts, railways or roads – was following the standard practice of American 'neighbourhood units'. In Cape Town, as in many American and colonial cities, townships were strictly racialised. But what was more insistent in South African planning was an awareness, particularly from the 1960s, that maintaining white supremacy might require force. As early as 1947 a prescient book called *When Smuts Goes* – written by the

Bonteheuwel, despite its careful planning, lacked the community warmth of District Six. Older residents mourned their lost homes while young people, often alienated by the apartheid system, formed part of the gang culture, which became increasingly violent in the apartheid years. (SAL Cape Times collection)

historian Arthur Keppel-Jones – described a black uprising engulfing two urban localities in the 1970s. One was Soweto; 'the other, stretching from District Six to Maitland and Langa, isolated central Cape Town'.[41] In the year that District Six was declared a 'White Group Area', an expert in race relations commented that 'The older non-white shanty towns with their maze of narrow, tortuous alleys were often located close to white residential or business districts; they are now systematically being razed as a major military hazard ... The new ghettos are typically situated several miles from the white towns, with a buffer zone in between.' Five years later another academic noted that African townships were designed and located so that they could be easily cordoned off, and resistance rapidly broken in their 'open streets'.[42] As we shall see, controlling African Capetonians became a particular obsession with the local architects of apartheid.

The Coming of Apartheid

'Apartheid is nothing new. Apartheid is the policy that has been applied in South Africa ever since Jan van Riebeeck landed there three hundred years ago.' These were the words of a National Party member in the House of Assembly in 1948.[43] Apartheid – racial separate development – had been a central part of the NP's victorious election platform.[44]

Part of what came to be seen as apartheid involved the extension, or more rigid enforcement, of existing policies and practices. Nonetheless, apartheid *was* something different. A major innovation was legislation requiring the registration of a person's 'race' – particularly significant in Cape Town with its large 'mixed race' population. Segregation could now be pursued with obsessive thoroughness. As a coloured Capetonian wryly observed, only roads and telephones were allowed to remain non-racial.[45] Apartheid also included the Nationalist fantasy of ridding the entire western Cape of Africans, who would become citizens of their own homelands, or bantustans.

In planning and implementing apartheid, the government was often helped by local authorities. In the case of greater Cape Town, this generally included the willing collaboration of the northern suburbs and Cape Divisional Council. In contrast the Cape Town municipality refused to help in drawing up Group Areas. But its racialised housing schemes on the Cape Flats became depositories for the victims of apartheid evic-

Employment in Leading Industries in Greater Cape Town, 1960

Industry	Employment
Clothing and textiles	31 000
Food and drink	26 000
Paper and printing	10 000
Chemical industries	7 600
Engineering	5 800

tions. Less innocently, the municipality remained actively involved in controlling the African presence in the city. In 1949 it even for a brief time adopted powers of arrest over 'illegal' Africans. In the 1950s its officials helped to screen such 'illegals' in settlements like Windermere and expel them to the eastern Cape.[46]

With a majority of only five seats in parliament, the Nationalist government began cautiously after 1948. As an 'experiment', limited segregation was introduced on Cape Town suburban railways in the belief that many whites wanted it – including those who supported the United Party. This was probably so, even if some opposed enforced segregation on principle. In 1947 the UP had ordered the construction of 800 'Europeans only' signs. Minister Sturrock had admitted at the time that this was 'in connection with the segregation of passengers on the suburban line', although not 'in keeping with any present policy'.[47]

'Frequently Natives and Coloured people deliberately seat themselves next to White women ... simply to show that they stand for absolute equality ... Respectable European women ... who not only have colour but odour next to them, have to resort to motor cars, and that has not only imposed a large additional burden on their shoulders but has contributed ... to the traffic congestion in Cape Town.'

D.F. Malan, 1948

In 1948, the new prime minister, D.F. Malan, justified train apartheid on the pretext that it would protect white women – an old ploy of segregationists – and solve the growing traffic problem: 'frequently Natives and Coloured people deliberately seat themselves next to White women ... simply to show that they stand for absolute equality ... Respectable European women ... who not only have colour but odour next to them, have to resort to motor cars, and that has not only imposed a large additional burden on their shoulders but has contributed ... to the traffic congestion in Cape Town.'[48] Apparently a 'noticeable' number of coloureds now travelled first class and many whites spilled over into second-class carriages during rush hour.[49] So the government began by reserving some first-class carriages for 'Europeans only' while the rest were left 'mixed'.

Post office apartheid followed in 1949. Initially 'Europeans' and 'Non-Europeans' had to queue separately before converging at the same window. But soon the system was 'perfected' with the establishment of separate counters.[50]

Early regulations and legislation generally observed these fault-lines. The main concern was clearly to protect whites, to keep the white race pure, rather than worrying too much at first about differentiating among blacks. This was made abundantly clear by the Prohibition of Mixed Marriages (1949) and Immorality (1950) Acts. They extended to coloureds and Indians the prohibition against sexual relations with whites that already applied to Africans.

Since Cape Town historically had the highest rate of miscegenation, these two laws probably hit its citizens the hardest, although there are no geographical statistics for the 20,000 prosecutions under the Immorality Act.[51] Numerous accounts – including John Carr's *An Act of Immorality* – testify to the humiliation, suffering and tragedy that was caused.[52] On one occasion the punishment meted out had Soviet overtones: a Cape Town ex-magistrate was ordered to undergo at least two years' psychiatric treatment for contravening the Immorality Act.[53]

The Population Registration Act of 1950 officially divided South Africans into 'White', 'Coloured', 'Asian' or 'Native' (African). All Capetonians over 16 had to carry identity cards specifying their race. People deemed difficult for the state to classify – who may have previously enjoyed a degree of individual and changeable choice – were now allotted a race, whether they liked it or not. 'Race inspectors' determined awkward cases.[54]

The 1951 census provided the initial basis for classification. In addition to asking people what race they belonged to, it required information on each individual's background and current circumstances. Once registered, people could object to their own classification or pay £10 and object to someone else's. A national Race Classification Appeal Board

THE MIXED MARRIAGES ACT

A particularly tragic case was the suicide of a 20-year-old coloured youth in 1974 because he could not legally marry his pregnant white girlfriend, Sonya Shepherd. He threw himself under a train at a suburban station, leaving his total wealth of R30 to pay for baby clothes. The money was used by the girl's father to pay for an abortion, only legal because the youth was coloured. Sonya then tried to commit suicide by cutting her wrists. Her boyfriend's name was not revealed by the newspaper because his family was trying-for-white. He was cremated to avoid being buried in a coloured graveyard.[55]

Although they were theoretically illegal, the state was less concerned about 'mixed' marriages between Africans and coloureds, as in the family illustrated here. Nevertheless, where such families lived or where the children could be educated would be severely affected by marriage of this kind. (Mayibuye Centre)

was established in 1959; provincial boards followed. In 1967, descent was made the critical factor in classification. If one could not prove one's antecedents, race 'tests' were carried out which included examining hair, nails, eyelids and babies' bottoms.[56]

Not surprisingly, a particularly large number of controversial cases occurred in Cape Town. They included a man initially classified 'Cape Coloured', reclassified as 'Indian' by race inspectors and eventually deemed 'Cape Malay' by the Appeal Board. In another incident the 'White' 47-year-old daughter of a National Party organiser was ironically reclassified 'Coloured'.[57] Pragmatic reasons often explained which race people tried to belong to: who they wished to marry, or where they wanted to live and have their children educated.

Race legislation involved contradiction. The Group Areas Act (1950) announced that there were three main racial groups – 'White', 'Native' and 'Coloured' – rather than the four of the Population Registration Act. But under a subsequent Group Areas proclamation, Chinese and Indians were declared to be subgroups of 'Coloureds'. So were some 'Malays', but only if they lived in specific magisterial districts like Cape Town, Simon's Town, Bellville or Wynberg.

The State defines a Capetonian's race

Some of the definitions of racial groups in the Population Registration Act were positively Orwellian and showed the state's continuing problems with making such classifications. A 'White' was defined as 'a person who in appearance obviously is, or who is generally accepted as a White person, but does not include a person who, although in appearance obviously a White person, is generally accepted as a Coloured person ... [provided that] ... a person who in appearance is a White person shall for the purposes of the Act be presumed to be a White person until the contrary is proved.' A 'Native' was simply 'any member of an aboriginal race or tribe of Africa' while a 'Coloured' was a person who was neither a White nor a Native. Proclamation 123 of 1967 expanded this negative definition: 'The Cape Coloured Group shall consist of persons who in fact are, ... except in the case of persons who ... are members of a race or class or tribe referred to [elsewhere] ... generally accepted as members of the race or class known as the Cape Coloured.'[60]

The Group Areas Act aimed at removing what remained of racially mixed suburbs, like Salt River or Lincoln Estate in Athlone, and destroying already semi-segregated pockets like the Valley in Mowbray or Tramway Road in Sea Point. The fact that the Act was only implemented over a long period, and in different places at different times, minimised the risk of serious disruption or resistance.

The first Group Areas were demarcated in 1957. Before that the government tried to maintain the status quo while building up its knowledge of the city's racial geography. From 1951 a complicated permit system regulated property transfers and changes of occupancy from members of one race to another. Applicants had to provide detailed information on the people, property and area involved. The absence of a permit could prevent owners from occupying their own property. The system was administered by a Land Tenure Advisory Board (LTAB – later renamed the Group Areas Board, or GAB), which held public monthly meetings. Those who attempted to ignore the system were subject to discovery by Group Areas inspectors, who became known as the G-men, often acting on the complaints of local residents.[58]

Unlike many other municipalities, the Cape Town City Council refused to help its local LTAB by providing racial zoning plans. But with the help of information gleaned from its administration of the permit system, the LTAB gradually established its own feel for how Cape Town might be demarcated. It was helped by the solicited and unsolicited advice of a variety of civil organisations and individuals. A Chinese applicant at one hearing, wishing to buy property in Grassy Park, was asked where 'the Chinese' wanted their Group Area; Indian fruit-sellers claimed that the city council had, since the 1920s, leased stalls on the Parade only to people of their race.[59]

The permit system may have been mild compared with the subsequent mass removals when Group Area boundaries were finally announced. But it still managed to cause considerable individual hardship, frustration and the stifling of small business enterprises. Michael Kalembe, classified as 'Native', was not allowed to occupy a shop in Retreat from which to operate his dairy business: the LTAB did not consider this to be an African area. Yet Kalembe was the sole supplier for hundreds of African squatters there, and had been told by health inspectors that he could no longer keep milk in his house. None of the larger dairies bothered to service the shanties because of the unmade roads.

In March 1953 the LTAB announced its first proposals. A meeting was held to hear objections. In many suburbs not yet designated, the refusal or acceptance of permit applications was revealing the LTAB's future intentions. Capetonians were being persuaded to move 'voluntarily' if they belonged to the wrong race, thereby easing the government's task ahead of further demarcations and reducing the need for naked force.

Divided Defiance

The government was soon able to discover that resistance to its gradual application of apartheid was extensive, but very divided. This was hardly surprising given that it was experienced in widely different ways by people of various racial and economic status.

Opposition politics in Cape Town became famous for its pervasive fractiousness. The ferocity of recriminations grew in pace with the dizzying number of political acronyms. Thus the NEUM, which now controlled the ever-diminishing APO, denounced members of the larger, moderate Coloured People's National Union (CPNU) as 'quislings', 'leeches', 'bootlickers, doormats, hat-in-hand crumb-picking serfs', because some served on the government-nominated Coloured Advisory Council (CAC).[61]

The NEUM also criticised the Communist Party (CPSA) and ANC for participating in government structures: they were accused of conducting 'sectional' (racially exclusive) campaigns and denounced as 'opportunist' and 'adventurist' for advocating mass action. In return the NEUM's and Anti-CAD's 'principled' stance was rejected as inactivity that protected its bourgeois adherents. As the Simonses were to write: 'the main achievement of the Anti-CAD was to immobilize a generation of Coloured intellectuals, immunize them against Marxist theory, and isolate them from the rest of the liberation movement.'[62] Both sides were guilty of disrupting the other's meetings.

Yet the early signs had been promising. The CPSA joined with the NEUM, APO and Teachers' League of South Africa (TLSA) in the Train Apartheid Resistance Committee (TARC) in 1948. TARC helped organise a mass meeting on the Parade on 5 September and backed early attempts to defy the new regulations.[63] But ideological and personal tensions helped limit its effectiveness.

The National Party quickly took steps to make effective opposition even harder. An early salvo was the Suppression of Communism Act (1950). This was enacted despite the declaration by the ANC and CPSA that 1 May 1950 would be marked by a worker stay-away. The fact that communists like Ray Alexander and Pauline Podbrey had been active in organising local unions – and had kept the tradition of May Day commemoration alive – played a part in ensuring that 'Freedom Day' was well supported in Cape Town. The Communist Party MP Sam Kahn addressed a crowd of 6000 on the Parade, most of whom subsequently marched through the streets shouting 'Down with apartheid, we want freedom'.[64] Such demonstrations only strengthened government resolve. The Suppression of Communism Act made not only the CPSA but any kindred party illegal, and allowed for office-bearers or supporters to be 'named' and their activities and movements restricted. Furthering 'any political, industrial, social or economic change ... by the promotion of disturbances or disorder' was enough to brand one a communist under the Act; so was 'provoking hostility' between whites and blacks.[66]

The following year, the government felt able to introduce the Separate Representation of Voters Bill. This aimed at removing coloureds from the common voters' roll, in part because most supported the United Party. Members of the now banned CPSA

The Unity Movement

The fact was that neither the Non-European Unity Movement nor the Coloured People's National Union was very effective in organising mass resistance. In the case of the CPNU, members were concerned with remaining respectable and worried about losing hard-won privileges. The members of the NEUM, largely middle class, were usually better at talking about workers than mobilising them. Their principle was 'non-collaboration', and their preferred tactic the boycott. Although this mustered considerable support for the Anti-Coloured Affairs Department (Anti-CAD) movement and the stay-away during the Van Riebeeck tercentenary, NEUM boycott campaigns 'came to mean no more than a series of indifferently attended public meetings' by the late 1950s. Nonetheless the movement's legacy involved a new sense of 'power and of pride' among many coloured intellectuals, the questioning of divisions amongst blacks and an enduring spirit of non-collaboration.[65]

Resistance to Train Apartheid

Only a few hundred volunteers came forward to defy the introduction of train apartheid on suburban lines. TARC initially did better with a challenge to the edict's legality, but the National Party merely responded with new railway regulations. Eventually TARC fell apart amid predictable recriminations from both sides, and the NEUM gradually retreated into political isolation and impotence.[67]

On 5 September 1948, after a protest rally, coloured commuters tried to force their way onto 'Europeans only' coaches. (*Cape Times*, 6 September 1948)

took the lead in forming the Franchise Action Committee (FRAC), an alliance of many civil organisations.

FRAC was led by Sam Kahn, Reggie September, Cissie Gool and Johnny Gomas. Initially it even received the backing of the CPNU, if not the NEUM. The campaign against the disfranchisement of coloureds also gained substantial indirect support from white organisations like the Civil Rights League and Torch Commando. For the first time in South African history a broad multi-racial front appeared to be emerging to oppose legislated racial discrimination.

In March 1951 FRAC organised a rally on the Parade of over 10,000 people who pledged to defend the vote with 'determination and courage'. Meanwhile the Civil Rights League was collecting 100,001 signatures against the Bill. FRAC then upped the stakes by calling for a work stayaway on 7 May. Despite active opposition from the NEUM, this gained considerable support from both coloured and African workers. In the same month, 50,000 ex-servicemen of the Torch Commando marched in protest to parliament, some getting involved in fights with the police in the process.[68]

The autumn of 1951 witnessed a high-water mark of divided but multi-racial and multi-organisational opposition to the National Party, not seen again until the 1980s. The CPNU soon worried about FRAC's strategy of mass mobilisation, while the Torch Commando fell apart amid internal disputes following National Party victory in the elections of 1953. Many United Party whites had been prepared to oppose coloured dis-

Sam Kahn (middle) and Cissie Gool (right) leading a FRAC protest rally. (SAL Cape Times collection)

franchisement to prevent the National Party from entrenching its power. Fewer were willing to do much about the introduction or extension of other segregatory practices, even if they had been perfectly content with the status quo before 1948.

Not many whites outside the CPSA would countenance any acts of civil disobedience in the cause, preferring to act within the law and not risk punishment. In this respect they were not dissimilar to members of the CPNU. Both were influenced by Christian, liberal orthodoxy and the need for constitutional action.[69] Nonetheless, the 1950s saw the emergence of an articulate and principled white liberalism in institutional form, however cautious and numerically small, whose words and actions were favourably publicised in the *Cape Times* and *Cape Argus*. Organisations (often with overlapping membership) like the Civil Rights League, the South African Institute of Race Relations, the Black Sash and the multi-racial Liberal Party played a significant role as the conscience of non-communist white Capetonians, something that the United Party – ever compromising on apartheid – conspicuously failed to be. They also provided practical support for the disfranchised. As church leaders gradually accepted both the theory and practice of non-racialism, their ideological contribution became increasingly important over time.

Geoffrey Clayton, the Anglican archbishop of Cape Town, was a particularly prominent and articulate critic of early apartheid laws. Fearing that violence might result, he nonetheless promoted the view that civil disobedience was justifiable if one believed a law to be contrary to the will of God. (SAL Cape Times collection)

By 1953 FRAC had fallen apart. On 26 June 1952, it had helped launch the ANC's national Defiance Campaign against discriminatory laws on the Grand Parade. Partly because of the opposition of the CPNU and NEUM, the campaign only attracted a couple of hundred volunteers in the western Cape. One was Hendrik Bestenbier, arrested for demanding service in the white section of the Elsies River post office; George Lusu met a similar fate for refusing to leave a 'European' waiting-room on Cape Town station.

The Torch Commando

During demobilisation, the Springbok Legion emerged as a radical organisation representing service personnel. Some members helped establish the War Veterans Action Committee in 1951 – with high-profile 'non-political' leaders like the Battle of Britain hero 'Sailor' Malan – to protest against the Separate Registration of Voters Bill. The subsequent 'Torch Commando' consisted of veterans who opposed this tampering with the constitution. Some did so out of principle, others in protest at the diminishing political significance of English-speaking whites – aware that the clause protecting the status of English as an official language could be similarly removed. Their intention was to force the National Party into another election before it could entrench its power. One of the most dramatic demonstrations followed the arrival in Cape Town on 28 May 1951 of columns of jeeps and cars from all over the Union, the 'Steel Commando'. An orderly demonstration on the Parade and outside parliament, which included coloured ex-servicemen, led to rioting and a clash with the police in which 160 people were hurt. But the Torch Commando had no coherent strategy. It was effectively hamstrung after joining the United Democratic Front under UP leadership to fight the 1953 election.[70]

(SAL Cape Times collection)

As the government cracked down on defiers country-wide, the campaign became more violent, particularly in and around some African townships.[71] In Langa, in December, the Native Affairs Department offices and two churches were set on fire.[72]

Both the NEUM, in perhaps its finest hour, and the ANC were busy organising meetings all over Cape Town in the second half of 1951 against this 'orgy of herrenvolkism'. As A.C. Jordan said at a gathering in Langa, 'Can we celebrate our enslavement?' A wide range of organisations decided to boycott the tercentenary of Jan van Riebeeck's settlement at the Cape, from the Wetton Ratepayers' Association to the Langa Rugby Club and half the 'Malay' choirs. The Parade yet again became a focal point of protest, with about 6000 people congregating there on 30 March to listen to Unity Movement speakers. And when the ANC launched the Defiance Campaign at the same spot on 6 April, Cissie Gool remarked that in the people's pageant 'one float was missing, and that was the Float of Truth'. The *Torch* (pro-NEUM) and *Guardian* (pro-ANC) newspapers duly published their versions of the truth, including Eddie Roux's '1652 and all that', which

'One float was missing, and that was the Float of Truth.'
Cissie Gool, on the Van Riebeeck tercentenary procession

The Black Sash

The Black Sash began in the Transvaal in 1955 as the Women's Defence of the Constitution League. White, mainly English-speaking women – 'those ladies with their hats and gloves' – camped in the grounds of the Union Buildings or stalked cabinet ministers, wearing a black sash with the legend 'Eerbiedig ons grondwet' to symbolise their mourning for the constitution. At its peak in 1956 the Sash had a membership of 10,000 nationwide, but this shrank to less than 2000 by the early 1960s. Yet in the process, and driven by its Cape Town branches, the organisation that began with 'a scent of snobbery' turned into an important pressure group for human rights, sparing it the fate of the Torch Commando. Links were forged with ANC-aligned organisations through the Cape Association for the Abolition of Passes for South African Women (CATAPAW). The Sash monitored pass cases in the Langa court on a daily basis from 1958, after discovering 46 African women had been imprisoned with their babies. Particularly horrified by the government's disregard for family life, the organisation raised bail money and arranged legal defence for the accused. An advice office was opened in Athlone in 1959. By this time the leadership of the Sash was located in Cape Town.[73]

In this stand in Parliament Street the Black Sash was protesting against the Extension of Universities Act of 1957, which removed the freedom of universities to admit students on merit alone. (SAL PHA)

The 1952 Van Riebeeck Tercentenary

A protest that coincided with the launch of the Defiance Campaign – and that may have gained strength from it – was the NEUM- and ANC-inspired black boycott of the Jan van Riebeeck tercentenary celebrations. These lauded the origins of a white South African nation, and were calculated to cut across divides in white society. To the same end, Van Riebeeck had been accorded the status of founding figure in school histories since the nineteenth century. Rhodes had presented a statue of Van Riebeeck to the city, and Van Riebeeck had featured in the pageants both of 1910 and of 1934. Consequently Cape Town was lauded as the 'mother city' in countless Cape Peninsula publicity brochures.

The tercentenary planning committee included provincial administrators, the principal of UCT (T.B. Davie) and members of the Federasie van Afrikaanse Kultuurverenigings. A huge stadium and exhibition halls were built on the reclaimed foreshore, Beaudouin's 'Gateway to Africa', at a cost of £450,000. Here white achievement in the fields of agriculture, mining and industry were contrasted with displays of 'Bushmen' shown fashioning bows and arrows or 'Bantu' building huts and polishing pots. A pageant displaying 'Malay' and 'Griqua' history included the coming of Sheikh Yusuf, the Battle of Blouberg and 'Malay' fishermen. On 3 April, a procession through the streets of Cape Town told the story of how 'Africa dark and unknown' (the title of the first float) had benefited from Western civilisation. This 'people's pageant' featured 70 floats, 400 horses and 2000 humans, and celebrated 300 years of white history, giving attention to both Boer and British contributions. Five floats were devoted to Jan van Riebeeck alone, and he was the centre of another pageant two days later. Starting at Granger Bay, this featured Van Riebeeck (the actor André Huguenet) stepping ashore, planting a flag, giving presents to 'Strandlopers', and scrolls (representing religion, law, freedom and commerce) to modern South African dignitaries. He then went by carriage to the Castle, where he and his wife waved to the crowds.[74]

The 'Malay' element of the pageant, the meeting of Simon van der Stel and Sheikh Yusuf in 1694, was played out in an empty stadium. (UCT Macmillan)

Left: At a fancy-dress garden party, the minister of posts and telegraphs and his wife greeted guests. (UCT Macmillan)

The first float, presented by the Drama Department of the University of Cape Town, represented 'Darkest Africa', symbolising the 'primitive shackling of the human soul'. (*Van Riebeeck Festival in Pictures*, Cape Town, 1952, p. 5) denounced the arrival of Van Riebeeck as leading to land-grabbing and slavery. Archbishop Clayton's chosen text for his tercentenary sermon was 'Forgive us our trespasses as we forgive those who trespass against us'.[75]

The government brought an end to the Defiance Campaign with the vigour of its response. In November 1952 the *Government Gazette* announced regulations 'to control meetings and curb excitement', with penalties of up to £300 or three years' imprisonment. Township violence was partly a response to the beatings and arrests that accompanied the enforcement of this measure. Early in 1953 the Criminal Law Amendment Act made it an offence to break a law 'by way of protest, or in support of any campaign against the law'. Thus if one unwittingly sat on the 'wrong' park bench one's fine would not be very high; but if it was considered an act of protest one might have to pay £500, be imprisoned for five years or receive ten strokes of a cane.

Soon the Public Safety Act was added to the armoury. This enabled the government to proclaim a State of Emergency, overriding any remaining legal restraints on its actions against protesting citizens.[76] In separate legislation, it was also made illegal for African workers to strike. Although they could still form trade unions, employers were not obliged to negotiate with them.

Having crushed the Defiance Campaign, the National Party secured a larger majority in the election of 1953. Both these events enabled it to proceed more confidently in implementing thorough segregation. Equally they helped to deter the kind of mass, multi-racial opposition that had briefly arisen in 1951. This did not mean that cross-racial alliances were entirely ended. But few issues before the 1980s could again inspire equal enthusiasm among all racialised groups. Influx control remained a burning issue for Africans, but not for coloureds, Asians or whites. On the other hand the Group Areas Act was generally more keenly felt by coloureds and Asians than by Africans. It predictably affected very few whites.

This helps to explain why an ANC-led Congress Alliance came into existence in the course of the 1950s. It consisted of separate organisations for each of the four 'national groups', concerned with mobilising people around issues that most directly affected them. Thus in the second half of the decade, the ANC in Cape Town concentrated on

Political education in Blouvlei

Amy Thornton remembers: 'I went out there over a few years, every Monday night ... Blouvlei was a squatter camp, one long sand dune, up and down ... we would rendezvous at a different place ... [and] meet in a different *pondokkie*. We'd sit around on handmade benches, with a candle in the middle ... it was mainly the men who participated; the wives would be nursing babies on the outskirts of the ring of light ... as the weekend for the Congress of the People came closer, people began electing delegates. I was elected by the Congress of Democrats. When I told the study class ... they presented me with four shillings, which they had collected among themselves. That was a lot of money in those days. You can imagine how honoured and moved I felt.'[77]

anti-pass campaigns. In contrast, its ally SACPO, the South African Coloured People's Organisation – led in the city by the former FRAC members Reggie September and Johnny Gomas – campaigned on issues like Group Areas. Both were hampered by internal disputes over strategy, while the white and Indian congresses attracted only a handful of supporters. The alliance's one cross-racial component was the South African Congress of Trade Unions (SACTU), formed in 1955 by unions that refused to exclude Africans so as to meet the requirements of industrial conciliation legislation. However, SACTU's national membership was only about 20,000, with the Food and Canning Workers' Union its most important affiliate in Cape Town. SACTU enjoyed some success in raising wages, and helped to draw workers into the political struggle through stayaways and a campaign for a £1 a day minimum wage. But political involvement ensured that SACTU would become a victim of state suppression in the 1960s.[78] Meanwhile, the ANC, SACPO, the South African Indian Congress and the small (white) Congress of Democrats had all co-operated in arranging the Congress of the People and Freedom Charter in 1955. In the lead-up to these events, a torchlight procession was held on Green Point Common and a conference of western Cape delegates met in the City Hall.

Separate Amenities and Separate Suburbs

Fresh from its recent victories, the National Party felt able to increase the pace and scope of apartheid implementation. It wasted little time in passing the Separate Amenities Act in 1953, which contained the important provision that a separate facility no longer had to be 'substantially equal'. This undercut possible legal objections.[79]

The way was paved for statutory segregation and inequality in every facility imaginable: from maternity wards to graveyards, shop entrances to restaurants, taxis to ambulances, beaches to parks, and park benches to pedestrian subways and bridges. The new subway at Salt River, for instance, enabled 'White workers and non-White workers to arrive at the [Salt River railway] workshops and leave them through different subways. But having arrived through their different subways, White and non-White workers will continue to work side by side inside the workshop.'[80] And at a drive-in cinema in Wetton in the early 1960s, 'The parking space, which holds about 1000 cars, is being divided into two. One half will be for Whites and the other half for Coloureds, but they will see the same film.'[81]

In 1956 segregation was introduced on buses, despite a SACPO-organised boycott. Regulations became Byzantine in complexity: 'in the new system [of 1959] the front four rows of seats and the longitudinal seats over the off-side wheel in the lower saloon are reserved for Europeans, and the long seats over the near-side wheel for non-Europeans ... the system changes slightly on Sundays when non-Europeans have both of the long seats over the rear wheels, the Europeans having the first four rows.'[82]

At much the same time the Group Areas Act was amended to prevent anyone attending entertainment or partaking of refreshment 'in any land or premises not zoned for his own group' – an attempt to force apartheid on private social gatherings, clubs and multi-racial organisations. Only a few, like the Liberal Party and National Union of South African Students (NUSAS), decided to carry on regardless, risking heavy fines or imprisonment. The government went as far as introducing a clause into the Native Laws Amendment Act of 1957 that made it illegal for an African to attend church services in white areas. Yet with even the Dutch Reformed Church demurring, it was not enforced and progressive churches became rare public places where cross-racial socialising still

WHITES
BLANK
WHITE

Segregation in Sport

There had been little participation across the colour line in sport since the 1890s – albeit white tennis stars would go to the coloured tennis courts at Trafalgar Park in the 1930s to 'have a knock'.[83] After the war, white boxers also hired their coloured counterparts as sparring partners. Apartheid legislation all but ended the possibility of even limited contacts. The Separate Amenities Act forced stadiums and other places of entertainment to provide segregated facilities. In 1965 blacks were banned from 'white' recreation altogether, unless a special permit had been granted and separate entry gates and toilets installed. The government could even ban multi-racial sports on private property. Such arrangements, together with professionalism, may explain why white attendance at Hartleyvale – the home of the National Football League's Cape Town City – reached its zenith in the late 1960s and early 1970s.[84]

The government's refusal to allow a coloured Cape Town cricketing exile, Basil D'Oliveira, to be included in a visiting England team in 1968 speeded the country's international sporting isolation. (SAL Cape Times collection)

occurred. Ironically, about the only others were city-centre clubs like the Catacombs and Navigators' Den, notorious for prostitution and drug-dealing. Although frequently raided by the police, these were allowed to remain open because they catered primarily for foreign sailors.[85]

However, through additional legislation, apartheid was imposed on technical colleges in 1955 and universities in 1959. The University College of the Western Cape, for coloureds, was built in what became Bellville South. The University of Cape Town was allowed to admit black students only if a course was not available at 'bush' campuses.

The government moved ever closer to thorough residential segregation with the Group Areas Development Act of 1955. This set out guidelines for disposing of people's property if they did not belong to the correct race. 'Affected property' had to be offered to the Group Areas Development Board for purchase before being considered for private sale. The Act allowed for the payment of a 'depreciation contribution' if properties were sold below a predetermined value, but in practice many owners were to lose a great deal.

Following the initial Group Area proposals of March 1953, more were published before the first official demarcations in 1957. In August 1954 plans were advertised for Woodstock, Maitland, Milnerton and Brooklyn within the Cape Town municipality. So were schemes for Goodwood, Parow and Bellville. There the LTAB had the willing assistance of the National Party-supporting councils of all three municipalities. They proposed that all blacks (except domestic servants) should be removed to the south of the

Opposite: 'Whites' and 'Non-whites' were also separated on overpasses. (Mayibuye Centre)

Beach apartheid

In 1969 Shirley Parks wrote guides to Cape Town specifically for coloured and African visitors. These revealed the paucity of their amenities compared with those for whites in terms of accommodation, entertainment and recreation. For instance Africans were allowed only on Mnandi beach. Coloureds may have had more set aside for them, but many were decidedly untempting. Thus Sunset Beach, Sea Point, was 'largely covered at high tide'. Melkbos had 'no shelter, water, or a bus service, and there may be a dangerous undertow'. And the nearest 'concentration of Coloured people' lived twenty miles away. The coastline to the west of Hout Bay was also for coloureds, but had no sandy beaches, the land fell steeply to the sea and was lined with slippery boulders. Parks concluded, 'No bathing or even paddling is possible.'[86]

Boulders Beach, Simon's Town, where Richard Rive and his friends had frolicked, was now closed to them. (Mayibuye Centre)

railway line (to the interior), leaving the area to the north for whites only.

Five months later, suggestions for the southern suburbs were publicised amid a storm of protest. As with the northern suburbs, it was again envisaged that the railway would be an important divide between black and white. The plan was to move all blacks save domestic servants to the east of the Simon's Town line. This would effectively clear an area for the sole use of whites that had previously been inhabited by almost exactly the same number of blacks, mostly coloureds – albeit largely in those pockets we have described. In addition, the intention was to remove yet more blacks from the area between the suburban and Cape Flats lines.

All the proposals were discussed at public hearings held in 1956. Many Capetonians boycotted proceedings. The CPNU preferred negotiating for the best deal possible for coloureds. In contrast SACPO had initiated a Group Areas Co-ordinating Committee which opposed the very concept of legislated segregation, and saw to it that individuals sent 2500 letters stating this view to the LTAB. At the hearings, counsels for both the Co-ordinating Committee and the Wynberg Dutch Reformed Mission Church expressed the same opinion, but also argued over the details of implementation.

They won a few concessions. These included the zoning of lower Wynberg for coloureds in an anomalous arrangement that allowed 'Malays' to stay there as well, despite the existence of separate 'Malay Group Areas'. But in the main the LTAB proposals were implemented as planned. Supposedly less 'contentious' areas – those involving fewer 'disqualified people' or those in the northern municipalities – were the first to be declared. The government was still faced with the problem that people could only be forced to move if alternative accommodation was available. By 1962 the Group Areas

Development Board had built but 250 houses on the Cape Flats. Crucially, however, the city council began to make its own housing available by the end of 1959, seduced by a sense of inevitability as well as by offers of government money towards its own 'slum-clearance' schemes.[87]

'Contentious' areas – like District Six or the 'pockets' in the southern suburbs – were generally decided only after the declaration of a national State of Emergency in 1960. Most were demarcated in favour of whites. Strategic and aesthetic considerations played a decisive role, with white areas eventually embracing virtually the entire inner city and Peninsula mountain chain. But there were a few exceptions. Schotsche Kloof had already been declared a 'Malay Group Area' in 1957, probably thanks to the intervention of I.D. du Plessis. Respectable Walmer Estate was eventually demarcated for coloureds and 'Malays' in 1975, possibly to counter international outrage over what was happening to District Six.[88]

By 1976 the only remaining 'controlled', or undecided, area consisted of part of Woodstock. This locality challenged the government's racial certainties throughout apartheid's heyday. The colour line was more frequently indistinct among its largely working-class population than anywhere else in pre-apartheid Cape Town. In the late 1960s, the principal of the local white school, Queen's Park High, had accepted fair-skinned 'pass whites' without asking for identity documents. Staff members believed at the time that about 80 per cent of all pupils were probably 'coloured'. The school became a convenient depository for borderline classification cases from other parts of the Peninsula, although the same principal fought to exclude even children officially classified as white when they had particularly dark skins. Not surprisingly, both school and

The Municipal Franchise

In 1958 the National Party began an assault on non-racial municipal franchises in the Cape, finally abolishing Cape Town's in 1970. The idea was for coloureds to vote separately for their own 'management boards' – which would initially advise white municipalities – in preparation for theoretical self-government. But as Nationalists pointed out, Cape Town's non-racial franchise in the 1950s was already far from democratic. Apart from location residents, people living in property worth less than £200 and municipal tenants paying weekly rentals were excluded. As in Goodwood, ward boundaries also limited the likely numbers of coloured councillors. Yet Congress-aligned organisations as well as the Black Sash and Civil Rights League united against what they called another 'injustice imposed by the Transvaal'. So did most Cape Town councillors, with 31 out of 45 rejecting the scheme in 1958 – the others were absent. Cissie Gool remarked that she could hardly recall 'such unanimity inside and outside the council'. But in the early 1960s the Nationalist administrator of the Cape was given sweeping powers to establish management boards, even without the consent of existing councils, with purely advisory powers. Existing voting rights were not yet removed. By the end of 1964 there were management committees for Goodwood, Parow and Bellville. Cape Town voted narrowly to co-operate – with those in favour arguing that they would make the system less onerous – and helped to establish committees for Duinefontein, Kensington and Wittebome in 1965. These had achieved little by 1970, when Prime Minister Vorster announced that the municipal elections of 1972 would be held on whites-only parliamentary rolls.[89]

There were 55 coloured and 3 Indian families living in Tramway and Ilford roads, Sea Point – which was now declared a 'White Group Area' in 1957. Of 250 people, almost a third had lived there for more than 30 years. Mohammed Allie Parker, an Indian property owner, had been there for 60. Most of the residents worked in the area as domestic servants, washerwomen, waiters, gardeners or artisans. All were given two years' notice. One, Frederick Mitchell, responded by committing suicide. Most joined the Tramway Residents Association (TRA), which negotiated for more time to allow residents to find accommodation as close as possible to where they worked, and to be able to stay together as a community. They were eventually given until November 1961 to vacate. This was probably more to do with lack of alternative housing than compassion. Some left on their own initiative before 1961, to places like Walmer Estate, Salt River or Woodstock. Others went to government accommodation at Duinefontein or the city council's housing development at Bonteheuwel. The last family left a South African flag flying at half-mast from a lamppost.[90]

Right: Members of the Tramway Road families Lambert, Ramsammy, Phillips, Mitchell and Barros and their friends outside No. 7. (District Six Museum)

Above: Leonard Lopes, a former resident, revisits the area as chairman of the Tramway Road Land Interim Committee in 1997. (Argus library)

GROUP AREAS DECLARED BY 1977, WITH SELECTED DECLARATION DATES

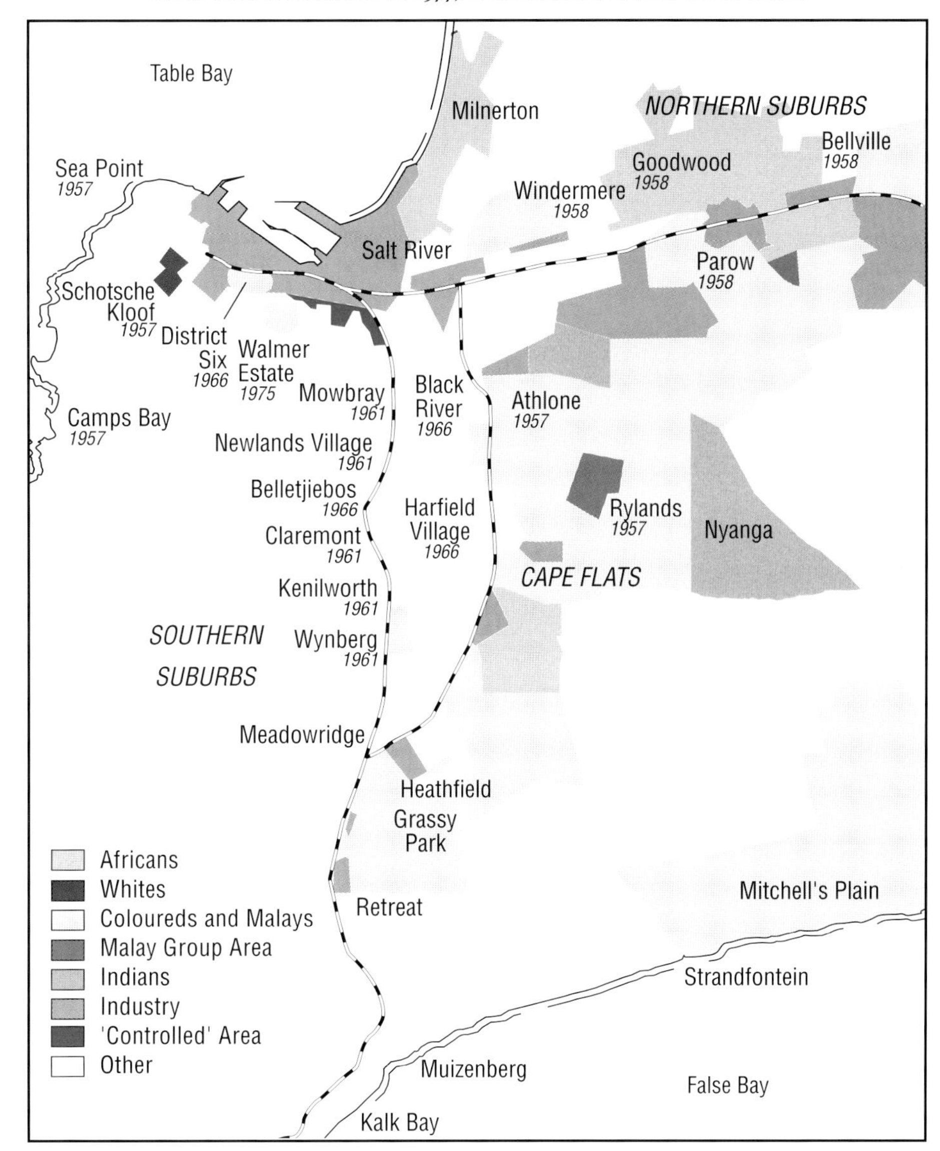

suburb attracted the detailed attention of foreign sociologists. All of this, together with the fact that inhabitants did not want change, may explain why no decision was taken on the area's fate until 1979. In that year a section was proclaimed for coloureds and 'Malays', but the rest was allowed to remain 'controlled'.[91]

The security crackdown that accompanied the State of Emergency in 1960 had helped to stifle effective opposition and to produce the so-called silent sixties. These developments are usually associated with the shooting of 69 African pass protesters at Sharpeville, a township near Vereeniging in the Transvaal. In fact they had as much to do with mass protest by Africans in Cape Town, prompted by increasingly ruthless government policies towards them in the 1950s.

A City without Africans?

Cape Town became a test case for the apartheid ideal of reversing African urbanisation. If proved impossible here, it would be impossible everywhere else. After all, this was the South African city furthest from any African reserve – the nearest was over 500 miles to the east. The new minister of native affairs, Dr E.G. Jansen, put the government's view bluntly in September 1948: 'Whatever claim, morally or otherwise, the Natives have in other parts of the Union, they have no real claim to be here in the Western Province at all. It is within the memory of many people today that there was a time that a Native was unknown in the Peninsula.'[92]

In 1950, legal work-seeking was reduced to only 72 hours. Police in the Peninsula stepped up raids for 'illegals', and pass or permit prosecutions shot up to well over a thousand a year. The government also replaced almost 2000 African employees in the western Cape region with coloureds and whites. The labour bureaux system, which registered prospective workers, was gradually extended throughout the Peninsula and linked to rural bureaux. Urban employers had to pay a fee of 2s 6d for recruits, the money helping to pay for locations.[93]

But there was still little capacity to enforce removals. Africans also forged papers or were sometimes able to use those of a friend or relative, because the holder's photograph was not yet required. Oral history has revealed that people got round existing restrictions on rail-ticket purchases from the eastern Cape in a number of ways, including bribing officials. Some bought tickets to Boland towns, and made their way to Cape Town from there; others travelled by road to Mossel Bay before catching a train, or clubbed together to hire a truck for the entire journey.

The ever-burgeoning shanties on the fringes of Cape Town bore testimony to the continued failure of influx control as well as the inadequacy of housing schemes.[94] Local authorities still balked at demolishing shacks, once the roof was on, for fear of having to supply alternative accommodation.[95] The Prevention of Illegal Squatting Act – applied to all magisterial regions in greater Cape Town in 1952 – was the government's response. This forced local authorities to co-operate in the process of establishing 'emergency camps' – where shanty dwellers could be 'concentrated and controlled' – and allowed them to demolish 'illegal' shacks.

Apartheid ideologues from the South African Bureau for Racial Affairs (SABRA) initiated meetings of Native Affairs officials from all local authorities to co-ordinate their efforts. SABRA was pushing for the prevention of any further African settlement, the sole use of migrant labour and the gradual elimination of African employees in the area altogether. The Cape Divisional Council and northern municipalities – sympathetic to Afrikaner nationalism – almost immediately began relocating Africans to an extended Nyanga. The more hesitant Cape Town municipality – effectively controlled by United Party supporters – was told to cater for a further 17,000 migrant labourers at Langa. No more purpose-built family houses were erected in either location after 1954.

As with other elements of apartheid, any reluctance on the part of local authorities to enforce government policy could be met with legislation. The 1952 amendment to the Natives (Urban Areas) Act was particularly significant. Central government rather than local authorities now decided which were 'proclaimed' areas under the 1923 Act, and thus where national restrictions on urban Africans would apply. Three years later the minister of native affairs was given the power to deproclaim a location. Eventually the government's Bantu Affairs Administration Boards took complete charge of influx control and locations throughout the Peninsula in 1973.

The 1952 Act already contained substantial further restrictions on African urbanisation. Notably, the seek-work period was reduced from a fortnight to only three days, and control over African women in Cape Town began in earnest: they were issued with work permits for the first time in 1954. Yet the Act's infamous Section 10 was tempered by constraints of cost and the concerns of employers for a more stable workforce. This

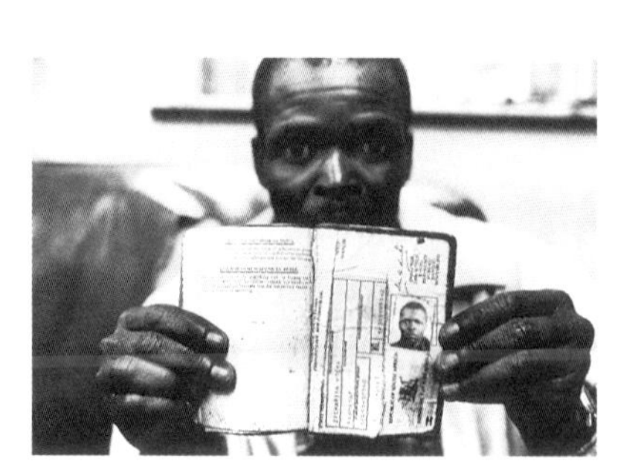

This pass was an example of the document which was so vital to the urban existence of Africans. (Mayibuye Centre)

meant that some Africans were actually granted 'permanent residence' rights in the city.

The Orwellianly named Natives (Abolition of Passes and Co-ordination of Documents) Act was the other crucial innovation of 1952, introducing 'reference books' for all Africans over the age of 16. Issued in Cape Town from August 1955, they replaced and consolidated all the previous documents Africans had had to carry, whether passes, permits or contracts. Those previously exempt from influx legislation were issued with a green version, the rest with a brown one that included the bearer's fingerprints. Both contained a photograph of the holder – making multiple use more difficult – and a copy of Section 10.

Police raids for 'illegals' and bootleg liquor continued to escalate. One massive raid took place on 1 December 1953: 800 police swept through Windermere, arrested 200 inhabitants and destroyed 4000 gallons of home brew. A raid even took place on Christmas Eve. As Mr I.Z. well remembered: 'the police were very active chasing about people. Like dogs you know ... If the dog catchers come around and they see a dog without a collar bearing a licence on it, they'd chase that dog and catch it and take it to the pound. That's how we were chased around at Windermere.'[96] To back up the police, location inspectors were granted powers of search and arrest in 1958. In total, more than 18,000 men and almost 6000 women were 'endorsed out' of Cape Town between 1954 and 1962.[97]

Such figures were in keeping with government plans for the region. In 1954 Dr Jansen's successor, Dr Verwoerd, announced that the western Cape was a Labour Preference area for coloureds. The Institute of Race Relations soon reported that influx control was being imposed more severely here than in any other part of South Africa. At the same time Verwoerd was busily implementing 'Bantu education' with a curriculum intended to equip Africans 'in accordance with their opportunities in life' and a knowledge of 'their' culture. Control of education was wrested from provincial governments.

Influx Control

Subsequent amendments to the 1952 Natives (Urban Areas) Act eroded rights granted under Section 10. From 1957, for instance, those who had previously qualified through length and continuity of employment had to go on working continuously in Cape Town to retain this privilege. In 1959 a Mr Jafta was 'endorsed' out of the Peninsula for spending a year with his family in the Transkei, having previously lived and worked in Cape Town for 45 years. His shack in Nyanga was demolished, and he remembers simply being told, 'Jy kan gaan waar jy wil.' Section 10 had the ironic effect of encouraging, even forcing, many migrant labourers in Cape Town to seek more permanent settlement there.[98]

Harassment by white policemen was the daily experience of almost all urban Africans. (Mayibuye Centre)

The ANC's Women's League marched in Cape Town against passes in 1956 and 1957. (SAL Cape Times collection)

Through reduction of their subsidies, mission schools were forced to close or join the state system. No private schools were allowed without state permission.

Although the ANC called for a boycott of the new system, it drew a weak response in Cape Town. But on the evidence of Langa High School, where two NEUM-aligned teachers were dismissed, it seems that the coming of Bantu education led to the demoralisation of staff and the deterioration of pupil discipline. Although on the one hand the politicisation of scholars increased, so did alcohol abuse, teenage pregnancies and poor academic results. Previously vibrant extramural activities such as rugby, acting or debating all but disappeared.[99]

By 1960 the situation for the city's 100,000 Africans had reached crisis point. Up till 1958, the majority still lived in shanties or undemarcated areas, and retained some control over their own accommodation. But in 1958 Group Area removals began affecting places like Elsies River and Windermere, and even the previously exempt now had to live in locations or premises licensed by the government. The only exception was made for domestic servants. Forging papers or faking identity was becoming much harder – by 1 February 1960, the deadline for compulsory possession, 62,000 men had been issued with the new reference books.

At the same time the clearance of remaining shack settlements was accelerating, from Hout Bay to Elsies River. More than 5000 'bachelors' were ordered into hostels, while thousands of 'illegals' were 'endorsed out' of the city.[100] Most were women, and by the end of October 1959 they were also being issued with what was dubbed the *dompas* or *domboek* ('stupid pass/book'). At the same time, despite the furious opposition of many employers, the Native Affairs Department decided that no further Africans at all could be recruited for work in Cape Town.[101]

All this was happening while conditions in the eastern Cape reserves were making it more desperately important than ever for people to find urban employment. Migrancy introduced the problems and politics of the countryside to Cape Town. Some Africans began expressing their resentment with physical violence, usually against official cars or policemen.

The combination of urban and rural upheavals underpinned a major crisis that lasted longer in Cape Town than anywhere else in South Africa. A new political party in the city, the Pan Africanist Congress (PAC), tapped into the mood of popular militancy. The PAC was formed in 1959 by 'Africanists' within the ANC. They wanted more aggressive opposition to the state and were unhappy with multi-racial co-operation. The PAC's relative success in Cape Town was aided by ongoing tension within the local ANC –

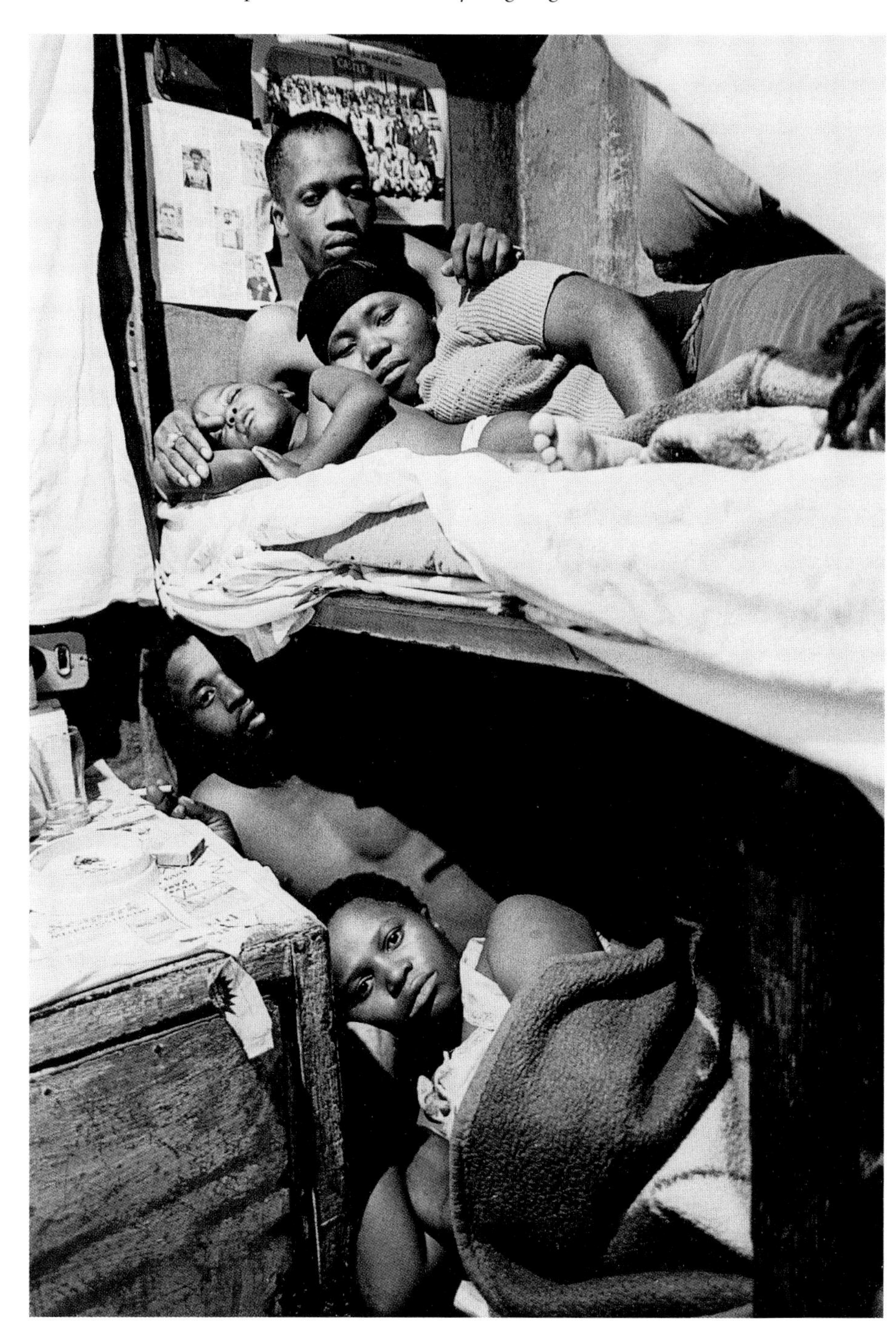

Largely because of the late 1950s removals, more than 70 new barracks were built at Langa and, in 1958, a new township was established at Nyanga West. It was renamed Guguletu ('Our Pride') in 1963. No families were allowed to own their home, only 30-year leaseholds were on offer. All the houses were designed for future conversion to single quarters. The reality of life in the Guguletu barracks for many families was shared accommodation in a single bed. Consequently Mamphela Ramphele entitled her study of Cape Town's migrant labour hostels *A Bed Called Home* (Cape Town, 1993). The accompanying photograph, by Roger Meintjes, was part of a series, sanctioned by the hostel dwellers themselves, whose aim was to highlight their plight and their need for proper accommodation, both for themselves and for their families.

BARRACK STREET

The 1960 March

Early in 1960 there were signs of a growing crisis. Police patrols had come under attack in Windermere and Langa. Cartons of Rembrandt cigarettes, seen as Afrikaner nationalist products, were burnt on Salt River station. ANC and PAC volunteers were campaigning vigorously in the townships.[102] On 18 March, the PAC pre-empted the ANC by announcing that its anti-pass campaign would start three days later under the slogan 'No bail, no defence, no fine'. The idea was for thousands of Africans to leave their passes at home and present themselves at police stations for arrest. They would fill prisons to overflowing and make influx control unworkable. Along with the Transvaal township of Sharpeville (affected by its own recent crises), Cape Town was one of the few places to respond enthusiastically to the PAC call.

In Nyanga, while women mocked those going to work, groups of male volunteers offered themselves for arrest at Philippi police station. In Langa a morning attempt to march to the police station was aborted for fear of violence, but thousands reconvened in the evening to 'hear news' from the PAC national office. In dispersing the crowd, the police killed two people. Rioting went on through the night, possibly fuelled by the news that 69 people had been killed in a pass demonstration at Sharpeville, and roads were barricaded in both Langa and Nyanga. The mutilated body of a *Cape Times* employee, Mr Richard Lombard, who had driven journalists into Langa, was found the next morning.

Opposite: The flaring press headlines, 'Natives march to the city', expressed the fears of nervous non-African Capetonians. (SAL PHA)
Above: The young Philip Kgosana, still wearing shorts in an age when long trousers were a mark of manhood, led the march from Langa. (SAL PHA)

Support for a work stayaway grew steadily over the next few days until it involved most location residents and had seriously affected services and industrial production. The Congress of Democrats, the Liberal Party and the Black Sash helped supply residents with food. The PAC-led campaign soon faltered everywhere except in Cape Town. Here it achieved the temporary suspension of the pass laws throughout the country by the evening of 24 March. But six days later the government declared a State of Emergency and arrested 1500 people.

Early that morning, 30 March, police launched a brutal attack on Langa residents in an attempt to break the strike. In response, 30,000 Africans from both locations marched to Caledon Square police station. The crowd dispersed after the police chief, Colonel Terblanche, had promised the PAC leader, Philip Kgosana, that he would meet the minister of justice later in the day. When Kgosana turned up for the appointment he was arrested. Within a few days the townships had been cordoned off with the help of the military and food supplies blocked. Resistance was broken by arrests and beatings, with residents alleging that police had worked with vigilantes from the bachelor hostels distinguished by 'white sheets round their bodies and white *doeke* on their heads'. By 11 April the strike had been broken, the pass laws restored and the cordon lifted.[103]

particularly over whether to support white Native Representatives in elections. The PAC may have benefited from the penetration of NEUM ideology among members of the Cape African Teachers' Association. Moreover, the ANC had recently been weakened by the arrest and banishment of leaders when Africanists – 'dressed in black and wielding knives and batons' – disrupted a party gathering in 1958. Three ANC branches – Langa New Flats, Crawford and Kensington – defected to the PAC.

PAC leaders used lively language, often spiced with rural idioms, to attract support and goad people into action. As Mrs Molokoti, the wife of the PAC leader in the western Cape, told one conservative male audience: 'You men ... give us your trousers and we will give you our dresses.'[104]

The main role of both parties in the critical autumn days of 1960 was to focus grievances and set a timetable for action. The ANC decided that a new anti-pass campaign should begin on 31 March. But the PAC went further. Its anti-pass plans included a national strike and the demand for a minimum wage. PAC leaders confidently declared that national liberation would be achieved by 1963.[105] Instead, the ensuing confrontation led to the government's declaring a State of Emergency and banning both the PAC and ANC. National liberation was delayed for 24 years.

Robben Island

Between 1931 and 1960 Robben Island had become a military outpost securing the approaches to Table Bay. But in 1959 its role as place of banishment was restored. The government placed it under the Prisons Department as a 'maximum security institution'.[106] Thousands of black political prisoners were sent there from 1962. The most famous were Nelson Mandela (ANC) and Robert Sobukwe (leader of the PAC). Although the vast majority of prisoners came from their two parties, a wide range of organisations was represented including the NEUM-affiliated African People's Democratic Union of South Africa, Black Consciousness and even the Liberal Party. Conditions were particularly atrocious in the early years, owing to poor food, racist warders and hard labour in the quarries. Notorious gang members among the non-political criminals were also a threatening presence. Nonetheless political organisation and education took place from the start. Gradually conditions improved, partly because of hunger strikes, the testimony of released prisoners, international pressure and the energy of Helen Suzman, the only member of the liberal Progressive Party in parliament. Academic study, sport and recreation became possibilities. 'Monopoly' was a special favourite of Mandela's. Hard labour in the quarries ended in 1977, some prisoners were allowed newspapers in 1980, and visits from children were permitted the following year. The last political prisoners left in 1991, ordinary criminals at the end of 1996.[107]

This official photograph of prisoners breaking stone in the prison courtyard was intended to show the world a well-conducted prison. (Mayibuye Centre)

Imam Haron

Hadji Abdullah Haron became imam of Al-Jaamia Mosque in Claremont in 1956 and 'honorary editor' of *Muslim News* in the 1960s. He played an important role in persuading particularly younger Cape Town Muslims to take a more active stand against apartheid. It was within this more defiant mood that the Muslim Judicial Council declared, in May 1961, that Islam could not condone apartheid, and active mission work began in the locations. The *Muslim News* published articles on Islam in Xhosa, and identified with African suffering. Haron was forced to move from Claremont to a 'Coloured Group Area' in 1966. During the crisis of 1960 he helped organise food supplies to the townships and served on a committee raising funds for political detainees. As his political involvement deepened, he supported the Coloured People's Congress (the successor to SACPO) in their call for a three-day stayaway to protest against South Africa becoming a Republic in 1961. In 1965

(Mayibuye Centre)

the CPC was dissolved and some members, including Haron, joined the PAC. He became involved in a plan to recruit young men for guerrilla training outside of the country. Although this came to nothing, Haron attracted increasing attention and harassment from the security police. He was detained in 1969 and died from injuries sustained during interrogation. The official cause of death was 'an accidental fall down a flight of stone stairs'.[108]

Peaceful protest grew correspondingly difficult as the government became less tolerant of any extra-parliamentary opposition. Though there were gatherings on the Parade and a SACTU-mobilised work stayaway in May 1961 – to oppose South Africa becoming a Republic and to commemorate the 1960 crisis – demonstrations and public meetings were ever more rigidly restricted. Eventually even Black Sash placard holders could only stand silently and alone – two would have constituted an illegal gathering.

Apartheid Heyday

Between 1960 and 1976 apartheid reached its apogee. The National Party banned or imprisoned many of its main opponents; others were banished to remote parts of the country, or forced into exile or underground. The Prevention of Political Interference Act of 1968, prohibiting multi-racial parties, put paid to the Liberal Party and deterred other initiatives along such lines. Cape Town's socialist newspaper, *New Age*, was closed down – only the second time this had happened to a paper since the days of Lord Charles Somerest. House arrest, threats and secret surveillance were additional weapons at the state's disposal.

The government gave itself powers to hold people for progressively longer periods without trial. Deaths and torture in detention became increasingly common: the Cape Town activist Looksmart Solwandle Ngudle became the first fatality in October 1963.

It was under these circumstances that the 'armed struggle' began. Both the ANC and PAC launched their armed wings – uMkhonto weSizwe (MK) and Poqo – and established secret training camps in the Cape Town area. Between 1961 and 1963 both managed a number of attacks, destroying government property and killing a policeman. But the police foiled a Poqo plan to murder the inhabitants of a Jewish old-age home and the Helmsley Hotel in the Gardens. Some white students – including the novelist Jonty Driver – formed the African Resistance Movement (ARM), and blew up electricity pylons. But the armed struggle fizzled out, partly as a result of mass arrests in 1963. With even strikes now defined as sabotage, the government was able to convict many SACTU officials and paralyse their movement by mid-decade.[109]

All of this eased the government's task of further refining apartheid, be it revisiting the idea of an African-free western Cape or dealing with 'contentious' Group Areas. So did the fact that the economy was booming. This made social engineering more affordable while helping to dampen discontent. The only problem was that it also meant a growing demand for African labour. Yet from 1966 the state refused to build any more houses for Africans in Cape Town. As P.W. Botha put it, the ultimate ideal was for the western Cape to be a 'safe White homeland' which also offered 'a future for Coloured people'. Africans would eventually vanish to their own homelands like the Transkei, which was granted 'independence' in 1976.[110]

The Peninsula was divided into two 'proclaimed areas' in 1960, supposedly to streamline administration. One included Nyanga and was controlled by the Cape Divisional Council and the northern municipalities. Cape Town municipality formed the other, administering both Langa and Guguletu. Africans were supposed to work only in the proclaimed area served by the location they lived in. Since they also required official permission to visit friends or relatives in the other proclaimed area, this caused predictable chaos and misery. Elected Urban Bantu Councils, with extremely limited administrative duties and even less legitimacy among residents, replaced the location Advisory Boards from 1961.

After 1965 African workers had to return to their 'homeland' at the end of a contract period, and re-apply for admission to the Peninsula from there – thereby preventing new acquisitions of 'permanent residence'. By the end of the decade those 'endorsed out' were being sent to 'resettlement camps' in the eastern Cape. The Bantu Affairs Department could now overrule Section 10 rights if a person was deemed 'idle and undesirable'. Meanwhile, and after years of opposition, municipal beer halls and bottle stores had been imposed on Cape Town locations: alcohol sales helped to pay the administrative costs of segregation.[111]

Despite all these devices, the numbers of Africans in Cape Town had grown considerably beyond 'natural increase' by the early 1970s. The government was forced to allow more 'legal' employment for the sake of the local economy, while employers were also prepared to break the law to meet their labour needs.[113] Influx control merely slowed the rapidly rising rate at which Africans sought jobs in the city. The desperate state of the rural reserves and infamous resettlement camps in the eastern Cape like Dimbaza kept driving people to the Peninsula in their thousands, including those who had already been 'endorsed out'. Mr Murray-Rawbone, an official administering influx control, later recalled that 'it was like trying to stop the sea ... you'll never be able to cope, even if you've got hundreds of thousands of policemen. I'm sure they didn't leave.'[114] Even government figures showed the 'legal' African population rising from about 70,000 in 1960 to 160,000 by 1974, with 'illegals' estimated at a further 90,000.[115]

By the early 1970s new shantytowns were appearing to the north and south of the airport, visible proof that the apartheid experiment was failing. They included Unibel (1972), Crossroads (1974), KTC and Modderdam (both 1975). Yet a recession was lessening the demand for labour. The government made a final effort to prevent the inevitable. With Bantu Affairs Administration Boards (BAABs) in place from 1973, annual pass prosecutions reached 24,000 in 1975 alone. Two years later an amended Illegal Squatting Act allowed shack demolitions even without a court order, and this meant the end of Unibel and Modderdam.

Developments in Coloured politics

With radical initiatives suppressed, two overtly coloured political parties were formed in the 1960s. The pro-apartheid Federal Coloured People's Party (FCPP) of Tom Swartz (founded in 1964) stood for 'pride of identity and independence among the Coloured people'. In 1966 Richard van der Ross became the first leader of the anti-apartheid Labour Party. In 1968 the government ended the indirect representation of coloureds in parliament and established a Coloured Persons' Representative Council with limited powers over education and 'community development'. Although the Labour Party took part – ostensibly to fight from within the system – and easily won majorities, the government appointed additional FCPP members and later replaced a Labour chairman. Eventually even the FCPP came out in favour of direct coloured representation in parliament and the Representative Council was abolished in 1980.[112]

Although KTC – placed between Nyanga and Guguletu – continued to be tolerated, the imminent threat of bulldozers hung over Crossroads. Demolition was not confined to shanties. In the course of the 1960s most of the remaining 'contentious' cases under the Group Areas Act were 'resolved'. The predominantly coloured 'pockets' in the southern suburbs were now reserved for whites. Many houses in areas like Newlands, Mowbray and Claremont were bought up by property companies. After suitable gentrification they were sold to whites, usually at a huge profit, rather than being knocked down.[116] But the fate of houses in District Six was different, as Achmat Dangor put it in *Waiting for Leila*: 'Brrrat-a-tat-brrr. Jackhammers picking like crows at his gut. All around him they were breaking down his city, brick by brick, stone by stone. District Six – Rock of My History.'[117]

The demolition of District Six involved the removal of perhaps 60,000 people.[118] It also meant the destruction of a kind of mother city within the Mother City for many

Mechanical monsters
with rapacious lust have ravished
the beauty of district six
seven steps
where gladiators provide circus
and flowers flourished
in fields of filth
familiar landscape effaced
now grey ghosts
in once hallowed places
exiled pilgrims worship
at desecrated shrines
solitary seagull awheeling
its melancholy mew
last rites chanted
at the death
of a spirit
that was district six

James Matthews, 1979

Cape Town's monument to social engineering

'You can take the people out of District Six, ou pellie, but you'll never take District Six out of the heart of the people.'[119] The remaining, unbuilt land so close to the city centre, dotted with churches and a mosque, was a powerful memorial to apartheid suffering. Organisations like the Hands Off District Six Committee attempted to ensure it would remain so. But the place was being immortalised in other ways. These included newspaper articles, films like Lindy Wilson's *Last Supper at Horstley Street*, photo exhibitions and published collections, written reminiscences and the oral testimonies of ex-residents collected by the Western Cape Oral History Project (UCT). Its destruction also inspired powerful poetry by James Matthews, Adam Small and Dollar Brand (Abdullah Ibrahim), as well as novels by Richard Rive and Achmat Dangor. However, it was probably the 1980s musicals of David Kramer and Taliep Pietersen – the most successful ever staged in the city – that did most to promote the local legend of District Six.[120] In the 1990s a District Six Museum was opened in Buitenkant Street to keep its memory alive. With the demise of apartheid, most Cape Town guidebooks now found a place to commemorate the place in favourable terms.[121]

The creation of a wasteland. Churches and mosques still stood as memorials to a lost community. (Mayibuye Centre)

The demolition of Modderdam squatter camp

During the week of 8 August 1977, two bulldozers destroyed Modderdam: 'As the camp was razed, squatters chanted hymns and freedom songs, charged columns of policemen, and hurled furniture onto Modderdam Road. Many burnt down their own shacks ... several squatters were hospitalised with dog bites.' Unlike the Rand's organised land invasions, most squatter camps in Cape Town were the relatively spontaneous initiatives of individual families. Forms of organisation, including Sunday morning courts, then developed. Some camps were still racially mixed; 10 per cent of Modderdam's population was coloured. As a resident told the journalist Andrew Silk, 'We were just passing by one day and saw people putting up shacks. I asked them who owned the land and they said they didn't know – everyone was just building.' Silk found that accommodation varied enormously. Mr V.'s one-roomed shack 'swarmed with flies and stank of old cooked food and shit'. But Mr P. had three rooms, the walls papered with *Darling* magazine articles – aimed at white women – with titles like 'Is living together a lousy idea?' People sold items such as live chickens or cigarettes from their homes. Pick-up trucks served as illegal taxis – a burgeoning township industry since the late 1960s – or brought in food, water and fuel.[122]

(Mayibuye Centre)

Opposite: By the 1980s Crossroads was superficially a more organised community in which each shack was numbered. In their shanty houses Crossroads residents struggled to create respectable homes, which they could not do in the Guguletu barracks. (SAL, photos by Chris Schoeman)

Crossroads

Crossroads grew up on land bounded by Lansdowne Road, Mahobe Drive and Klipfontein Road. It was started by shack residents forced to move from Brown's Farm. As one remembered: 'We were told ... that during the day white men had come to say that all blacks must move. We asked, "But where to?" We were told ... "to the Crossroads" ... unfortunately when we came there it was just bush. A lot of trees and a few houses ... there were less than fifteen families there.'[123]

Not only 'illegals' lived in Crossroads. In the early years, about 10 per cent of women and 50 per cent of men were 'legal'.[124] Many had been lodgers in the increasingly overcrowded locations, eager to be 'free' and avoid rent. Average official occupancy of a three-roomed house in Nyanga had risen from 4.7 to 5.9 people during the 1960s. Actual numbers may have been even higher. In addition, male migrants left the hostels in order to live more easily with 'illegal' wives.

A 1977 Crossroads survey counted 18,000 inhabitants. Household heads had usually lived in Cape Town for more than 18 years, their spouses for over 11. Nearly 15 per cent of shacks had a single adult in charge, almost all of whom were women.[125] The authorities had initially allowed Crossroads as a temporary camp, but by 1975 officials were issuing eviction orders, though a stay of execution was granted the following year. This was partly because both a Men's and Women's Committee had been formed to fight for the right to stay. Residents donated 20c each to the cause. The Women's Committee was particularly successful in inspiring resistance and involving outside support. Liberal organisations like the Black Sash joined in a Save Crossroads campaign from 1978. So instead of its being demolished under the new Prevention of Illegal Squatting Act, the Cape Supreme Court ruled that Crossroads be declared an 'emergency camp' – and that the Divisional Council should supply water taps, and remove refuse and night-soil for a nominal fee.[126]

coloured Capetonians.[127] Local residents had been led to believe that the District was secure in 1961, when it was 'investigated' as a Group Area for coloureds.[128] But in the following year the government blocked the city council's belated plans to upgrade the area, and in 1965 appointed its own committee on 'rehabilitation'. Hettie Adams recalled that her family began to fear the worst when Group Area inspectors started a house-to-house survey: 'They came to us: "Who is staying in this house? How many in a family?" ... For months we had it hanging over our heads we would have to move. As the men looked around our house and in the street and wrote things, we wondered: What's going on? At that stage we were not told anything definite.'[129] On 11 February 1966, District Six was declared a 'White Group Area' and 'they chucked us out of Cape Town ... they took our happiness from us'.[130] By 1976, two-thirds of the residents had been moved to the Cape Flats at a cost of some R30 million.[131]

The Northern Suburbs

For Afrikaner nationalists at least, these were halcyon days. Mark Behr provides a vivid if unsympathetic portrayal of their pride and prejudices in *The Smell of Apples*, a historical novel about the Erasmus family of St James.[132] However, it was the northern suburbs, linked by Voortrekker Road and dotted with rugby posts, that became the real bastions of nationalism – in an urban environment otherwise more reminiscent of America than Britain. Opulent middle-class enclaves emerged on the slopes of the Tygerberg.

Durbanville was a municipality as early as 1901. Goodwood, Parow and Bellville gained this status in successive years from 1938. During the war, their white populations became predominantly Afrikaans-speaking. In the 1950s costly modernist municipal centres bore testimony to combined ethnic and civic self-confidence, as well as to rapid economic growth. Prime Minister D.F. Malan was granted the freedom of Parow in 1956 after opening its civic centre, complete with library and substantial theatre, amid great festivities. The same year he laid the foundation stone of D.F. Malan High in Bellville. Tygerberg Hospital, linked to Stellenbosch University, was the first to teach medicine and dentistry in Afrikaans. The Afrikaner financial giant Sanlam moved its headquarters to Bellville in 1962, initiating numerous commercial ventures. In 1971 the opening of Parow's Sanlam shopping centre symbolised the contemporary strength of Afrikaner capitalism. Fittingly, the Dutch Reformed church in Bellville, constructed in 1975, became the biggest in the Cape.[133]

In Bellville, bustling Voortrekker Road and Karl Bremer Hospital each represented aspects of Afrikaner commercial and technocratic success. (SAL PHA)

Removals were facilitated by government loans to the city council for new housing schemes at Rylands, Belhar and Hanover Park (the last name a cruel reminder of the District's principal street). Group Area legislation also compelled local governments to set aside at least 40 per cent of all newly constructed homes for removed persons. Numbers on Cape Town's municipal waiting-list duly swelled to 24,000 by the early 1970s. Room occupancy in many parts of the new townships rose accordingly, hardly solving the 'slum' problem.[134]

District Six was renamed Zonnebloem by the government in 1970 after the original Dutch farmstead. But this failed to attract the hoped-for private developers willing to turn the place into a cluster of high-rise apartments and town houses for whites. Protest organisations ensured that Zonnebloem became tainted ground. By 1979 the only sign of redevelopment was the Oriental Plaza, a sop to dispossessed Indian traders. So the government intervened by building the Cape Technikon and apartments for its own employees. In 1985 District Six's population of 3500 consisted largely of middle-income, Afrikaans-speaking whites.[135]

Perhaps 150,000 Capetonians had been relocated under Group Areas legislation by the end of the 1970s, of whom only a handful were white and the vast majority coloured.[136] When residents of Black River, Rondebosch, were interviewed by the press in 1961, before their removal, many were defiant. John Davis said, 'This is my home – and if they want to get me and my family out of it they will have to bring their tanks and Sten guns.' In the event, little naked force was necessary.[137] Most resistance was similar to that of the smaller removals of the 1950s: protest meetings, prayers, petitions, letters to the press and delegations. In District Six there was also a brief placard demonstration by students and the distribution of thousands of 'I am from District Six' lapel stickers. This publicised a sense of grievance to white Capetonians: many clerics and groups like the Progressive Party and Black Sash responded with their support. But the net result was that some evictions were delayed, not prevented.[138]

One reason continued to be the staggered nature of Group Area declarations and different time periods within which people had to leave various places. This eroded potential solidarity. It also gave those who had already witnessed successful removals a sense of the inevitable. State power loomed particularly large in people's minds after 1960. Special Branch policemen deliberately made themselves conspicuous to threatened communities: the feared 'Spyker' van Wyk haunted the streets of doomed District Six.[139]

As a resident of Mowbray explained: 'After all those years it wasn't easy to leave, but we had to go, we had to obey. That man [the government official] said, "if you don't want what we have to give you, you can sit in the street."'[140] Some people chose to go before they were evicted, to get the best alternative housing: 'We left when we knew we were going to have to go. The longer you wait, the further in [to the Cape Flats] you'll have to go – now they're building out at Mitchell's Plain,' said another Mowbrayite in the mid-1970s.[141] Others waited until the last moment, but by then the potential for united resistance had gone.

But even in their heyday, communities were not usually as united as memory would have it: racial, religious and class divides and different interests existed. Some coloureds successfully 'passed for white', and Africans 'passed for coloured', to escape removal. Many better-off people wanted to retain respectability and feared the consequences of over-vigorous opposition to the government. Some of the poor may not have wanted to resist. Sub-tenants especially may have welcomed the possibility of renting their own flat or house in a better estate like Heideveld.

Living Conditions in Heideveld

Heideveld was developed in 1962 on a former dairy farm. Accommodation ranged from five-roomed detached houses on sizeable plots through three-roomed flats in three-storey buildings to two-roomed 'sub-economic' dwellings. The Epping, Elsies River and Bellville South industrial areas were conveniently close at hand. A UCT study in 1968 found that the average household size was 6.2 persons, with a birth rate that was likely to increase this further – given that 70 per cent of household heads were under the age of 39. Yet more than half the residents questioned – including Group Areas victims – thought that living conditions were better than those experienced by their parents; only 10 per cent thought the opposite. The main complaints were inadequate public transport, absence of shops and parks, and distance from work – most respondents were still employed in the city centre.[142]

Many people missed what they had left behind: familiar surroundings, institutions, closeness to work and facilities and, in some cases, better homes in leafier suburbs. Women in particular regretted the loss of kin and neighbourly networks that had provided both social and economic support – through household production of foodstuffs among other things. Members of Hettie Adams's family, for instance, had all lived together in the same house in District Six. Thereafter they were scattered between Heideveld, Belhar, Elsies River, Bishop Lavis and Netreg. New housing on the Cape Flats was designed with nuclear families in mind. Its uniformity was reinforced by the fact that only a small number of construction companies were involved. By 1981 the Afrikaner-owned firm Besterecta alone had 42 per cent of contracts over R100,000 – worth in total almost R13 million.[143]

What almost everyone came to long for most was the greater safety of pre-removal days.[144] A major factor contributing to the spiralling rates of domestic and public violence by the 1970s was the break-up of old, settled communities. Members were now being dispersed across the Cape Flats in anonymous townships swollen by urban migrants and the refugees of shack demolition. Poverty also accelerated in mid-decade owing to recession, declining real wages and continued high birth rates, while the lifelines of additional income from household production or corner-shop credit had all but vanished.

Societies that were more communal and face-to-face in nature had provided at least some restraints on the growth of violence. Juvenile delinquency in particular was likely to flourish when there were fewer relatives or well-disposed neighbours on hand to help working parents with child-care, especially in view of the paucity of crèches. And even low-rise flat development probably hampered the growth of new supportive street cultures.

In April 1970 the Cape Divisional Council began a ten-year 'replanning programme' for the Elsies River area, aided by a R25 million loan from the government. The idea was to provide accommodation for about 75,000 coloured people in 13,000 'dwelling units'. Research for the Second Carnegie Commission into Poverty revealed a much sorrier story than the surveys of Parkwood in the 1940s or Heideveld in the 1960s. Only 5775 homes had been completed by 1983, mostly three-storey flats, and the population was nearer to 82,000. Altogether 4813 families, numbering about 28,000 people, were still waiting for their own accommodation. Average room occupancy was 5.6 persons. Many houses were without electricity. There were no playgrounds and only one library, one community centre, three dance halls and five crèches. Male unemployment was almost 60 per cent, female 75 per cent. The average head-of-household income was R173 per month (compared with R183 for all coloureds) while the official 'household subsistence level' was R231. Roughly 100 people a day attended the TB clinic. Many parents abused alcohol or drugs; many children ran away, joined gangs or sniffed glue. By this stage Elsies River had one of the highest crime rates in South Africa: including 100 murders, 147 rapes and 790 other violent assaults in a year. As Mrs T., of Clarke's Estate in Elsies River, commented: 'you suffer – you're not certain of your life or anything else.'[145]

There may also have been a growing disrespect for order that accompanied the experience of apartheid 'justice'. Few coloured, Asian or African families were untouched by Group Area removals, shack demolitions or pass convictions. For many youths, the frequent absence of parental authority or recreational alternatives hastened their graduation from peer 'playgroups' to 'street defence gangs'. Some were recruited by both new and old 'mafias' specialising in protection rackets.

The Mongrels was one of the best-known 'mafia' gangs in District Six and was centred on the April family. Here gang members have photographed themselves in their new place of residence, Hanover Park. (UCT Macmillan)

ZANE BROWN

Zane Brown was just one of many talented Capetonians who chose to leave the city. In 1961, at the age of 17, he left his parents' home in District Six and went to Canada, contributing to the considerable post-1948 coloured diaspora. He eventually became his adopted country's leading consumer watchdog. His visit to Cape Town in 1997 was only his second in 36 years. (*Argus* library)

If they ended up in reformatories, others were drawn into the two 'super gangs' – the Cape Town Scorpions and Born Free Kids – and looked to make money on release from sentences of robbery and housebreaking. As one explained: 'I was very small ... when my mother and father they threw me away. There was no more money ... I found myself in a stony place of sadness and madness where each dog was hustling for his own bone, you see. That's why I realised that there's only one thing for me: if I will survive I must play dirty.'[146]

And it was easy to land up in prison. Between 1971 and 1976, some 80,000 South Africans were jailed for dagga offences alone, mostly for possession. Merchant 'syndicates' controlled the sale of dagga and mandrax, as well as more expensive stolen goods. Some may have used drugs and alcohol to help numb life under apartheid. Others, who were able, escaped the age of social engineering through emigration, chiefly to Australia, Canada and Britain. Particularly in the immediate aftermath of the 1960 State of Emergency, emigrants included many armageddon-fearing whites. Yet until 1976 white immigrants, attracted by the Mediterranean climate and Californian standard of living, exceeded those departing.

LITERATURE AND LIFE UNDER APARTHEID

Few aspects of life were untouched by apartheid. It almost ended the New Year Carnival, that affirmation of coloured claims to central Cape Town. Apart from the devastation wrought by Group Area removals, the banning of the 1968 carnival from Green Point Stadium and the restrictions put on street parades by the Gatherings and Demonstrations Act of 1973 proved almost fatal, though damage was also caused by stringent municipal traffic regulations. Between 1977 and 1989 parades disappeared from the city centre.[147]

Yet individuals experienced apartheid Cape Town in predictably varied ways. Lyndall Gordon has recounted her sheltered Jewish upbringing in Sea Point, at a time when the southern suburbs in particular still had their 'elite of [English] colonials whose consciously refined accents and distancing manners intimidated all other groups'. Her teenage years in the 1950s were full of sunbathing, friendships, fashion and

ALEX LA GUMA

Like his father James, Alex La Guma (born in 1925) was a communist frequently imprisoned for his politics. As with Richard Rive's, Alex La Guma's writing was inspired by the poverty, language and popular culture of District Six. But La Guma's fictional Cape Town – notably in his novels *A Walk in the Night* and *The Stone Country* – was more wretched and violent. His 'Up my alley' column in *New Age*, between 1956 and 1962, sometimes offered a lighter tone. Thus 1950s dance halls were 'Kwela. Commercial quadrilles ... Sambas all the way from Brazil. The girls are gay, wild, ecstatic. Their brilliant skirts whirl and their hairdos are awry; red lips parted, panting; eyes bright as jewels. The boys are sharp in their zootsuits, yellow socks and Tony Curtis haircuts. They swagger between the dances, showing off their patterned neck-ties and jingling their silver wrist chains.'[148] In 1962 La Guma was prohibited from publishing, and four years later went into exile. He died in Cuba in 1985.

(George Hallett)

boys, with the conservative schooling of Good Hope Seminary contriving to suppress political awareness if not youthful rebellion.[149] Gordon's was a life of privilege, but even the most oppressed sought what meaning and fulfilment they could. Contemporary literature begins to reveal this complexity. It was undergoing something of a golden age, notably in the writings of Richard Rive and Alex La Guma. Even in his newspaper columns, La Guma gave a sense of the variety of coloured experience:

> Herded into slums, shivering in shanties, scattered along the hillsides, rocking in buses to housing schemes, living comfortably in bright homes: Frigidaire, His Master's Voice, Edblo. They toil in thousands in big factories and push vegetable barrows, dig up roads and teach in schools, grow flowers and run shops. They steal and sometimes murder, they beg or carry loads from the markets. They drink, curse, make love and beat their wives or cheat their husbands. Heroes and cowards, villains and gentlemen, saints and sinners, people.[150]

'Herded into slums, shivering in shanties, scattered along the hillsides, rocking in buses to housing schemes, living comfortably in bright homes: Frigidaire, His Master's Voice, Edblo. They toil in thousands in big factories and push vegetable barrows, dig up roads and teach in schools, grow flowers and run shops.'

Alex La Guma, 1956

Unsurprisingly, much of the literature is political. The semi-autobiographical novels of Jonty Driver and Richard Rive – *Elegy for a Revolutionary* and *Emergency* respectively – both describe the dangerous lives of activists in the city. Albie Sachs, a young lawyer with left-wing sympathies, published a *Jail Diary*, recording his 168 days of solitary confinement mostly in Maitland police station. La Guma's *The Stone Country* also draws on personal experience of detention to portray the ghastly conditions in Roeland Street jail, and provide an allegory for working-class life outside: 'This was a world without beauty; a lunar barrenness ... no trees grew ... the only perfume it knew came from night-soil buckets and drains. In the summer it broiled, and it chattered in the winter ...'[151]

But these works are not entirely consumed with politics or suffering. Even for activists or the poor, apartheid Cape Town was also about family, school, work and recreation, about *Living, Loving and Lying Awake at Night* – as the title of a collection of stories by Sindiwe Magona affirms. Alex La Guma said he was 'all shook up' after watching teenagers rocking to juke-box records of Elvis Presley and Little Richard in his favourite Hanover Street café. But he willingly listened to local jazz musicians, complaining when they sounded too American. The novelist J.M. Coetzee found his Plumstead childhood dull but developed a passion for cricket.[152]

Cross-racial musical contacts were made in residential areas like District Six, through the racially mixed composition of bands, and in 'liberal' clubs and halls before apartheid made this much harder. Langa's Ngcukana family and the Merry Macs played central roles in spreading knowledge of African big-band sounds beyond the locations. Some whites became part of the movement. Pianist Chris McGregor, determined to decide 'what, how and with whom I play', worked with black musicians including the tenor saxophonist 'Cup and Saucer' Nkanuka: 'I realised that we had a common ground in the folk songs I had been aware of from childhood'. Venues included the Zambezi Club in upper Darling Street, decorated with bamboos and palm trees. Like carnival, jazz declined in pace with inner-city removals.[153]

Albie Sachs courted prison when still a UCT student – by sitting on 'non-white' post office benches during the Defiance Campaign – and was a member of the left-wing and non-racial Modern Youth Society. But most of the time of the society's members was spent not just in 'endless woolly discussions' but also in 'frantic searches for houses in which to hold parties ... we also read philosophy, climbed mountains and went into trances at musical evenings'.[154] When released, Sach's first act was to run to beautiful

The 1950s and 1960s saw two styles of jazz emerge from the wide-ranging and popular dance band traditions of Cape Town. One was modelled on American varieties and practised at places like the Weizmann Hall in Sea Point or St John's Bop Club in Waterkant Street. As Vincent Kolbe put it: 'we would scoff at the "peasant" music of the locals [like *vastrap*] ... we considered ourselves superior'.[155]

The other, which became known as Cape Jazz, stemmed from the belief that working-class dance music – be it 'African' *marabi, kwela* and *mbaqanga* or 'coloured' *vastrap* and *klopse* – should form the basis of local jazz. Its most important pioneers were Kensington's Dollar Brand (later famous as Abdullah Ibrahim) and his Jazz Epistles. According to saxophonist Kippie Moeketsi, they started to experiment after an audience in Langa grew restless during purely American renditions. In developing his own syncretic forms, Dollar Brand was affected by the political sentiments of pan-Africanism. Tremolo ornamentation, supposedly influenced by the sound of the fish-horn and practised by Cape dance band saxophonists, became a noticeable feature. 'Manenberg', named after the gang-ridden suburb created by the Group Areas Act, was Cape Jazz's most famous number – the 'national anthem' of the Cape Flats.[156]

Inset: Winston 'Mankunku' Ngozi playing at the Luxurama, Wynberg, in 1968.
Above: Basil Coetzee and Abdullah Ibrahim rehearsing for a performance at Strandfontein, 1970. (Basil Breakey)

Welfare in Cape Town in the 1960s

By the early 1960s there were 288 welfare agencies in the city of which less than half were now run by religious organisations. They offered a wide range of services including home tuberculosis care, providing Kosher food in hospitals, helping indigent Muslims with burials or 'genteel Whites' to maintain their 'accustomed standard of living'. Of the charities 96 were for whites only, 68 for blacks, and the remainder for both. In all, 76 per cent were managed entirely by whites.[157]

Not surprisingly, a common way that blacks experienced more liberal, middle-class whites outside the workplace was through church and charity work. Magona remembered the toys given by white women from 'another world' at CAFDA children's parties she attended. Both CAFDA and SHAWCO – which grew to be the largest student welfare institution in the world – also ran soup kitchens, and supplied shelter and clothing when periodic floods hit the city. In 1952 CAFDA even bought land in Retreat for its own coloured housing scheme, though some town councillors thought this was aiding Group Areas. Cafda Village was officially opened in 1958. It consisted of several hundred houses with a converted cowshed as the community centre. As with CAFDA industrial training centres (for weaving or shoemaking), the emphasis was on 'rehabilitation' through 'cleanliness', 'personal discipline' and 'sympathetic, but firm, guidance'.

CAFDA's workshop for sheltered employment. (SAL Cape Times collection)

Together with medical clinics, SHAWCO had its own community centres on the Cape Flats. They were paid for through the sale of *Sax Appeal* magazines and money collected on Rag day. By the 1950s drum majorettes had been introduced into the city centre procession. Scantily clad women riding on floats called 'Inn the nude' or 'Gin and sin' caused an uproar. Feminist criticism led to the disbanding of 'drummies' in 1987.

Much of the earlier criticism of welfare had come from Marxists who argued that social work treated the symptoms rather than causes of poverty, and softened the proletariat's resolve to fight. The increased political and social tension after 1960 brought greater racial hostility and vandalism against 'white' welfare work. The rise of Black Consciousness at the end of the decade gave intellectual input to such suspicions. Experience eventually taught the organisations to work much more in consultation with local communities.[158]

Clifton beach for a swim.

Magona grew up both in poverty and in the 1950s, but her autobiography tells of a predominantly happy childhood within a close family. Her parents made great personal sacrifices to buy the books and uniforms for her education. They found the strength to do so through religion, in their case Christianity. When asked why they took no part in political demonstrations, Magona remembers that her father would reply: 'I am hard put to it remaining human, maintaining and conducting myself as a person, getting up each day, going to work, bringing the pay packet home on pay days, cherishing my spouse, respecting my neighbour, refraining from crime, and, above all, remaining intact mentally.'[159]

Magona's own life became considerably more stressful as she herself grew older. In the process she challenged her parents' authority, an increasingly common stand by youth of all races in post-war Cape Town. In 1961 her family was moved from Blouvlei to Guguletu: 'in ... nearly three decades ... I have never seen one squirrel'.[160] Here gangsters or 'spoilers' robbed, raped and killed fellow residents. Yet the turning point of Magona's early adulthood was an unplanned child. This brought enormous shame to her relatives. The crisis was eventually resolved by a traditional Xhosa marriage and the impecunious father promising to pay *lobola* at a future date. Magona lost her teaching position – in charge of a class of 72 at a Nyanga primary school – and was forced to become a domestic worker.

Above: The 'Hippy' Market in Loop Street, consisting mainly of stalls selling craft wares, was the commercial centre of Cape Town's counter-culture. An observer commented: 'Pop music blares through the loudspeakers and penetrates the smoky, incense-scented atmosphere ... bellbottoms, Afro-hairstyles and leather sandals are the order of the day.' The selling of peace symbols was appropriate, given the introduction of nine months' conscription for all young white male Capetonians in 1967 – just as youth rebellion was reaching its zenith in the West. (B. Katzen, *Looking at Cape Town*, Cape Town, 1972, pp. 73–5)

Left: Donald Paarman belonged to one of Cape Town's most famous surfing families. Both he and his brother Jonathan were members of the Springbok team that went to Australia in 1970. Although there had been previous forms of wave riding, modern surfing in Cape Town was pioneered by John Whitmore. Having seen a picture of an American surfboard, be constructed and marketed his own variety in 1955 – 10 feet long and costing £20. By the late 1960s there were international contests, with the sport and culture that surrounded it popularised by imported American films like *Endless Summer*. This culture was predominantly Californian, and embraced distinctive clothing, music and magazines – and, frequently, the smoking of marijuana. (Private collection)

Domestic employment was the usual way that black and white Capetonians came into intimate contact, especially as most servants 'lived in'. These relationships were often as complicated as they were varied, albeit that accommodation for the servant was typically in a physically separate 'maid's room' at the back of suburban houses. Magona worked for four employers in as many years. They ranged from a temporary resident from Britain – who lent her books and allowed her baby into the house – to a 'screeching' Greek immigrant for whom she worked for over 18 hours a day. The former treated her as a person; others referred to her as 'the girl' and to themselves in the third person: 'if Master phones, tell Master [that] Madam will be back around three o'clock'.[161] Magona grew increasingly resentful, like many other domestics she met.

Work concerns and ambitions consumed the minds of many. Dr Jean Walker's research was on the skin diseases associated with tuberculosis, still rife in the city. One of her postgraduate students was the Karoo-born Afrikaner, Christiaan Barnard. When first at UCT, because of lack of money and the seriousness with which he took his studies Barnard 'never went to dances; I had no dress suit or car – nor time to make friends with boys who had cars. I ducked the students' cheering section at the annual inter-varsity match.' He went on to perform the first heart-transplant operation at Groote Schuur in 1967 (C. Barnard and C.B. Pepper, *One Life*, Cape Town, 1969, p. 50).

Yet from oral accounts, both employers and workers often expressed fondness for one another, particularly if they (and their families) had been together for a lengthy time. Loyalty could be rewarded. A superior 'lady's maid', Mrs E.C., worked for the same wealthy Newlands family for fifty years: 'I really enjoyed it, I enjoyed the parties, all the beautiful ladies, can see their beautiful gowns.' She remembered that when Dr Verwoerd came to dinner her services were not required: 'we had all ... European waitresses there that night'. But she was given many 'presents' and even a house on retirement.[162]

There could be pride, resentment or resistance in most forms of employment. African stevedores, whether living in the converted Breakwater prison (which replaced the Docks Location) or other accommodation, frequently indulged in macho rivalry. As one recalled: 'The *serang* [gang leader] was responsible for the pace of work – our role was working together as a team, that way we could maintain the pace. This depended on your attitude and sense of competitiveness, because people were proud of beating the other half of the gang or the other gangs in the vessels.'[163]

In contrast the workforce in clothing factories was almost exclusively female and, since the war, coloured. Paternalism played its part in helping it to become something of a sheltered community within the apartheid world. As one manager told a worker in the 1960s, '"Isabel, the girls must always remember that we [are] family." And I told him that we knew that – that he was like the second father.'[164] The fact was that new recruits usually were 'family' or friends of existing workers. Factory netball teams, charity work and the celebration of birthdays all helped in maintaining a communal spirit. So did the favours granted by women supervisors on a daily basis, be it cigarette breaks or allowing seams for workers' own garments to be stitched on factory machines. And the Garments Workers' Union, which operated within industrial conciliation legislation, was a so-called sweetheart union.[165]

For increasing numbers, work was not merely a matter of subsistence. But possession of the desired products of twentieth-century industrialism was predictably influenced by class and race. In the late 1960s, after almost a decade in which the real wages of industrial workers had grown by above 4 per cent each year, there was a 'high proportion' of radios, fridges and washing machines in every Heideveld household. (Television only came to South Africa in 1976.) There were also 16 cars per thousand residents in the township, among the highest rates in black areas. The average in white areas was already about 300 per thousand. For households with cars, a trip to the drive-in cinema now provided an alternative to the increasingly ubiquitous weekend *braai*.[166]

The greater pace and dehumanising nature of life in the age of social engineering underlay the success of antiquarian histories of the city in this period. Older English-speaking whites in particular – estranged from the present by the triumph of Afrikaner republicanism and the subsequent decline of the United Party – enjoyed retreating in

Police unsuccessfully attempt to arrest the UCT student Patrick Harries after baton charging a demonstration of students on the steps of St George's Cathedral in June 1972. The protest was against university apartheid. (J. Kuus, *South Africa in Black and White*, London, 1987)

their imagination to gentler, slower times full of British achievement. They eagerly consumed the veritable explosion of offerings by writers like Lawrence Green, P.W. Laidler, C. Pama and H.W.J. Picard.

Meanwhile, the attractions of Western counter-culture provided an alternative means of escape for some of their offspring. By the late 1960s the better-educated in particular were impressed by the actions of youth in the United States and Europe – be it Vietnam War protests, free love or the Paris 'revolution'. White UCT students staged sit-ins and demonstrations – earning their institution the nickname of Moscow-on-the-Hill – while a few graduated to trade-union activism. Yet it was urban rebellion of a different kind – by black schoolchildren in 1976 – that was to be far more important in heralding the demise of apartheid.

CHAPTER FIVE

Reclaiming the City

Cape Town since 1976

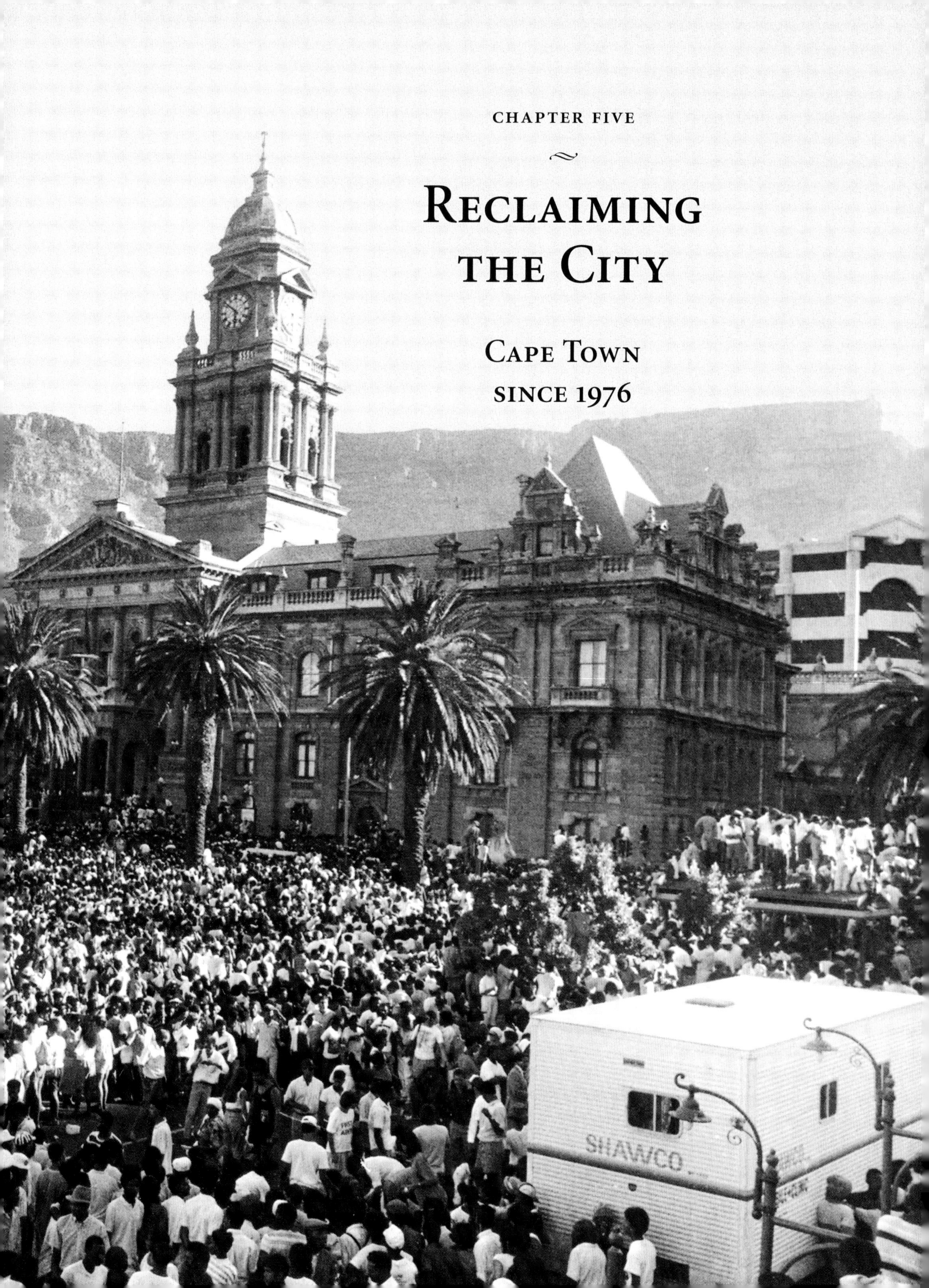

In September 1989 peace marchers reclaimed their right to Cape Town's streets when they took the familiar route from parliament and St George's Cathedral down Adderley Street to the Grand Parade. (*Argus*, 13 September 1989)

IT was lunchtime on Wednesday 13 September 1989 – a particularly hot spring day in Cape Town. After a short service of 'peace and mourning' at St George's Cathedral, thirty thousand people packed the streets en route to the Parade. They were reclaiming the right to peaceful protest and, symbolically, equal citizenship of Cape Town. The city was witnessing its largest and most peaceful march since that led by Philip Kgosana in 1960. Participants carried scores of banners demanding 'Bread not bullets', the release of Mandela and 'De Klerk, stop killing our people'. The largest of all proclaimed 'Peace in our city, Stop the killings'.

Unlike most demonstrations since 1960, not a single uniformed policeman was in obvious attendance – although a force was mustered near the Oriental Plaza. What was also striking was the composition of the crowd. At its head were Archbishop Desmond Tutu, Mayor Gordon Oliver, Dr Allan Boesak (president of the World Alliance of Reformed Churches), Sheikh Nazeem Mohamed (president of the Muslim Judicial Council) and Jakes Gerwel (rector of the University of the Western Cape). Behind them walked a multi-racial throng from all walks of life, including the chairmen of oil companies, civil rights leaders, workers, schoolchildren and unemployed township residents. Archbishop Tutu declared, 'We are a new people, a rainbow people, marching to freedom.'

At their destination, those who could packed into the City Hall. Thousands of others waited outside. A minute's silence was held for people killed in recent violence. A wide range of speakers commented on the fact that the government had at last conceded such a march, in defiance of its own laws. And, as the civil rights lawyer Dullah Omar put it,

Previous pages: Crowds gather in front of the City Hall in anticipation of Nelson Mandela's arrival, after his release in February 1990, to address the nation. (*Argus* library; *inset:* Nic Bothma/iAfrika Photos)

'when the batons, guns and quirts are absent there is no violence'. Amid cries of 'Long live the mayor' and deafening applause, Gordon Oliver announced, 'Today Cape Town has won. Today we all have the freedom of the City.'[1]

These events, made possible by national and international developments, were of enormous practical and symbolic significance. Days later they were emulated in most other major towns of South Africa. Echoing what was happening simultaneously in Eastern Europe, the days of 'Pretoriastroika' had arrived.[2] After four dehumanising decades, Cape Town was entering a period of reclamation.

What occurred on 13 September marked the triumphant climax of a new defiance campaign that had only recently gathered momentum. The new National Party leadership of F.W. de Klerk, who had ousted P.W. Botha on 14 August, allowed the march to take place. The end of apartheid was close.

'We have Soweto with us'

By the mid-1970s the opposition United Party was in terminal decline. At 3 a.m. on 24 April 1974 Frederik van Zyl Slabbert of the Progressive Party found himself 'on the roof of a Volkswagen Combi ... surrounded by screaming, cheering and crying people' (Slabbert, *The Last White Parliament*, Johannesburg, 1985, p. 10). Slabbert had just been elected as Progressive Party MP for Rondebosch. His party stood against apartheid and in favour of a complicated but multi-racial and unitary form of parliamentary representation. Apart from Rondebosch, it also won Sea Point and five seats in other cities. Formed in 1959 as an offspring of the United Party, the Progs had been represented in parliament by a lone MP, Helen Suzman, since 1961. This explains the almost millenarian excitement of Slabbert's largely English-speaking supporters, at the possibility that the tide was turning at last in favour of English liberalism and international acceptability. What also contributed to their fervour was Slabbert's youth and Afrikaner background. Here was a more liberal Smuts for the seventies, someone who could bring sufficient of the *volk* to see the errors of their ways, and thereby save South Africa. As the United Party disintegrated, the Progressive Party picked up some deserters. In 1977 it changed its name to the Progressive Federal Party (PFP). (*Argus*, 24 April 1974)

De Klerk's 'Damascus conversion' to democracy – of which Cape Town's march provided an early outward sign – can best be explained as the result of 13 years of urban turmoil and economic decline. After the boom years of the 'silent' 1960s, South Africa – and Cape Town – had experienced two decades of slower growth, violence, isolation and inefficiency. The starting point was economic recession in the mid-1970s, precipitated by a falling gold price and rising inflation in the wake of the OPEC oil-price hike. This spawned unemployment, illegal strikes and the reawakening of a more militant black trade unionism. It was also a factor in the urban uprisings of 1976.

The immediate cause of the demonstration by fifteen thousand Soweto schoolchildren on 16 June 1976 was the government's decision that half the curriculum in African schools should be taught in Afrikaans. But tension was already high because of rapid growth in black school attendance – more than quadrupling in the previous twenty years to over 4 million – and facilities in black schools were far inferior to those for whites. In the Cape, annual government expenditure on education for every African child was R28.56, on every coloured child R199, and on every white child R496. Job prospects for school-leavers were increasingly poor; unemployment had grown to 12 per cent of 'legal' African urban dwellers.[3] The rise of the Black Consciousness movement and the success of anti-colonial movements in neighbouring states had added to feelings of discontent. Even two Cape Town gangs, the Dirty Kids and Panorama Boys, changed their names to the Cuban Kids and MPLA Terrors in solidarity with the forces then fighting an invading South African army in Angola.[4]

Coloured and African student numbers in Cape Town had been boosted by high population growth – by the late 1970s about half of the city's population was under 21 – and the expanded provision of schooling, however flawed. Their radicalism was fuelled by poor job prospects, a result of both recession and racism. Together with recent school-leavers, they formed a new generation full of 'optimistic desperation'. In the struggle against discrimination, they believed that they could succeed where their parents had failed.[5]

When police killed several protesting children in Soweto in June 1976, they sparked off months of violent unrest that eventually swept across the Rand and down to Cape Town. But beyond the headlines in local newspapers, the initial reaction of Capetonians was muted. Significantly, the extent of violence grew dramatically after the beginning of new school and university terms. It was at these institutions that political ideology was most easily transmitted by teachers and older students alike to a new generation of youth, helping to mould their sense of common destiny. With demonstrations banished from other public open spaces, educational institutions provided one of the few venues where mass protest was relatively easy to organise. It is hardly surprising that they became 'sites of struggle', battlegrounds between police and students, into the 1990s.

On 11 August schoolchildren from Langa, Nyanga and Guguletu marched defiantly through the streets of the townships. Influenced by events both on the Rand and at local tertiary institutions, they also had their own particular grievances. For 'security reasons' the police had recently prevented them from studying at night at their schools, where they could have electric light and enjoy more space than at home. Dogs and teargas were used to disperse the marchers, and the hitherto peaceful demonstration turned into full-scale rioting. This continued for 36 hours, with attacks on shops and government buildings, including bottle stores and beer halls, the revenue from which helped pay for segregation.

Police reinforcements were flown to Cape Town from the Witwatersrand and the townships sealed off on the evening of 12 August. But unrest now spread to many coloured schools – some students even went to Guguletu to express solidarity with their African counterparts and taunt the police.[6] Deficiencies of particular schools, especially in poorer areas, and experience of harsh discipline fed this defiance. So did Black Consciousness and youthful or masculine bravado.[7] But violence usually occurred only

The Black Consciousness Movement

The banning of the ANC and PAC criminalised the two main vehicles of black political opposition to apartheid. For some years, joining the multi-racial National Union of South African Students (NUSAS) seemed the only viable option for those at tertiary institutions. But as the 1960s drew to a close, many black members grew increasingly frustrated by what they saw as the cautious policies and white dominance of NUSAS. In 1968 a medical student at Natal University, Steve Biko, began to promote the idea of a parallel black association. The South African Students' Organisation (SASO) was duly established the following year with Biko as its president.[8] Influenced by Pan-Africanism and the American Black Power movement, SASO espoused Black Consciousness – the unity of all blacks, however classified, who needed to be self-reliant and proud of their heritage and culture. In 1972 the Black People's Convention (BPC) became the co-ordinating body for organisations adhering to this philosophy.

Black Consciousness found many adher-

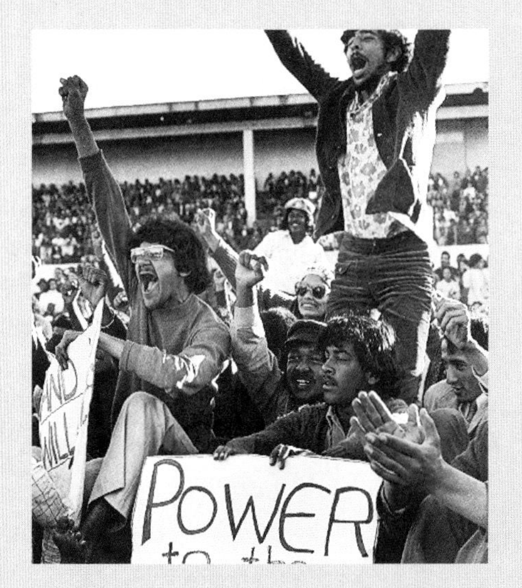

At a Black Consciousness meeting in Athlone in 1973, about 12,000 people attended representing all 'races' in South Africa except whites. (*Argus*, 7 July 1973)

ents in the western Cape especially among teachers, scholars, professionals and the clergy. The ideological legacy of the Non-European Unity Movement had undoubtedly ensured fertile ground. Unity Movement ideas had been recently invigorated by the formation of the South African Council on Sport (SACOS) in 1973. SACOS promoted non-racialism and non-collaboration, and set up its own sports leagues and competitions, though having to make do with hugely inferior funding and facilities. Its local affiliates included a large number of coloured primary and secondary schools.[9] Black Consciousness also found purchase because the experience of removal and social segregation as 'non-whites' – alongside Africans – had helped (at least temporarily) to erode the salience of coloured ethnicity for many. So did the common experience of living on the Cape Flats, novel to those from District Six or the southern suburbs. Black Consciousness was generally more attractive to the young and better-educated from more privileged backgrounds, who felt less threatened by working-class African competition. Indeed, many adopted Afro hairstyles and listened to black American music, while others were attracted to Rastafarianism by the music and lyrics of Jamaican reggae.[10]

By 1972 the majority of members of the Students' Representative Council at the University of the Western Cape (UWC) belonged to SASO. This helps to explain why, on 30 July, a thousand students decided to boycott lectures and 'educate ourselves to the realities of the situation'. One of the matters they wished to consider was the government's rejection of the Theron Commission report on coloured South Africans. This had recommended 'satisfactory' forms of direct representation and the repeal of the Immorality and Mixed Marriages Acts.

On 4 August – the day the government announced a nation-wide ban on open-air meetings – hundreds of UWC students stormed on to Modderdam Road, carrying placards that read 'Save the children of Africa' and 'Fight for freedom'. They were angry at the reaction of some staff members to their boycott, as well as at the detention of one of their number. Although the students moved back to campus when the riot police arrived, the administration block was destroyed by fire bombs on 5 August. UWC remained a 'site of struggle' into the 1980s. (UCT Carnegie collection)

once the police arrived.[11] Thus Bonteheuwel was turned into a battlefield after students demonstrating on school property were teargassed and beaten up. 'Peaceful students protest, but police riot' became a popular slogan on the Cape Flats.[12]

The ban on outdoor meetings was lifted for only one day, 1 September, when a thousand African pupils marched peacefully through central Cape Town. Similar attempts by coloured students over the next few days met with teargas, beatings and birdshot. Demonstrators and opportunistic gangsters then stoned passers-by and smashed car windows as violent confrontations escalated throughout the Peninsula.

White experiences and responses varied. Some whites, like blacks, became victims of violence. Sympathy for black grievances came largely from members of liberal organisations and staff and students at UCT. Several lecturers were banned or detained; while others established a history workshop to monitor events and attempt explanation. A newly founded, multi-racial Women's Movement – aimed at fostering cross-racial contact – expressed concern. In contrast many whites, particularly in the northern suburbs, undoubtedly supported both government policies and police practices.

If most whites were passive spectators, few could ignore what was happening. On finding her car damaged by rioters, the Austrian consul's wife exclaimed: 'One can't even go to the hairdresser these days without encountering trouble.'[13] White tension was heightened in the run-up to worker stayaways planned for 15 and 16 September. After stories circulated that every black had been told to 'kill a white', local newspapers were inundated with calls. Many whites rushed to buy guns, took shooting lessons and patrolled their suburbs, while nightwatchmen were posted at most schools after rumours of arson arose. In the event the docks, bakeries, building sites and clothing factories were hard hit, but the stayaway – observed by about 100,000 African and coloured workers – was largely peaceful.[14] Yet foreign embassies were besieged with enquiries about emigration.[15] The change from 1960 was that fear for many in the suburbs was now ongoing, emigration a dinner-party topic and escalating practice into the 1990s.

By mid-November, a tense calm had been restored to coloured areas; on the other hand African students had successfully called for a boycott of exams. What finally broke even their resistance was the murderous Christmas onslaught of migrant labourers ('bachelors') against townspeople in Nyanga. As in 1960, there were many reports of active police collusion.[16]

The urban uprisings of 1976 shook both the nation and the international community. In all, 128 Capetonians were reported killed, and about 400 injured.[17] The call for change from white businessmen in the country – including government-supporting Afrikaners – intensified in pace with increased foreign outrage and the threat of sanctions. Such businessmen established the Urban Foundation, towards the end of 1976, to help improve housing and community facilities in the locations. By now even a columnist on *Die Burger* was arguing that Africans outside the homelands should be accommodated politically as South African citizens.[18] So did several Stellenbosch professors.[19]

The Diary of Maria Tholo

Maria Tholo was a domestic worker living in Guguletu in 1976. Her accounts of daily life at the time were tape-recorded by a journalist, Carol Hermer. Tholo told of the mixture of respect, admiration and fear that many adults felt when confronted with the township schoolchildren. Of 11 August she related: 'It's happened ... We have Soweto with us ... At first the children were orderly but when the teargas came they saw red. They threw stones at any car that came their way. The buses were also attacked and the lorries – the lot. So there are no more buses coming into Guguletu ... on the road we met a mob of youths, singing and wielding axes and sticks. At first they didn't want to let us through. I waved my fists ... and said "Power!" ... "Black Power" is like a password now.'

Police chase a young boy through Guguletu township. (Mayibuye Centre)

Tholo went on to describe events as they unfolded over the next six months – police shootings, deaths, massively attended funerals, stonings and looting. The story is initially one of excitement mixed with fear, leading to eventual weariness. Men suspected women of telling students where to locate and destroy shebeens and the alcohol that supposedly made men compliant to white supremacy. 'Bachelors' from the single quarters attacked children who tried to prevent them from drinking, and also parents who ignored the stayaway on 15 September. Children attacked real and imagined 'informers', people in cars and anyone disobeying their decisions – be it for stayaways, a boycott of shops outside the townships, or mourning over Christmas.

But Maria Tholo's diary is much more than a chronicle of the troubles. It gives insight into the values and tribulations of a 'respectable' urban African woman in the mid-1970s. Tholo tells of fights over the disappearance of Tupperware party money, of female relatives being forced into marriage, and of menfolk coming home late after a night's drinking. She also details a complex mixture of Western and 'traditional' Xhosa culture in the townships: from Christian and 'traditional' religious beliefs, through the mock stick-fights of young males after circumcision rites, to loudspeakers placed on roof tops while parties raged inside, or trips to Kenilworth horse-races and the Big Walk starting at Simon's Town.[20]

Whites provided most of the media commentaries on civil unrest. Sensing the spatial significance of the city centre – from which the New Year Carnival was now restricted and where the police were less likely to kill demonstrators – a *Sunday Times* journalist believed in September 1976 that 'rioting in the Mother City is a combination of Cloud Cuckoo Land, carnival and mayhem ... never negate the very real violence ... but floating above it all ... is a feeling of excitement, rather akin to a Derde Nuwejaar'. On the same occasion the National Party-supporting newspaper *Die Burger* stated that 'cunning people' had deliberately wished to move rioting beyond black areas, to involve whites and attract more publicity. (*Argus* library)

And there was also considerable concern that whites had managed to alienate their potential coloured allies, that something should be done to remedy this situation. As a Muslim reporter put it while describing the Bonteheuwel riots, this was 'a day people said would never happen. Soweto, yes. Guguletu, Langa, Nyanga, yes. But never a Coloured township. But then it happened.'[21]

'The Past is Theirs, the Future is Ours'

Over the next 13 years the government responded with a combination of repression and reform that deeply affected many aspects of life in Cape Town. As an immediate result of the uprisings, the introduction of Afrikaans as a means of instruction in African schools was abandoned. Instead the government promised to improve teachers' salaries, and provide compulsory schooling and free textbooks. The Department of Bantu Education became the Department of Education and Training (DET). Improvements were also promised in coloured education, though little materialised before renewed disturbances in Cape Flats schools in 1980.[22] Similarly the prime minister, B.J. Vorster, acknowledged the need for African participation in township government. In 1977 financial and administrative authority was given to Community Councils, albeit that they were still under the aegis of white officials.[23]

P.W. Botha, prime minister from 1978, developed the idea that there needed to be a 'total strategy' to deal with the 'total [revolutionary] onslaught' against South Africa. A remodelled State Security Council, first established by Vorster in 1972, became in the 1980s something akin to an alternative cabinet. Yet, encouraged by the captains of white industry and pressurised by growing economic sanctions, Botha made some concessions.[24] His plans to accommodate blacks politically, without conceding the substance of white supremacy, were positively Byzantine. Botha persevered with the concept of independent homelands and influx control, while granting Section 10 urban insiders local self-government through the Black Local Authorities Act of 1982. On the other hand whites, coloureds and Asians were brought within a single parliamentary system, in which the coloured Labour Party decided to participate. In 1983 a whites-only referendum approved the establishment of a tricameral legislature in Cape Town, despite the opposition of the PFP on the left and the newly formed Conservative Party on the right. Crucially, the white majority party controlled the election of an executive state president who was given wide-ranging powers. Botha was duly elevated to this position.[25]

'We do not want chaos in South Africa.'

P.W. Botha, refusing to open cinemas to all races, 1983

As prime minister and then president, Botha demonstrated that he was prepared to abandon much 'petty apartheid' that was 'hurtful and unnecessary'. The process of moving away from the segregation of sport and public amenities had begun in the early 1970s. Many of the initial steps were aimed at escaping international isolation. Thus a 'multi-national' sports policy was unveiled in 1971: international teams could now be mixed, while permits could be granted for matches between South Africans of apartheid's different 'nations'. This allowed the first 'multi-national' life-saving championships to be staged at Milnerton in 1974.[26] Permits were also granted for desegregated spectating at such events.

After the 1976 uprisings the dismantling of 'petty apartheid' accelerated in Cape Town, if often in confusing fashion and without threatening the 'hearth and home' segregation of residential areas and state schools. 'Multi-national' sport was now permitted at provincial and club level – with both mixed and segregated leagues acceptable – and gradually extended to schools. At international level, representative teams could include South Africans of all races.[27] Hotels, clubs and restaurants were able to apply for 'international' status, enabling them to admit all who could afford them. But, demonstrating the bewildering nature of such concessions, a prohibition remained on mixed dancing in licensed premises.

Theatres and Apartheid in the 1970s

In 1975, after local outrage at the provincial government's lavish expenditure on Cape Town's whites-only Nico Malan Theatre – built in 1971 – a permit system was extended to theatres. This allowed the management to apply for government permission to admit multi-racial audiences without imposing segregation. But the principle of segregated audiences was maintained at other places of entertainment. As late as 1983 P.W. Botha still refused to open cinemas to all races because 'We do not want chaos in South Africa'.[28]

The Space Theatre, situated above shops in Charles Freeman's YMCA building in Long Street, was one place that refused to apply for a permit and operated as a private club. Founded by Athol Fugard, Yvonne Bryceland and Brian Astbury in 1972, The Space played a central role in the development of socially conscious and experimental South African music and drama – with Fugard's plays pre-eminent. Apart from Bryceland and Fugard, actors included John Kani, Winston Ntshona, Percy Sieff and Paul Slabolepsky. David Kramer, Amampondo and Steve Newman were some of the musicians showcased there. The theatre changed its name to The People's Space in 1979, but struggled to overcome the difficulty of being situated in the nocturnally moribund city centre. Ill served by public transport and facing competition from UCT's impressive and well-placed Baxter Theatre (built in 1977), The People's Space closed in 1983.[29]

The Space Theatre in the old YMCA building, shortly before it opened in 1976. (*Argus* library)

By the mid-1980s multi-racial political parties were legal, private schools could admit all, and the Mixed Marriages Act and racially discriminatory clauses of the Immorality Act had been abolished. Yet there was often no formal legislation eliminating different kinds of segregation. Much initiative was left to private owners and local authorities. Thus the privately owned Cape Town bus service desegregated in 1977, having learnt that government would not interfere if there was 'no fuss or bother'.[30] But although the Cape Town City Council opened its beaches to all, adjacent councils persisted with segregation into the late 1980s. And even in January 1990 the Volks Hospital in the Gardens

The Aftermath of 1976 and Radical Politics

At a National Party meeting in Maitland protesters heckled the minister of justice, Jimmy Kruger. (*Argus*, 11 November 1977)

The 1976 uprising and government repression made some whites more politically radical, as did the fact that white males now faced two years' military service and the possibility of fighting in Angola. Jimmy Kruger, the minister of justice, was greeted with cries of 'Sieg, heil' and 'Who killed Biko?' by hundreds of UCT students when he addressed a meeting in Maitland in November 1977. For the first time in several decades, a National Party gathering was seriously disrupted and the event closed with a rousing rendition of 'We shall overcome'. Within white Cape Town's social geography, Observatory gradually emerged as the left-wing student quarter, full of communes and activists. It was the 'coolest place' to be.[31]

Biko, defying his banning order, had made a secret visit to Cape Town earlier in the year as part of broader attempts to unify black organisations. Politicians from the Unity Movement tradition refused to see him – arguing that they needed a mandate from supporters before doing so – and he was arrested on his journey back to the eastern Cape. Any faint hopes of black political unity ended with Biko's subsequent death at the hands of the security police on 12 September. A few weeks later Kruger banned 17 Black Consciousness bodies. The formation of the Azanian People's Organisation in 1978 was an attempt to resuscitate the movement, but AZAPO's leaders were swiftly arrested and the party was unable to gather much popular support.

Even in the western Cape this support increasingly went to 'Charterist' organisations, so named because of their adherence to the Congress movement's Freedom Charter. The exiled ANC had benefited from the organisational chaos of the rival PAC and recruited most of the students fleeing from state repression. In turn this helped uMkhonto weSizwe to raise the profile of the ANC within South Africa through escalating guerrilla incursions. These included the much-publicised attacks on Sasolburg oil refinery and Voortrekkerhoogte military base at the beginning of the 1980s – just as a Johannesburg newspaper, *The Post*, was running a Release Mandela campaign and popularising the Freedom Charter. At the same time the slightly more relaxed political atmosphere of the early Botha years meant that living icons of the ANC's 1950s defiance, like Helen Joseph and Oscar Mpetha, resurfaced to inform the new militant generation of their party's traditions.[32]

refused to admit a domestic servant who needed urgent surgery 'because the three beds reserved for blacks ... were full'.[33]

Many black Capetonians were unimpressed by both social and political reforms. In February 1977 Maria Tholo commented, 'So you can go to the same toilet ... but you can't go to the same school which is much more important when our schools are so crowded and have less funds.'[34] Most supporters of the South African Council on Sport held similar sentiments, hardened by the events of 1976. Hassan Howa, SACOS cricket president, claimed that through their participation in the uprising 'our children have given us a clear mandate not to co-operate [in the new sports dispensation] ... we cannot ignore them'. Talks with white officials of the South African Cricket Association over possible unification were abandoned. Instead SACOS coined the slogan 'No normal sport in an abnormal society' and passed the 'double standard resolution'. This prohibited a person from playing one sport under SACOS jurisdiction and another in a 'multinational' league. But particularly in Cape Town, many SACOS supporters took it to mean that they should not frequent any establishment that respected the new permit system, whether stadiums, theatres or cinemas, and ostracised people who did.[35]

The popularity of the SACOS slogan on the Cape Flats reflected the politically galvanising effect of the 1976 uprising. Another factor was the increasingly strong and well-publicised anti-apartheid stand taken by Muslim and Christian bodies, notably the South African Council of Churches, which was headed by Bishop Desmond Tutu from 1978. Mutually stimulating action by radical trade unions, by school students and by numerous 'civic' associations had thrust Cape Town to the forefront of the anti-apartheid struggle by the early 1980s. The strength of popular resistance was first demonstrated by the extent of both African and coloured community support for militant trade-union activity.

Group Areas removals had been a further element in coloured politicisation, with people involved becoming prominent in initiating civic organisations in their new localities. The largest on the Cape Flats was the model 'dormitory suburb' of Mitchell's Plain, about twenty miles from the city centre, which grew from 56 dwellings in 1976 to over 33,000 by 1989: 'Monotonous rows of small, neat houses stretched for miles between awesomely wide thoroughfares. The houses were in general dreary but, by black stan-

Below left: Mrs Magdeline Daniels in her Mitchell's Plain home. (*Argus* library, *c.* 1978)

Below: Housing in Atlantis reflected the bleak employment conditions of the area. (UCT Carnegie collection; photo by Chris Ledochowski)

Opposite: One person who felt the wrath of SACOS hardliners was the Cape Town cricketer Omar Henry, a member of the black Western Province team in the 1976/7 season. While in Durban for an away match he was one of several players who watched ten minutes of a South African Cricket Association game. On his return he was brought before a disciplinary hearing in front of 150 SACOS supporters who greeted him with cries of 'traitor' and refused to let him speak. Together with the other offenders, Henry was given a life ban and later received death threats. He switched to multi-racial sport and, relishing the far superior facilities, became the first black cricketer to play for the predominantly white Western Province team in 1980. He went on to play for South Africa and Scotland. (O. Henry, *The Man in the Middle*, Durban, 1994, p. 160)

dards, "middle-class" – the government liked to show off Mitchell's Plain to overseas visitors. Like apartheid itself, the huge, half-finished project had the slightly dazed, unlikely quality of cheapskate futurism.'[36] Another huge development was Atlantis – planned almost as a separate 'ethno-city', complete with its own huge industrial area – to the north of Cape Town. In 1977 it was 'envisaged that by the year 2010 Atlantis will house 500,000 people in six separate towns ... For the next four years, 2,000 homes a year are planned.'[37]

The gold-driven economic recovery of the late 1970s and early 1980s saw the revival of ex-South African Congress of Trade Unions affiliates in the western Cape, like the Food and Canning Workers' Union. They declined to apply for registration under the government's new labour dispensation. In April 1979, 78 workers went on strike at a Fatti's & Moni's pasta factory in Bellville South after 10 fellow workers had been dismissed for refusing to resign from the African Food and Canning Workers' Union. Many people throughout the Cape Flats, including the Western Cape Traders' Association, a body of African small retailers, supported a seven-month boycott of Fatti's & Moni's products and contributed to union funds. The company's profits were halved, and the strikers won the battle.[38] Two more 'communal' campaigns followed in 1980. Public donations to workers helped force Table Bay Cold Storage into allowing them to belong to the Western Cape General Workers' Union, after a struggle lasting from May to August. And although striking abattoir labourers failed to gain 'democratic representation', they received funding of R100,000 and communal support for a boycott of red meat.[39]

The red meat boycott in May – as well as a boycott against fare increases on City Tramways buses in June – received the active backing of school students, who used

Spring Queen Festival

In May 1980 there was a strike at the Rex Trueform clothing factory in Woodstock, which was soon settled when management brought forward a wage increase promised for the end of the year. But the family atmosphere that had characterised relations between management and workers in previous decades was under threat. This was partly due to the growing scale of plants, stagnating real wages and the gradual recruitment of 'struggle generation' school-leavers: 'They were rude! ... no respect for anyone ... These girls *mos* thought they knew everything.' But also important was the increasing militancy and success of 'community' unions in other industries, one of which, the Clothing Workers' Union, challenged the Garment Workers' Union's closed shop arrangement. It was apparently under these circumstances, and with SACOS endangering factory sports leagues, that managers gave increasingly enthusiastic and material support to an industry-wide Spring Queen Festival beauty pageant. First organised at the end of the 1970s, these became major events by the mid-1980s, with activities lasting from July to November. The contests themselves, usually held in Main Road's Space Odyssey disco by the end of the decade, were carnivalesque: 'supervisors dressed as Miss Piggy, mechanics dressed as beauty contestants, Hawaiian dancers, cabaret stars and even a director as a Zulu warrior.' According to an ex-manager, they allowed 'the healing of wounds', as rivalry between factories bred loyalty while the contestants themselves were drawn from the 'difficult' generation. These 'proletarian Cinderellas' could now aspire to become feminine 'royalty', fêted by management and colleagues alike, and win prizes of modelling contracts or holiday trips to Sun City.[40]

Janine Meyer from Wolpe, Jacqueline Paulse of Bonuit (Lansdowne) and Elize Gazar of Val-Hau were proud winners of the Spring Queen Festival in 1989. (*Argus* library)

school presses to print pamphlets. The students had been involved in new conflicts of their own since February. These began at much the same time in African and coloured schools, but over different problems. Students at Fezeka Senior Secondary in Guguletu complained about the expense of uniforms and the shortage of textbooks, issues that had been raised for all DET schools by the recently formed Congress of South African Students. Coloured pupils in Hanover Park and Parkwood Estate deplored the dreadful state of their schools, as well as the shortage of stationery. School buildings were mostly prefabricated and poorly insulated, without electricity. They had been erected during Group Areas removals and badly damaged during the 1976 riots, with desks and windows broken, and glass scattered across the playgrounds. On 12 February more than 100 students boycotted classes for twenty-four hours at Mount View school in Hanover Park, and two days later 800 Fezeka pupils did the same.[41]

Presumably because of the memory of 1976, these protests received swift remedial attention from the authorities. Repairs were immediately promised at Mount View, while fees were reduced at Fezeka and pupils given until April to buy their uniforms. But one of the differences in the nature of student protests in 1980, compared with 1976, was the early evidence of much greater organisation and direction. Both Charterist and AZAPO activists, along with religious leaders, were present at Hanover Park meetings held on 13 and 20 March against 'gutter education' and dissolute teachers. In addition,

The Emergence of Civics

The proliferation of civics, numbering about 32 by 1982, was encouraged both by the schools boycott and by the new monthly journal *Grassroots*. This was an avowedly 'alternative' left-wing newspaper with contributors like Trevor Manuel and Johnny Issel, both to become prominent political figures.[42] Civics were usually established by a small number of relatively affluent residents to fight cost-of-living increases and demand better facilities in their neighbourhoods. Early campaigns concentrated on bread and butter issues. They began with local demands – for the due dates of electricity accounts to be changed in Mitchell's Plain or for better council-house maintenance in Bonteheuwel – before escalating into a general campaign against rent increases. By 1982 three umbrella organisations had been formed to co-ordinate action: the Charterist-oriented (coloured) Cape Housing Action Committee and (African) Western Cape Civic Association, and the Unity Movement-aligned Federation of Cape Civic Associations.[43]

Above: Trevor Manuel. (Mayibuye Centre)

Right: Civics formed the core of the UDF, whose patron was Allan Boesak. (UCT Carnegie collection)

Coloured high schools and a 'Culture of Revolution'

William Finnegan, a 27-year-old Californian surfing enthusiast, spent 1980 in Cape Town pursuing his hobby and teaching. He described his experiences at Grassy Park Senior Secondary School, situated in a somewhat more prosperous part of the Cape Flats, in his book *Crossing the Line* (London, 1987). Finnegan discovered his pupils' enthusiasm for sport and organised religion: '"church" ... was choral societies, picnics, film shows, fund raisers, youth groups. "Mosque" ... an endless round of Koran classes, special observances, and social obligations.' They listened to Abba, Boney M and Michael Jackson. In the course of the boycott, Finnegan's students – like their counterparts at other schools – organised 'awareness programmes' with the help of sympathetic teachers. There were classes on 'the non-racial sporting movement ... the *sestigers* [1960s avant-garde Afrikaner writers, like André Brink] ... women's issues ... the fall of Allende's Chile ... Khoisan culture ... the tradition of black resistance ... [and] rock-'n'-roll music'. Screenings of films such as *If*, about revolt in a British school, and *Nicholas and Alexandra* were arranged. Students held rallies and 'songfests', and wrote and staged their own plays. Many featured security police 'buffoons ... destroyed by The People – a part usually taken by the audience itself'. Finnegan recounted both the students' intolerance of dissenting voices and the development, in language, 'signs and symbols', of a 'subculture of revolution'.

Above: Political meeting at South Peninsula High School, Diep River. (Mayibuye Centre)

Right: Nigel Penn, a teacher ('Alex Tait' in *Crossing the Line*), with students at Grassy Park Senior Secondary in 1980.

Two white motorists were stoned and torched to death by a large crowd of youths on Klipfontein Road on 11 August 1980. Tension was already high in African communities because of the school and bus boycotts. But on that day a church service was held at Nyanga's Assembly of God church to commemorate the beginning of the 1976 uprisings in Cape Town's townships. Youths reportedly left the service vowing to attack cars driven by whites. (*Argus* library)

a joint parent and student committee was formed to keep the issue alive. Matters came to a head with the dismissal of three white members of staff from Hanover Park's Crystal Senior Secondary School, for supposedly encouraging pupil disaffection. Amid a flurry of pamphlets denouncing 'education for domination', a broader meeting of 'student leaders' called for a boycott of classes until the dismissed three were reinstated, students' representative councils were allowed and education improved.

The boycott began on 14 April. By the end of the week it involved Fezeka and 30 coloured schools, with over 25,000 students affected. Soon a Commitee of 61 (later the Committee of 81) was elected by Peninsula schools, whether boycotting or not, to direct proceedings against what they called 'training for cheap labour'. Numerous local 'civic' organisations held meetings at which parents expressed solidarity.

Some parents or grandparents were activists themselves – 'the old-style politicians of the Cape Flats', whether from a Unity Movement or Charterist background – who displayed 'extraordinary eloquence in English. Bejewelled phrases, packed in tremendous Victorian sentences, tripped off their tongues.'[44] The meetings were also addressed by students as young as 13, and by religious leaders, notably Dr Allan Boesak of the Dutch Reformed Sendingkerk. The Students' Representative Council at UCT, teachers' associations and local SACOS affiliates pledged their support.[45] The rhetoric of student discussions and pamphlets shifted in the course of the boycott from a rejection of disadvantaged education – expressed in the singing of a British rock band's lyrics 'We don't need no education, We don't need no thought control' – to a Marxist analysis of apartheid: 'the struggle ... is ... not against white domination ALONE, but ALSO against the whole system of class exploitation which underlines it'.[46] This was undoubtedly encouraged by the convergence of strikes with the school boycott, as well as by the input of adult activists.

Fearing the bloodshed of 1976, the Committee of 61 insisted that demonstrations be confined to school grounds. But many pupils expressed the desire to 'do something', and to take the struggle to 'the white areas'. When they tried – with a march in Athlone on 21 April and a demonstration in the Golden Acre shopping precinct in central Cape Town in May – their gatherings were predictably, and violently, broken up by police. And if protests at schools occurred within 'sight of a highway', they faced the same fate. By June the mood among parents and many adult activists had turned against the boycott, which stalled in coloured schools just as it was gathering momentum in African ones. After the winter break, coloured schoolchildren returned to classes while an

Up to 15,000 people, including 1500 delegates, attended the UDF's national launch at Rocklands Community Centre in Mitchell's Plain on 20 August 1983. Allan Boesak, a UDF patron, declared: 'We want all our rights, we want them here and we want them now.' Of the 565 registered affiliates – largely student and youth groups, women's organisations and civics – 358 came from the western Cape. Although this region's executive committee was predominantly coloured – and included Trevor Manuel, Cheryl Carolus and Chris Nissen – Oscar Mpetha was elected president and Andrew Boraine, of NUSAS, one of the treasurers. Slogans became simple vehicles for expressing UDF ideology. Two of the more popular were 'Apartheid divides, the UDF unites' and 'The past is theirs, the future is ours'.

Early UDF activities included a 'People's weekend' of motorcades and mass meetings, as well as religious, sporting and musical events. According to Trevor Manuel, their purpose was 'to relate people's individual conditions to oppression' (cited in Francis, 'The past is theirs', p. 32). (UCT Carnegie collection; photo by Paul Weinberg)

African boycott lasted until March 1981.[47]

The events of 1980 paved the way for the re-emergence of broad political movements. In 1982 both Charterist and Unity Movement organisations were represented on a Disorderly Bills Action Group. Its purpose was to oppose new government legislation aimed at entrenching divisions between homeland Africans and those with Section 10 rights to reside in South African cities. But Charterist organisations withdrew once Unity Movement supporters objected to working with black business groups and whites in NUSAS and the Black Sash – 'the children and wives of factory bosses'.[48]

The Unity Movement rump renamed itself the Cape Action League (CAL). Its guiding spirits were the ex-Robben Islander Neville Alexander and the SACOS president, Frank van der Horst. Alexander played a prominent role in June 1983 in the launch of the National Forum, which linked CAL with AZAPO against Botha's new tricameral constitution. But, with echoes of the 1950s, their efforts were surpassed by those of the more popular Charterist organisations. At the instigation of Allan Boesak, these were soon combined in the United Democratic Front (UDF).[49]

Unlike the National Forum, the ideologically catholic and non-racial UDF plunged immediately into a series of campaigns that suggested it was not just a talker but a doer. They included a largely successful call for a boycott of coloured and African local elections, a drive to collect a million signatures against the new constitution, and a mass meeting against the removal of Crossroads squatters to Khayelitsha. Although most trade unions kept their distance and concentrated on work-place concerns, the UDF's strategy appealed particularly to young opponents of apartheid. National Forum advocates dubbed many UDF efforts 'populist' – predicting they would not lead to social revolution – yet had few attractive alternatives to offer of their own. After co-operating briefly with the UDF in working for a boycott of the tricameral parliamentary elections, the Forum ceased to have much public impact.

The Western Cape Rebellion

Although 14 UDF leaders were detained shortly before the elections in August 1984, only 29 per cent of all registered coloured voters in the country and 19 per cent of Indians went to the polls. The percentages were even smaller in Cape Town. In September violence broke out in Transvaal townships – spearheaded by UDF-aligned civics and boycotting schoolchildren – aimed at the recently elected, often corrupt black community councillors. The cause was supported by the powerful Federation of South

Khayelitsha

In the spirit of P.W. Botha's other reform initiatives, the Bantu Affairs Department was first renamed Plural Relations and then Co-operation and Development. Botha's new minister, Dr Piet Koornhof, promised more enlightened treatment for black urban insiders while persisting with influx control. He embarked on negotiations with Crossroads residents aimed at either upgrading the settlement or providing an acceptable alternative. Some brick houses were built nearby at New Crossroads, and rented out to 'legals' who could afford them. The unintentional result was to attract squatters recently removed from other parts of the Peninsula, refugees from overcrowded townships and more job-seekers from the eastern Cape. Despite intensifying pass raids and arrests, this led to a proliferation of shanties in the vicinity of Old Crossroads – KTC, Nyanga Extension, Nyanga Bush and Portland Cement – and the overall population grew to around 80,000 in the mid-1980s. In 1983 Koornhof appeared to backtrack on his promises to Crossroads residents by announcing that all 'legal' residents of the Cape Peninsula – whether in squatter camps or existing townships – would be accommodated in a vast 3220-hectare site to the south-east, between the N2 and False Bay, to be called Khayelitsha, or 'New Place'. In 1984 the National Party's Cape Congress resolved to drop the Coloured Labour Preference policy, and to allow Khayelitsha residents to apply for 99-year leaseholds. But the estimated 100,000 'illegals' in the Peninsula would be 'repatriated' to their homelands.

Early Khayelitsha. (Mayibuye Centre)

The initial intention was to create four towns, each with 30,000 residents in brick houses, some of which would be privately owned. Space was allotted for schools, clinics and shops – but not industries – and a rail link to Cape Town was planned. By 1986, some 8300 people occupied 4150 site-and-service plots at 'Site C' and a further 13,000 rented 5000 tiny core houses on plots of 160 square metres in 'Town 1'. At Site B, 99-year leasehold housing was also being developed.

In 1990 the population of Khayelitsha was estimated at 450,000 and unemployment at 80 per cent. Roughly 14 per cent lived in core houses, 54 per cent in serviced shacks, and 32 per cent in unserviced ones. Hardly anyone had electricity, and most inhabitants had to fetch water from taps. Social control was largely maintained by unofficial, popularly elected councils – serving a limited number of streets or houses – with powers to use physical punishment on children and adults.[50]

African Trade Unions (FOSATU), which organised a massive stayaway of over a million workers in November. Councillors used 'vigilante' hirelings to protect themselves, and the death toll rose as insurgency spread to many parts of the country. In January the ANC lent its support by urging 'the people' to 'render South Africa ungovernable'. The government responded by sending troops into the townships and, on 21 July 1985, imposing a State of Emergency on the Witwatersrand and eastern Cape.

As a result of the heightened political activity of recent months, UWC and UCT students as well as pupils from a large number of coloured and African schools in Cape Town were boycotting classes and organising rallies within a matter of days. The sense of desperation in black communities introduced by the political crisis was deepened by

On 16 October 1985, the day after the 'Trojan horse' deaths, there were bloody clashes at a mosque. A large crowd had gathered to demand the bodies for immediate burial, and another man was shot. Many Muslims began to wear 'Arafat scarves', as Richard Rive described them, with the militant connotations of Middle East conflicts – useful for concealing identity and affording some relief against teargas. (UCT Carnegie collection; photo by D. Hartman)

a prolonged economic depression that had begun in 1982, when unemployment already stood at 6 per cent overall, and up to 14 per cent in some coloured areas.[51] Most of the growing number of unemployed thereafter were between 16 and 25 years old: 'Every fourth person in Mitchell's Plain, every second person in Atlantis,' as a student pamphlet put it.[52] The official housing backlog for greater Cape Town, already estimated at 46,000 in 1980, was also increasing.[53]

But there was a strong sense among many of the insurrectionists of 1985 that at last the government was vulnerable, that the end of apartheid was at hand. This feeling was inspired by P.W. Botha's resort to the State of Emergency, and because his rejection of foreign calls for fundamental change had precipitated a financial crisis. Consequently some white businessmen met the ANC in Lusaka, which only nourished the idea that the government was undergoing a widespread crisis of legitimacy. So did Tony Heard's editorial decision to defy censorship laws and publish an interview with Oliver Tambo, the ANC president-in-exile, in the *Cape Times*.[54]

Anticipation of early victory was reflected on the Cape Flats in new slogans like 'Liberation before education' and leaflets that saw the Emergency as 'the last kick of a dying animal'.[55] A galvanising moment came on 28 August. Having banned the Congress of South African Students (COSAS) and detained Allan Boesak, the police blocked UDF marchers – heading from Guguletu, Athlone Stadium, Kromboom Road and UCT campus – intent on reaching Pollsmoor Prison in Tokai. They were demanding the release of Nelson Mandela, moved there from Robben Island to be closer to medical facilities. Resulting clashes left 8 people dead, scores wounded and 29 arrested, including several nuns. One clergyman, Jan de Waal of the Dutch Reformed Sendingkerk, had his glasses smashed by a police baton and lost the sight in his right eye.[56] Protests now developed into violent revolt – well described by Richard Rive in his novel *Emergency Continued* – with parents assisting their children to set up street barricades in numerous Cape Flats streets. Such direct action – absent in 1976 and 1980 – was encouraged by what residents experienced or heard of shootings and torture by police. Marlene Bailey, the mother of

After a protest march against the State of Emergency, UCT students tried to protect themselves from quirt-wielding policemen on the Main Road in Rondebosch. (Mayibuye Centre)

The 'Trojan horse' incident in Athlone. Ten security force members hid in crates on the back of a truck driving down Thornton Road. When attacked by stone-throwers, they opened fire, killing Michael Miranda (11), Shaum Magmoed (16) and Jonathan Classan (21). (*Argus* library)

a 13-year-old boy killed in Mitchell's Plain on 29 August, recalled that after finding her son's body a policeman told her: 'Los die vark af' [Leave the pig alone].[57] Lines of a student song became increasingly popular: 'Al die mammas and die pappas, die boeties en die sussies, die oumas en die oupas, die hondjies en die katjies – almal is saam in die struggle.'[58]

In desperation the government closed coloured schools on 6 September, only to reopen them on 1 October, after parents and students had already effected a 'reoccupation'. The revolt in coloured areas reached a climax following the 'Trojan horse' shootings in Athlone on 15 October. But rioting was eventually brought under control after the State of Emergency was extended to the western Cape on 26 October, conferring almost limitless powers on the security forces – embracing the ability to ban even indoor meetings – and restricting media coverage. Students also faced end-of-year exams. When some attempted to disrupt these, thousands were detained, including an entire Lotus River school.[59]

At the same time violence was increasing in African areas, fanned both by security force actions and by internal conflicts. By November 1985, one clinic in Crossroads alone had treated 500 people for shotgun wounds.[60] On 3 March 1986 seven uMkhonto weSizwe guerrillas were ambushed by police outside a men's hostel in Guguletu. Several witnesses saw one man shot after raising his hands to surrender, while another was 'finished off' at close range. About 30,000 people attended the funeral, ANC flags were displayed and speakers defied a ban on political orations.[61]

Scores of people had been killed by 12 June 1986, when the government announced a new, nation-wide State of Emergency. Yet in April 1986, almost unnoticed in the drama of surrounding events, Botha had made his most important retreat from apartheid. Although retaining the concept of homeland citizenship, he had abolished influx control.

'Christmas against the Emergency'. Although relative calm had descended on coloured areas by the end of 1985, many households lit candles at Christmas time in protest against the continued State of Emergency. (UCT Carnegie collection; photo by D. Hartman)

Crossroads conflicts and the end of influx control

Conflict in the Crossroads area had its origins in the rise to power of Johnson Ngxobongwana as head of a residents' committee consisting exclusively of males in 1979. This he turned into his personal fiefdom, raising numerous taxes by means of which he could reward himself and his male enforcers with salaries and 'community cars'. As a Women's Committee member recalled, 'the men decided to have one committee and kick the women away ... when I look deep into things it was this ... that brought all the corruption.' In the early 1980s a power struggle developed between Ngxobongwana and some of his past supporters, notably his former vice-chairman, Oliver Memani. This developed in 1983 into bloody clashes that soon spread into surrounding camps like KTC. Ngxobongwana's supporters distinguished themselves by wearing bits of white cloth, or *witdoeke*. Some people fled to Khayelitsha to avoid the violence. Yet, ironically, the UDF welcomed Ngxobongwana – now head of the Western Cape Civic Association – into its fold as the leading opponent of forced removals to Khayelitsha.

Right: Crossroads and surrounding informal settlements.

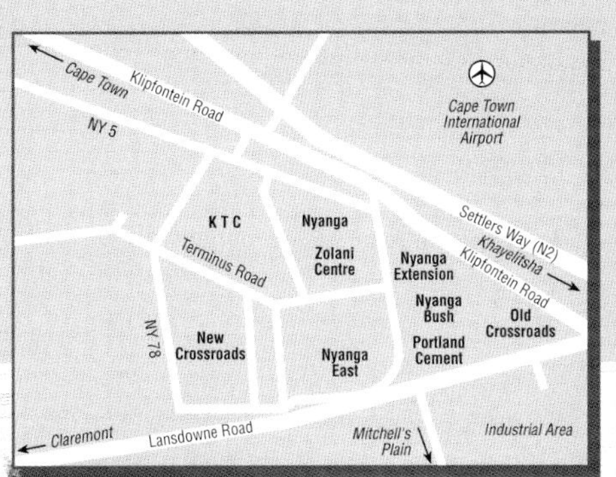

Below: Witdoeke, wearing their distinguishing white armbands, supported by the police, seen here attacking KTC residents. (Mayibuye Centre)

In January 1985, UDF affiliates – the Cape Youth Congress (CAYCO) and United Women's Organisation – helped organise a rent boycott in New Crossroads. This led to Ngxobongwana's arrest. In his absence, CAYCO extended its influence into Old Crossroads and publicised the way community taxes had been spent by Ngxobongwana's committee. Initially they gained the support of the headmen, who administered small sections of the camp. But on his return in July, Ngxobongwana won back the headmen's support – partly by turning on his own committee members – and began a campaign to root out the UDF-supporting *amaqabane*, or 'comrades'. Lending urgency to his efforts was a new government promise of R2 million for the upgrading of Old Crossroads and the belief that this would require more land.

Ngxobongwana regained some popular following, particularly among older people, when the comrades used violence in compelling residents to boycott white shops – transgressors were beaten or made to drink fish oil or washing powder. Comrades also killed a number of 'sell-outs', some by the notorious 'necklace' method – a flaming car tyre hung around their neck – endorsed by Winnie Mandela. In March 1986, nine of Ngxobongwana's supporters and two policemen were killed in the Crossroads area. This seems to have cemented co-operation between members of the security forces and the *witdoeke*, who were allowed to use their own illegal guns as well as those taken from dead comrades. The security forces sealed off the vicinity and, between 17 May and 12 June, protected Ngxobongwana's followers as they set fire to all the shanty settlements surrounding Old Crossroads, rendering about 60,000 people homeless. Many moved 'voluntarily' to a tent town near Site C in Khayelitsha nicknamed Green Point. Others, sheltered temporarily by churches and mosques, attempted to rebuild their shacks in the Crossroads area in subsequent months. In all, at least 59 people had been killed in the winter onslaught; the security forces requested R3000 for a 'victory celebration' by the *witdoeke*. In 1987 Crossroads officially acquired the status of an African local authority, under an Act of 1982, with Ngxobongwana as its first mayor. He was ousted in 1990 by a former fellow *witdoek* and new convert to the ANC, Jeffrey Nongwe. Nongwe was at the centre of renewed violent struggles for control of the area towards the end of 1993, but was incapacitated by a traffic accident in 1995. By then residents were combining in reconstruction programmes like the Crossroads Development Forum, and hoping that conflict lay in the past.[62]

The State of Emergency declared on 12 June 1986 brought thousands more detentions and was renewed annually until 1991. Under its provisions the media could no longer report 'unrest incidents' directly, but only relay the brief official bulletins. A National Security Management System was imposed on African areas until 1988, able to override any other form of local authority. Control was bolstered by the swift recruitment of township policemen (*kitskonstabels*) and continued sponsorship of conservative vigilantes. The UDF was effectively banned in February 1988, and the same fate befell the radical Cape Town newspapers *Grassroots* and *New Era*.[63]

The events of 1985 and 1986 seemed to have presaged a dreadful future for Cape Town and the country at large. Rebellion may have been contained by 1988, but international pressure, a severely ailing economy and the government's failure to accommodate black South Africans in a satisfactory political dispensation meant that deadlock had been reached.

Yet the very impasse between government forces and their opponents was the reason why a negotiated settlement became possible – the more so when military reversals in

A significant moment came in September 1986 when Desmond Tutu – a leading opponent of the government since his election as general secretary of the South African Council of Churches in 1978 – was enthroned as archbishop of Cape Town. He urged whites to become more involved in peaceful protests and all Christians to disobey unjust laws, and held 'political' services in St George's Cathedral. In February 1988, together with the Catholic archbishop and Methodist president, he was briefly arrested while attempting to march to parliament in protest against the banning of political organisations. While immensely popular among blacks, Tutu often provoked unfavourable reactions from whites during the apartheid era. Graffito on busy Edinburgh Drive, near his Bishopscourt home, read, 'I was an Anglican until I put Tu and Tu together'. Yet by the late 1990s Tutu, then chairman of the Truth and Reconciliation Commission, was hailed even by most former opponents for his tireless advocacy of inter-racial understanding. In 1998 he became a freeman of the city of Cape Town. (Katy Raddatz)

End Conscription Campaign

(UCT Carnegie collection)

In 1983 a small number of white conscientious objectors – who faced severe penalties for refusing to serve in the defence force – heeded a call from the Black Sash and launched the End Conscription Campaign (ECC). In August 1984 the ECC 'declaration' maintained that conscripts were used to defend apartheid, assist the illegal occupation of Namibia, and wage war on the frontline states. Most Cape Town ECC recruits were English-speaking, middle-class university students, and over half were women. In August 1985, despite the arrest of its regional chairman, Michael Evans, the western Cape ECC conducted a highly publicised Troops Out (of the townships) campaign. The centrepiece was a 21-day fast by Ivan Toms – a Crossroads clinic doctor who was later jailed for resisting conscription – in St George's Cathedral. This culminated in Toms's addressing a packed City Hall meeting in April 1986. In January, the Cape Town ECC had used innovative publicity techniques in opposing the annual call-up. A dummy was tied to the war memorial on the Heerengracht and 40 supporters wearing 'Stop the call-up' T-shirts built a gigantic sandcastle in the shape of the Castle – headquarters of the defence force's western Cape command – on Clifton's Fourth Beach. Police ordered them to destroy it. The May 1986 Emergency outlawed calls for an end to conscription, which greatly hampered subsequent ECC campaigns, and gave security police free rein to intimidate members. The organisation was effectively banned in August 1988.[64]

The versatile academic Keith Gottschalk wrote a poem to commemorate the police shooting of Ashley Kriel (an uMkhonto weSizwe cadre) on 7 July 1987 in Hazendal, and his subsequent funeral in Bonteheuwel (*Upfront*, 8 February 1988). One stanza read:

Our movement is moved to action by
your dying:
when they handcuffed you, beat you,
threw you out the door face down,
shot you in the back–
the killing of a comrade means much
work.

Stephen Watson, a liberal opponent of apartheid, defended cultural aestheticism. Watson's collection of poems *In This City* (Cape Town, 1986) provided portraits of Cape Town in the mid-1980s. These are the last two stanzas of the final poem, 'Coda':

For years you've walked a place,
through a peninsula of light,
passing through days and lives that
are nothing but their pain.
For years you've lived divided,
darkened by the same divisions,
have lived so long with these
extremes torturing each other,
tearing you apart,
that a city can now start, can finally
speak through you

Of that bleakness like no other in its
wind and blander lives,
of the beauty that is seasonal in its
big-clouded winters,
of this city of your origins, this city
where you'll surely end,
and of the life it gave you, that, for
the first time now
lives joined in you, is life itself:
painful, incomparable.

Angola in 1987–8 led to the waning influence of the 'securocrats' in the National Party. Unbeknown to Capetonians, the minister of justice had visited Nelson Mandela at the Volks Hospital in the Gardens in November 1985. This set in motion a tortuous process of secret talks between the government and the ANC. At the same time Mandela was prepared for release with surreptitious trips around the city – one of his warders even took him for a stroll on the Sea Point beachfront.[65]

Given the restrictions placed on lay opposition, religious leaders, church buildings and funerals played an increasingly prominent role in Cape Town resistance during the 1980s. So did drama, music and poetry, at a time when the ANC was promoting an international academic and cultural boycott of South Africa. By 1987 both the Congress of South African Writers and the South African Musicians' Alliance helped harness local 'culture' to the UDF cause. The concept of 'people's education' was promoted in schools and universities.[66] Yet some liberal opponents of apartheid were concerned that such developments could submerge artistic aesthetics beneath 'relevance' or propaganda, and lead to political and cultural intolerance. The violent disruption in October 1986 of a UCT lecture given by the Irish academic Conor Cruise O'Brien – who had described the academic boycott as 'Mickey Mouse stuff' – sharpened this opinion, and the debate over what constituted academic freedom in an unfree society.[67] One student pamphlet calling for action had certainly been uncompromising: 'to the oppressed and exploited masses, O'Brien is a stinking scoundrel ... Down with racism and "liberalism"!!! Kick O'Brien out, now!!!'[68]

Picnic at Blouberg

One of the classic postcard images of modern Cape Town is the view of Table Mountain from Bloubergstrand. Its whites-only beach was the site of a protest 'picnic' on 19 August 1989. A participant, Tony Karon, described how 'Frisbees floated lazily through the air. Anti-military sandcastles were built. The beach was a carnival of games – everything from relatively serious football to hop-scotch. Mothers on large woollen blankets dispensed goodies to their *laaities* ... a solitary banner proclaiming defiance looked almost incongruous amidst the tranquillity.' Then police waded in with quirts, to the cheers of brandy-and-Coke-swilling locals. The same fate befell protesters gathered at the Strand, near Somerset West, who had struggled to gain access to the beach. The authorities had cordoned it off for 'police dog-training'.[69]

(*Argus* library)

A water cannon spewed jets of purple dye – dubbed 'purple rain' by the public (after the title of a song by Prince) – and knocked protesters and onlookers alike off their feet. Anyone marked by this dye was arrested. Altogether 500 people – including 51 journalists and some startled tourists – were ferried to Caledon Square police station. The graffito soon appeared on a wall in Observatory: 'The Purple shall govern'. (Obed Zilwa)

Notwithstanding friction between liberals and radicals, opponents of apartheid were in the numerical ascendancy throughout Cape Town – outside of the northern suburbs – by 1989. The PFP's successor, the Democratic Party, won all the city, southern and Atlantic suburbs seats in the white general election of that year. Cape Town's mayor and councillors had already come out in favour of an 'open city' and on 11 June, together with two thousand other people, had walked from Rondebosch to District Six for the cause – keeping just within the law. There they were entertained by David Kramer, one of the composers of the recent (and hugely successful) musical that lamented the destruction of District Six.[70]

It was with the likelihood of considerable white support that a pro-ANC Mass Democratic Movement (MDM) – successor to the banned UDF and bolstered by the

inclusion of the Congress of South African Trade Unions (COSATU) – launched a new defiance campaign against remaining social segregation on 2 August.[71]

The defiance campaign intensified as parliamentary elections, scheduled for 6 September, drew close. On 1 September several groups of clerics and academics gathered to demand the right to protest. All were arrested, and some of the clerics were badly beaten by the police. So were many members of COSATU as they demonstrated throughout the Peninsula against a new Labour Relations Act. On 2 September attempted marches to parliament were broken up by police using teargas, quirts and a water cannon.[72] On election night itself, most Cape Flats townships were turned into battlefields. Police used teargas and shotguns to disperse crowds that had formed largely in response to their presence. As many as 23 people were killed, about 100 more wounded.[73] This made the peaceful march of 13 September all the more remarkable.

Because of the secrecy surrounding talks with the ANC, President De Klerk's unbanning of all political organisations in February 1990 – and ensuing release of political prisoners – took Capetonians and the world by surprise. The abolition of the Group Areas Act followed in 1991, and in 1992 the government unveiled plans that began the gradual process of removing statutory discrimination from state schools.

But the years of negotiations were marked by frequent violence instigated by forces across the political spectrum. Three events in the second half of 1993 rocked Cape Town in particular. In July, members of the PAC's Azanian People's Liberation Army (APLA) used rifles and hand-grenades to attack a multi-racial congregation in St James's Church, Kenilworth – later claiming in mitigation that whites had in the past used Bibles and churches to oppress Africans. In all, 11 worshippers were killed and a further 58 injured. A month later, an American Fulbright scholar, Amy Biehl, was stoned and stabbed to death by young PAC supporters inspired by the party's slogan 'One settler, one bullet'. And at the end of the year another APLA attack, on the Heidelberg Tavern in Observatory, led to more deaths and injuries.[74]

Given the extent of the bloodshed in the country as a whole, it is no wonder that the

UCT academics, standing peacefully in St George's Mall, were serenaded by this busker's rousing rendition of 'Nkosi Sikelel' iAfrika'. (Mayibuye Centre)

peaceful elections of 1994 seemed 'miraculous'. Almost equally surprising though, after all they had suffered under apartheid, was the fact that a majority of coloured Capetonians voted for the newly multi-racial National Party. Having also gained the largest number of white votes, ahead of the Democratic Party, the NP was able to control the Western Cape provincial government (one of nine regional authorities created

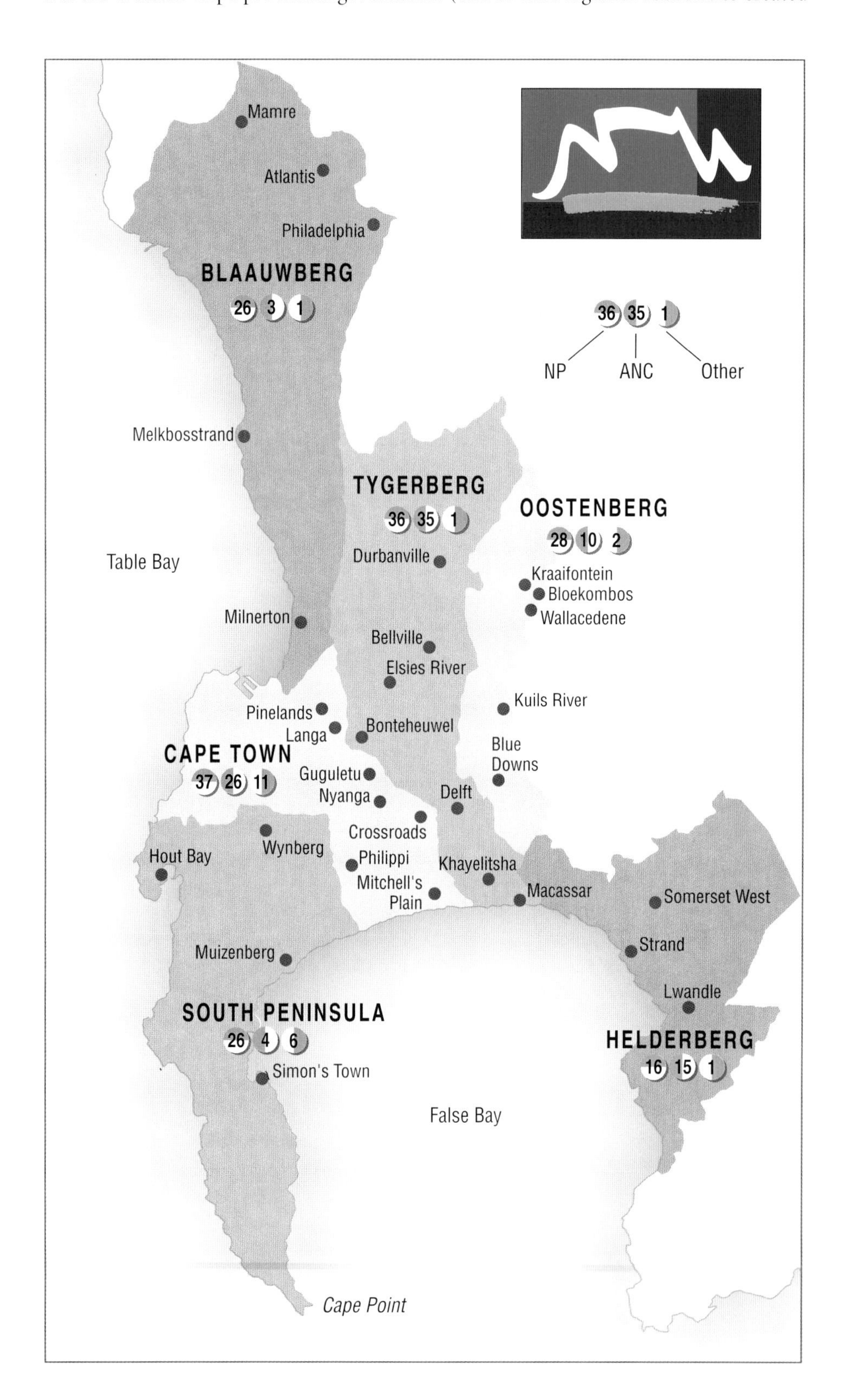

The six municipalities of Cape Town's metropolitan areas in 1996, showing political representation after the first democratic local elections. In 1998 national legislation stipulated that these municipalities would lose most of their executive powers to a 'megacity' council.

Images like this one, of a happy multi-racial voting queue in Claremont, epitomised the 'miracle' of April 1994. The National Party won 53.3 per cent of the vote in the Western Cape, the ANC 33 per cent, and the DP 6.6 per cent. (*Argus* library)

by the new constitution). It would seem that the UDF – with its accommodation of numerous racially distinct affiliates – had largely failed to overcome the ethnic particularism so carefully fostered by apartheid planners. The ANC also began to be perceived by some former coloured supporters as more narrowly Africanist than the UDF. The ANC's appointment of Allan Boesak as provincial leader was aimed at attracting coloured backing; it could count on most African votes. But the break-up of Boesak's marriage, and a well-publicised extra-marital affair, upset many potential supporters, especially churchgoers. More importantly, most working-class coloureds were fearful of losing jobs or even homes to African 'newcomers', whose numbers they had seen increasing rapidly since the abolition of influx control. National Party electioneering played on such concerns, encouraging both white and coloured racism with its accompanying dread of 'African' chaos, corruption and violence.

Similar reasons explain the outcome of the first democratic local government elections held in 1996. The racially distinct local authorities of apartheid days were abolished. Instead, greater Cape Town was split into six independent municipalities, with a total of 174 wards, within an umbrella Metropolitan Council. The National Party won five of the six municipalities, but without capturing a single ward in previously African areas; the ANC only fared marginally better in previously coloured and white ones. Political reclamation did not prevent most Capetonians from continuing to have a sense of community that interacted with ethnicity, despite the erosion of residential apartheid and the appearance of newly built, racially mixed developments like Summer Greens in the northern suburbs.[75]

Paradise or Adamastor's Den?

What kind of city had the new councillors inherited? The population of metropolitan Cape Town, now the capital of the Western Cape, had risen to 3 million people. About 50 per cent were officially described as coloured, 27 per cent as white and 23 per cent as black (African).[76] Contemporary guides and glossy books all featured beautiful photographs of people relaxing on beaches, of the sublime mountains and glorious flora and fauna, of old Cape Dutch buildings and the wonderful new Waterfront development. Flower-sellers and 'Malays' were represented, as were Coon troupes – if some-

America's *National Geographic* magazine of March/April 1997 described Cape Town as 'one of the most beautiful and compelling places to visit on the planet'. The 15,000 readers of *Harper's Travel* supported this judgment by voting Cape Town the third most desirable destination in the world, after San Francisco and Vancouver. (Mark van Aardt)

times euphemistically referred to as 'Cape minstrels'. Many similar pictures had adorned countless Cape publicity brochures since the Second World War. But now there were also depictions of coloureds who were not flower-sellers, Coons or Malays, and of Africans who did not present any obvious stereotype. These included a sculptor and a street waif, well-dressed shoppers, buskers, hawkers, Rastafarians, fishermen, and participants in street games and theatre.[77] At least one publication also depicted whites and blacks harmoniously together, picnicking at a wine farm, in voting queues and making physical contact as 'South African sisterhood' in a section on feminism and gay places of entertainment.[78]

Altogether these modern images presented a safe liberal paradise, recently cleansed of the apartheid serpent. This was what attracted increasing numbers of tourists as well as many wealthy new citizens after 1994 – whether from within southern Africa or, like Princess Diana's brother, Earl Spencer, from overseas. Those fleeing the greater dangers of suburban crime in Gauteng dubbed the city 'Escape Town'.[79]

Yet one of the first sights greeting any newcomer arriving by air was the shacks of KTC and Nyanga. Built in part on an old city rubbish dump, they overlooked the N2 freeway into the city centre and were separated from it by a concrete fence usually lined with thousands of plastic bags. These shacks formed the north-west fringes of a huge area of shanty settlement that had burgeoned since the end of influx control and now reached as far as Macassar to the east and False Bay to the south. And there were other shack settlements scattered throughout greater Cape Town: be it Marconi Beam in Milnerton, Mandela Park in Hout Bay or the small 'Bridge Hotel' under the unfinished Table Bay Boulevard flyover which sheltered some of the thousands of 'street people' in the city.

Particularly in the cold, wet Cape winter, these shanty dwellers remained acutely aware of Adamastor's storms. A 1992 survey calculated that about 440,000 people lived in 88,664 shacks scattered throughout the metropolitan area; only 31 per cent of Capetonians were described as 'adequately housed'.[80] Not surprisingly, lung diseases remained rife in the city. Cape Town had the highest rate of tuberculosis in the world in the 1990s. In 1993 there were almost 28,000 cases, and hundreds still died every year from the disease.[81]

Some shanties were old settlements: somehow Vrygrond, near Lavender Hill, had managed to survive the entire apartheid period. But after the ending of influx control, shacks spread particularly rapidly across previously uninhabited parts of Khayelitsha. In the early 1990s, an estimated 2000 settlers arrived every month from the eastern Cape, helping to swell its population to well over 500,000 by 1995.[82] Until such shacks had the benefit of electricity, the use of paraffin and candles meant that fire was a continual

Julia Teale's painting 'Bitter Fruit' questions the conventional tourist image of Cape Town, and shows something of the city behind Table Mountain.

threat: in summer the south-easter ensured that, once started, a blaze spread swiftly.

Much of the Cape Flats continued to suffer from the ravages of gangs, alcohol and drug addiction, as well as domestic violence. This resulted in horrendously high rates of murder, rape and child abuse. In 1995 almost half of the city's 1962 homicides took place in five townships – Khayelitsha, Guguletu, Mitchell's Plain, Nyanga and Bishop Lavis – although the extent of violent crime varied considerably even within each of these areas. Given inadequate state protection – 306 policemen had to maintain law and order among 650,000 Khayelitsha residents, spread across 42 square kilometres, in 1997 – it was hardly surprising that vigilante activities increased. These were both of a spontaneous and more organised and enduring nature.[83]

If the Cape Flats had by far the highest incidence of violence, fear of crime – fanned by dramatic newspaper headlines – was common throughout Cape Town. By 1995 the Western Cape's 182 car hijackings were well below the 7637 of Gauteng, but they had

Taxi Wars

Minibus taxis block the Strand Street entry into Cape Town. (*Argus* library)

A ubiquitous presence on Cape Town roads in the late twentieth century was the Kombi minibus taxi. They had initially been an illegal response by individual black entrepreneurs to the inadequacies of other forms of public transport serving townships and informal settlements. Despite the relatively cheap and convenient service they rendered, dangerously driven minibus taxis came to constitute a particular hazard on the already fairly lawless Cape Town roads. But passengers – mainly poorer black commuters – also frequently risked death when bloody clashes erupted between rival organisations. These came to prominence in the 1980s when Webta (the Western Province Black Taxi Association) and a body called Lagunya – two predominantly African bodies – were battling to control lucrative routes from townships to white areas. In 1992, after a particularly violent year, they agreed to unite in the Convention for a Democratic Taxi Association (Codeta) and share all routes. Peace lasted until some former Webta members launched the Cape Amalgamated Taxi Association (Cata). In the ensuing conflict, both Cata and Codeta employed hit squads. One estimate suggested that as many as 339 people were killed in 1996 alone. Thereafter violence was at least temporarily reduced by an accord in terms of which all taxis had to display their agreed routes.[84]

risen from only 39 in 1992 and some involved murder.[85] Much more frequent were muggings, vehicle break-ins and burglaries. Many households protected themselves with high walls, window bars, dogs, guns and alarm systems – which often included an armed response component. The security industry flourished, while the development of cluster housing behind electric fences gained in popularity.[86] Cape Town's middle classes were also troubled by many of the other issues that affected their counterparts in cities the world over, like pollution and environmental degradation. A 'brown haze' covered the Cape Flats on windless winter days. Development, while needed to create employment, remained a constant threat to the Peninsula's beauty.

Despite the repeal of the Population Registration Act and President Mandela's attempts at nation building, distinct racial and ethnic identities not only persisted in the

Cattle being herded across pedestrian bridges over the N2 freeway, a common sight in the 1990s. It epitomised the strong rural ties, and blurred the distinction between rural and urban, still typical of many Capetonians in the late twentieth century. For urban farmers in Crossroads, keeping cows to supply fresh and sour milk to shanty inhabitants provided a considerable income. (Eric Miller/iAfrika Photos)

The New Immigrants

The Cape of Good Hope continued to draw thousands of the rural poor at the end of the twentieth century. For some the decoration and expansion of their shanties were symbolic of urban aspirations rather than despair. Equally, Paul and Merriot Mohare of Guguletu may have had to live on bread and water, but Paul dreamt of eventually becoming a lawyer. Dreams or desperation meant that people came to Cape Town from throughout sub-Saharan Africa, but mainly from the eastern Cape, where many still had additional homes. A survey in 1995 found that 20 per cent of African households, which averaged about 4.5 members, expected to be joined soon by at least one other relative. In all, 66 per cent of household heads had arrived since 1980. Most counted Cape Town as their home, but 33 per cent said that it was the eastern Cape. The latter were mainly male hostel dwellers like Mr Gugu Sifuba, who had rented a small room in an old block overlooking the Langa taxi rank for 22 years and remained depressed 'to wake up every day to smell poverty all over the Cape Flats'. As many as 40 per cent of households were headed by women, who now constituted 57 per cent of the population. Average monthly household incomes were about R1250, 20 per cent had incomes below the poverty datum line, and 33 per cent of adults were unemployed – compared to a figure of 17 per cent unemployment for the western Cape as a whole.[87]

New residents arriving in the city crowded at the Langa bus station. (*Argus* library)

city but received new encouragement in the late 1990s through laws and policies aimed at correcting past injustices. Many white, coloured and Indian Capetonians believed that such affirmative action discriminated in favour of Africans. Most white Capetonians also believed that the ANC's attempts to achieve rapid egalitarianism were leading to 'declining standards', especially in public health and formerly white educational institutions. Such concerns were encouraged by newspaper articles that highlighted the growing financial problems facing institutions like Groote Schuur, as money was redistributed to clinics, or the 'levelling down' perceived to be involved in the 'transformation' of education.[88] For their part many black Capetonians believed that the legacy of racially based deprivation was being redressed too slowly. A number went further, and denounced any concerns about declining standards as 'racist', as the defence by whites of traditional privileges.[89] Whether these views were merited or not, there was nonetheless an awkward and unresolved paradox in the ANC's efforts to redress past discrimination by continuing to reify racial categorisation above class deprivation – whether in political rhetoric or the national census questionnaires of 1996.

An intended housing scheme at Oudekraal – on the unbuilt mountain slopes south of Camps Bay – created a particularly vociferous popular outcry that embraced environmentalists, Muslims (worried about despoilation of historic *kramats*) and New Agers alike. (*Argus* library)

Cape Town newspapers gave prominence to lively debates about ethnicity. These included articles on whether 'rainbow nation' diversity was a strength or a weakness, and whether 'Africanism' could or should embrace all 'races'. Interviews conducted for a *Cape Times* survey on the third anniversary of the 1994 elections suggested that Western Cape ethnicities were complex and fluid.[90] Thus 'whites' described themselves as 'African' or 'South African', as well as 'white South African', 'Afrikaner' or 'English-speaking'. 'Africans' called themselves 'black', 'Xhosa' or 'mainly Xhosa'. And 'coloureds' used a variety of terms beyond that one to describe themselves, including 'South African', 'indigenous South African', 'Griqua' and 'Rastafarian'.[91]

In fact, of all identities, the actual or appropriate one for 'coloured' Capetonians was probably the most hotly debated and researched by middle-class pundits, particularly around election times.[92] In the process, it was stressed that some coloureds preferred to call themselves 'brown' or 'black'. Foreign academics looked for, and found, numerous sub-identities that encompassed 'respectability', religious adherence, association with particular neighbourhoods, and 'maleness'.[93] The Rastafarian philosopher Zebulon Dread distinguished between anglicised 'sturvies' (snooty people) from places like Wynberg or Greenhaven and 'grassroots' (ordinary people) whose 'Coca-Cola culture' included 'Coons, gangsters and gossip'.[94]

'You have the middle-class "sturvies" who steer away from the rude Cape Flats slang towards the anglicised realm and perceive themselves as "cultured" – that whole status thing from the people in the Greenhavens, the Fairways, the Wynbergs. But the grassroots is Lavender Hill, Kalksteenfontein, Bishop Lavis, Elsies River, Manenberg.'

Rastafarian philosopher Zebulon Dread, 1996

Yet whether coloured Capetonians were, or were not, more than simply 'people', as Alex La Guma had described them, small groups emerged vowing to defend their interests. These included the Kleurling Weerstandsbeweging (KWB, or Coloured Resistance Movement) and the Cape People's Congress.[95] Seemingly as a result of the new democracy, some coloured Capetonians also claimed or reclaimed 'ancestral' slave or Khoi identities. But this process itself involved controversy, including disputes over the correct name for the Khoi, with Xhoi, Xoi-Xoi and Quena among suggested alternatives.[96] In the case of the First of December movement – which revived the commemoration of slave emancipation – it also involved reclaiming a forgotten, Capetonian history.[97]

Indeed, post-apartheid Cape Town witnessed numerous efforts to reclaim and commemorate hitherto neglected aspects of the city's past, from slave sites to places of importance in the fight against apartheid. The Mayibuye Centre, at the University of the Western Cape, preserved and publicised records of 'the struggle', already revisited daily in the media through hearings of the Truth and Reconciliation Commission. Robben Island was turned into a popular museum, with ex-prisoners employed as guides, while

PAGAD AND CORE

In the last quarter of the twentieth century Cape Town gangs were increasingly armed with guns, acquired in part from suburban burglaries. Firearm deaths rose from 600 in 1976 to 1300 in 1995, though many were the result of domestic conflicts or suicide and knives still accounted for the majority of murders.[98] By the 1990s, the two largest gangs in coloured areas were the Americans and the Hard Livings. Both used the opportunities offered by South Africa's difficult period of transition to expand their operations. They forged links with international crime syndicates which saw South Africa as a potentially lucrative new market. Drug runners into the country took advantage of border controls that were utterly inadequate at a time of rapidly increasing imports: Cape Town harbour had only two drugs officials to check on 2500 incoming containers daily.

It was in this context that Cape Town gangs sold increasing amounts of cocaine, crack and LSD as well as mandrax and marijuana. The initiative was taken by the Americans and their allies, the Sexy Boys. But the Hard Livings soon followed suit and took the opportunity to reduce costly turf battles among their own smaller allies by drawing them into an organisation called the Firm – For It Requires Money – in 1994.

The period between 1994 and 1996 was an especially lucrative one for the Firm. Its considerable interests and assets, besides drugs and prostitution, included race horses, taxis, shellfish poaching and investment in fixed property. A leading member, Colin Stanfield, reputedly accumulated R30 million, including a house in Constantia.[99] But on 4 August 1996 the co-leader of the Hard Livings, Rashaad Staggie, was shot and set alight by militant members of a vigilante organisation called People Against Gangsterism and Drugs (PAGAD). This helped to persuade the Americans and Sexy Boys to join the Firm.[100]

PAGAD apparently originated in July 1995 on the initiative of ten concerned friends. After several successful community meetings in which the number of adherents escalated rapidly, they invited religious leaders of all denominations to become involved. Although some Christians responded, including a Catholic priest, PAGAD evolved as a predominantly Muslim organisation whose rhetoric, 'marches, scarves and slogans evoked scenes from international Islamic movements'.[101] Its militancy was enhanced by the involvement of Achmat Cassiem's Qibla, a group that had produced Libyan-trained insurgents in the 1980s.[102]

PAGAD first received wide media coverage in 1996. On 11 March supporters marched to parliament. A week later, some armed with guns entered the Rylands home of the minister of justice, Dullah Omar, to publicise their cause. This was the suitably symbolic beginning of PAGAD's decision to take the law into its own hands. The following months saw a series of marches during which the houses and cars of drug dealers and gangsters were damaged, leading to the killing of Rashaad Staggie in London Road, Salt River. If most Capetonians had hitherto supported PAGAD's aims, the photographs of Staggie's death caused considerable shock. Popular backing for the organisation was further eroded when demonstrations at the Waterfront and airport in November and December 1996 were marred by violence, which led to the arrest of several PAGAD leaders.[103]

Faced with such opponents, the Firm responded in novel manner. Rashaad Staggie's twin brother Rashied played a central role in organising meetings and marches aimed at demonstrating that gangsters wanted peace, and establishing the Community Outreach Forum (CORE). CORE claimed that gangs would soon be disbanded and demanded talks with the government about alternative occupations. However, the drug trade continued apparently unabated, and so did the low-level war between PAGAD and CORE, characterised by assassinations and pipebomb attacks, in which innocents were often caught in the crossfire. Renewed gang warfare after November 1997 added to the violence.[104]

Members of CORE fire a salute on the site where Rashaad Staggie was killed the previous year, renaming the street in his honour. (Benny Gool)

A PAGAD march. (Benny Gool)

Reclaiming Identities

Right: Lumka and Tony Yengeni at the opening of parliament in 1997. (*Argus*)

Far right: The founders of the First of December movement commemorate emancipation at the site of the old slave tree in Spin Street. (Benny Gool)

Below: Coons reclaiming the city centre. (*Argus* library)

Bottom: In keeping with the new liberal ethos of the 1990s, Rastafarians were allowed to stage demonstrations outside parliament to promote the legalisation of marijuana. And a number established their own Marcus Garvey informal settlement camp at Philippi. (Mike Hutchings)

Visual and written histories of the city's substantial gay culture also made an appearance in the 1990s. These highlighted traditional outdoor meeting places like Graaff's Pool, Bachelor's Cove and Sandy Bay as well as more historically transient indoor venues such as clubs or cafés. In this photograph gays are seen celebrating the Twinkly Sea Mardi Gras at the River Club in Observatory. (Mike Hutchings)

tours to Khayelitsha enabled outsiders to gain a momentary glimpse of township life. A District Six Museum was established as a memorial to Cape Town's most infamous removal, and as a nostalgic celebration of the place.[105]

Reclaiming history was closely connected for many to reclaiming lost rights, or seeking compensation for past injustices. The new government established a land claims court that undoubtedly encouraged this connection and enabled Capetonians displaced by enforced segregation to apply for restitution or reparation. In the case of District Six, and after lengthy disputes, two facilitators – Neville Alexander and Elaine Clark – brokered a deal with the municipality on behalf of the District Six Civic Association. This provided for at least some former residents to take part (through a communal trust) in the re-development of the remaining barren land, and envisage their imminent return. Yet others, former tenants, felt sidelined by this outcome and briefly erected shacks on the land. Believing that other stakeholders like the Cape Technikon and the churches had not been consulted, the government delayed the process until a settlement was finally reached in 1998.[106]

There was also a sense of reclamation for many Capetonians in urban renewal, which appeared to be creating a more human, and humane, built environment. This was per-

Charismatic revivalism offered spiritual renewal to many Christian Capetonians in the 1980s and 1990s, and therewith the strength to cope with contemporary urban conflict and change. One new church, His People, began in 1988 when three people met in the house of its founder, Paul Daniel. By 1997 the multi-racial Cape Town congregation had grown to 6000, filling four separate Sunday services in the Baxter and Nico Malan theatres. (Private collection)

In a bizarre 'new South African' moment at the Storm Supermodel Fashion Party in 1997, British billionaire Richard Branson and 'catwalk queen' Kate Moss swayed to the strains of Peter Gabriel's song 'Biko' – played to commemorate the twentieth anniversary of the Black Consciousness leader's death. The same factors that boosted tourism aided the city's fashion industry – attracting international modelling and advertising agencies, as well as film crews – even though ordinary clothing factories laid off workers in the face of tariff reductions and global competition. (*Argus* library)

haps first noticeable in the slow renaissance of the city centre, which had its roots in the late 1970s, despite the simultaneous spread of offices and shopping malls to the suburbs. The Golden Acre complex (1979) and adjoining underground concourses provided shoppers with a city centre alternative in the 1980s to Tyger Valley or Claremont's Cavendish Square.[107] At the same time young Capetonians began making their own contribution to revitalisation by frequenting new multi-racial nightclubs – a development facilitated by P.W. Botha's relaxation of petty apartheid. Among the earliest was a Shortmarket venue called Scratch (later The Base), opened in 1979. This showcased

Recreation in Cape Town in the 1990s

Recreation in Cape Town took diverse new forms towards the end of the twentieth century. Rave parties with elaborate light shows, designer drugs and acid rock were patronised mainly by white youth; their black counterparts enjoyed hip-hop or *kwaito* music. The suburban middle classes kept fit by jogging, or with aerobics and weight lifting at luxury gymnasiums. Amid dusty games of soccer or cricket, a few played golf in Khayelitsha or learnt ballet in Guguletu. Apart from going to the beach or walking up the mountain, most kinds of entertainment (whether old or new) were highly commercialised, international and professional. Entertainments often involved mass participation, be it in road races like the Two Oceans Marathon, or pop concerts and sports events in large stadiums – a collective involvement momentarily calculated to overcome the atomisation of modern urban societies. There were elements of reclamation or renewal to be found in 1990s recreation, beyond racial integration in sport or the fact that Dollar Brand, who had taken the name Abdullah Ibrahim, returned from exile. Boat races – albeit now including motor power and cross-gender 'dragon' crews – returned to the Waterfront. Melodrama and pantomime resurfaced in television soap operas and professional wrestling matches. And the nation-building ceremony at the opening of the 1995 Rugby World Cup – with 'Cape minstrels', multi-racial groups of children and African gumboot dancers all performing in front of a benevolent President Mandela – had at least some echoes of royal celebrations in the nineteenth century.[108]

Two Oceans Marathon. (*Argus* library)

local bands – whether they played jazz, reggae or ska – and introduced patrons to 'world music'.[109] And from the early 1980s the Greenmarket Square flea market developed as a daytime successor to Loop Street's Market, accommodating both craft sales and New Age culture.

By this time town planners were beginning to implement some of Sir William Holford's suggested remedies for the ills of modern Cape Town. Initial results were vis-

Urban renewal also found expression in the growing popularity of post-modernist architecture. As in Woolworths House behind the City Hall, this borrowed from a range of styles and attempted to ensure that new buildings were in harmony with their surroundings while making an aesthetic contribution to the urban landscape. It was also evident in the careful restorations or refurbishments of old edifices like the Civil Service Club in Church Square or the Standard Bank in Adderley Street. (Douglas Roberts & Peter Loebenberg)

The Waterfront Development

(Mark van Aardt)

The decline of Cape Town harbour and success of waterfront projects elsewhere in the world prompted redevelopment plans. In 1980 a prominent architect, Gawie Fagan, proposed converting part of the old harbour into a yacht basin and tourist area. Four years later UCT's School of Architecture suggested that the city's links with the sea be re-created. Such ideas were greeted enthusiastically by local newspapers and the city council.[110]

Redevelopment was initially thwarted by the government's refusal to give up control of the harbour area. But in 1988 the newly privatised port authority, Portnet, together with the council and private developers, was represented in the establishment of a Victoria and Alfred Waterfront Company. This was allowed to lease 83 hectares in the older harbour area. The first part to be redeveloped was the 1.5 hectares in the vicinity of the Pierhead. Old buildings were restored or added to, while new buildings imitated their style, all in a deliberate attempt to recapture Cape Town's 'Victorian heritage'. The North Quay warehouse was turned into a hotel and shopping arcade. The old power station and Robinson Dry Dock pumphouse were converted into a theatre and bar complex. The Breakwater Prison – a migrant workers' barracks since 1926 – became UCT's Graduate School of Business. A Victoria Wharf, incorporating existing warehouses, took shape as a massive complex of shops, restaurants and cinemas. By the late 1990s heritage concerns were less evident as further development produced an aquarium, marina, six hotels and a luxury housing scheme.

The Waterfront development received initial criticism from the ANC and some journalists for excluding black traders because of its high retail rentals, and for promoting a laager mentality – by supplying an artificially safe and sanitised space – that allowed visitors to evade the city's social problems. 'The Waterfront is Cape Town scrubbed, perfumed and packaged', commented one newspaper.[111] But the Waterfront proved to be enormously popular with Capetonians of all races, as well as with tourists, precisely because of the security, style and setting it provided despite occasional outrages like the Planet Hollywood bomb. By 1997 it attracted, on average, more than 1.5 million visitors every month.[112]

ible by the late 1980s. St George's and Church streets were transformed into a busker-friendly pedestrian precinct. Street trading had also expanded there from the Parade, foreshadowing a formal relaxation of controls in the 1990s. By this decade, the fruits of a 1982 municipal plan called 'Greening the city' were evident in the creation of 'urban trails' and 'greenways', as well as in proposals to restore or conserve the vleis, flora and fauna of the Cape Flats. In a significant victory for environmentalists, the Table Mountain chain would become a national park. Meanwhile a long-held desire to restore links with the sea – shared by many citizens – was realised in a bold Waterfront development scheme.[113]

In 1996 Cape Town Cares, a joint project between private enterprise and the city council, was launched to fight 'grime and crime' in the city centre. This initiative involved employing homeless people to help sweep the streets, and allowing other unemployed individuals to act as informal parking attendants. It also entailed sponsoring additional police and setting up satellite police stations.[114] Thanks partly to such initiatives, Cape Town's central business district remained prosperous in the late 1990s, while those of other South African cities experienced decline. But undoubtedly contributing to this result was Cape Town's dramatic geographical setting. Beautiful views helped retain 30,000 'high-income earners' among the 100,000 residents of the city bowl, and thereby their support for local (and diverse) retail outlets and services.[115]

Once apartheid had ended, Cape Town's exceptional scenery – combined with its Mediterranean climate and the low value of the rand – enabled foreign tourism to assist commercial growth and thereby urban renewal. By 1996 some 600,000 overseas travellers were spending R4 billion a year in the city and surrounding areas. Cape Town airport, now handling three million passengers annually, was extended and upgraded. So

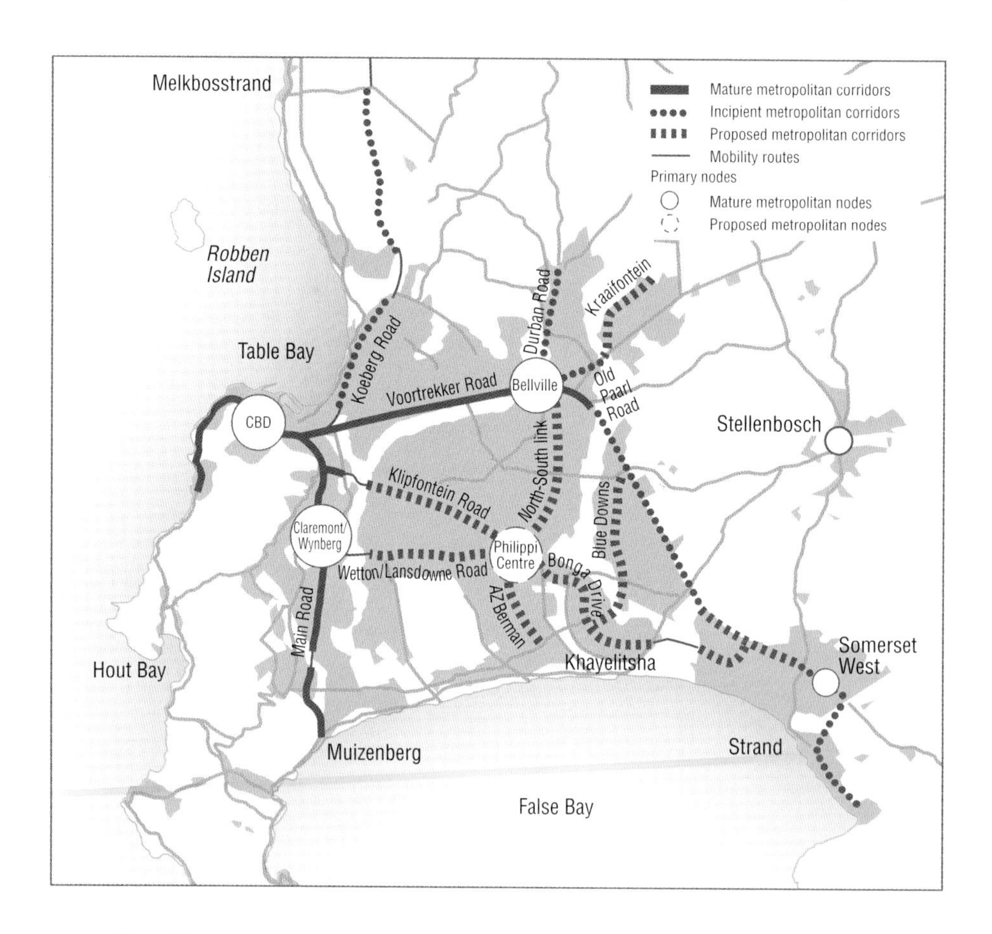

Following the painter James Ford's romantic creation a century earlier, the Cape Metropolitan Council produced a modernist *fin de siècle* vision of Cape Town's future, suitably in keeping with the late twentieth century.

were facilities at popular tourist sites like Kirstenbosch and Cape Point, while Table Mountain's cable-car system was modernised. Shortage of accommodation led to the burgeoning of bed-and-breakfast and backpacker establishments throughout the Peninsula, as well as multi-million-rand hotel projects. All played a part in rejuvenating the city bowl area, with foreshore redevelopment plans (including a proposed canal) promising to link the Waterfront more securely to the central business district.[116] The rate of economic growth and redevelopment in Cape Town also benefited from the fact that the proportion of professional, technical and skilled personnel in the Western Cape was more than 20 per cent higher than the national average.[117] Together with Cape Town's bid for the 2004 Olympics – in which it came third after Athens and Rome – this helped attract more than R8 billion in direct foreign investment to the region in 1996.[118]

But as Cape Town's six municipalities received their formal independence on 1 July 1997, urban renewal had touched only parts of metropolitan Cape Town. Some older residential areas like Maitland and parts of Sea Point had even declined in recent years, while Muizenberg had wallowed in a kind of dilapidated charm since before the Second World War though a multi-billion-rand science park promised commercial renaissance. Only pockets of prosperity existed on the Cape Flats. The new municipalities immediately established their own housing departments, yet their general role in reconstruction was hampered by the fact that they had inherited rent and rates arrears of some R1.5 billion.[119]

The uneven distribution of power and wealth, and its approximate correlation with gender and race, remained dramatically visible. Yet disadvantage was, increasingly, more a matter of class than of colour. Political change and affirmative action policies were hastening the emergence of a substantial black middle class, some of whom were successfully pursuing 'black economic empowerment' through companies like the Cape Town-based Mnyama Holdings. But the majority of blacks were still poor, and perhaps 10 per cent of whites had fallen into this category.

Then again, particularly from the 1970s, feminists had successfully challenged the remaining male exclusivity in occupations. But with many notable exceptions – like the leading estate agent, Pam Golding; the vice-chancellor of UCT, Mamphela Ramphele; the magazine editor Jane Raphaely; or the Speaker of parliament, Frene Ginwala – relatively few women rose from the lower occupational levels into positions of authority.[120] And in the 1990s crimes of violence against them were higher than ever.

So as the twentieth century drew to a close, was Cape Town more like paradise or Adamastor's den? Perhaps one answer is that suggested by the city poet Stephen Watson in 1993. People's experiences of the place, both in the past and in the present, were and are too diverse to be encompassed within a single myth. 'My Cape Town may well not be your Cape Town; ... its ways are many, its realities multiple'.[121]

Abbreviations

ACVV	Afrikaanse Christelike Vroue Vereniging
AME	African Methodist Episcopal
ANC	African National Congress
APO	African Political Organisation
ARM	African Resistance Movement
APLA	Azanian People's Liberation Army
AZAPO	Azanian People's Organisation
BAAB	Bantu Affairs Administration Board
BPC	Black People's Convention
CA	Cape Archives
CAC	Coloured Advisory Council
CAD	Coloured Affairs Department
CAL	Cape Action League
CAFDA	Cape Flats Distress Association
Cata	Cape Amalgamated Taxi Association
CATAPAW	Cape Association for the Abolition of Passes for South African Women
CAYCO	Cape Youth Congress
CIA	Cape Institute of Architects
CMA	Cape Malay Association
Codeta	Convention for a Democratic Taxi Association
CORE	Community Outreach Forum
COSAS	Congress of South African Students
COSATU	Congress of South African Trade Unions
CPC	Coloured People's Congress
CPCO	Cape Peninsula Charity Organisation
CPNU	Coloured People's National Union
CPSA	Communist Party of South Africa
CTHP	Cape Town History Project
DET	Department of Education and Training
DP	Democratic Party
DSAB	*Dictionary of South African Biography*
ECC	End Conscription Campaign
FCPP	Federal Coloured People's Party
FOSATU	Federation of South African Trade Unions
FRAC	Franchise Action Committee

GAB	Group Areas Board
GWU	General Workers' Union
JSAS	*Journal of Southern African Studies*
KWB	Kleurling Weerstandsbeweging
LBS	Ladies' Benevolent Society
LTAB	Land Tenure Advisory Board
MAPP	Musical Power for People's Power
MDM	Mass Democratic Movement
MK	uMkhonto weSizwe
NCW	National Council of Women
NEUF	Non-European United Front
NEUM	Non-European Unity Movement
NLL	National Liberation League
NUSAS	National Union of South African Students
PAC	Pan Africanist Congress
PAGAD	People Against Gangsterism and Drugs
PFP	Progressive Federal Party
RDB	Reddingsdaadbond
SABC	South African Broadcasting Corporation
SABRA	South African Bureau for Racial Affairs
SAC	South African College
SACOS	South African Council on Sport
SACPO	South African Coloured People's Organisation
SACTU	South African Congress of Trade Unions
SAL	South African Library
SANNC	South African Native National Congress
SAR&H	South African Railways and Harbours
SASO	South African Students' Organisation
SAVC	South African Vigilance Committee
SAWAS	South African Women's Auxiliary Services
SDF	Social Democratic Federation
SHAWCO	Students' Health and Welfare Committee
TARC	Train Apartheid Resistance Committee
TLSA	Teachers' League of South Africa
TRA	Tramway Residents Association
UCT	University of Cape Town
UDF	United Democratic Front
UWC	University of the Western Cape
UNIA	Universal Negro Improvement Association
UP	United Party
WCOHP	Western Cape Oral History Project
WCTU	Women's Christian Temperance Union
WEL	Women's Enfranchisement League
Webta	Western Province Black Taxi Association
WFC	Women's Food Committee
YMCA	Young Men's Christian Association
ZACVV	Zuid-Afrikaansche Christelyke Vrouwe Vereniging
ZAVF	Zuid-Afrikaansche Vrouwe Federatie

References

PREFACE

1. P. Podbrey, *White Girl in Search of a Party* (Pietermaritzburg, 1993), 97.
2. *Cape Times*, 9.4.1996.
3. *Mail & Guardian*, 28,8,1998–3.9.1998.

CHAPTER 1

1. G.W. Steevens, *From Capetown to Ladysmith* (London, 1900), 3–4.
2. Ibid., 7–8.
3. E. Smithers, *March Hare: The Autobiography of Elsa Smithers* (OUP, 1935), 168–73.
4. *Cape Times*, 7.2.1900.
5. *Cape Times*, 26.10.1899.
6. *Cape Times*, 5.2.1901.
7. *Cape Times*, 16.10.1899.
8. *Cape Times*, 17.2.1900.
9. *Cape Times*, 22.5.1900.
10. CA, 3/CT 1/1/1/50, 22.3.1900.
11. W.J. Simpson, *Lecture on Plague* (Cape Town, 1901), 8–9.
12. CA, MOH 27–214, Creed's report, 26.9.1901.
13. *Cape Times*, 9.3.1901, 11.3.1901.
14. C. Saunders, 'The creation of Ndabeni: Urban segregation and African resistance in Cape Town', *Studies in the History of Cape Town* (Cape Town, 1984), 1, 166.
15. CA, NA 457 [Stanford commission].
16. *Cape Times*, 4.6.1900.
17. *Cape Times*, 26.7.1900.
18. E. Wallace, *Unofficial Dispatches* (London, 1901), 14.
19. *SA News*, 29.3.1901.
20. CA, PM 96, 11.9.1901.
21. *SA Review*, 6.2.1903.
22. J.J. van-Helten and K. Williams, '"The crying need of South Africa": The emigration of single British women to the Transvaal, 1901–10', *JSAS*, 10, 1 (Oct. 1983), 23.
23. *The Shield*, 5, 55 (June 1902), 31.
24. *Cape Times*, 27.11.1899.
25. *Cape Times*, 25.5.1900; *SA News*, 28.6.1900.
26. CA, 3/Wsk-8, 30.7.1900, Mayor's minute for 1900.
27. *SA News*, 22.8.1903.
28. E. Mantzaris, 'The cigarette makers' strikes and the first workers' co-operative society in South Africa' (4th Cape Town History Workshop, 1983).
29. *Cape Times*, 19.6.1900.
30. Quoted in R. Hallett, 'The hooligan riots', *Studies*, 1, 49–50.
31. Saunders, 'Ndabeni', 183.
32. *Cape Times*, 2.8.1917.
33. M. du Toit, 'Women, welfare and the nurturing of Afrikaner nationalism: A social history of the Afrikaanse Christelike Vroue Vereniging, c.1870–1939' (Ph.D. thesis, UCT, 1996), 87.
34. Ibid., 92.
35. Ibid., 85 quoting from K. Schoeman, *Only an Anguish to Live Here: Olive Schreiner and the Anglo-Boer War 1899–1902* (Cape Town, 1992), 206.
36. *Cape Times*, 7.5.1904.
37. *Cape Times*, 14.5.1904.
38. *Cape Times*, 27.10.1904; *SA News*, 1.11.1904, 3.11.1904.
39. *Cape Argus*, 4.5.1906; *Cape Times*, 4.5.1904, 24.4.1906.
40. *Cape Argus*, 30.7.1906.
41. *Cape Times*, 30.7.1906.
42. Hallett, 'Hooligan riots', 55.
43. Ibid., 57.
44. Ibid., 78.
45. *Cape Times*, 19.10.1909.
46. *Cape Argus*, 6.3.1905; *Cape Times*, 27.10.1905.
47. CA, CO 7469-551, 20.7.1903.
48. *Cape Times*, 27.7.1903.
49. CA, CO 7393–6.7.1902.
50. *Cape Argus*, 3.4.1906.
51. R. Hallett, 'Policemen, pimps and prostitutes – public morality and police corruption', *Studies*, 1, 7.
52. *Cape Times*, 3.11.1903.
53. *Cape Times*, 24.8.1904, 18.10.1904.
54. *SA Review*, 24.3.1905.
55. J.R. Finch (comp.), *The Cape of Good Hope* (Cape Town, [1926]), 125–30.
56. *Cape Argus*, 10.4.1890.
57. *Cape Times*, 27.10.1906.
58. *Cape Times*, 11.8.1906.
59. A. Badham, 'St Mary's Anglican Church as a "window" on turn-of-the-century Woodstock' (B.A. Honours thesis, UCT, 1985), 79.
60. *Cape Times*, 7.7.1902, 18.11.1907.
61. G39–1893, 140–1.
62. D.F. Adonis, '"Today's boys, tomorrow's men": A short history of the Boys' Brigade of Britain, with further reference to the Boys' Brigade in South Africa (circa 1880s–1980s)' (M.A. thesis, UCT, 1995), 97.
63. *Cape Times*, 12.11.1884, 28.1.1903.
64. *Cape Times*, 23.11.1876, 25.12.1876, 5.1.1878, 9.1.1878.
65. *Cape Times*, 11.8.1896.
66. Gerald Stone, 'An ethnographic and socio-semantic analysis of lexis among working-class Afrikaans-speaking coloured adolescent and young adult males in the Cape Peninsula, 1963–1990' (M.A. thesis, UCT, 1991).
67. George Manuel, *I Remember Cape Town* (Cape Town, 1977), 56–7.
68. G19–1909, 66.
69. CA, NA 457, 5.3.1901.
70. CA, NA 264, 4.7.1901.
71. S. Gray (ed.), *Three Plays* (Johannesburg, 1984), 125.
72. *Cape Times*, 6.7.1912.
73. H. Wittenberg, 'Rhodes Memorial: Imperial aesthetics and the politics of prospect' (UCT, African seminar, 1996).
74. H. Phillips, *The University of Cape Town 1918–1948. The Formative Years* (Cape Town, 1993).
75. *Cape Times*, 5.8.1914.
76. *Cape Times*, 10.8.1914.
77. *Cape Times*, 10.9.1914.
78. Cape Town. Peace Celebrations Committee, *The Celebration of Peace, August 2 to 5, 1919: Official Programme and Souvenir Booklet* (Cape Town, 1919), 35–6.
79. *Cape Times*, 11.8.1915.
80. *Cape Times*, 24.8.1916.
81. *Cape Times*, 1.9.1914.
82. *Cape Times*, 14.4.1916.
83. *Cape Times*, 14.4.1916.
84. *Cape Times*, 15.6.1915, 28.6.1915, 22.11.1915.
85. *Cape Times*, 27.5.1916.
86. *Cape Times*, 21.8.1915, 11.3.1915.
87. *Cape Times*, 21.8.1915; NCW, 1/1/3, CT branch minutes, 4.2.1915.
88. *Cape Times*, 9.12.1916.
89. A.J. Hunter, 'Anti-German riots in Cape Town, 1915' (B.A. Honours thesis, UCT, 1980), 52–3.
90. *Cape Times*, 31.8.1918.
91. D. McIntyre, *The Diocesan College, Rondebosch, South Africa: A Century of 'Bishops'* (Cape Town, 1950), 57.

CHAPTER 2

1. *Cape Times*, 2.2.1930.
2. *Cape Times*, 5.10.1929.
3. M. Nicol, 'A history of garment and tailoring workers in Cape Town, 1900–1939' (Ph.D. thesis, UCT, 1984), 60.
4. Ibid., 96, 97.
5. Ibid., 111.
6. Unpublished interview by M. du Toit for CTHP.
7. *Cape Times*, 1.11.1940.
8. *Cape Times*, 21.11.1940.
9. *Cape Times*, 25.9.1924.
10. B. Nasson, 'Oral history and the reconstruction of District Six' in S. Jeppie and C. Soudien (eds.), *The Struggle for District Six Past and Present* (Cape Town, 1990), 59.
11. P. Corgatelli, 'Tapes and testimony: Making the local history of Italians in the Western Cape in the first half of the 20th century' (M.A. thesis, UCT, 1989), 209.
12. M. Kondlo, 'Squatters in Cape Town, c.1950–1960' (M.A. thesis, UCT, 1992), 43–4.
13. *Cape Times*, 13.6.1939.
14. J. Carruthers, 'Swingler and the supply of electricity to Cape Town', *Studies*, 5 (1984), 209–36.
15. S. Jeppie, 'Popular culture and carnival in Cape Town: The 1940s and 1950s' in Jeppie and Soudien, *The Struggle for District Six*, 67–87.
16. Corgatelli, 'Tapes and testimony', 185, 199.
17. P. Machado, '"Little Madeira": The Portuguese in Woodstock c.1940–c.1980' (B.A. Honours thesis, UCT, 1992).
18. K. McCormick, 'Language in the Jewish community of District Six 1880–1940 (unpublished paper, UCT, 1990).
19. A. Kreitzer, *My Yiddische Mama: Anecdotes from the Life of a Jewish Mother* (Cape Town, 1991).
20. L.J. Brenner, 'Moving up: Adaptation and change amongst the Cape Town Jewish community, 1920–1939' (B.A. Honours thesis, UCT, 1991).
21. B. Feldman, 'Social life in Cape Town Jewry, 1904–1914; with special reference to the East European community' (B.A. Honours thesis, UCT, 1984).
22. P. Furlong, *Between Crown and Swastika: The Impact of the Radical Right on the Afrikaner Nationalist Movement in the Fascist Era* (Johannesburg 1991), 37. For a larger discussion of Jewish immigration and anti-semitism see M. Shain, *Jewry and Cape Society* (Cape Town, 1983); M. Shain, *The Roots of Anti-semitism in South Africa* (Johannesburg, 1994).
23. Cape Town, Mayor's Minute for 1924, 17.

24. Quoted in P. Merrington, 'Pageantry and primitivism: Dorothea Fairbridge and the "aesthetics of Union,"' *JSAS*, 21, 4 (Dec. 1995), 653.
25. *Cape Times*, 27.3.1924.
26. Cape Town, Mayor's Minute for 1924, 19.
27. R. Hill and G. Pirio, 'Africa for the Africans: The Garvey movement in South Africa, 1920–40' in S. Marks and S. Trapido (eds.), *The Politics of Race, Class and Nationalism* (London, 1987), 218.
28. Merrington, 'Pageantry and primitivism', 654.
29. *Cape Times*, 27.3.1924.
30. *DSAB*, 5, 218.
31. D. O'Meara, *Volkskapitalisme: Class, Capital and Ideology in the Development of Afrikaner Nationalism, 1934–1948* (Johannesburg, 1983), 101.
32. *Cape Times*, 8.8.1938.
33. *Cape Argus*, 9.8.1938.
34. Furlong, *Between Crown and Swastika*, 17, 20–2, 34.
35. O'Meara, *Volkskapitalisme*, 193.
36. R.R. Edgar (ed.), *The Travel Notes of Ralph Bunche, 28 September 1937–1 January 1938* (Johannesburg, 1992), 76.
37. *Cape Times*, 23.6.1936.
38. C. Kadalie, *My Life and the ICU, the Autobiography of a Black Trade Unionist in South Africa* (London, 1970), 41.
39. S. Jeppie, 'I.D. du Plessis and the "re-invention of the Malay" c.1935–1952' (B.A. Honours thesis, UCT, 1988).
40. *Cape Times*, 23.9.1942, 21.9.1942.
41. B. Nasson, 'The Unity Movement tradition: Its legacy in historical consciousness' in J. Brown (et al.), *History from South Africa: Alternative Visions and Practices* (Philadelphia, 1991), 145.
42. Edgar, *Ralph Bunche*, 79, 332–3.
43. F. Khan, 'The origins of the Non-European Unity Movement' (B.A. Honours thesis, UCT, 1976), 27, 33.
44. *Cape Times*, 6.2.1922.
45. *Cape Times*, 6.2.1922, 9.2.1922.
46. Cited in C. Saunders, 'From Ndabeni to Langa' in *Studies*, 1, 194–230.
47. M. Musemwa, 'Aspects of the social and political history of Langa Township, Cape Town, 1927–1948' (M.A. thesis, UCT, 1993), 35.
48. R. Levin, 'Marriage in Langa native location' (M.A. thesis, UCT, 1946), 65.
49. Ibid., 19.
50. W.D. Hammond-Tooke, 'Six native churches: A preliminary survey of religion in an urban location' (M.A. thesis, UCT, 1948), 17–8.
51. Edgar, *Ralph Bunche*, 77.
52. N. Mohamed, 'Langa High School: the struggle for existence: The first twenty years in the history of Langa High School' (B.A. Honours thesis, UCT, 1989), 72.
53. Saunders, 'Langa', 202.
54. Hill and Pirio, 'Africa for the Africans', 219.
55. *Umteteli wa Bantu*, cited in ibid., 231.
56. Ibid., 232.
57. D. Gordon, 'The Cape Town renaissance and the genesis of African nationalism, 1918–1926' (B.A. Honours thesis, UCT, 1993), 21.
58. *Cape Times*, 15.7.1940.
59. *Cape Times*, 2.5.1942.
60. Phillips, *University of Cape Town 1918–1948*, 225–45.
61. J. Crys-Williams, *A Country at War 1939–1945: The Mood of a Nation* (Rivonia, 1992), 142.
62. *Cape Times*, 18.11.1941.
63. *Cape Times*, 12.12.1942.
64. *Cape Times*, 22.3.1944.
65. *Cape Times*, 30.3.1944.
66. *Cape Times*, 14.12.1942.
67. *Cape Times*, 9.5.1945.
68. E. Everett, 'Zainunnissa (Cissie) Gool 1897–1963' (B.A. Honours thesis, UCT, 1978), 72.
69. *Cape Times*, 15.7.1940.
70. Cited in Musemwa, 'Langa', 175.
71. *Cape Times*, 8.10.1918.
72. H. Phillips, ' "Black October": The impact of the Spanish influenza epidemic of 1918 on South Africa' in *Archives Yearbook for South African History*, 53, 1 (1990), 133.
73. A. Walker, 'Out on a limb' (unpublished report to CTHP), 47.
74. P. Alexander, *Roy Campbell: A Critical Biography* (Cape Town, 1982), 235.
75. R.B. Miller, 'Science and society in the early career of H.F. Verwoerd', *JSAS*, 19, 4 (Dec. 1993), 645.
76. M. du Toit, ' "Co-workers of state and church"? Female Afrikaner nationalists and gender conflict in the making of state social welfare policy, 1928–1939' (UCT, Africa seminar, 1996), 10.
77. Unpublished interview by M. du Toit for CTHP, 8.11.1991.
78. P. Rabkin, 'A socio-economic study of Parkwood Estate, Cape Flats' (M.Soc.Sci. thesis, UCT, 1941).
79. *Cape Times*, 6.9.1924.
80. D. Pinnock, 'From Argie boys to skolly gangsters: The lumpen-proletarian challenge of the street-corner armies in District Six, 1900–1951', *Studies*, 3 (1984), 131–74.
81. Edgar, *Ralph Bunche*, 78, 332.
82. Crys-Williams, *A Country at War*, 143.
83. C. Walker, *Women and Resistance in South Africa* (London, 1982), 80.
84. *Cape Times*, 2.5.1944, 12.11.1941.
85. *Cape Times*, 4.2.1943.
86. *Cape Times*, 31.8.1945.
87. *Cape Times*, 29.6.1943.
88. *Cape Times*, 22.6.1944.

CHAPTER 3

1. J. Packer, *Valley of the Vines* (London, 1955), 201.
2. P. Podbrey, *White Girl in Search of a Party* (Pietermaritzburg, 1993), 96–7.
3. P. Ntantala, *A Life's Mosaic* (Cape Town, 1992), 128.
4. There are over 400 interviews (conducted from 1984 onwards) by the Western Cape Oral History Project (WCHOP) collection, Archives and Manuscripts section, Jagger Library, UCT.
5. S. de Villiers, *A Tale of Three Cities* (Cape Town, 1985), 39.
6. *Cape Times*, 4.9.1946.
7. Podbrey, *White Girl*, 150–1.
8. H.V. Morton, *In Search of South Africa* (London, 1948), 11, 32.
9. D. Reed, *Somewhere South of Suez* (London, 1950), 200.
10. Morton, *In Search of South Africa*, 17.
11. Reed, *Somewhere South of Suez*, 163.
12. *Cape Argus*, 4.4.1949. This and the two following *Argus* references are cited in A.K. Marquard, 'The political significance of the liberal media coverage of District Six from 1949 to 1970' (M.A. thesis, Rhodes University, 1996), which has informed my remarks.
13. *Cape Argus*, 6.4.1949.
14. *Cape Argus*, 23.3.1949.
15. Morton, *In Search of South Africa*, 18.
16. UG 51-1949, Census of the Union of South Africa for 1946, I, 'Population'. Unless otherwise indicated, statistical details for Cape Town in 1946 are drawn from the census of that year.
17. M. Budow, 'Urban squatting in Greater Cape Town 1939–1948' (B.A. Honours thesis, UCT, 1976), 8.
18. Y. Muthien, *State and Resistance in South Africa* (Aldershot, 1994), 16.
19. K. Ward, 'The road to Mamre: Migration, memory and the meaning of community c.1900–92', (M.A. thesis, UCT, 1992).
20. Podbrey, *White Girl*, 128.
21. See V. Bickford-Smith, *Ethnic Pride and Racial Prejudice* (Cambridge, 1995).
22. *Cape Times*, 24.7.1946.
23. P.A. Millar, 'Aspects of the history of Goodwood c.1925–1955' (B.A. Honours thesis, UCT, 1996).
24. G. Manuel, *I Remember Cape Town* (Cape Town, 1997), 30.
25. *Cape Argus Centenary Supplement* (Cape Town, 1956), 22.
26. S. Patterson, *Colour and Culture in South Africa* (London, 1953), 71.
27. Ibid., 74–5, 114–17.
28. K. Greenbank, ' "You chaps mustn't worry when you come back": Cape Town soldiers and aspects of the experience of war and demobilisation 1939–1953' (M.A. thesis, UCT, 1995), 83–125; J. Western, *Outcast Cape Town* (Cape Town, 1981), 56.
29. B. Kinkead-Weekes, 'Africans in Cape Town: State policy and popular resistance, 1936–1973' (Ph.D. thesis, UCT, 1992), 117–18.
30. H. Fast, 'Vacation in Nyanga: Removals, evictions and spatial dynamics' (unpublished paper, SA Historical Society Conference, 1995), 4–13.
31. Bickford-Smith, *Ethnic Pride and Racial Prejudice*, 150–1; U.S. Mesthrie, ' "No place in the world to go" – control by permit: The first phase of the Group Areas Act in Cape Town in the 1950s', *Studies*, 7, (1994), 187.
32. Edgar, *Ralph Bunche*, 58–9.
33. Western, *Outcast Cape Town*, 48–58; K.M. Kondlo, 'Miserable hovels and shanties on waterlogged wasteland: Political economy of peri-urban squatting around Cape Town, circa 1945–1960' (M.A. thesis, UCT, 1991).
34. Muthien, *State and Resistance*, 49–58; Kinkead-Weekes, 'Africans in Cape Town', 15, 97–105; Ntantala, *Life's Mosaic*, 132–5. H. Fast, 'An overview of African settlement in the Cape metropolitan area to 1990' (UPRU Working Paper no. 53, December 1995), 9.
35. W. Taliep, 'A study in the history of Claremont and the impact of the Group Areas Act, c.1950–1970' (B.A. Honours thesis, UCT, 1992), 11–13; Western, *Outcast Cape Town*, 162; U.S. Mesthrie, 'The Tramway

Road removals, 1959–61' (unpublished paper, South African and Contemporary History seminar, UWC, 1994).
36. A.M. Smalberger, 'Lady Anne Avenue, Newlands' (unpublished third-year project, UCT, 1992), 1–2; Mrs S., interview in R. Hill's video, *Some Aspects of the History of Newlands Village* (third-year history project, UCT, 1989); *Cape Times*, 9.4.1996.
37. Edgar, *Ralph Bunche*, 59.
38. P. Scott, 'Cape Town a multi-racial city', *Geographical Journal*, 121 (1955), 149–57; Ntantala, *Life's Mosaic*, 136; Kinkead-Weekes, 'Africans in Cape Town', 19; K. Daniels, '"Claremont was a little pocket of nice people": An examination of the community of Harfield' (WCOHP, UCT, 1994), 13–15; Western, *Outcast Cape Town*, 47–57.
39. Podbrey, *White Girl*, 134.
40. Patterson, *Colour and Culture* remains the best source for what was, and was not, segregated in Cape Town on the eve of apartheid.
41. Edgar, *Ralph Bunche*, 95.
42. Mrs C., interview, in Hill, *Newlands Village*.
43. *Cape Times*, 22.11.1946.
44. *Cape Times*, 25.7.1946.
45. T. Heard, *Cape of Storms* (Johannesburg, 1990), 174.
46. Podbrey, *White Girl*, 136.
47. A. Paton, *Apartheid and the Archbishop* (Cape Town, 1973), 201.
48. *Cape Times*, 5.11.1949.
49. Patterson, *Colour and Culture*, 139.
50. Ibid., 97–8, 267.
51. *Die Burger*, 14.9.1949, cited in Patterson, *Colour and Culture*, 284, n.5.
52. Ntantala, *Life's Mosaic*, 136.
53. Ibid., 136.
54. Quote is from Patterson, *Class and Colour*, 127; Ntantala, *Life's Mosaic*, 138; Heard, *Cape of Storms*, 57.
55. Patterson, *Colour and Culture*, 103–4, 275.
56. *Cape Times*, 27.1.1947, 28.1.1947.
57. *Cape Times*, 26.9.1946.
58. *Cape Times*, 26.9.1946, 3.12.1946, 16.4.1947, 17.4.1947.
59. Ntantala, *Life's Mosaic*, 142.
60. Podbrey, *White Girl*, 100, 111.
61. R. Rive, *Emergency* (Cape Town, 1988); R. Gool, *Cape Town Coolie* (Oxford, 1990); A. Brink, *Looking on Darkness* (London, 1988). Also Patterson, *Colour and Culture*, 297–8, mentions inter-racial social intermingling in 'intellectual' circles.
62. Podbrey, *White Girl*, 133.
63. WCOHP interview: Mr A., Coloured politics files.
64. Edgar, *Ralph Bunche*, 66.
65. J. Walker, *Skin Deep* (Kommetjie, 1977), 103.
66. Greenbank, 'You chaps mustn't worry', 127–50.
67. Rive, *Emergency*, 74–5.
68. WCOHP interview: Mrs M.S., Claremont files; also cited in Daniels, 'Claremont', 5.
69. WCOHP interview: Mr S.A., Claremont files; also cited in Daniels, 'Claremont', 4.
70. Rive, *Emergency*, 23–4.
71. Taliep, 'Claremont', 12, 46–7 and 'Appendix with transcripts', R.O. Dudley interview, 1–2.
72. Taliep, 'Claremont', 22; Daniels, 'Claremont', 13.
73. Taliep, 'Claremont'; Dudley transcript, 1–3; Mrs C. and Mrs S. interviews in Hill, *Newlands Village*.
74. Western, *Outcast Cape Town*, 184–5; U.S. Mesthrie, 'Swallowing the gnat after the camel: The Fraserdale/Black River Group Area proclamation of 1966 in Rondebosch' (unpublished UCT History Department seminar paper), 17.
75. A.G. Weiss, 'The Cape coloured woman: Within an industrial community and at home' (M.Soc.Sci. thesis, UCT, 1950).
76. Taliep, 'Claremont', 'Appendix with transcripts', M. Galant second interview 1992, 2.
77. Edgar, *Ralph Bunche*, 79.
78. Patterson, *Colour and Culture*, 155, 309.
79. Rive, *'Buckingham Palace', District Six* (Cape Town, 1987), 51.
80. Stone, 'Ethnographic and socio-semantic analysis of lexis'.
81. K. McCormick, 'The vernacular of District Six' in Jeppie and Soudien, *The Struggle for District Six Past and Present*, 88–109.
82. C. Keeton, 'Aspects of material life and culture in District Six, c.1990s–1950s' (B.A. Honours thesis, UCT, 1987).
83. Cited in McCormick, 'The vernacular of District Six', 96.
84. And see V.A. February, *Mind Your Colour* (London, 1991), 160–3, for a discussion of this issue in Rive's novel.
85. Mrs S. interview in Hill, *Newlands Village*. See also J. Branford, *A Dictionary of South African English* (Cape Town, 1987), 273, 398–9. See also G. Watson, *Passing for White* (London, 1970).
86. M. Wilson and A. Mafeje, *Langa* (Cape Town, 1973), 67–9.
87. Ntantala, *Life's Mosaic*, 137.
88. Wilson and Mafeje, *Langa*.
89. Cited in Muthien, *State and Resistance*, 20.
90. M. Qotole, ' "We will provoke the bees," ' (draft M.A. thesis, UCT, 1996).
91. *Cape Times*, 26.7.1946.
92. *Cape Times*, 7.8.1946.
93. *Cape Times*, 10.8.1946.
94. See for instance *Cape Times*, 1.8.1946, 8.8.1946, 7.9.1946.
95. Sergeant Nel, cited in D. Pinnock, *The Brotherhoods* (Cape Town, 1984), 24.
96. Residents' views on gangsters and crime are discussed in Keeton, 'District Six', 59–61.
97. WCOHP interview: M.F., District Six files.
98. WCOHP interview: A.P., Claremont files; also cited in Daniels, 'Claremont', 11.
99. WCOHP interview: G.A. and D.M., Claremont files; also cited in Daniels, 'Claremont', 10, 13.
100. WCOHP interview: J.J., District Six files.
101. WCOHP interview: G.J., District Six files. See also L. Baxter, 'History, identity and meaning: Cape Town's Coon Carnival in the 1960s and 1970s' (M.A. thesis, UCT, 1996), on how and why carnival was remembered as non-violent and non-commercial, despite contemporary evidence to the contrary.
102. WCOHP interview: F.S., District Six files.
103. *Cape Times*, 15.11.1946. For more on the gangs of this period, see Pinnock, 'From Argie boys to skolly gangsters'.
104. S. Field, 'From the "peaceful past" to the "violent present": Memory, myth and identity in Guguletu', in A. Norval and D. Howarth (eds.), *South Africa in Transition* (London, forthcoming); H. Fast, 'Vacation in Nyanga'.
105. Taliep, 'Claremont', 'Appendix with transcripts', M.G. first interview 1992, 9.
106. Much of the following summary of newspaper accounts of District Six in the 1950s and 1960s is informed by Marquard, 'District Six', 67–76. See also *Cape Times*, 23.1.1950.
107. *Fairyland* and *District Six*.
108. A. La Guma, *A Walk in the Night* (London, 1967); D. Muller, *Whitey* (Johannesburg, 1977).
109. *Cape Times*, 24.1.1950, 25.1.1950, 26.1.1950.
110. Marquard, 'District Six', 71–6.
111. Pinnock, 'Argie boys', 162.
112. Particularly Western, *Outcast Cape Town* and Mesthrie, 'Swallowing the gnat'.

CHAPTER 4

1. *Cape Town Your City* (Cape Town, 1956).
2. R. Marks and M. Bozzoli, 'The urbanism of District Six' (unpublished paper presented at 'Africa's Urban Past' conference, London, 1996), 7; also H.A. Vokety, 'Cape Town and Montreal: A tale of two cities' (M.A. thesis, UCT, 1985) and Western, *Outcast Cape Town*.
3. A. Mabin, 'Dispossession, exploitation and struggle: An historical overview of South African urbanization' in D. Smith (ed.), *The Apartheid City and Beyond* (London, 1992), 13–24.
4. *Cape Times*, 6.2.1922, 9.2.1922.
5. Mayor's Minute (Cape Town, 1928), 51–67, cited in N. Barnett, 'Race, housing and town planning in Cape Town c.1920–1940: with special reference to District Six'(M.A. thesis, UCT, 1993), 12.
6. *Cape Times*, 26.3.1924.
7. G. Cuthbertson, 'A new town at Uitvlugt: The founding and development of Pinelands 1919–1948', *Studies*, 1 (1984), 107–24.
8. Edgar, *Ralph Bunche*, 67.
9. De Villiers, *A Tale of Three Cities*, 39; *Cape Argus Centenary Supplement* (Cape Town, 1957).
10. *Cape Times*, 31.5.1924.
11. CTHP interview, conducted by M. du Toit.
12. CA, 3/Cape Town 1/5/14/1/2, 'City Engineer memo, 5.11.1936'.
13. *Cape Times*, 28.11.1917, 5.12.1917.
14. Barnett, 'Race, housing and town planning', 72.
15. Ibid., 124.
16. Ibid., 53.
17. *Cape Standard*, 28.3.1939, 4.4.1939.
18. *Cape Times*, 7.8.1941, 30.4.1941, 10.9.1942.
19. *Cape Times*, 30.4.1940.
20. Barnett, 'Race, housing and town planning', 20.
21. *Cape Times*, 13.3.1939.
22. *Cape Times*, 22.3.1939.
23. *Cape Times*, 13.4.1940, 12.11.1940.
24. E.E. Beaudouin, *Outline of Scheme (Foreshore) for Cape Town (South Africa)* (Cape Town, 1940); SAR&H, *Report of the Town Planning Advisers on the Cape Town Foreshore Scheme* (Pretoria, 1940).
25. *The Cape Town Foreshore Plan: The Final Report of Cape Town Foreshore Joint Technical Committee, June 1947* (Pretoria, 1947), 19.
26. *Cape Times*, 25.9.1943, 29.9.1943, 20.1.1944.
27. *Cape Times*, 28.2.1945.
28. Cape Town City Engineer's Department, *Metropolis of Tomorrow: A Development Plan for the Central City and Foreshore Areas* (Cape Town, 1951), 13–14.

29. Cited in Vokety, 'A tale of two cities', 202.
30. V. Bickford-Smith and E. van Heyningen (eds.), *The Waterfront* (Cape Town, 1994), 57–8.
31. L. van der Post, 'The ambivalent Cape', in M. Venter (ed.), *The Spirit of Place* (Cape Town, 1992), 120.
32. Bickford-Smith and Van Heyningen, *Waterfront*, 59–61; N. Veitch, *Waterfront and Harbour* (Cape Town, 1994); P. Newall, *Cape Town Harbour* (Cape Town, 1993).
33. Cape Town City Engineer's Dept, *Report on Amended Provincial Town Planning Scheme, 1941* (Cape Town, 1941).
34. Cape Town City Engineer's Department, *Metropolis of Tomorrow*, 40.
35. *Cape Times*, 26.7.1940.
36. *The Sun*, 27.4.1940.
37. *Cape Times*, 24.2.1966.
38. Western, *Outcast Cape Town*, 70.
39. Marks and Bozzoli, 'District Six', 7.
40. J. Whittingdale, 'The development and location of industries in Greater Cape Town, 1652–1972' (M.A. thesis, UCT, 1973).
41. A. Keppel-Jones, *When Smuts Goes* (Cape Town, 1947), 121.
42. P.L. van den Berghe and H. Adam (respectively), cited in Western, *Outcast Cape Town*, 74–5.
43. Cited in B. Maclennan, *Apartheid: The Lighter Side* (Cape Town, 1990), 77.
44. N. Worden, *The Making of Modern South Africa* (Oxford, 1994), 87–94.
45. Heard, *Cape of Storms*, 61.
46. Fast, 'An overview of African settlement in the Cape metropolitan area', 12–16; Kinkead-Weekes, 'Africans in Cape Town'.
47. *Cape Times*, 7.3.1947.
48. Maclennan, *Apartheid*, 25.
49. R. Donaldson, 'The train-apartheid issue in the Cape Peninsula, 1948–1953' (B.A. Honours thesis, UCT, 1981), 2–5.
50. Maclennan, *Apartheid*, 25.
51. Heard, *Cape of Storms*, 82–3.
52. J. Carr, *An Act of Immorality* (London, 1988).
53. *Cape Times*, 10.12.1968, cited in Maclennan, *Apartheid*, 22.
54. A.J. Venter, *Coloured* (Cape Town, 1974), 125–6.
55. Stanley Uys report, *Guardian Weekly*, 7.9.1974, cited in Western, *Outcast Cape Town*, vi–vii.
56. Maclennan, *Apartheid*, 12.
57. Venter, *Coloured*, 123–7.
58. Information on the early implementation of the Group Areas Act in Cape Town is drawn from Mesthrie, '"No place in the world to go to,"' 184–207.
59. Ibid., 191–2.
60. Cited in February, *Mind Your Colour*, 4–5.
61. See G. Lewis, *Between the Wire and the Wall* (Cape Town, 1987), 220–66; I.A. Goldin, *Making Race* (Cape Town, 1987), 57–60, 108–18. Also, E. Roux, *Time Longer than Rope* (Wisconsin, 1964), 358–9; Kinkead-Weekes, 'Africans in Cape Town', 192, 270–80.
62. H.J. Simons and R.E. Simons, *Class and Colour in South Africa* (Harmondsworth, 1969), 546.
63. Donaldson, 'Train-Apartheid', 14–17.
64. *Cape Times*, 2.5.1950; *Guardian*, 4.5.1950; T. Lodge, *Black Politics in South Africa since 1945* (Johannesburg, 1985), 33–5.
65. N. Alexander, 'Non-collaboration in the Western Cape, 1943–1963', in W.G. James and M. Simons (eds.), *The Angry Divide: Social and Economic History of the Western Cape* (Cape Town, 1989), 188.
66. T.R.H. Davenport, *South Africa: A Modern History*, 4th edn (London, 1991), 333–4.
67. Lewis, *Between the Wire and the Wall*, 253, 266.
68. Ibid., 266–8; Goldin, *Making Race*, 109.
69. Lewis, *Between the Wire and the Wall*, 255.
70. M. Fridjohn, 'The Torch Commando and the politics of white opposition' (unpublished paper, Wits African Studies seminar, 1977).
71. Roux, *Time Longer than Rope*, 386–92.
72. Kinkead-Weekes, 'Africans in Cape Town', 283.
73. J. Macrobert, 'The emergence of the Black Sash Advice Office in Cape Town: A regional study of the Black Sash, 1956–63' (B.A. Honours thesis, UCT, 1988).
74. C. Rassool and L. Witz, 'The 1652 Jan van Riebeeck Tercentenary Festival: Constructing and contesting public national history in South Africa', *Journal of African History*, 34, 3 (1993), 447–67.
75. A. Paton, *Apartheid and the Archbishop* (Cape Town, 1973), 218.
76. Roux, *Time Longer than Rope*, 392–3; J. Pampallis, *Foundations of the New South Africa* (London, 1991), 181–3; Worden, *Making of Modern South Africa*, 97.
77. Cited in R. Suttner and J. Cronin (eds.), *30 Years of the Freedom Charter* (Johannesburg, 1986), 70–1.
78. Lodge, *Black Politics*, 189–99.
79. Donaldson, 'Train-apartheid', 9, 13, 51, 54, 56.
80. *Cape Times*, 13.12.1960, cited in Maclennan, *Apartheid*, 31.
81. *Cape Times*, 29.4.1961, cited in Maclennan, *Apartheid*, 32.
82. *Cape Times*, 18.8.1959.
83. Edgar, *Ralph Bunche*, 72.
84. R. Archer and A. Bouillon, *The South African Game* (London, 1982), 45–50, 252–4.
85. Paton, *Apartheid and the Archbishop*, 283–8.
86. S. Parks, *A Guide to Cape Town for Coloured People* (Pietermaritzburg, 1969), 14–19.
87. Mesthrie, 'The Tramway Road removals', 3–6, 21–2.
88. Western, *Outcast Cape Town*, 110–32; Mesthrie, 'Black River', 22–3.
89. G.C. Brown, 'The abolition of the non-racial municipal franchise in the Cape, 1958–1972' (B.A. Honours, UCT, 1981); Muthien, *State and Resistance*, 138–9.
90. Mesthrie, 'Tramway Road', 8–16.
91. Watson, *Passing for White*; J. O'Toole, *Watts and Woodstock* (New York, 1973).
92. Cited in Muthien, *State and Resistance*, 61.
93. Kinkead-Weekes, 'Africans in Cape Town', 140–2, 150–2, 222–3, 231, 249–56, 302–3, 313–18, 320–1.
94. Goldin, *Making Race*, 87; Kinkead-Weekes, 'Africans in Cape Town', 108–9, 240–2, 244.
95. Fast, 'African settlement', 9.
96. Cited in S. Field, 'The power of exclusion: Moving memories from Windermere to the Cape Flats, 1920s–1990s' (Ph.D. thesis, Essex, 1996), 128.
97. Fast, 'African settlement', 16.
98. Kondlo, 'Peri-urban squatting', 98.
99. N. Mohamed, 'Langa High School' (B.A. Honours thesis, UCT, 1989).
100. Kinkead-Weekes, 'Africans in Cape Town', 337–45.
101. Ibid., 322–3, 327–8, 371–4. Goldin, *Making Race*, 99–101.
102. Kinkead-Weekes, 'Africans in Cape Town', 330–6.
103. Lodge, *Black Politics*, 201–30; H.H. Fast, 'Pondoks, houses, and hostels: A history of Nyanga 1946–70, with a special focus on housing' (Ph.D. thesis, UCT, 1995), 200–15; P. Kgosana, *Lest We Forget* (Johannesburg, 1988).
104. Fast, 'History of Nyanga', 201–2.
105. Lodge, *Black Politics*, 201–3.
106. A. Davey, 'Robben Island and the military 1931–1960', in H. Deacon (ed.), *A History of Robben Island* (Cape Town, 1996), 77, 92.
107. F. Buntman, 'Resistance on Robben Island 1963–1976' and 'Robben Island after 1976' in Deacon, *Robben Island*, 93–166.
108. B. Desai and C. Marney, *The Killing of the Imam* (London, 1978); A. Davids, 'Politics and the Muslims of Cape Town: A historical survey', in *Studies*, 4 (1981), 211–12.
109. Lodge, *Black Politics*, 197, 231–55.
110. Kinkead-Weekes, 'Africans in Cape Town', 483–4.
111. Ibid., 497, 548; Fast, 'African settlement', 17–21.
112. Lewis, *Between the Wire and the Wall*, 271–6.
113. Kinkead-Weekes, 'Africans in Cape Town', 523–7.
114. Cited in Fast, 'African settlement', 22–3.
115. Kinkead-Weekes, 'Africans in Cape Town', 545.
116. Western, *Outcast Cape Town*, 185–201.
117. A. Dangor, *Waiting for Leila* (Johannesburg, 1995), 1.
118. D.M. Hart, 'Political manipulation of urban space: The razing of District Six, Cape Town', in Jeppie and Soudien, *The Struggle for District Six*, 26–7. Official figures showed that the population of District Six was only 33,500 in 1966; but estimates suggest that between 55,000 and 65,000 were forced to move. The discrepancy was partly due to the large number of people 'uncounted' by government inspectors, and the fact that as people moved out, others moved in until the buildings were demolished.
119. Resident, quoted in *Cape Times*, 8.3.1966.
120. For a comment on the novels, poetry, photos and films of District Six see R. Rive, 'District Six: Fact and fiction', in Jeppie and Soudien, *Struggle for District Six*, 110–16. Popular publications have included G. Manuel and D. Hatfield, *District Six* (Cape Town, 1967); C. Breytenbach, *The Spirit of District Six* (Cape Town, 1970); and T. Grogan, *Vanishing Cape Town* (Cape Town, 1976). The most recent novel to evoke '"coloured" Cape Town' nostalgically, drawing on memories of both District Six and the Valley, Mowbray, is P. Jooste, *Dance with a Poor Man's Daughter* (London, 1998).
121. For instance, D. Biggs, *This is Cape Town* (Cape Town, 1995); P. Venster (ed.), *Daynight Guide: Cape Town* (Cape Town, 1995).
122. A. Silk, *A Shanty Town in South Africa: The Story of Modderdam* (Johannesburg, 1981).

123. J. Cole, *Crossroads* (Johannesburg, 1987), 11.
124. Ibid., 12.
125. Fast, 'African settlement', 26–7.
126. Cole, *Crossroads*, 13–25.
127. Western, *Outcast Cape Town*, 147–55.
128. Mesthrie, 'Black River', 32.
129. Adams and Suttner, *William Street, District Six*, 55–6.
130. G.J., District Six interview, WCOHP.
131. C. Soudien, 'District Six: From protest to protest', in Jeppie and Soudien, *Struggle for District Six*, 155; Hart, 'Razing District Six', 126.
132. M. Behr, *The Smell of Apples* (London, 1995). The novelist J.M. Coetzee's autobiography *Childhood* (London, 1997) explains how he escaped the 'threat' of being 'consigned to an Afrikaans life' in Cape Town, in part by attending a Roman Catholic school, St Joseph's, in Rondebosch.
133. *Parow* (Parow Municipality, 1956); *Cape Argus*, 28.9.1967, 11.9.1979, 11.9.1985; *Die Burger*, 19.11.1956, 1.8.1975; *Cape Times*, 14.8.1971; *Tygerberg News*, 3.11.1961.
134. Hart, 'Razing District Six', 126–7. S. Jensen and S. Turner, 'A place called Heideveld: Identities and strategies among the coloureds in Cape Town, South Africa' (M.A. thesis, Roskilde University, 1995), 110–11.
135. Hart, 'Razing District Six', 131–7; Soudien, 'From protest to protest', 155–77.
136. An estimate from Western, *Outcast Cape Town*, ix, x, 72.
137. Mesthrie, 'Black River', 28–42.
138. Soudien, 'From protest to protest', 144–55.
139. Ibid., 150.
140. Western, *Outcast Cape Town*, 217.
141. Ibid., 216.
142. D.S. Mabin, 'A study of attitudes and values of coloured residents in the Heideveld Public Housing Estate, Cape Town' (M.A. thesis, UCT, 1968).
143. Pinnock, *Brotherhoods*, 53.
144. Western, *Outcast Cape Town*, 172–85; Jensen and Turner, 'Heideveld', 100.
145. P. Jansen, A. du Plooy and Faika Esau, 'Elsies River' (unpublished paper, Second Carnegie Inquiry into Poverty and Development in Southern Africa, Cape Town, 1984), 23.
146. Pinnock, *Brotherhoods*, 9.
147. Baxter, 'Coon Carnival', 200–5; *Cape Times*, 4.1.1989.
148. *New Age*, 30.8.1956.
149. L. Gordon, *Shared Lives* (Cape Town, 1992), 70.
150. *New Age*, 30.8.1956.
151. A. La Guma, *The Stone Country* (London, 1974), 18.
152. *New Era*, 13.2.1958, 29.1.1959; Coetzee, *Childhood*, 144–5.
153. V. Layne, 'A history of dance and jazz band performance in the Western Cape in the post-1945 era' (M.A. thesis, UCT, 1995), 90–130. See also M. McGregor, *Chris McGregor and the Brotherhood of Breath* (Michigan, 1995).
154. A. Sachs, *The Jail Diary of Albie Sachs* (Cape Town, 1990), 45.
155. Quoted in R. Gassert, '"Bop till you drop": An oral study of popular musical cultures in Cape Town' (third-year history long paper, UCT, 1988), 26.
156. Layne, 'History of dance and jazz band performance'; B. Breakey and S. Gordon, *Beyond the Blues: Township Jazz* (Cape Town, 1997).
157. B. Helm, *Social Work in a South African City* (Cape Town, 1962).
158. *Cape Times*, 22.4.1952; *Cape Argus*, 27.1.1955; L. Taylor, 'The Cape Flats Distress Association: A history, 1944–94' (B.A. Honours thesis, UCT, 1994); T. Turkington, 'A history of SHAWCO' (B.A. Honours thesis, UCT, 1992).
159. S. Magona, *To My Children's Children* (Cape Town, 1990), 41.
160. Ibid., 127. For a novelised account of the experiences of a 'coloured' woman coming to Cape Town from the platteland for a superior education see Z. Wicomb, *You Can't Get Lost in Cape Town* (London, 1996).
161. Magona, *To My Children's Children*, 127.
162. WCOHP interview: E.C., domestic worker files.
163. Cited in Bickford-Smith and Van Heyningen, *The Waterfront*, 75.
164. P. Johnson, 'Talking the talk and walking the walk: The spring queen festival and the eroding family cult in the Western Cape garment industry' (unpublished paper, UCT Centre for African Studies, 1993), 8.
165. Weiss, 'The Cape coloured woman'.
166. Mabin, 'Heideveld', 31, 35.

CHAPTER 5

1. *Cape Times*, 14.9.1989, *Cape Argus* (Late Final) 13.9.1989.
2. *Weekly Mail*, 21.12.1989 to 18.1.1990, 'Year in review'.
3. C. Hermer, *The Diary of Maria Tholo* (Johannesburg, 1990), 4, 141.
4. R. Hallett, 'New winds of change: South Africa, 1966–76' (unpublished paper, Cape Town History workshop, 1976), 3; N. Worden, *Making of Modern South Africa*, 118–20.
5. Lewis, *Between the Wire and the Wall*, 276–9; Lodge, *Black Politics*, 324–5; C. Bundy, '"Action, comrades, action!": The politics of youth–student resistance in the Western Cape, 1985', in James and Simons, *The Angry Divide*, 206–17.
6. Hermer, *Maria Tholo*, 36–7.
7. M. Fernandez, 'Ideology challenged: Aspects of the history of St Columba's High School (1941–1990) and their application to the classroom' (M.Phil. thesis, UCT, 1996), 31.
8. Reader's Digest, *Illustrated History of South Africa*, 443.
9. Archer and Bouillon, *The South African Game*, 229–30.
10. S. Borchadt et al., *I-Story* (B.A. Honours Video, UCT, 1996).
11. Prof. H.W. van der Merwe, UCT Centre for Intergroup Studies, evidence to Cillie Commission, *Cape Times*, 27.11.1976.
12. *Cape Times*, 1.12.1976.
13. *Cape Times*, 8.9.1976.
14. Hermer, *Maria Tholo*, 65.
15. Ibid., 94.
16. Cillie Commission evidence, *Cape Times*, 21.6.1977
17. J. Western, 'The geography of urban social control: The Group Areas and the 1976 and 1980 civil unrest in Cape Town', in D.M. Smith (ed.), *Living under Apartheid* (London, 1982), 217–29.
18. 'Dawie', *Die Burger*, 10.11.1976.
19. *Argus*, 11.11.1976.
20. Hermer, *Maria Tholo*; the quote is from 10–13.
21. *Cape Herald*, 31.8.1976.
22. P. Kallaway (ed.), *Apartheid and Education* (Johannesburg, 1988), 351–2.
23. Worden, *Making of Modern South Africa*, 124.
24. Lodge, *Black Politics*, 338; W. Finnegan, *Crossing the Line* (London, 1987), 43–4.
25. Davenport, *Modern History*, 434.
26. E. Rosenthal, *Milnerton* (Cape Town, 1980), 105.
27. Archer and Bouillon, *The South African Game*, 212.
28. Davenport, *Modern History*, 541. P.W. Botha in the House of Assembly, cited in Maclennan, *Apartheid*, 51–2.
29. *Cape Times*, 24.2.1997; Andrea Fine, telephonic interview 2.9.1997; see also B. Astbury (ed.), *To Bear Witness* (Cape Town, 1998).
30. Heard, *Cape of Storms*, 180.
31. J. Richards, *Touching the Lighthouse* (London, 1997), 5.
32. A.W. Marx, *Lessons of Struggle* (Cape Town, 1992), 73–105; Lodge, *Black Politics*, 339–56.
33. *Cape Times*, 27.1.1990.
34. Hermer, *Maria Tholo*, 194.
35. Archer and Bouillon, *The South African Game*, 231–5, 262.
36. Finnegan, *Crossing the Line* (London, 1987), 136; Cape Town City Planner's Department, *Cape Town City Council's Involvement in Providing Housing for its Poorer Citizens* (Cape Town, 1993), 12.
37. *South African Digest*, 21.1.1977, cited in Western, *Outcast Cape Town*, 66.
38. L. McGregor, 'The Fatti's and Moni's Strike', *South African Labour Bulletin*, 6 & 7 (March 1980), 122–31.
39. Lodge, *Black Politics*, 348; M. Francis, '"The past is theirs, the future is ours": A study of the United Democratic Front in the Western Cape' (B.A. Honours thesis, UCT, 1984), 7–8.
40. Johnson, 'Talking the talk'.
41. F. Molteno, 'The schooling of black South Africans and the 1980 Cape Town students' boycott: A sociological interpretation' (M.Soc.Sci. thesis, UCT, 1983), 105–14.
42. T. Lodge and B. Nasson, *All, Here and Now: Black Politics in South Africa in the 1980s* (Cape Town, 1991), 40; G. Whittle, 'State strategy and the rise of the UDF in the Western Cape, 1979–1984' (B.A. Honours thesis, UCT, 1992), 33.
43. Francis, 'The past is theirs', 19.
44. Finnegan, *Crossing the Line*, 174. For a novel that focuses on the 1980 crisis see M. du Plessis, *A State of Fear* (Cape Town, 1985).
45. Molteno, 'Schooling of black South Africans', 116–56. Finnegan, *Crossing the Line*, 188.
46. Cited in Finnegan, *Crossing the Line*, 180.
47. Molteno, 'Schooling of black South Africans', 141–8, 202–5. Worden, *Modern South Africa*, 124.
48. Lodge and Nasson, *All, Here and Now*, 221.
49. Ibid., 142–51, 223.
50. G.P. Cook, 'Khayelitsha: New settlement forms in the Cape Peninsula', in Smith, *Apartheid City*, 125–35; Davenport, *Modern History*, 404–5; Cole, *Crossroads*, 71–82.

51. F. Wilson and M. Ramphele, *Uprooting Poverty* (Cape Town, 1989), 91–7.
52. Bundy, '"Action, comrades, action!"' 212.
53. K.S. Chetty, 'Urbanization and health: Evidence from Cape Town', in Smith, *Apartheid City*, 219.
54. *Cape Times*, 4.11.1985; Heard, *Cape of Storms*, 185–94.
55. Bundy, '"Action, comrades, action!"' 213.
56. See *Cape Times*, 29.8.1985; *Cape Argus*, 27.11.1996; local newspapers reported extensively on the numerous Truth and Reconciliation Commission hearings, held between 1996 and 1998, into 'gross human rights' violations' committed in Cape Town before the 1994 elections.
57. *Cape Argus*, 27.11.1996.
58. Bundy, '"Action, Comrades, Action!"' 212.
59. *Cape Times*, 8.11.1985.
60. *Cape Argus*, 11.6.1997.
61. *Cape Argus*, 18.2.1997, 19.2.1997; *Cape Times*, 24.4.1996, 28.11.1996, 14.2.1997, 18.2.1997.
62. Cole, *Crossroads*, 43–156; M.J. Murray, *The Revolution Deferred* (London, 1994), 60; *Cape Times*, 10.6.1997, 11.6.1997; *Cape Argus*, 12.6.1997; *Weekend Argus*, 14/15.7.1995, 14/15.6.1997.
63. Lodge and Nasson, *All, Here and Now*, 87–92; Marx, *Lessons of Struggle*, 148–9.
64. S. Anderson, 'The End Conscription Campaign in Cape Town, 1983–1989' (B.A. Honours thesis, UCT, 1990).
65. A. Sparks, *Tomorrow is Another Country* (Johannesburg, 1995), 21–39.
66. *South*, 19.3.1987–25.3.1987; the art pages of *South* are a useful guide to such events and publications.
67. See *Cape Times*, 9.10.1986, 10.10.1986, 13.10.1986, 15.10.1986, 18.10.1986, 6.11.1986; *Sunday Times*, 19.10.1986.
68. Azanian Students' Organisation pamphlet, *The Academic Boycott* (Cape Town, October 1986).
69. T. Karon, 'Blouberg Beach memoirs', *Upfront* (November 1989), 14–5.
70. *Cape Times*, 12.6.1989.
71. Reader's Digest, *Illustrated History of South Africa*, 486.
72. *Weekend Argus*, 2.9.1989; *Cape Times*, 2.9.1989; *Sunday Star*, 3.9.1989; *Weekly Mail*, 8.9.1989–14.9.1989. See also D. Smuts and S. Westcott (eds.), *The Purple Shall Govern* (Cape Town, 1991).
73. *Weekly Mail*, 8.9.1989–14.9.1989.
74. *Argus*, 26.7.1993; *Cape Argus*, 8.7.1997; *Cape Times*, 9.7.1997, 10.7.1997, 11.7.1997, 18.11.1997; *Weekend Argus*, 12/13.7.1997.
75. *Cape Times*, 3.9.1996, 19.9.1996.
76. Cape Metropolitan Council, *Metropolitan Spatial Development Framework* (Cape Town, 1996), 16.
77. *DayNight Guide* (Parklands, 1995), 71, 107, opp. 141, 162, 168; D. Biggs, *This is Cape Town* (Cape Town, 1995), 54, 56; *Captour Tourist Guide*, 36.
78. *DayNight Guide*, 107, 208–12.
79. *Sunday Times*, 16.2.1997; *Sunday Times Metro*, 11.5.1997, 20.6.1997; *Cape Times*, 12.8.1997; *Cape Argus*, 5.2.1997.
80. *Metropolitan Spatial Development Survey*, 16, 18.
81. *Cape Argus*, 13.2.1997, 17.2.1997.
82. *Metropolitan Spatial Development Survey*, 16, 18; Murray, *Revolution Deferred*, 50; *Cape Argus*, 27.1.1997.
83. *Cape Times*, 10.1.1997, 29.1.1997, 30.1.1997, 12.3.1997, 19.5.1997, 26.5.1997, 7.8.1997, 29.8.1997; *Cape Argus*, 10.2.1997, 23.5.1997, 1.8.1997.
84. *Weekend Argus*, 27/28.7.1996; 16/17.11.1996; *Argus*, 17.1.1996; *Cape Argus*, 11.3.1997; *Cape Times*, 27.3.1996, 31.10.1996, 1.11.1996; *Sunday Times Cape Metro*, 29.6.1997.
85. *Cape Times*, 2.10.1997.
86. *Weekend Argus*, 14/15.12.1996; *Argus*, 31.5.1996; *Peninsula Times*, 23.4.1997; *Cape Times*, 22.10.1996, 3.4.1997, 30.4.1997, 20.5.1997, 9.6.1997, 11.7.1997, 18.7.1997.
87. *Cape Argus*, 13.2.1997, 17.2.1997.
88. *Weekend Argus*, 29/30.4.1997, 19/20.4.1997, 10/11.5.1997, 17/18.5.1997; *Cape Argus*, 29.1.1997, 13.3.1997, 23.5.1997, 23.6.1997, 3.7.1997, 16.7.1997; *Sunday Times Cape Metro*, 20.4.1997; *Cape Times*, 12.3.1997, 4.4.1997, 17.7.1997, 30.7.1997, 22.8.1997, 8.9.1997, 19.9.1997, 2.10.1997.
89. See e.g. *Cape Times*, 10.4.1997, 17.4.1997, 23.4.1997, 7.7.1997, 8.10.1997; *Cape Argus*, 1.7.1997, 7.8.1997; *Sunday Times*, 6.7.1997.
90. *Cape Times*, 2.12.1996, 6.2.1997, 3.4.1997, 11.4.1997, 17.4.1997, 23.4.1997, 29.4.1997, 29.5.1997, 18.7.1997, 24.7.1997, 7.8.1997, 1.9.1997.
91. 'True colours' supplement, *Cape Times*, 25.4.1997.
92. *Cape Times*, 18.3.1996, 9.4.1996, 3.5.1996, 3.6.1996, 5.6.1996, 8.7.1996, 11.12.1996; *Argus*, 27.5.1996; *Sunday Independent*, 12.11.1995; *Sunday Times Cape Metro*, 18.6.1995.
93. Jensen and Turner, 'Heideveld'; E. Pullen, 'Race and self: A community study of self-identity among women classified as "coloured" in Cape Town' (UCT History Department Seminar, 1996).
94. *Cape Times*, 11.12.1996.
95. *Weekend Argus*, 16/17.9.1995.
96. *Weekend Argus*, 17/18.6.1995; *Cape Argus*, 26.3.1997; *Cape Times*, 29.9.1997, 2.10.1997.
97. *Cape Times*, 16.10.1996, 17.10.1996, 21.10.1996, 2.12.1996; *Weekend Argus*, 7/8.12.1996; *Sunday Times Cape Metro*, 1.12.1996.
98. *Sunday Times Cape Metro*, 10.3.1996.
99. W. Scharf and C. Vale, 'The Firm: Organised crime comes of age during the transition to democracy', *Social Dynamics*, 22, 2 (1996), 30–6.
100. *Cape Times*, 5.8.1996, 4.9.1996; *Sunday Times Cape Metro*, 18.8.1996; *Cape Argus*, 26.3.1997; *Weekend Argus*, 1/2.3.1997, 23/24.8.1997.
101. A.I. Tayob, 'Jihad against drugs in Cape Town: A discourse-centred analysis', *Social Dynamics*, 22, 2 (1996), 24.
102. Lodge and Nasson, *All, Here and Now*, 195–7; Tayob, 'Jihad', 23–9.
103. *Cape Argus*, 4.11.1996, 5.11.1996, 17.12.196, 19.3.1997; *Weekend Argus*, 9/10.11.1996; *Cape Times* 18.3.1996, 1.10.1996, 24.10.1996, 12.8.1996, 21.10.1996, 23.10.1996, 24.10.1996, 4.11.1996, 7.11.1996, 8.11.1996, 11.11.1996, 18.12.1996, 5.8.1997; *Sunday Times Cape Metro*, 10.11.1996.
104. *Cape Times*, 12.8.1996, 5.9.1996, 9.10.1996, 17.10.1996, 3.12.1996, 28.5.1997. *Cape Argus*, 23.10.1996. Very useful summaries of events can be found in *Cape Times*, 16.2.1998, 17.2.1998, 18.2.1998.
105. *Weekend Argus*, 1/2.7.1995; *Southern Argus*, 13.2.1992; *Argus*, 29.1.1996, 25.4.1996; *Cape Argus*, 18.8.1997; *Cape Times*, 9.4.1996, 9.10.1996, 18.4.1997, 21.4.1997, 14.7.1997, 12.9.1997; *Sunday Times Cape Metro*, 6.4.1997. N. Worden and E. van Heyningen, 'Signs of the times: Tourism and public history at Cape Town's Victoria and Alfred Waterfront', *Cahiers d'Etudes Africaine*, 141–2, 36 (1996), 215–36.
106. *Cape Times*, 11.7.1997, 4.8.1997; *Cape Argus*, 4.8.1997.
107. *Metropolitan Spatial Development Framework*; De Villiers, *Tale of Three Cities*, 63.
108. *Argus*, 22.1.1996; *Cape Times*, 25.3.1997, 3.4.1997; *Mail and Guardian*, 27.3/3.4.1997.
109. *ADA: Cape Town*, 11 (Cape Town, 1993), 90.
110. Bickford-Smith and Van Heyningen, *The Waterfront*.
111. *Weekly Mail*, 4/10.12.1992, cited in Worden and Van Heyningen, 'Signs of the times', 224.
112. Statistics supplied by Nina Tshandu and P.S. van Zyl of the Victoria and Alfred Waterfront Company.
113. De Villiers, *Tale of Three Cities*, 63–91; Worden and Van Heyningen, 'Signs of the times', 219–22; *Sunday Independent*, 17.8.1997.
114. *Weekend Argus*, 14/15.12.1996.
115. *Sunday Independent*, 17.8.1997.
116. *Cape Times*, 16.10.1996; *Cape Argus*, 28.1.1997, 25.2.1997, 12.9.1997; *Weekend Argus*, 1/2.2.1997; *Weekend Argus*, 9/10.11.1996; *Sunday Times Business Times*, 24.11.1996.
117. *ADA: Cape Town*, 42.
118. *Cape Argus*, 11.2.1997.
119. *Sunday Times Cape Metro*, 23.3.1997; personal information from Hans Smit, director of housing for the South Peninsula Municipality.
120. L. Clowes, 'Mothers, wives and workers: White South African women, 1974–1984' (unpublished paper, UCT History Department seminar, Cape Town, 1996).
121. *ADA: Cape Town*, 77.

Index

J

K

L

M

T

U

V